Kate Fortune's Journal Entry

That old clapboard New England home holds such special memories for me. I'm so pleased that my granddaughter Jane and her son, Cody, are making good use of it. She and her little boy have had a rough time of it. When Cody's father abandoned Jane before Cody was even born, I knew the road ahead would be difficult. But her family has always been there to support her. Now I hope some of the "magic" of the house weaves its spell around her. And that she'll finally be able to discover true love....

A LETTER FROM THE AUTHOR

Dear Reader,

It isn't often I get the chance to speak directly to you at the beginning of a book, and I'm so glad my editors at Silhouette gave me that opportunity with *A Husband in Time*. I'm very excited to be a part of this special series, and was even more thrilled when I learned the *type* of story I would be asked to write. When you read it, I'm sure you'll see why.

A Husband in Time is my twelfth novel with Silhouette. From the very first book, I've felt the warmth of those of you who read them. Through the letters you send me, and the books you buy, you let me know that the work I put into these stories is worth the effort, because someone, somewhere, is getting pleasure from reading them. That's what makes it all worthwhile. And it's also what keeps me punching away at the keyboard, day after day. As long as you keep enjoying them, I'll keep writing them.

Happy reading!

Maggie Shayne

A Husband in Time

MAGGIE SHAYNE

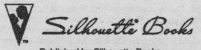

Published by Silhouette Books

America's Publisher of Contemporary Romance

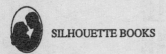

SILHOUETTE BOOKS

A HUSBAND IN TIME

Copyright © 1997 by Harlequin Books S.A.

ISBN 0-373-50183-8

Special thanks and acknowledgment to Maggie Shayne for her contribution to the Fortune's Children series.

MAGGIE SHAYNE,

a national bestselling author who *Romantic Times* magazine calls "brilliantly inventive," has written twelve novels for Silhouette, including a popular vampire romance trilogy, *Wings in the Night,* and a spin-off novella in the 1995 Shadows anthology, *Strangers in the Night.* Maggie, who lives in a rural community in central New York with her husband and five children, also writes mainstream romance fiction. Look for her next novel, *Born in Twilight,* a brand-new single title based on her vampire series, from Silhouette Books in March.

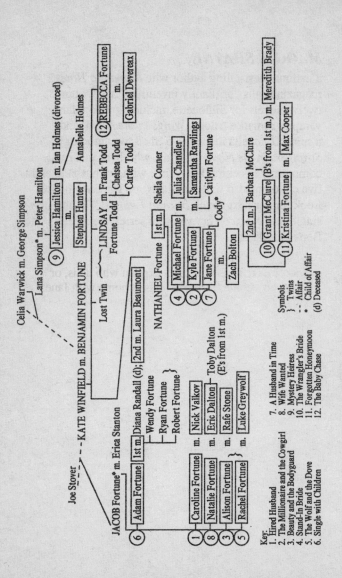

Key:
1. Hired Husband
2. The Millionaire and the Cowgirl
3. Beauty and the Bodyguard
4. Stand-In Bride
5. The Wolf and the Dove
6. Single with Children
7. A Husband in Time
8. Wife Wanted
9. Mystery Heiress
10. The Wrangler's Bride
11. Forgotten Honeymoon
12. The Baby Chase

Symbols
⎫
⎬ Twins
⎭
-- Affair
* Child of Affair
(d) Deceased

FORTUNE'S Children

Meet the Fortunes—three generations of a family with a legacy of wealth, influence and power. As they unite to face an unknown enemy, shocking family secrets are revealed…and passionate new romances are ignited.

JANE FORTUNE: The single mother secretly dreams of finding a husband, and a father for her six-year-old son. She has almost given up hope until a mystery man comes to her out of nowhere.…

ZACH BOLTON: He can't explain who he is, or where he's come from. He feels at home with Jane and her son, but can he stay with them—forever?

MONICA MALONE: She now owns major shares in Fortune Cosmetics. What further havoc will she create to claim the rest of the Fortune wealth?

JAKE FORTUNE: The hardworking family man is hiding a deep, dark secret. Is he in cahoots with Monica? Once his secret is discovered, the Fortune empire might come tumbling down.…

NATALIE FORTUNE: Kindhearted schoolteacher. Could a farmhouse and St. Bernard inherited from her grandmother lead to the exciting romance with a dashing man she's been dreaming of?

LIZ JONES— CELEBRITY GOSSIP

Is anyone but me wondering why Jake Fortune sold Monica Malone sizable shares of stock in Fortune Cosmetics? After all, Monica is just a faded starlet coasting on her former glory and fame. Do you suppose Jake and Monica are having a torrid affair? Or perhaps the shrewd Monica is holding some juicy secret over Jake's head and blackmailing him? Rumors are running rampant.

The rest of the Fortunes are up in arms. Now Monica owns a big piece of the business, and who knows what type of control she'll want to wield.

This is going to be a battle to the bitter end. And I'm putting my money on the Fortunes!

One

August 4, 1897

Six-year-old Benjamin Bolton rested against a stack of pillows in his bedroom—the first room on the left, right at the top of the stairs. He couldn't get out of bed very often, not at all without his father's help. But Father had turned his bed around and tied the curtains open so that Ben could see the sky as he lay there. And tonight, as he stared up at the sparkling night sky, he saw a shooting star...and then another, and a third. They zipped across their blue-black home, leaving white-hot trails, and though it wasn't very scientific at all, Benjamin closed his eyes and wished with everything in him.

"Three shooting stars, that's three wishes for me. I wish..." He bit his lip, thinking hard to be sure he'd word the wishes right, and not waste them. "I wish to be well again, so I can run and play outdoors, and ride my pony, and not die like they all think I'm going to, even though they don't say it out loud."

He drew a breath, heard the wheezy sound it made as it whistled into his weakened lungs. His head hurt. He ached most everywhere, and he was dog-tired. His eyes tried to close, but he forced them open. This was important, and he still had two wishes to go.

"I wish for a mother. A real mother, who will love me and read to me ... And who isn't afraid of bullfrogs, like Mrs. Haversham is." He smiled after he made the wish, because he was sure he'd worded it just right.

Licking his lips, Benjamin squeezed his eyes tight, and made the third wish, the one he'd been wishing for all his life. "And I wish for a big brother. I promise I won't ever fight with him or tease. I would like for him to be smart, and brave, and strong, just like my father. I'll even share my pony with him."

Ben opened his eyes, gazing out the window. No trace of the stars remained. But they'd been there. He'd seen them. And now an odd, warm feeling settled over him, just like a big woolly blanket. Somehow, he just knew everything was going to be all right.

August 4, 1997

Cody Fortune glanced up from the laptop computer his mom had given him for his tenth birthday, turning his head just in time to see the three shooting stars arching over their car as it rolled over the narrow, deserted roads of Maine, heading for the coast and their new home.

"Wow," he whispered, craning his neck for a better look. Of all the things he'd seen on this trip from Minnesota, this was the most incredible. Three at once. It had to be an anomaly.

"Did you see that, Mom?"

"What?"

"Three shooting stars, right in a row!"

She smiled at him, only taking her eyes from the road for a second. "So, why don't you make a wish? Or are you too skeptical for that?"

Cody Fortune was far too intelligent to believe in any such thing as wishing on stars. But he knew his mom didn't like him taking life too seriously, and some touch of whimsy moved him to close his eyes and whisper the things that had been on his mind the most lately. "I wish I had a dad," he said softly. "And a little brother, because it gets so darn boring being an only child. We'd have great times together. And I wish..." He licked his lips, opened his eyes and stared up at the sky. His eyes watered just a little bit, but he blinked them dry again. "I wish for my mom to be happy. Really happy. 'Cause I know she isn't. I can't remember when she was."

He lowered his head, and his mother's soft hand stroked his hair. "Of course I'm happy, Cody. I have you, and a new house in a small town, just like I've always wanted. What more could I need?"

Cody smirked. He knew better, of course, but he'd never get her to admit her life was less than perfect. "You realize I've just wished on three hunks of burned-out rock, don't you?"

"It was still generous of you to use up a whole wish on me."

He shrugged and turned to the laptop again. It wasn't so bad that he'd lapsed into childish fantasies for a second there. It was like his mom was always saying, he was still a kid, even if he did have the brain of a full-grown nuclear physicist.

"So, have you thought about what I told you?" he asked, and saw her brows rise.

"About what, Cody?"

Cody sighed. When he spent the weekend with his grandparents, he'd stumbled on something he knew must be important, but his mother, as usual, couldn't care less about the family business. "What I overheard when Grandpa took me to work with him last week. Don't you remember? That witch Monica was there, and—"

"Cody, that isn't very nice."

"So? Neither is Monica. Anyway, she was being really nasty to Aunt Tracey. Said she knew some secret, and she'd tell if Tracey and her boyfriend, what's his name—? Wayne. Yeah, that's it. Monica said she wanted them to go away, or she'd tell some secret."

Jane shrugged. "I wouldn't worry about it, Cody. We all know Monica's been wanting to get her hands on the business. She probably sees Aunt Tracey as one more competitor for it."

"Yeah, but Aunt Tracey only just found out she *was* a Fortune."

"If she's a Fortune, Cody, she can handle empty threats from Monica Malone." She sent him a sideways glance. "This is just one more example of why I want no part of the family business, pal. All the scratching and clawing and fighting to hold on to it." She gazed out the window at the rugged coastline as they passed it. "It's going to be so much better here."

Cody sighed. It was no use talking to his mother about business. She just didn't care. He stared at the dark ocean, and the whitecapped waves crashing to the shore, and then he thought maybe she was right. It was kind of pretty here. "So how much longer till we get there?"

"I think... I think this is— Oh, my, Cody, this *is* the place. Look at it!''

Cody looked up at the house their headlights illuminated as the car turned into the gravel drive. "Looks like something out of a Stephen King novel."

"Isn't it *great?*''

He grimaced at his mother's enthusiasm as she brought the car to a halt and killed the engine.

"I thought you liked Stephen King novels," she said.

"Yeah, but I don't want to live in one."

She smiled at him. Then he turned his gaze to the house once again, and froze. From the corner of his eye, he'd seen some kind of flash in an upstairs window. Like... lightning or something. His mom was already opening her door, but he put a hand on her arm, stopping her. "I think... somebody's in there."

"What?" She frowned and looked where he pointed. "I don't see anything."

"Maybe it was just a reflection." But he didn't think so. He folded up the laptop and pulled his penlight from his pocket. He never went far without it— not that it would make a very good weapon, but at least he'd be able to see whatever horrible creature sneaked up on him. "Better let me go in first, Mom, just in case."

She ruffled his hair, which he hated. "My hero," she said, but he could tell she wasn't one bit nervous about going into that big, empty, dark house. She must be nuts.

Headlights spilled through the rear windshield, and Cody turned to see a second vehicle bounding over the gravel drive. A police car. He bit his lip before he could say, "Thank God!" Though he was still a bit nervous. In Stephen King novels, the small-town sheriffs of Maine never failed to be good guys, but they usually got killed off pretty early on, leaving the innocent mother—and her son, who knew all along something wasn't quite right, but who couldn't get anyone to listen—to fend for themselves.

Sure enough, a reed-thin man in a gray uniform with a shiny badge, stepped out of the car, and came over just as Mom stepped out of theirs.

"Quigly O'Donnell, ma'am. You must be Ms. Fortune. You're right on time." He had the same accent as the old man who'd lived across the street from the main characters in *Pet Sematary*. Cody shivered.

"Call me Jane," his mom said, and shook the sheriff's hand. "And this is my son, Cody."

Cody nodded, but didn't shake. He was too busy watching the house. "I thought I saw something up there," he said, pointing, hoping the sheriff would go against character and check it out, hoping the guy would survive the experience.

"Ayuh, I wouldn't worry about that, son. Probably just the ghost."

"Ghost?"

"Some say the ghost of Zachariah Bolton still rattles around the old place. Not that I'd give it much credence, mind you. It's just a tale the old folks like to tell now and again. Gives 'em something to talk about over checkers, it does."

"Checkers," Cody said, raising a brow. "Gee, Mom, thanks for bringing me to such a cultural mecca."

"Mind your manners, Cody. Sheriff O'Donnell, if you brought the key along, I'll—"

"Got it right here," he said, and the last word sounded like "hee-ya." Mom would call that accent charming and say it was local "flavor." Cody found it irritating as all get-out. The sheriff held up a big old key on a brass ring. Like a jail-cell key from an old western. Or the key to the dungeons in a horror flick. Cody felt the tone slipping from King to Poe. This was not a good sign. "I'll help you with your things, if you like. Power's been turned on, and everything should be ready for you."

"That was kind of you, Sheriff."

"Yeah," Cody put in. "I'm glad to know we've got pow-uh."

His mom's elbow dug into his ribs, but the doomed sheriff didn't seem to notice Cody's mimicry. He just nodded. "Least I could do for your grandmother, ma'am. Kate Fortune was one hell of a lady, if you'll pardon the expression. When she asked me to watch after the place for her, I was more than happy to do it. Pity we've lost her now."

Jane nodded. "I miss her terribly." She slipped an arm around Cody's shoulders and squeezed. "We both do."

The sheriff nodded, cleared his throat. "Well, come on and follow me. I'll show you around. And while I'm at it, I'll tell you all about our town's one and only claim to fame. This place's original owner, and resident ghost, if you believe in that kind'a thing. Zachariah Bolton." He walked as he spoke, in that slow, lazy pattern that left every sentence sounding like a question. They followed him up the porch's wide steps and across it to the front door, which was tall, and dark, and to Cody's way of thinking just a little bit scary.

Then Quigly O'Donnell opened the front door, and he decided he'd been wrong. It was a *lot* scary.

Quigly O'Donnell snapped on a light.

It was *fabulous!* Everything Jane had ever wanted in a home was in this house. Oh, she knew most of her family thought her hopelessly old-fashioned, but she wasn't fond of modern society and all its trappings. Modern-day values were what had landed her pregnant and alone ten years ago, and that shock had gone a long way toward guiding Jane to her own perhaps outmoded system of morality.

This house was the embodiment of the life she wanted for her and Cody. A simple, old-fashioned life. With one notable exception. There would be no father in this traditional American family. Jane was mom and dad and everything in between. Everyone said she couldn't do it all, that she was pushing herself too hard. But she could. And she'd do it without her family's money. She wanted no part of the family business or the wealth that went with it. It was a rat race, everyone fighting to hold on to their share of the pie and always worrying about someone trying to take it from them. No. That wasn't anything she wanted to be involved with.

This, though—this would be perfect.

"I never thought my modern-minded grandmother had a clue what to make of me," she whispered as she moved through the modest entry hall and into the Gothic living room, with its high ceilings and intricate, darkly stained woodwork. "But Grandma Kate knew me better than I ever imagined. She must have, to have left me this place." All around them, furniture stood draped in white sheets, like an army of ghosts.

"And that guest house out front will be perfect for my antique shop." She couldn't stop smiling. The place was her dream come true.

"The house isn't the half of it, ma'am," Sheriff O'Donnell offered. "It's the history that goes along with it that makes it so special." He'd carried in two of their suitcases, and he set them on the hardwood floor. "You've heard of quinaria fever, of course?"

"Heard of it?" Jane glanced behind her, but Cody was already off exploring nooks and crannies, flashing his ever-present penlight into closets and cupboards. Her heart twisted a little in her chest at the mere mention of the disease. "I nearly lost my son from it," she said quietly. "He was exposed as a baby. Thankfully, we caught it in time."

Frowning, the sheriff tilted his head. "Well, now, if that don't beat all..." Then he shrugged. "Hell of a coincidence, ma'am, if you'll pardon the expression."

"Why's that, Sheriff?"

"Well, Zachariah Bolton was the man responsible for finding the cure. Tryptonine, you know. Same drug we use today, with a few modifications, of course. If it hadn't been for him— Ah, now here's the dining room. Floor-to-ceiling hardwood cupboards on two walls. See there? Same as in the kitchen. And the ones here on the wall in between..." He opened a cupboard door, left it wide, then meandered into the kitchen. Opening the cupboard from that side, he peered through at her. "See that? Accessible from either side."

"That's very nice." But she was more interested in the tale he'd been telling before.

Cody joined them then, having heard the tail end of the sheriff's comments. "You're dead wrong about tryptonine, Sheriff," he said, then grinned innocently at his mom and added, "if you'll pardon the expression."

"Cody!"

"Come on, Mom. Everyone learns this stuff in fourth grade. The quinaria virus was cured by Bausch and Waterson in 1898."

Jane scrunched her eyebrows and shook her head. "Are you a walking encyclopedia, or what?"

He shrugged and looked past her to Sheriff O'Donnell.

"Well, now, that's a bright young fellow you have there, Ms. Fortune. Cody, is it? Well, Cody, m'boy, you have part of it right. But you don't know the whole tale. Did you know, for instance, that Wilhelm Bausch and Eli Waterson spent most of their time competing against one another? Great researchers, sure enough. But more focused on getting the jump on each other than on the importance of their work. Blinded by ambition, you might say."

Jane saw Cody's eyes narrow suspiciously. But he listened.

"It was their friend Zachariah Bolton who finally brought them together. And only by working together were they able to find the cure." He waved a hand to indicate that they **should** follow him and turned back toward the living room, then headed up the stairs. "Come on, I want to show you something."

Jane knew she was grinning like a loon, but she couldn't help herself. "Isn't this great, Codester? A house complete with a ghost and a historical past?"

"Mom, you're too into history. Get with the nineties, willya?"

"Yeah, yeah. Hurry up, I want to hear the rest of this." She followed her son, noticing the way he paused just outside the door of the room at the top of the stairs. He stood still for a moment, staring at that door. Then shivered and rubbed the back of his neck with one hand.

"You okay, pal?"

"Yeah. Sure, fine. C'mon."

Sheriff O'Donnell headed into a bedroom farther down the hall, snapped on a light and waved his arm with a flourish when they entered.

Jane caught her breath. "My God," she whispered, blinking at the portrait on the far wall. "It looks like a Rockwell!" She moved closer, ran her fingertips lovingly over the ornate frame, then touched the work itself. "But it can't be. This has to be at least a hundred years old."

"You have a fine eye, Jane."

"I know antiques," she said with a shrug. "It's my business. This is unsigned. Do you know who did it?"

"Ayuh, unsigned, and no, I don't know who the artist was," O'Donnell said. "But it's yours, along with everything else in the house. Including the old safe in the attic, still locked up. Might even be some of Zachariah Bolton's old notes and such tucked away in there. Yours to do with as you please, just as your grandmother's will specified.''

Jane couldn't take her eyes from the portrait on the wall. A very Rockwellian painting of a dark-haired man, eyes passionate and intense, hair rumpled, white shirt unbuttoned at the neck. In one hand he held a small contraption with springs and wires sprouting in all directions, and in the other a tiny screwdriver. Gold-rimmed glasses perched on his nose, and those piercing, deep brown eyes stared through them at his work. And beside him, right beside him, dressed in identical clothes—though in a much smaller size—sat a little boy who couldn't be more than five or six. He had carrot-colored curls and bright green eyes, and he was tinkering with a tiny screwdriver of his own. The two sat so close they had to be touching. And the connection between them was so strong it was palpable, though they weren't even looking at one another. At the bottom of the painting was a single word: Inventor.

"That there is Zachariah Bolton, ma'am," Sheriff O'Donnell told her. "And the boy is his son, Benjamin."

"Benjamin," she whispered. "That was my grandfather's name and this child looks enough like Cody to be his..." Jane's voice trailed off.

"Little brother," Cody finished, stepping farther into the room.

"Bolton was a friend and colleague to Wilhelm Bausch and Eli Waterson. In fact, they both said publicly that they considered him one of the greatest scientific minds of their time. One of the few things they agreed on, it was. Well, sir, when little Benjamin died of quinaria fever—''

Jane gasped, her eyes snapping back to the mischievous green ones in the painting. "Oh, no. That sweet little boy?''

"Yes, ma'am. And the day the boy passed, Zachariah Bolton went plumb out of his mind. The grief was too much for him, they say. Locked himself in the boy's bedroom and refused to let anyone in. When they finally forced the door, he was long gone. And he'd taken the poor little fellow's body right along with him. Bolton was never heard from again. Now, Bausch and Waterson were distraught enough over it that they vowed to find a cure for the disease that took little Benjamin. And by heaven, that's just what they did.''

Jane blinked away the inexplicable tears that came to her eyes as she heard the story. "That's so incredibly sad.''

"Yes, ma'am, that it is. I can take that painting down, store it somewhere, if it's going to bother you.''

"No,'' she answered quickly. "No, leave it right here.'' Her eyes found those of the inventor again, and she could almost feel his pain.

"The place hasn't changed much over the years,'' the sheriff mused. "Aside from some fresh paint and paper, it's almost exactly the way Bolton left it. Almost as if it's been . . . waiting . . . or something.''

Jane frowned at the man. "But it's been a century.''

"Ayuh. After Bolton vanished, his friends, Bausch and Waterson looked after the place. Kept the taxes paid up and so on, always insisting Bolton would come back someday. Course, he never did." Quigly shrugged and heaved a sigh. "The house was left alone for a short while, of course, after the two men passed. Went to the town for taxes, and naturally the town kept it up, hoping to sell it one day. Never did, though. Not until your Grandma Kate came along. And even when she bought it, she refused to change a thing."

Jane could understand that reluctance to change this place. It had a soul to it, as if it were a living entity—or was that the lingering presence of the long-dead scientist she felt in every room?

"Hey, Mom?"

She turned, surprised that Cody's voice came from a distance and not right behind her, where he'd been standing only seconds ago. "Codester? Where are you?" She stepped out of the master bedroom, into the hall. Cody stood two doors down, in front of that room at the top of the stairs. The one that seemed to have given him a scare before.

"I want this room, if it's okay with you," he said. Frowning, Jane went to where he stood near the now open door. He looked in at a rather ordinary-looking bedroom, with no furniture to speak of, and nothing exceptional about it except for the huge marble fireplace on one wall.

"I kind of thought this room . . . gave you the willies. Isn't this where you thought you saw something before?"

"That's why I want it," Cody said. He looked at her and shrugged. "If there is some kind of ghost hanging out around here, I want to know about it."

"Gonna analyze it until you convince it it can't possibly exist?"

"Maybe," he said, grinning. "So when are the movers gonna get here with my Nintendo?"

Two

1897

Thunder rumbled and growled in the distance, and Zachariah got up from the chair where he'd been keeping constant vigil to light the oil lamp on his son's bedside table. Benjamin had always been afraid of thunderstorms. Just as Zach fitted the glass chimney into place, Ben stirred, as Zach had known he would.

"Father... Oh. You're right here."

"Where else would I be?"

"Working on the device, of course. You waste an awful lot of time sitting here with me, you know."

"I like sitting with you." Thunder cracked again, and Benjamin reached for his father's hand, found it, and held tight.

"There, now. No need to be afraid, son. You know thunder can't hurt you."

"That doesn't make it any less noisy, though," Benjamin said, quite reasonably. "How much longer will it last, Father? It's been storming all night."

Zachariah pulled the gold watch from his vest pocket, opened it and then turned its face toward his son. "It's only 9:08, my boy. It hasn't been storming all night, only a couple of hours. And it will end any time now, I'm cer—"

His words were cut off by the loudest, sharpest crack yet, this one so loud it even made Zachariah jump a bit. At the same instant, the night sky beyond Benjamin's window was ripped apart by a blinding, jagged streak.

"Father, the lightning! It's hit something!"

Zach moved to the edge of the bed and gathered his son in his arms. "There now..." he said. "It wasn't as close as it seemed." But he kept his gaze focused on that one spot in the night where the lightning seemed to have struck. And as he watched, he rocked his son, whispered to him, stroked his hair.

Within seconds, a pinprick of light danced in the distant sky. And then it began to grow, and spread, until Zach recognized it for what it was. A fire. And from what he could see, it was the old Thomas barn, nearly three miles away, that had been hit, and that was now burning. No great loss. It was an old, decrepit building and hadn't been used in years. The only thing inside, so far as he knew, was some musty old hay.

Benjamin fell asleep in Zachariah's arms, and Zach remained right where he was all night long, holding his precious child and watching the growing blaze in the distance. Soon it illuminated the entire night sky. The barn was old, tinder-dry, and had gone up like a matchstick.

Zach ought to be working. He knew he should, for so very much depended on the success of the current experiment. And he was so close. So close.

Right now, though, Benjamin needed him. And right now he couldn't bring himself to leave.

But as the sun rose high the next morning, and spirals of smoke still rose from the charred remains of the old Thomas barn, Zach gently tried to extricate himself from the bed without disturbing Benjamin. And he did. A bit too easily. As he got to his feet, it hit him that, sick as he was, Benjamin was normally a very light sleeper. He should have at least stirred when Zach got up from the bed.

A cold chill crept up his spine as he turned to face his son, who hadn't so much as stirred in his sleep all night.

And then Zachariah Bolton's heart froze over. He shook Ben's frail shoulders gently, tapped his pale cheek. But there was no response. His son had slipped into a coma. The state that marked the final stages of his illness. Death was only twenty-four hours away now, perhaps less.

There was no more time. None whatsoever. He must act now, and if the experiment had side effects, then so be it. He'd suffer whatever he must in order to save his son's life.

He reached into his vest, and removed the device from its pocket. There was no longer any reason to stay by his son's side. Benjamin wouldn't wake again. Not unless . . . Not unless this worked.

Leaning over the bed, he stroked his son's coppery curls, kissed his forehead. "I'll be gone for a little while, my Ben. But I'll try to arrange it so it's only an instant for you. I don't want to leave you, but I must to get you healthy again. Understand?"

Benjamin's auburn lashes rested on his chalk-white cheeks, and his breath wheezed in and out of his rail-thin body.

Zach straightened and pushed his hands through his hair. He looked like hell. He knew it without a glimpse at the looking glass. His clothes were rumpled, vest unbuttoned and gaping. The thin black tie he'd worn the day before hung loose from his collar. He'd planned, though. There was a small satchel in Benjamin's wardrobe, with a change of clothes and the things he'd need. Including proof, should he be questioned. He took a moment to retrieve the satchel. No time to change. Not now. Ben could very well expire while his father worried over such trivial matters. But once Zach was gone, time would virtually stand still for his son. Time enough to bathe then. If he was displeasing to those he met, well, too bad for them. Not that he was likely to meet anyone at all. Each time he'd opened the portal, it had shown him an empty, unlived-in version of his own house. Not that he cared right now who he might meet, or what they might think of him.

He wasn't thinking of himself. Not at all. He wasn't thinking of society, either, or of the repercussions he knew full well might come from his tampering with nature this way. He flatly refused to consider those. The only thing on Zachariah Bolton's mind was his son. His precious Benjamin. The only thing that mattered right now was finding a way to save his child's fragile life. The child who was, right now, precariously close to death. And he could do it. Zachariah Bolton could do it. He could travel backward through time. He could go back to a time before his son had been exposed to the killing virus that was trying so hard to take him. And when he arrived there, he'd take Benjamin away, somewhere safe. So

that when the virus pummelled Rockwell, Ben would
be far away. He'd never be exposed. And when the
danger had passed, he'd bring Ben home safe and
sound. He'd never become sick. He'd never die. He'd
be all right. Zach would return here, to this time, to
find his son healthy and well again. With no memory
of having been sick at all.

Zach's heartbeat escalated as he pointed the device toward *that spot* in the very center of his son's
bedroom. He had no idea what the spot was. A wrinkle in the fabric of time. A rent. Whatever it was, it
was only here, in this room, and he suspected it had
been here, hovering in the air above the ground, even
before the house was built. He'd attempted the experiment in numerous locations, but here and here
alone had he found success. One night, when he'd
been working in here so as to be with his ailing child,
he'd discovered the portal purely by accident.

With his thumb, he depressed the initiator button.
And a pinprick of light appeared in midair, at the
room's center. Holding the device steady, he turned
the expander dial, and the light grew bigger, brighter,
until it was a glowing sphere that extended beyond the
ceiling and the floor. A mist-filled, glowing orb. But
even that began to change. The mists cleared and took
on forms, and in moments Zach was looking into
what appeared to be a huge mirror. And the mirror
reflected this very room back at him. Only in another time. He could clearly see that the wallpaper
was different, and the curtains in the windows were
different, and the furnishings. Everything. Right
down to the small body bundled beneath the covers
in the bed. Benjamin? Before he was taken ill, when

he was well and strong and healthy? This was going to work. It was going to work!

He only hoped it didn't kill him. Every test so far indicated there would be side effects. The tea cup Zach had pushed through the portal a few days ago had shattered. He'd made adjustments to the device and tried again. The apple he sent through had withered, and he'd made still more changes. The mouse... the mouse had died. And though Zach had recalculated and made even more changes, he couldn't be certain he had it right this time. So, yes, there might be side effects. Serious ones. He just didn't know what they would be, yet. But—he smiled a little—he was about to find out. "You're going to be all right, Benjamin. I swear to you. You'll be well again!" And Zachariah Bolton stepped into the light, and promptly felt a post wallop him right between the eyes.

Jane Fortune couldn't sleep. There was simply too much on her mind. Oh, not the house. The house was perfect, she'd known that the second she saw it. The aging but elegant Victorian, standing like a guardian of the sea. The rocky Maine shoreline below. The songs of the waves that would sing her to sleep under ordinary circumstances.

Her new antique shop—Jane smiled at the words— was now a reality. She'd researched the area, made new contacts and stocked up on local finds. She'd been open for several weeks now, and business was brisk. The guest house—a miniature copy of the main house, perched at its feet as if the house had given birth to a pup—was perfect, just as Jane had known it would be. Even the nearby town, appropriately named Rockwell, was picture-perfect. The epitome of the New England fantasy. A place time and progress seemed to have forgotten. It boasted a corner drugstore complete with a soda fountain and a barbershop with an old-fashioned candy-cane pole outside. When she walked along Rockwell's sidewalks, she half expected to round a corner and spot four men in flat-topped straw hats and handlebar mustaches singing about strolling through the park.

But as Grandma Kate used to say, when things seem too good to be true, look out, because they probably are. What if the business failed? What would she do then? Go running back to Minneapolis with her tail between her legs?

No. No, this move had been hard enough on Cody. She wouldn't uproot him again. She'd make this work, somehow. She had to, for her son's sake.

But financial worries were not the only things troubling Jane's mind tonight. She was more concerned about her son than about anything else. Cody's wish for a father had gnawed at her heart from the second he uttered it in the car that night. He was an intelligent child—gifted, the school officials called him. He knew he'd had a father once. But while Jane didn't believe in lying to her son, she hadn't told him the whole truth about Greg. He knew only that his father had been a talented musician who died when Cody was still a baby. She'd left out the rest. She'd never told Cody how taken in she'd been by Greg's idealism and sincerity, and the beauty and meaning behind the songs he wrote and played in clubs around Minneapolis. God, when she thought now about how quickly she'd fallen in love with him...

She'd been a fool. Greg's idealism had fled the second some L.A. big shot heard him play, and offered his band a recording contract. A pregnant young girlfriend who had made it clear she wanted no part of her family wealth, hadn't fit in with his new and improved plans. She wouldn't have wanted such a shallow and irresponsible man raising her son, anyway. She knew that now. But she also knew her son ached for the lack of a father in his life.

Oh, if only...

She looked wistfully at the painting on the wall beside her bed. Zachariah Bolton. His soft sable hair fell across his forehead, his brown eyes gleamed. The narrow black tie hung in two thin ribbons, and his vest was unbuttoned. The top of a gold watch peeked up from a small pocket.

The boy's resemblance to her own son struck her again, and she figured that might be a lot of the reason she liked the piece so much. The two sat very close to one another, at a wooden table with an oil lamp at either end. Each intent on his own work, but still, somehow, aware of the other. You could almost feel the love between them. Father and son, she'd have known that even without Quigly O'Donnell's narration. A father whose work meant the world to him, she thought, but who had never once allowed that work to come before his son.

If only Cody could have a father like that one.

Jane sighed, and relaxed deeper into her pillows. It was no use dreaming. She'd never find a man with those century-old values in the nineties. Not even in this nostalgic town. And she wouldn't settle for less. She didn't want another man whose career meant more to him than his own child. And she didn't want an ambitionless bum, or an immature, irresponsible overgrown kid, either.

She wanted . . .

Her gaze wandered back to the man in the painting. His full lips were parted just slightly, his strong jawline was taut, as if he were grating his teeth, and he was shoulder-to-shoulder with the little boy. The passion in his eyes was for his work. But it was intense enough to make her wonder if it had ever been there for a woman. His wife, the boy's mother, perhaps?

She smiled and shook her head. She was gifting the mysterious inventor with qualities he'd probably never had. The day after she and Cody moved in, Jane had made a trip to the Rockwell Public Library and borrowed several books on the town's history. The chapters on Bolton all read much the same. He'd been a notorious womanizer. The Don Juan of the nineteenth century, one author had dubbed him. None had mentioned his wife. Poor, long-suffering woman.

And yet that passion in the eyes of the inventor called to her.

Oh, but all this speculation was silly. The man was no longer living. And that probably wasn't passion at all in his eyes, but perhaps the beginnings of insanity. Once a man considered to be a genius, and far ahead of his time, Bolton had, the books claimed, crossed that fine line between brilliance and insanity. And from what she'd read, Jane thought the mad-ness had begun to take over long before the death of his precious son. Two accounts said that Bolton had claimed he'd discovered a way to travel through time. He'd been ridiculed for that claim, and soon after he'd refused to discuss it. Some said it was that ridicule that had sent him into seclusion, as much as the loss of his son. Whatever the reason, he'd dropped out of sight in 1890-something, never to be heard from again.

A shame. A crying shame.

"Mom! Mom, hurry!"

The alarm in Cody's voice pierced straight through every thought, to her very soul. Something was wrong. She jumped out of bed and ran into the hall, down it, and her heart was in her throat even before she exploded through his bedroom door and froze in place.

The moonlight spilled through the window and bathed the two forms in its pale, liquid glow. A rumpled, tousled man knelt on the floor, holding her son in his arms, so tightly she wondered if Cody could breathe. The man's back was toward Jane, and his shoulders shuddered and convulsed as if he were sobbing. Cody stared at her from the darkness, wide-eyed, as the man rocked him back and forth.

"My son," he kept whispering, his voice raw and coarse. "My boy, my son. Thank God..."

Jane's heart seemed to grind to a halt. Without a second's hesitation, she stepped into the room, snatched the baseball bat from where it leaned in the corner, lifted it and moved forward.

"Mom, no!"

Cody's shout made the lunatic who held him pause and stiffen, as if just realizing someone else had come into the room. And Jane hesitated. Instead of bringing the bat crashing down on his head, she just held it there, ready, poised. Her throat was so dry that the words sounded raspy and harsh when she said, "Let him go. Let him go, right now, or I swear..."

And he turned very slowly, still hugging Cody tight, to face her. The movement bringing him out of the light, so that his face was in shadow. His brows drew together, and he seemed puzzled. Confused.

"Please," Jane said, and her voice wasn't quite as demanding or as confident this time. Her hands shook, and her grip on the baseball bat was none too steady. "Please, take whatever you want. Just don't hurt my son."

"Hurt him?" he said, his voice barely more than a whisper. Tormented, pain-filled, and weak. "No, I could never... I love him. He's *my* son, my Benjamin, my..." Blinking as if to clear his eyes, he turned to stare at Cody's small, frightened face.

Jane lowered the bat, reached out a hand, flicked on the light switch. She saw the man jerk in shock, saw the fearful glance he sent up at the light fixture on the ceiling above him. Then his gaze returned to the top of Cody's head, because he held him too closely to see much else.

"He's my son," Jane said, calmly, gently, and her eyes were fixed to Cody's. The man was obviously insane. "His name is not Benjamin, it's Cody. He's my son. Please..."

The man gave his head a shake. With deliberate tenderness, he clasped Cody's small shoulders and moved the boy away from him, just a bit. Enough so that he could stare down into Cody's face.

"You're...you're not Benjamin...." he whispered, and the pain in his voice had tears springing to life in Jane's eyes.

"I'm Cody, mister. Cody Fortune. I had a dad once, but he died when I was a baby. That's my mom." Cody pointed. "Her name's Jane."

The man's brows rose. He shook his head slowly, and tears filled his eyes. "Lord," he whispered. "You're not... But...I thought..." Blinking repeatedly, he gripped the bedpost, pulled himself to his feet, but remained bent over, his free hand pressing to his forehead. Finally, he straightened, and turned to face Jane fully, right beneath the overhead light.

She saw his face, and her jaw fell. She caught her breath, forced her shock into submission. But then she noticed the clothes he wore, and her heart flip-flopped all over again.

Dear God, he was the image of the man in the painting.

"I'm sorry," he said, glancing down at Cody. Then facing Jane, he repeated, "I'm so sorry I frightened you both. I..." He took a step toward her, but swayed a little, and grasped the bedpost to hold himself up.

"Th-th-that's okay," Jane said, and she wiggled her hand at her son. Cody ran to her, and she held him tight, never taking her eyes off the stranger. "Um...look, how did you get in here?"

He frowned, and looked around the room as if for the first time. "It's...it's different." He closed his eyes, pinched the bridge of his nose between thumb and forefinger.

Jane gently pushed Cody behind her, then took a backward step. She forcibly ignored his resemblance to the inventor she'd been mooning over so recently, and refused to think about his clothes. "You're, um . . . sick or something, aren't you," she said, almost as if to convince herself of it. "You're disoriented and you wandered in here by accident. I understand, all right? I'm not going to press charges, or anything like that."

The man's eyes opened. They were a bit dazed, clouded with pain, but they were also intelligent, perfectly sane and utterly sincere brown eyes. Brown eyes that looked so familiar it was downright uncanny. "What year is this, Jane?"

What year—

Jane swallowed hard and refused to so much as allow the thought to enter her mind. "Nineteen ninety-seven," she told him, as casually as if it were a question she answered every day. She nudged her son with her as she took another backward step into the hall.

The man's head jerked up fast and his eyes widened. "Nineteen . . ." Then he looked above him, at the light fixture in the ceiling, and when he lowered his head again, he grimaced in agony. "No. . . No, I went the wrong way. I came forward instead of going back. This can't be, I . . ." Still ranting, he lunged forward, toward Jane, but he never made it. He went down like a giant redwood, in a heap at her feet.

And that was when she noticed the gold wire-rims on the floor beside him. The satchel in the middle of Cody's bedroom floor. The little black box. She swallowed hard and told herself she was letting her imagination run wild. She bent down over him, reached into his vest pocket and pulled out the pocket watch—the exact same pocket watch she'd seen in the painting. And then she looked more closely at the small black box on the floor. An odd-looking remote control that looked an awful lot like the box the inventor was tinkering with in the painting.

"He asked what year it was. Said he'd *come forward*," she muttered. And she mentally revisited what Sheriff O'Donnell, and the library books, had told her about the genius scientist who'd lived here. That he'd claimed to have invented time travel...and then he disappeared.

"But that just can't be..."

"Mom?"

She rose, and turned to face her son.

"Can we keep him?"

Jane braced her hands on the edge of the bed, bending almost double as she tried to catch her breath. The man was no lightweight, that was for sure. Getting him into the bed had been no easy job. And whoever he was, he could use a shower, a shave and a clean change of clothes.

None of which, she reminded herself, was her problem. All she had to do was go downstairs, call Sheriff Quigly O'Donnell and have this intruder taken away to a jail cell.

Except that she hadn't placed that call just yet. And she was in no hurry to, for some reason.

"Mom, is he sick?"

She glanced at her son, shrugged. "I don't know. Probably. You'd better go wash your hands, Cody. It might be catching."

Cody didn't go. "Maybe he's not sick, Mom. Maybe he's hurt."

Jane slipped her arm around her son's shoulders and squeezed. "You must have been scared to death."

"Nah. At first I thought he really was my dad. That he'd come back somehow—even though I know that's impossible. The way he was hugging me and all." His chin lowered just a bit. "It was kinda nice."

Jane's throat tightened. Time to change the subject. "How did he get in here, sweetheart?"

Cody shook his head. "There was this big light, right in the middle of my room. Round. Like . . . sort of like a train tunnel, only light instead of dark. Really light. It hurt my eyes." Jane frowned, but her son kept on talking. "Then the light was gone, and he was laying on the floor."

"Lying on the floor," she said automatically, her gaze pinned to the man in her son's bed.

"That's what I said. Mom, you think he's a *ghost?*"

"No, Cody, I don't think he's a ghost." She frowned at her son. "And I didn't think you believed in anything as non-scientific as that."

"I don't. But what about—?"

"Come on," she said, feeling uneasier by the second. A train tunnel, indeed. "Let's go call Sheriff O'Donnell."

"Mom, we *can't!*" Cody pulled his hand free. "He needs help! He's sick or hurt or something! You can't go putting him in jail!"

"Honey, he broke into our house—"

"He's my friend!" Cody crossed his arms over his chest, lower lip protruding.

"How can he be your friend? You don't even know him."

"He hugged me," Cody said firmly. "*And* he said he loved me. And I'm not going to let you put him in jail."

Jane closed her eyes and sighed. "Codester, sweetie, we can't just keep him."

"Why not? He could help with the tree house I want to build in the backyard. When he's better, I mean. It would be great. And we could—"

"For all we know, Cody, this man could be a dangerous criminal. We can't just let him stay. He could be—" She looked down into her son's huge green eyes and felt like Attila the Hun. "Cody..."

"Please, Mom? We at least have to find out who he is, where he came from. What that flash of light was all about. I think he needs help, Mom."

She sighed. "I'll think about it."

Cody smiled. Then he yawned and rubbed his eyes.

"Come on. You'd better get some sleep now. In my room, okay?"

"Okay." Grinning, Cody raced down the hall and shot right into her bedroom.

Jane looked at the man who slept in her son's bed. There was, of course, no way she was going to let him stay here. She'd simply have to wait until Cody went to sleep to call the sheriff. She'd figure out a way to explain it to him later. Meanwhile, she wouldn't take her eyes off the guy. If he so much as glanced in Cody's direction...

She picked up the baseball bat and pulled up a chair. She'd give Cody fifteen minutes to fall asleep. Then she'd place that call.

Zach awoke in the darkened room. His son's bedroom, of course. He must have tired himself out working today, and fallen asleep reading to the boy. It was a wonder Ben hadn't shaken him awake to get him to finish the story, the way he usually did.

But where on earth was Benjamin?

He closed his eyes, shook his head. Of course. Benjamin was still visiting his grandparents in Boston. How could he have forgotten?

Well, then, as long as he was awake, he might as well get some work done.

Oh, bother.

Zach poked into his shirt pocket in search of his spectacles, but didn't find them there. He reached to the small stand beside the bed for an oil lamp, but he must not have left it there. All he had to go by was the moonlight streaming in through the window behind him as he scanned the room in search of the lamp. But what was this? There was an incredibly beautiful young woman asleep in a wooden chair beside the bed. She wore a pale nightgown, with short sleeves that revealed her shapely arms. Her head was tipped sideways, resting upon her shoulder. And her hair rolled in waves of red-brown satin, halfway to the floor. My word, she was something. But what on earth was she doing here? How had she...

Slowly Zach recalled his colleagues Wilhelm and Eli, and their penchant for practical jokes. They'd been teasing him about working too hard, about having no life, no interests, aside from his son and his work. He'd once been something of a rogue, engaging in affairs with some of the town's most notoriously improper young women. But he'd been slacking off lately, and devoting all his time to the current experiment. One that would change the world, if he ever made it work.

Once, those two clowns had suggested he'd been so long without a woman that he wouldn't know what to do with one if she showed up in his bed. So they'd decided to hire some doxy to prove their point, had they? My, she was beautiful. Unfortunately, he wasn't so desperate to prove his manhood that he'd risk disease to do so. He much preferred to choose his own lovers. A shame, such a shame.

He sighed. No doubt she'd report back to those two childish pranksters that he'd failed to show any interest in her...charms.

Well, he could at least avoid the ribbing he'd take over that.

Sliding from the bed, wondering only briefly why he felt so weak and slightly dizzy, he tiptoed to the chair where she slept, nearly tripping over the baseball bat his son must have left lying about. Amazing he hadn't spotted it before. He shoved it out of the way with his foot and stepped closer to the trollop, and touched that long hair, rubbed it between his fingers. Soft as down. He bent slightly, inhaled her scent and smiled. Oh, they'd gone all out. Must have paid extra for a clean and lovely girl. This one looked as fresh as a daisy, and smelled even better.

As he stood bending over her, she sighed and moved a bit. Her lips parted and her head tipped back. And Zach realized with a pang how very long it had been since he'd kissed a woman. And, aside from the common cold, perhaps, he didn't fear catching anything by kissing this one.

So he did. He bent lower, lifted her chin with the tip of his forefinger and fit his mouth to hers. Her lips were warm and moist and pliant, and they felt good beneath his. Better when a gentle sigh escaped them, one he inhaled. He nudged those soft lips apart, to taste more of her, and they opened willingly, easily. She was starting to come awake now. Starting to respond, kissing him back. He slipped his arms around her small waist and pulled her to her feet, cradling her between his legs and against his chest as he deepened his kiss. Her drowsy response ignited feelings in him that he'd long since forgotten. Feelings he hadn't thought he'd ever know again. Passion flared in his veins, and her body pressed closer, head tilted farther, lips opened to his questing tongue. Her hands crept up his back, clung to his shoulders, and his heart beat a wild tattoo in his chest. No, none of his halfhearted dalliances had produced this strong a response in him.

Not since Claudia...

And then a mighty shove sent him staggering backward, and Zach was too surprised to even wonder why he was so weak that a mite of a woman could send him flying.

She stood panting, glaring at him. "That's it," she fairly growled at him. "That's it. I was thinking about going easy on you, mister, but you've pushed me too far."

"Rough or easy," he told her, "doesn't much matter. I'm not interested in having sex with you, Miss, so you might as well be on your way." It was a lie, of course. He was *very* interested. If only he had one of those condoms on hand, he might even oblige her.

"Not . . . interested . . . *Sex?*" She blinked as if in shock.

"Oh, it isn't you, love." He smiled at her, reached out a hand to smooth her hair out of her eyes. She only stood there, apparently too shocked to move. "Actually, I'm more tempted than I've been in a very long time. You're lovely. But I've no wish to expose myself to . . . Well, you understand."

She shook her head. "No. I don't understand, and I don't think I want to. Listen, you're nuts. You're certifiable. I'm taking you downstairs right now, and I'm calling the sheriff. But don't bother waiting around for him, okay? Just get out."

He frowned, tilted his head. "Pardon?"

"I said get out," she told him. She was grating her teeth and her fisted hands were shaking at her sides. "Get the hell out of my house. Now."

"My word," he told her. "You really should consider a career in the theater. I've no idea what you're up to, darling, but this is my house, and it's you who really ought to be leaving."

She blinked. The anger was rapidly fading. It was fear he saw replacing it in her eyes.

"I'm sorry," he said, thinking perhaps she'd be beaten if it became known she'd failed. He almost reconsidered his decision to abstain. Sex with this fiery woman would have to be something to experience. "What if I let you stay a couple of hours, hmm? Will that be enough to convince them we had ourselves a good tumble?"

Her hand connected with his face in a streak, and he didn't have time to duck it. It thoroughly amazed him when her blow knocked him off balance. He landed on the bed, blinking up at her. Lord, why was he so weak? So dizzy? Had he been ill recently?

"Get out," she ordered.

"Enough," he said softly, still baffled by his physical state. "Are you daft? Must I prove to you that this is my home? Shall I send for the sheriff to have you carried out? Is that what you want?" He shook his head, lifted a hand and pointed toward the table near the window, its shape just visible in the darkness. "There is a worktable. Not the main one, of course, but I do keep one here in Benjamin's room. Some of my experiments are there. My tools. My notes. They're secret, naturally, but a common doxy like you could make neither heads nor tails of them anyway, so go ahead and look." He pointed to the far wall. "There is the hearth, and upon the mantel are a pair of oil lamps and some matches. Do light one, so you can see for yourself where you are, woman. And then kindly remove yourself. I have work to do."

The woman only stared at him, completely puzzled. And then, slowly, she moved to the wall. She touched an appendage there, and the room was suddenly flooded with light. Zachariah Bolton nearly fell on the floor in shock.

Three

Jane searched the floor, spotted the baseball bat and snatched it up again as she watched an apparently bewildered man gazing around Cody's bedroom as if in disbelief.

"What is this?" he shouted. "Where is the slate board? My notes? Lord, woman, who installed this confounded electrical illuminator in here, and what have you done with my notes?"

"Look," she said, holding the bat up in front of her. "I don't know who the hell you are, or what you're talking about, but—"

"My tools!" he yelled, turning this way and that, pushing a hand through his nearly black hair. "What in tarnation have you done with my tools? And my worktable? Woman, where is Aunt Hattie's credenza?"

The man was sick. And not just mentally, either. His face was pale, and thinner than it should be, and dark circles ringed his deep brown eyes.

"Thank heavens," he said at last, and fell to his knees on the floor, grasping that small box. "The device is safe, at least. The device..." He looked even more confused than before. "But...but I hadn't finished it yet."

She wanted to run from the room. Right that second, run down the hall to grab Cody, and then take him right out of this house. But the man on his knees in the center of the floor was looking at her, and she thought, maybe, he was remembering... The pain that slowly shadowed his face said more than words could. But he spoke all the same, staring hard at her.

"You're Jane."

She nodded, not moving. Telling herself to leave, call for help. And telling herself *not* to go to him and try to ease the confusion from his brow.

"And the boy... he's your son... He's not Benjamin."

"That's right. You remember, then," she whispered.

He closed his eyes. "I remember. Benjamin... my little Benjamin... he's..." His head bowed, and his shoulders began to shake. "He's dying. How could I forget that, even for a moment?"

Jane blinked. Dying? He had a son, who resembled her own, and that son was dying? "My God," she whispered, and the bat fell to the floor with a bang. "My God, no wonder you're so messed up." Warily she moved forward. And when she stood close to where he knelt, she touched his hair, stroked it away from his face and felt the tears that dampened it.

His arms closed around her legs, his head resting against her thighs. "I meant to go back, Jane. I meant to go back, so I could save him. Before he was ever exposed to the blasted virus. I meant... But I failed. A miscalculation. Something. I failed, and now I might have lost him forever."

Crazy talk again. But then, how sane would she be if she ever lost her Codester? A little chill raced up her spine, but she went right on stroking his hair. His entire situation resembled the history of Zachariah Bolton. No wonder he'd wandered here in confusion. "It's all right," she whispered, because there was a lump in her throat that prevented her speaking louder. "It's going to be all right. I'll help you. Okay?"

He said nothing. But she knew he was devastated. He clung to her, shaking, crying perhaps, confused and in terrible pain.

"What's your name?" she asked him.

"Zach," he muttered. "Zachariah Bolton."

She stiffened, and he must have felt it, because he straightened away from her. He pressed a hand to his forehead, as if trying to rub away a pounding headache, and then he slowly got to his feet. "I'm sorry. I'm falling apart. What must you think?"

"I think," she said, choosing her words carefully, "that you've been through something horrible and it's left you...confused."

"Insane, you mean."

"Of course not."

He shook his head and paced away from her. "You look at me as if you believe I'm insane."

"I...well...look, it's just that Zachariah Bolton would be over a hundred and thirty years old today."

He stopped pacing and stood, toying with the black box in his hands. "Zachariah Bolton," he said softly, "is thirty-five years old, Jane. He was born in 1862."

"That doesn't make any— What is that thing you're playing with?"

He looked up, blinked. "So the house belongs to you now?"

"Yes. My son and I, yes."

"Your husband...is he at home? May I speak with him?"

"I don't have—" She bit her lip, averted her gaze. Since when did the handbook on survival in the nineties advise women to tell insane housebreakers that they were all alone? "He's not here right now."

The man who claimed to be Zachariah Bolton frowned, and his gaze shifted downward. To her left hand, she realized belatedly. "You're not married, are you?" She didn't answer. He shook his head in wonder, and looked down at the box in his hand once more. And then he swayed a little, blinked as if his vision were blurring.

"You're not well," she told him.

He drew a fortifying breath and eased himself down onto the edge of the bed. "No. No, physically, I'm not at all myself. Side effects, I suppose. I hadn't expected them to be quite so severe."

"S-side effects...to what?"

He looked her squarely in the eye. "You'll run off to send word to the local asylum if I tell you. But I don't suppose I have much of a choice right now, do I? I need you, Jane. I need you to... Ah, but I can't make you understand this way. Come here."

She blinked, took a step backward, eyeing him as he patted the spot on the bed beside him.

He frowned, and then his brows went up and he nodded. "Yes, I don't suppose I behaved as a gentleman when I found you here earlier, did I?" And his eyes, for some reason, fixed on her lips, and remained there a moment too long. "I don't know what that was, Jane. A memory lapse of some sort. Side effects, as I said. I was remembering a time when two of my colleagues hired a..." He gave his head a shake. "No matter. I apologize for that. Please, come over here, just for a moment. If you stand there, you might be hurt when I show you what this device does."

She tilted her head. "What is it, some kind of stun gun?"

His eyes narrowed. "I don't know that term, but no, that's not what this is. I only want to show you how I got here, Jane, because if I tell you, you'll think I'm insane and throw me out before I can offer proof."

She took a step toward him. He held out a hand. "I am Zachariah Bolton, Jane, and if you'll just come over here, I'll prove it."

Sighing, she picked up her baseball bat. He glanced down at it, lifting one eyebrow. Jane went to him, sat down beside him on the bed. "I suppose you're going to tell me you traveled a hundred years forward in time, and that this little remote control gone haywire is your time machine."

He frowned hard. "How on earth could you know—"

"Oh, everyone around here knows about Zachariah Bolton. He was a genius. A man light-years ahead of his time. But he got a little crazy after his..." Her voice trailed off, and she lost her breath.

"After his son died? Yes, I suppose I will go a bit crazy if that happens. But, Jane, I have no intention of letting it happen." Her eyes widened as she stared at him. He glanced down at himself. "I've been wearing these clothes all night, as I sat up with him. No wonder you were so afraid of me. I look like a common tramp. I hadn't expected anyone to be here...except for Ben and perhaps Mrs. Haversham."

She stood up, shook her head. "Stop. Just stop talking this way. It's..."

"Crazy?" He nodded. "I know. I know. That's what all my colleagues kept saying. That time travel was physically impossible. That I was wasting my talents working on it. I was close, oh, so very close, for months. When Benjamin took ill...it did something to me. Gave me something...extra."

She was still shaking her head, still backing away. But his hand came up and caught her wrist, holding her still, bringing her close to him. With the funny-looking remote, he pointed. "That spot, right there, Jane. A spot some thirty-five feet above the ground, a spot that this house ended up being built around... There's a wrinkle there. An invisible wrinkle in the fabric of time. A doorway, Jane. And I can open it."

His thumb touched a button on the remote, and she heard a low-pitched hum. A pinprick of light appeared in the air halfway between the floor and the ceiling, at the room's center.

"My intent was to go back, and only a few months. I wanted to go to my Benjamin before he'd ever been exposed to the virus, and take him away before he could become infected. I wanted to save him. Surely you can understand that, can't you, Jane? Only hours ago you were willing to face me down with nothing but a wooden bat in order to save your own child. You'd do anything for him. You know you would."

She didn't like the way his eyes were blazing, or the tightness of his grip on her forearm. She pulled, but he got to his feet, gave one good tug, and she was pressed tight to him. His free arm snapped around her waist like a padlock's hasp, and he held her immobile. The fingers of his other hand worked the dial on the little black box, and the box began to hum. But the light remained the same.

"I messed it up, Jane," he said, his voice close to her ear, as he slowly turned a dial with his free hand. "My calculations were off somehow, and I came forward instead of going back. And not just a few months, but a century. A hundred years."

He gave the dial another twist, his grip on her waist tightening. She shook her head, but stopped pulling against his embrace. "This can't be," she whispered. "This just can't be."

Zach twisted the dial once more, but the light only flashed brighter for an instant and then died. For a long moment, Jane just stared at the spot where it had been.

He fiddled with the box, twisting the knob again, but nothing happened.

"Damn. I'm forgetting... I'm not insane," he whispered, and she realized, a little belatedly, that he was still holding her. Her back nestled intimately against the front of him, and his hand remained, lightly now, but snugly, at her waist. "The device needs time to recharge. How I let that slip my mind, I don't know. Three days, Jane, and I'll show you a wonder you'll never forget. I am exactly who I say I am. I swear to you. And I need you, Jane. I need you to let me stay here until the device can recharge and I can get back to my son.''

She turned in his arms, stared up into his eyes and knew, without any doubt, that this man fully believed every word he was saying. This poor, beautiful, sick man.

''You won't turn me away. I know you won't. There's kindness in your eyes, Jane. I see it there. You won't—''

''You need help,'' she whispered. ''Let me help you find it.''

He closed his eyes, his shoulders slumping forward as if he were too exhausted to go on. ''At least,'' he whispered, ''let me stay until morning. I'll think of a way to make you believe me by then. I'm too tired now. I can't think....''

''All right.'' Stupid, she told herself. Stupid to let an insane man stay the night. But she couldn't turn him away, not with that pain in his eyes. She just couldn't.

The relief in his face, in his eyes when he opened them again, was incredible. He pulled her closer, hugged her, rested his cheek in her hair. ''Thank you, Jane,'' he told her. ''Thank you.''

She was, he mused, perhaps the kindest woman he'd ever known. She'd suggested he get some rest, expressed concern over his health before she retired to her bed. Truth to tell, he was more than a bit concerned himself. That memory lapse...and this incessant weakness, and the recurring vertigo... Coming through the doorway had altered him physically, and he still wasn't certain of the extent of the damage. He'd fallen asleep instantly, and only awakened just now, to the sun rising high in the east. And he still felt exhausted and battered. His head ached intensely. But he had no time to waste lying in bed and waiting to recover. For all he knew, he might get worse, rather than better. Best, he decided, to get to work right away.

Work? But what work? What the hell could he do? Nothing, he realized slowly. Nothing but wait. He couldn't return to his own time until the device had recharged. So for three days he'd be here, unable to do a thing to help his son.

It wasn't hopeless. Merely a setback. He'd wait, and then he'd return. He'd return to the exact time whence he'd come. Benjamin's condition would not have had time to worsen. And from there, Zach would simply start over. Make a few adjustments, and try again. In the meantime, there was very little he could do. His main task, it seemed, was proving himself to Jane, convincing her to let him remain right here, for there was no other place....

Yes. He'd have to convince Jane to let him stay. Fortunately, Zach thought, influencing reluctant females to his way of thinking was one of his areas of expertise. Second only to science, in fact. Or had been, once. He wondered briefly whether he could drum up enough of his legendary charm to sway her. He had to try. There was more at stake than conquest here. There was Ben. Benjamin was safe... for the moment. So Zach was free to pursue the matter at hand.

But first...

He glanced down at his rumpled clothing and wrinkled his nose. First a bath, and a change of clothes. His carpetbag still lay on the floor, where he'd dropped it when he first came through. So at least he had the most recent notes—torn hastily from his journal in case he might need them—a few basic tools, a change of clothes and some toiletries. He carried these with him into the bathroom down the hall, and then marveled at the wonders to be found there.

At first he wondered how he'd manage without a lamp or a candle. But then he recalled the electric illuminator in Benjamin's—er, Cody's—room, and searched the spot on the wall just inside the door, where the control for the other one had been. He found the switch, moved it, and the bathroom filled with light. Zach simply shook his head in wonder, and explored further. The tub was huge, with spigots fixed into it. Water, hot, as well as cold, ran into the giant shining tub at the touch of a knob. Far more advanced than his own bathroom had been, and his had been the very latest in technology. Judging by the force with which the water spewed from the spigots, he knew there must be more power behind it than mere gravity. The necessary, too, was sparkling-clean and water-filled. Warm air blew gently from a register low on the wall. He smelled no wood smoke. Something else was obviously heating the water, and the house, as well. The very essence of day-to-day living, he realized slowly, had changed. Drastically changed.

He ran water into the tub, and soaked for a long time as he tried to imagine what other advances he'd discover in this new era. Automobiles... Had they proved practical, or been a passing fancy, as so many of his colleagues had predicted? Had this new generation of humanity wiped out disease? Achieved world peace? And this woman, Jane, owning this house filled with modern wonders and raising a son all on her own. Was this common today? Zach frowned as he considered it. Something told him that nothing about Jane was common.

He'd kissed her. Yes, he'd been in the throes of some sort of delirium when he did it, but not so much so that he couldn't recall every instant of that kiss. And her sleepy response to it. Her soft breath in his mouth, her hands splayed on his shoulders. She'd set a fire in him that he hadn't felt in a very long time. Perhaps ever. Oh, there'd been passion between him and Claudia, one he suspected was based more on his own youth and energy than anything else. But they'd really had very little in common. And, of course, he'd learned later that he'd been no more than an amusing diversion to her. She hadn't cared for him in the least. He'd been young, with little money and few prospects. She'd been married to a wealthy man, a woman of social standing who couldn't risk it all by admitting to her frequent affairs with naive young men. Much less admitting that she had become pregnant as a result of one of them.

She'd gone abroad to visit an aunt, or so the story went. Months later, Benjamin had been dropped upon Zachariah's doorstep, with a note promising Zach he'd be ruined, both socially and financially, if he ever breathed a word about the child's mother.

She'd never wanted to lay eyes on the baby or on his
father again.

And so she never had.

It had been, Zach mused, the best education he
could ever have. Oh, he'd learned all about women.
They were practical creatures. No woman would be
truly interested in a man who was less than wealthy—
particularly if he was less wealthy than she. Claudia's interest had recently been renewed. No doubt
due to the fact that her rich husband had passed,
leaving most of his money to a nephew. And in the
years in between, Zach had acquired his own wealth
and social standing. But he was no longer interested
in Claudia. For a time he'd become a user of women,
the way he'd once been used by one of them. Once he
understood how the game was played, he'd suffered
no further delusions about romance or love.

Perhaps the lovely Jane had learned the lesson, as
well, in a manner much the same as he'd learned it
himself. Or perhaps she was simply a lonely widow.
Though most widows of Zach's acquaintance continued to wear their wedding bands. That gave him
pause.

Jane. Beautiful, brave, passionate Jane. She looked
like an angel. But she kissed like a woman too long
without a man. He could, he mused, take care of that
problem for her. His thoughts surprised him, since
he'd given up his roguish ways long ago. But then,
he'd been very long without a woman's touch, and
hers had been . . . incredible. He had three days here,
after all, and little else to do besides wait.

Oh, yes. And a well-planned seduction would
probably go a long way in helping to convince the lit-

tle skeptic that he was who he said he was. Or at least convincing her to let him stay.

He swallowed hard at the thoughts racing through his mind. Was it some added side effect of the time travel making him addle-brained, or was it *her?* Either way, it didn't matter. He thought he had come up with a far simpler means to convince her now.

As he soaked, there was a knock at the door, followed by Jane's voice. "Are you decent?"

Some devil came to life inside him, all over again, and it was that devil who made him call, "Come in." Perhaps he was testing her to judge her reactions, so that he might gauge what sort of woman he was dealing with. A test, much like the many other experiments he'd performed in his day. He ignored the tiny voice in his brain that told him that theory was nothing more than self-deception. The woman got to him, in a way that disturbed him far too much to admit, even to himself.

The bathroom door opened, and the woman he'd been thinking about stepped inside. Aside from an initial start of surprise, she showed no reaction at all. Keeping her eyes averted, she moved through the room, extracting big, emerald green towels from a cabinet, and then a small pink plastic item, and a can of some sort. "If you were trying to shock me, you chose the wrong method," she said. "I was raised with brothers." She set the towels and the other items on a shelf beside the tub, and still without looking at him, turned to go.

"Jane?" She stopped, her back to him. She wore a robe now, over the thin nightgown of the night before. Pity. But that glorious hair still hung loosely down her back, making him ache to run his hands through it once again. "What is this?" he asked.

"I thought you'd want to shave." She still didn't turn.

Frowning, Zach leaned forward and picked up the pink thing, turning it this way and that. "This bit of a thing is a razor?" He could clearly see, upon closer inspection, that that was precisely what it was.

"Of course it is."

He sighed loudly, and achieved the desired results. She turned, but kept her eyes carefully glued to his face. "Could you...could you show me how it works, Jane? They've changed drastically in the past hundred years."

Her eyes narrowed as they searched his, and he tried desperately to keep the mischief hidden. He started to get up. "Stay where you are," she told him.

"I'll need a mirror—"

"Not if I'm doing the shaving," she said. Then she knelt beside the tub, picked up one of the towels and handed it to him. "Cover your—yourself," she told him.

"And soak this wonderful towel?"

Frowning at him, Jane dropped the towel into the water, so that it landed right in his lap, no doubt concealing the parts of his anatomy she'd rather not be tempted to look at too closely. Then she took up the can, shook it and depressed a button on its top. Mounds of white foam oozed from the spout and into her palm. Zach felt his eyes widen. Then she leaned over and smoothed the lotion onto his face. Her touch was warm, and trembling, and so good that he closed his eyes and relished it.

When she finished, she dipped her hands into the water to rinse them clean. Her fingertips brushed his thigh, and he knew then that certain bodily functions had not been damaged by the side effects of time travel. He hoped she didn't notice the change in the shape concealed by that towel.

"Now, you just take the razor and..." She demonstrated, by drawing the blade very carefully down over his cheek. "Just like that. You see?"

"Mmm..." he said. Then he opened his eyes and saw her scowling at him. "I mean, yes, of course. But...suppose I cut myself?"

"If you are who you say you are, then you've managed a straight edge in your time. And if you can handle that, you can handle this." She set the razor on the edge of the tub and got up to leave.

"I am who I say I am, Jane. And you'll believe it before breakfast. I promise."

She looked at him for a long moment, and this time her eyes betrayed her, dipping down to gaze at his chest and belly. Hastily she turned and left the room, closing the door firmly behind her.

Jane leaned back against the bathroom door and tried to steady her breathing. Whoever he was, the lunatic in her bathtub was incredible. And that made him dangerous. The sooner he was out of her house, the better. She closed her eyes, but still the image of that muscled chest, beaded with water, kept resurfacing in her mind. "The sooner the better," she muttered, and headed downstairs to start breakfast.

When she had the coffee brewing and Cody's favorite blueberry muffins in the oven, Jane went upstairs again to wake her son. But Cody was no longer in bed when she stepped into her room. For just a second, his absence startled her. And then she heard the reassuring sounds of his Nintendo game from down the hall, and sighed. As she dressed, she glanced up at the painting that hung on the wall above her bed...and then she went still, falling into the brown eyes of the man in that painting. The inventor. The time traveler.

He'd hopped right out of a Jules Verne novel and landed smack in the middle of her life.

Or so the man who'd somehow become her houseguest would have her believe. It was, to say the least, mind-boggling. The coincidence of it, anyway. He looked so much like the man in the painting. Even his clothes...

But it was impossible, of course. Still, something about the man pulled at her. She wanted to help him. And today she would. She'd convince him to let her take him into town, to see a doctor. Maybe he'd taken a blow to the head or something.

She hadn't warned Zach not to tell Cody where he thought he'd really come from, or who he thought he really was, and she should have. Lord, she could just imagine the call she'd get when Cody started sharing that tale with his fifth-grade class next week at school. Besides, it would only confuse him. He was far too young to grasp a concept like that, despite his above-average intelligence.

She finished dressing and went down the hall, then stood in Cody's doorway and stared for a moment. Cody stood near the desk, laughing uproariously as the man who claimed to be Zachariah Bolton, genius, worked the control pad, unerringly marching the little Mario on the screen right off a cliff and into oblivion.

He made an aggravated sound in his throat.

"Don't feel bad," Jane said. "I've been trying for months, and I still can't get past World Two."

Both of them turned to face her, and both were smiling. Zach's eyes glittered with something like wonder. "This," he said softly, "is amazing."

"And addictive. Be careful, or you'll find yourself glued to that thing like a fly in a spider's web." His smile broadened and she caught her breath. Clean and shaved, he was even more breathtaking. Especially when he smiled. Her errant mind chose that moment to recall the way that smiling mouth had felt when it made love to hers last night, and she quickly averted her eyes. Too late, though. He'd seen it. She saw the way his gaze lowered to her lips for just an instant. And she felt the air between them change.

She cleared her throat. "And, Cody, what have I told you about Nintendo before breakfast?"

"I know, Mom. But Zach's never seen anything like this. Have you, Zach?"

"Certainly not."

"Heck, Mom, they didn't even have TV in 1897."

She grimaced and shot a glance at him. "You didn't tell him—"

"He figured it out all by himself, Jane. Of course, it took him several guesses. As I recall, the first one was that I was a traveler from another planet. And then that I was a ghost. And finally that I was a..." He frowned. "What did you call it, Cody?"

"A time cop," Cody said.

Jane sighed. "I knew I never should have let you rent that Van Damme movie."

"Jane, really," Zach said. "Your language."

Jane rolled her eyes. "Breakfast will be ready in fifteen minutes," she told them both. "Be there."

"We will, Mom."

She eyed them both, wondering whether it was truly safe to leave Cody alone with the man, as delusional as he was.

"Don't go just yet, Jane," the man said, and he set the control pad down and got to his feet. "I have something to show you. In my satchel." He went to the bed, where the bag rested, unbuckled it and reached inside. What he pulled out was a newspaper, and he turned to face her, holding it out. "I promised I'd prove myself to you before breakfast. Go on, take it."

Swallowing hard, Jane stepped forward and took the crisp newspaper. It was so new she could still smell the ink. The *Rockwell Sentinel*, it said across the front—31 August 1897.

She blinked and looked up at him. Cody had forgotten all about his game, and was standing close beside her. "Wow. It's really true," he said in awe.

"Cody, these things can be made to order. You know that." Her eyes met Zach's. "I'm sorry, but this isn't good enough."

"I was afraid it might not be. Fortunately, I have more." He came closer to her, took her arm and turned her slightly, pointing. "There is a loose floorboard, the fourth one from that wall," he told her, pointing as he did. "Beneath it is my journal. Records I kept of the work I was doing. I put them there for safekeeping out of habit. My field is wrought with competitors, not all of them honest men. The notes are there, with the exception of one page. One I tore out and brought with me. Notes and figures I would need should the device require adjusting or repair.''

She stared at him, then at the floor, where he was pointing.

''Come, let's look. We need to get your skepticism out of the way, if I'm going to be able to proceed.''

''Look, Mom,'' Cody begged. ''He's telling the truth, I know he is!''

Shrugging, Jane moved to the spot he'd indicated. She bent down, pressing on the loose board with her hands, gasping and drawing away when it moved. She glanced his way, licking her lips, and then attempted to pull the board up.

''Allow me.'' He bent down beside her and pulled the loose end of the board until it came up a few inches. He held it there while she thrust her hands beneath and pulled out a heavy leather-bound journal. Then she sat down on the floor, pulling it into her lap.

''I can't believe . . .''

''You must believe, Jane. Please, open it up. Look at it.''

She brushed the dust from the leather cover and opened the book. The pages had yellowed and curled with time. But the handwriting on them was still legible. She shook her head in wonder.

''Several pages in, find the place where a page is missing.''

Nodding quickly, Jane turned the pages, taking care with them due to their fragile condition. She found the spot where jagged, yellowed edges were all that remained, and looked up into his eyes. He pulled a folded page from his vest pocket, smoothed the sheet and handed it to her. It was white and crisp and new. She took the page from him, stared at it in wonder, and then laid its uneven edge against the jagged, yellowed place in the book.

And the edges lined up perfectly. She scanned the pages, and noticed that the handwriting was identical, as well.

"My God," she whispered. "My God, it's true."

Her hands, still holding the page, began to tremble.

"I'm sorry to shock you this way," he told her gently. "But, Jane, I must convince you to let me stay here. Work here, until I can find out what went wrong with the experiment. I have to go back."

Her head came up, her eyes meeting his. "To save your son."

"Yes. Yes, I must prevent him from dying. If I can go back, return to a time before Benjamin was exposed, I can take him away. He'll never become sick, never die. And, Jane, I must do it from here, from this very room."

"Why?" she asked him, and she slowly realized that she was believing this man. In shock over what he was claiming, but still *believing* it.

"There's something here, some force, some sort of wrinkle in the fabric of time, as I told you before. My device opens a doorway into that void, and allows me to travel through it. But I've attempted opening the doorway in other areas, outdoors, on the ground, in other rooms. It doesn't function, Jane. Only here. Only in this very room."

He sighed and lowered his head. "And I must admit, there's a distinct possibility that the doorway is limited. That my travel will only take me from this time to my own, and back again. I might return only to experience the death of my son, and be unable to stop it."

He seemed surprised when he looked down to see Jane blinking tears from her eyes. "I don't know what I would do if I lost Cody," she told him. "It would kill me, I think."

"Then you understand how important this is to me."

She nodded. "Of course I understand. I'm a mother. How could I not?"

"Then . . ."

Jane licked her lips, drew a fortifying breath, and then saw the plea in Cody's eyes, identical to the one in Zach's. "All right," she said at last. "All right, you can stay. For as long as you need to."

He sighed, every muscle in his body relaxing at once, as the tension was visibly washed away.

"Thank you. It isn't enough, I know, but . . ." He shook his head, as if words failed him. "Thank you."

Jane got to her feet, pressed his journal into his hands. "I just hope you can do this—go back far enough, I mean."

He closed his eyes as the agony of possible failure washed over him, nearly buckling his knees. "I have to."

"Maybe not," Cody said quickly. "What was it that killed your son, Zach?"

He sighed hard. "Quinaria fever," he said softly.

Cody grinned, but Jane's heart almost stopped beating. She'd forgotten. My God, how had she forgotten? She gripped Cody's arm to stop him. "Cody, no—"

"We can cure that now," he said. "You don't have to worry about trying to go back to a time before Benjamin got sick. All we have to do is get the medicine for you, Zach, and you'll be able to make him well again."

He stared at Cody, gaping. And then he grabbed Jane's son, and hugged him tightly to his chest.

Jane stood there, watching them, trying to breathe, though her chest felt tight and heavy. She knew that she couldn't let this happen. She had to stop Zach from saving his beautiful, sick little boy.

Because if he did, there was a good chance she'd end up losing her own.

Four

She left them. There was nothing she could do. Not now, not with Cody standing there listening to every word. She had three days. Three days to find a way to keep Zachariah Bolton from returning to the past and curing his dying child.

My God, she must be some kind of monster to be thinking this way! How could she? But Cody... Cody was everything to her. All she had, all she'd ever wanted. If she lost him...

She knuckled a tear from her eye and told herself she was right. Benjamin's death had saved countless lives. It was meant to be, and as painful as that knowledge was, it was there. It was meant to be. You couldn't just go around altering history.

She bit her trembling lip. Maybe there was another way....

Damn, she'd drive herself crazy thinking about this. It made her dizzy when she considered the magnitude of it all, the ramifications, the impossibility of it. She deliberately focused on taking the blueberry muffins from the oven, setting the table. She had time. Three days. For now, she just needed to get through breakfast.

Cody and Zach showed up in the kitchen a short time later, and Jane was relieved to see that Cody had

showered and dressed. She served up blueberry muffins and scrambled eggs, and as she shook out Cody's
daily vitamin tablet she decided Zach could use one
as well.

He took the little pill from her hand and eyed it.

"You're still not looking all that great," she told
him. "It's a vitamin supplement. It's good for you."
He shrugged and swallowed the tablet, washing it
down with his orange juice. The entire time he ate,
Jane noticed his curious gaze darting around the
kitchen, at the appliances, the light fixtures, the microwave. He was brimming with questions, she knew
he was. But he also kept looking at her, and though
she tried to hide the worry, she knew it must show in
her eyes. Because his were probing and questioning.
She avoided that disturbing gaze of his, bustling
around the kitchen, getting butter for the muffins and
refilling coffee cups and juice glasses before they were
half-empty.

"Jane," he said, when she finally ran out of things
to do, and sat down to eat. "Is something wrong?
Have you had second thoughts about letting me
stay?"

And then a car pulled into the drive, stopping near
the shop, and saving her from having to answer. She
couldn't tell him. Not yet. She wasn't even sure how
to tell him, and she certainly couldn't do it in front of
Cody. She needed to speak to him when they were
alone together, and only after she'd found the right
words to convince him to give up this insane quest.

"I have to..." she began, but her words trailed off,
because Zach was on his feet, rushing to the door,
gazing out at the car with amazement on his face.

Jane couldn't stop herself from smiling as she walked up behind him. "It's a car. Um...an automobile. They..." The horn sounded. "Gee, Zach, I have an impatient customer to tend to. The explanation is going to have to wait until later."

"Go on, Mom. Me and Zach'll be fine." Cody came to stand close to Zach's other side.

"Zach and I," Jane said. "A whiz kid is supposed to know grammar."

Cody made a face at her, then glanced up at Zach. "You've seen cars before, right, Zach?"

Zach nodded, his gaze remaining riveted to the late-model Cadillac out front. "Nothing like that one, my boy."

Jane sighed. There wasn't any time to lose. She moved past them, out the door and down the driveway to the little shop resting at the end. And she knew as soon as she saw the car's passenger that she was in for a long visit. Isabelle Curry, the town of Rockwell's librarian and resident gossip. Fortunately, she was also an avid antique collector. A good customer, but a trying one. "Give me strength," Jane muttered, and plastered a smile on her face.

"Amazing," Zach said, trailing his hand over the smooth, gleaming red finish of the automobile, peering through the windscreen. "The glass is darkened."

"To keep the sun outta your eyes," Cody explained. "Why don't you get inside it, Zach? Mrs. Curry won't mind. She's nice."

"I don't think..." Zach stopped speaking when Cody pulled the door open, giving him a better view inside the machine. He couldn't stop himself. He poked his head into the thing and ran his hand over the soft plush fabric of the seats. And then he jumped a bit, because the boy had opened the door on the other side and jumped into the car.

"C'mon, Zach. I'll show you how it works."

"Cody, that probably isn't—"

"Look," Cody said, pointing. "It has a radio, and a CD player, so you can listen to music while you drive."

Cody twisted a set of keys that were dangling from the steering wheel, and then punched a button. Loud music—or something that vaguely resembled music—flooded the vehicle.

Amazed, Zach slid inside, settling himself behind the wheel and ignoring the deafening sounds.

"It's really easy to drive it," Cody said loudly. "Even I know how."

"You?"

"Sure. I watch Mom all the time."

"Your *mother* owns an automobile?"

"Sure she does. How do you think we go anyplace? It's in the garage, over there." He pointed, and Zach noticed the small outbuilding near where the pony shed used to be. "Look, it's simple," Cody went on. "First, you turn the key, like this..."

Cody turned the key still farther, and the vehicle came to life. Zach felt a smile splitting his face as the vibration of the motor moved through him, smooth and efficient and quiet. Far removed from the autos he'd driven.

"Then you just move this shift, here," Cody went on, as if thrilled with his role as teacher. "Push that pedal to go, and the other one to stop. Simple."

"There's no choke? No clutch?"

"Nope." Cody's eyes had taken on a decidedly mischievous gleam. "Wanna try it?"

Zach chewed his lip, truly torn. On the one hand, this was not his machine, and he had no business experimenting with it. On the other . . . oh, the wonder of it! He could barely contain the excitement coursing through him.

The decision was taken from his hands a second later, when Cody yanked on the shifting lever and the auto lurched backward. Its hindquarters were pointed directly toward the guest house at the end of the drive, and Zach barely managed to turn the wheel and alter its direction in time to miss the building. He stomped on the pedal that he thought was supposed to stop the thing, but instead it went faster.

"Tarnation!" he exclaimed, steering madly as the auto raced backward in a loopy pattern across the lawn.

"I shifted wrong!" Cody shouted, and yanked on the lever yet again. There was a horrible grinding sound. The vehicle lurched and bucked, suddenly changing direction and heading forward now.

Jane and a heavyset, bejeweled woman had emerged from the guest house. Both waved their arms and shouted, though Zach couldn't hear what they said, with the music blasting in his ears and Cody's uproarious laughter. The auto bounded over the grass, across the drive, and pointed its beak right at the two women. They split as it rolled between them.

Zach glanced over his shoulder to see the older woman picking herself up off the ground. If her face was any indication, she was hopping mad.

He tried the other pedal, and the vehicle ground to a stop so suddenly that he had to grab hold of the boy to keep him from being flung forward and hitting his head. He didn't dare remove his foot from the pedal. Though when the two women came running toward him, he was tempted to do just that. Free up his feet for a quick escape.

Jane got to the vehicle first, yanked the door open and reached past him to move the lever once more. With a snap of her wrist, she twisted the keys and yanked them out of the car when the motor died.

"What in the name of God do you think you're doing?" she screamed at Zach. Then her face softened as she sought the eyes of her son. "Cody, sweetheart, are you okay?"

"Sure, Mom. I was just showing Zach how to drive, is all." He slanted a glance at Zach. "He's not very good at it, though, is he?"

The other woman had arrived now, spluttering and red-faced. "Who is this person, and what in the world is he doing in my car?"

"It's all right, Mrs. Curry," Jane said soothingly, turning to the woman. "No harm done. The car is fine, see?"

Cody got out his side, and Zach figured it would be a good idea to do the same. He was embarrassed beyond measure.

"It was my fault," Cody said, hurrying around the car. "I wanted to try driving your car, Mrs. Curry. I thought I knew how. Gee, if Zach hadn't jumped in and stopped it, I don't know what I would have done."

Jane's eyes widened to the size of saucers, and she glared at her son. "Cody Nicholas Fortune, you know better than to—"

"Oh, my!" said Mrs. Curry, rushing to Cody and hugging him against her ample belly until Zach wondered if the boy would be smothered. "You poor child. You must have been so frightened. Oh, Jane, you mustn't punish him for this. Boys will be boys, you know. I never should have left the keys in the ignition with a child of his age nearby. Whatever could I have been thinking?"

She released Cody, who sent his mother an angelic smile. And then Zach found himself embraced by the ubiquitous Mrs. Curry. "And you!" she ranted, squeezing him until his seams nearly popped. "A true hero. Chasing down that car and jumping in to save a little boy! What courage!"

"Thank you," he managed, but his words were muffled by her embrace.

She released him, beaming. "Jane, dear, aren't you going to introduce me to this modern-day superman?"

Jane—from behind gritted teeth, Zach suspected—said, "Of course. Isabelle Curry, meet Zachariah B—" She bit her lip.

"Bolton," Zach finished automatically. Jane made her eyes huge and sent him a look that would wilt fresh lettuce. "Er... the third," he added.

Isabelle blinked. "Of course! I would know you anywhere. My goodness, have you any idea how much you resemble your grandfather?"

"I've been told it's quite remarkable," Zach said.

"I should say so. Whatever brings you to Rockwell, Mr. Bolton?"

Zach frowned and searched his brain.

"He's, er...tracing his family tree," Jane said quickly.

"Yes. I was very eager to see what my... grandfather's house looked like today."

"Well, of course you are," Isabelle said. "Where are you staying while you're here, Zachariah?"

"Here," he said.

Jane's eyes burned holes through him.

"Here?" Isabelle repeated. Her excitement died a slow death, and something else replaced it in her eyes as she looked from him to Jane and back again. "With Jane?"

Jane lowered her forehead into her palm.

"Well, now, isn't that...nice?" Isabelle said. She turned to Jane, but when their eyes met, the smile left Isabelle's lips. "I really should be on my way. Lots to do, you know." She held out a hand to Jane. "My keys, dear."

Jane handed them over, then looked on as Isabelle got into the car and started the engine. The woman grimaced when the music blasted, and poked her thumb on a button a little harder than was probably necessary to shut the sound off. A second later, she was gone, spewing gravel in her wake.

Jane pushed her hair back with both hands, tipping her head skyward. "I don't even know where to begin."

"I apologize, Jane," Zach said. "I was so intrigued by the automobile that I used poor judgment."

"You," she said, poking him in the center of his chest with her finger, "are not to get anywhere near a car again unless I'm with you. Got it?"

He nodded, but couldn't help smiling a bit at her anger.

"And *you,*" she said to her son. "You lied to Mrs. Curry. How many times have I told you about honesty?"

"Well, gee, Mom, I couldn't tell her the truth. That Zach didn't know how to drive because he came from another time, and stuff. She wouldn't have believed me."

"You...you..." Jane looked helplessly at Zach. Zach shrugged.

"Besides, you lied to her, too."

"Well, yes, but..." She blinked slowly. "Cody, I..." And finally shook her head. "You're right. I lied, too, and it was wrong. Unfortunately, I had to."

"So instead of never telling lies at all, we should never tell lies unless we have to?" Cody asked innocently.

The child's intelligence was astounding. And Zach knew the boy was only teasing his mother at this point. Fortunately, Jane knew it, too. He could tell by the narrowing of her eyes. She dropped down to her knees and took her son by the shoulders. "There might be times, Cody, when you have to tell a lie to other people, especially if you're doing it to avoid hurting someone or causing a whole lot of trouble, or because you know you won't be believed anyway. But there will never, never, be a time when you will have to lie to me. Understand? No matter what you have to tell me, Codester, I'll believe you. So you'll never have to keep the truth from me. All right?"

Cody smiled. "Okay, Mom."

"Good."

"Can I go ride my bike now?"

She nodded, and he turned and raced away toward the back of the house.

Zach couldn't take his eyes from her.

"What are you looking at?" she asked when she met his gaze at last.

He shook his head slowly. "I..." He cleared his throat. "Your son is very lucky to have you for a mother, Jane Fortune."

A pink blush crept up her neck and spread into her face. Zach resisted the urge to reach out with his hand, and feel the warmth of it.

She blinked, perhaps in confusion. "Compliments aren't going to get you out of this, Zachariah. You screwed up."

"Mrs. Curry will get over it."

"Sure she will, but not before she's told everyone in town that I'm a shameless hussy who's captured herself one hell of a hunk and is parading him around right in front of her impressionable son."

"What," he asked, "is a hunk?"

Her blush deepened and she lifted her brows. "I didn't say hunk, I said skunk."

"I distinctly heard you say hunk."

"My reputation is ruined. They'll probably report me as an unfit mother."

"You think Mrs. Curry believes we're...er..."

"Having sex?" she inserted, and Zach blinked at her casual use of the words. "Of course she does. What else would she think?"

"I fail to see why she'd jump to such a drastic conclusion."

"Take a look in the mirror, Zach. Mrs. Curry isn't numb from the neck down, or blind, or gay. And she's probably pretty sure I'm not any of those things, either." She shook her head. "Lord, I hope it doesn't make the *Rockwell Daily Star*. 'Local Spinster Living in Sin. Read all about it!' "

Zach resisted the urge to laugh. She was sincerely upset over the blemish he'd caused to her reputation. Though it was difficult to focus on that, when he was fairly certain she'd just said she found him attractive. Unless he'd misunderstood.

"Gossip hasn't changed much, has it?"

"Nothing's changed in this little town, Zach. Anywhere else, it wouldn't matter if I paraded men in and out of my bedroom day and night. No one would care. Here, though, we have Isabelle Curry, Rockwell's answer to modern morality, and her partner in crime, Pastor McDermott. And they're both on the school board, too." She shook her head.

"I'm sorry," Zach told her, and he meant it. "Perhaps we could say I was renting a room from you, or..."

"No one would believe it, Zach."

Zach sighed, truly sorry for causing Jane so much strife. "I suppose the best thing I can do is get hold of that miracle drug of yours as soon as possible, and be on my way. Surely your reputation can survive a mere three days of living in sin?" She rolled her eyes.

"Meanwhile, Jane, would it be better if I were to stay here in the guest house?"

"It's not a guest house anymore."

Zach looked past her, at the guest house—or at what had been the guest house. Now bric-a-brac lined shelves beyond the windows, and a sign above the door read Times Remembered—Fine Antiques and Collectibles.

"Would you like to see it?" she asked softly. And though he really should have been beginning the search for this new drug, Zach found himself nodding. A few more minutes wouldn't matter.

"Yes," he said. "I'd like that very much."

The smile that touched her lips, and the light in her eyes, told Zach that this little enterprise meant something to her. And that she was proud of it. She led him through the front doors, and Zach didn't recognize the place. The entire building had been converted, partitions knocked down. It was one large room now, with a long counter across the back side, and rows of shelves everywhere else. The shelves were lined with too many items to name. Canisters, dishes, knickknacks, music boxes. There was an entire section of books, another with artwork. And a large corner had been left open, for several pieces of furniture that had been cleaned and polished until they shone. An oak rocking chair. A sewing machine. A pedestal table.

Each item in the shop had a price tag dangling from it. And on the counter in the back sat a large black cash register that had obviously come from his time, as well. Zach doubted he'd recognize its modern-day counterpart.

"I'm impressed, to say the least, Jane. A woman setting up and running her own business. Owning her own home and automobile. Raising her son alone."

She waved a dismissive hand at him. "Don't be impressed until I make enough money to expand."

"Are you...having financial problems, then?"

She smiled at him. "Zach, my family is one of the wealthiest in the country. I have trust funds and interest-bearing accounts enough to buy the moon."

Zach tilted his head. "I don't understand. Why—"

"Growing up in Minneapolis, I lived in my father's mansion. Servants at my beck and call. More clothes than I could wear in a year. Cars and private schools and money, money, money."

"And?"

"And I hated it. Zach, Fortune Cosmetics is a monster. My family think they're running the business, but the truth is, it's running them. My father is so jealous of my uncle Jake that they can barely speak without an argument. And they're brothers. My mother...all she cares about is money and scheming to get more of it. I just didn't want any part of that. Not for me, and especially not for Cody."

She shrugged and paced toward him, eyes dreamily scanning the aisles of her shop. "I've always been the old-fashioned one. My grandmother...she knew that about me. More than I ever realized. When she died, she left me this place. So I left home to come out here and try to find a simpler life." She looked up at him, and smiled fully. "And instead, I got a time-traveling inventor."

"Not exactly simple," Zach said. "I find it amusing, Jane, that you see yourself as an old-fashioned woman. To me you seem the opposite. Strong. Independent. A freethinker. Everything I always..." he stopped himself from finishing when he realized he was going to say "wanted." "Everything I always thought of as modern," he said instead. It was true, what he'd been thinking, he confirmed, a bit surprised. Oh, yes, he'd had his share of women since Claudia had broken his naive young heart. But all the while, he'd scoffed at their docile ways and insipid giggles. Their meek manners and false shyness. Their constant quest for wealthy husbands. Deep inside, he'd secretly wished for a modern woman. One who had her own opinions and lived as no man's servant. Not a fainting, timid, helpless child, but a woman like... a woman like Jane Fortune.

Not that he wanted any woman bound to him. Not even one like this. No, he'd learned his lessons too well for that. But just to know one. Just to be with her...

"Maybe I'm modern from a nineteenth-century point of view, Zach," she said. "But to a twentieth-century mind, I'm the one stuck in a time warp."

Zach drew in a breath, let it out slowly. "Tell me about... about Cody's father."

Jane's head came up quickly, her soft brows bending together. "No."

"I didn't mean to pry, Jane. I was just wondering how such an old-fashioned girl managed to—"

"I really should be working on the books," she told him. "Why don't you go back to the house and finish your breakfast?"

He'd touched on a tender subject, then. All right. He told himself he wouldn't ask again. Though, for some reason, he was dying to know about the man who'd fathered Jane Fortune's child.

"Yes, I suppose I will," he said. And he managed to take his eyes off her, turn and leave the shop.

"We have lunch at noon," she told him as he started through the door.

He nodded, and closed it behind him.

Jane had more customers that morning than she'd had since she'd opened the shop. A few of them even bought something. The rest, she was convinced, had come to see if they could catch a glimpse of the man Isabelle Curry had no doubt told them about. The man who was living in sin with an unmarried mother. Damn. It had been hard enough seeing the speculation in their eyes when she arrived here. Everyone wanted to know where her husband was. Most came right out and asked, though a few were subtler. She didn't blame them for being curious. She'd moved into their close-knit, old-fashioned midst, and they wanted to know what kind of person she was.

Lord, now they probably thought they did.

"I need a slate board," Zach said.

Cody tilted his head. "There's one in the attic."

Zach's head came up. He'd been muttering to himself, unaware of Cody's presence in the room. He'd stationed himself at a small table in Cody's bedroom. The tools he'd brought along with him lay scattered around him on the table. The device, too, was there. Its protective cover removed, and its insides exposed as he checked to be sure it hadn't been damaged coming through the portal. The leather-bound journal with his notes inside was open, and a newfangled ballpoint pen lay beside it. Zach had already filled three new pages with his account of his trip.

"Cody. Just the man I want to see."

"Really?"

"Yes, indeed. I'm having some trouble with your modern vernacular. Tell me, son, what does it mean when a woman refers to a man as a, uh, hunk?"

Cody grinned. "Means he's handsome."

Zach felt his brows lift in surprise. "Handsome?"

"Verrrry handsome," Cody said. "Did my mom call you a hunk, Zach?"

"Er...no. No, of course not. I read it in a book, actually."

"Uh-huh."

Zach actually felt his face heat. So Jane found him to be...handsome. Verrrry handsome. It wasn't such a major revelation. And it certainly shouldn't be this pleasing to have confirmation of what he'd already suspected. He cleared his throat. "You were telling me about the attic?" he prompted, in an effort to change the subject.

"Yeah," Cody was saying. "There's lots of neat stuff up there. A big safe, and some old furniture. But I don't know why you need a chalkboard."

"Ah, yes, my safe." Zach frowned. No doubt everything in it was worthless today. And it occurred to him that he was, for the second time in his life, lusting after a woman who was far wealthier than he. That thought troubled him more than it should. He cleared his throat. "The slate board. I need it for calculations, Cody. My work involves complicated mathematical problems, and it's easier to work them out if I have..." He let his voice trail off, because Cody had turned away from him and yanked open a drawer.

"How come you don't just use this?" He showed Zach a small unit, a bit smaller and thinner than Zach's device.

"What...?"

"It's a calculator," Cody told him. He turned so that Zach could view the tiny screen on the thing, and he pressed numbered buttons. "Watch this. One hundred fifty-three times forty-five divided by 56.9 plus two. Equals...." He pressed the button with the equal sign and held the box up to Zach.

It read 123.0017574. Zach shook his head slowly, and turned to the table, rapidly doing the figuring on a sheet of scrap paper. Amazingly, he came up with the same answer.

"It's gonna be a lot faster this way," Cody said, and he set the calculator down on the table beside Zach's journal. "I'm really sorry about Benjamin." Cody pulled up a chair, close beside Zach's, and sat down.

A huge lump rose in Zach's throat as he recalled, vividly, the way Ben used to work at his side before he became too weak from the illness to do so any longer. That was when Zach had moved his table and tools into his son's bedroom. So that they could work together the way they used to.

"I want to help," Cody said.

Zach blinked at his burning eyes, and ruffled the boy's hair with one hand. "You're a good man, Cody. But I'm not sure what you can do."

"More than you think." Cody spun the chair he sat in around and wheeled it across the hardwood floor, stopping at the desk on the other end. "You haven't seen my computer yet."

"Another modern wonder?"

Cody nodded and flicked a switch. "I have a modem. We can talk to scientists all over the world, download all kinds of information. And you can feed in all your numbers, and try making changes on the computer before you try it on the real machine. That way, you might be able to figure out if something's gonna work before you go ahead and do it."

Zach braced one hand on the desk, blinking rapidly. "This machine...can do all that?"

Cody grinned. "Yeah."

"Are all children in this century as smart as you are, Cody?"

"Nah. I'm s'posed to be gifted."

Zach nodded, and drew his own chair over beside Cody's. "Well, it's a good thing. I'm beginning to feel decidedly uneducated. It does look as though this equipment of yours can save me a lot of time. So...will you teach me, Cody?"

Cody nodded hard, and it seemed to Zach the boy's spine lengthened and straightened. Zach watched and listened as Cody explained the machine to him. Part of him was wishing he could take the modern wonder apart to see what was going on inside it, what made it work. But he couldn't risk breaking it. Already he knew this piece of equipment would cut his research time by leaps and bounds. If he'd had access to this in his own time...

Perhaps he could find a way to avoid the side effects before he returned to the past. Or even a way to speed up the recharging process. And get back to his son all the sooner.

Jane found them together in Cody's room, hunched over the computer, and she stood there a moment, watching as Zach slowly punched keys and Cody looked at him with adoration in his eyes.

"Time to wash up for lunch, Codester," she said, startling them both.

"Okay, Mom." Cody smiled up at Zach. "We'll save this, Zach, and work on it some more later." Cody executed the save command, jumped out of his chair and rushed past Jane on his way to the bathroom down the hall. Zach got up, as well.

"Wait a minute," Jane said. "We need to talk."

Zach's brows rose, and he sat back down. Jane came into the room, glancing down the hall first, to be sure Cody was out of earshot. Then she took the seat her son had formerly occupied.

"Cody...he's a special boy."

"I can see that."

"His IQ is far above what's considered normal," she explained. "And from what I've read about you, I imagine yours is, too."

He shrugged, saying nothing.

"Zach, don't get too close to him."

He looked confused.

"Look, I don't want to see him get hurt. We both know you have to go back to your own time, eventually. But he's getting attached to you, I can see that already."

"Ah . . . I see what you're getting at. But, Jane, I need the boy's help. With the use of this machine, I can—"

"I don't care about the machine, Zach. What I care about is my son."

"Me, too," he said softly. And she felt a rush of guilt for objecting so strongly. Even more for what else was on her mind. She sighed, and lowered her head. "I know how important this is to you. I do. It's just . . . he's never had a father, Zach. And lately, all he's talked about is wanting one."

"I understand that," he said.

"No, you don't. You can't possibly. He's—"

"I understand, Jane." He sighed, and placed a hand on her shoulder. "Benjamin and Cody have more in common than you know. My Ben . . . he's never known a mother's love, and since he's been ill, it's all he's talked about. Wanting a mother. I understand everything you're saying."

He did, she realized slowly. She swallowed hard, looking him in the eye. "I'm sorry . . . about your wife, I mean."

Zach lowered his head, but not before she saw the bitterness flash in his eyes. She frowned at him. But he shook his head, seemingly eager to change the subject. "This drug," he said. "The one that can cure my son. Do you have any idea where I can obtain it?"

She drew a breath, lifted her chin. "I've been wanting to talk to you about that. Zach . . ."

"We can't get the medicine without a doctor help-ing us, can we, Mom?" They both turned to see Cody in the doorway, drying his small hands on a towel. "Don't you need a prescription?"

Zach's eyes met hers, and they were worried. "Yes," she said. "It's a powerful antibiotic, and a controlled substance. You can't buy it unless a doc-tor orders it."

"Then we'll contact a doctor," Zach said. "We'll explain, and—"

"And he'll have us all tossed into a rubber room," Jane said. It wasn't a good solution, and maybe it wasn't even a solution at all. More like a delaying tactic. When Zach only frowned, she explained, "He'll think we're nuts."

"Then we'll find another way." Zach's eyes were intense.

"We can look it up on the computer," Cody said. "Find out how to make the medicine, and—"

Zach shook his head. "We'd have the same set of problems, though. We don't have the supplies or equipment we'd need to create the drug. And if we didn't get it exactly right, it might not work at all. I can't risk failure."

Cody stood still, gnawing his lip. "Mom? You know how you said it was only okay to tell a lie when you really, really had to?"

She looked at her son through narrowed eyes. "Yeah?"

"Well, is it the same with, uh...with stealing?"

"Cody! You know it's never, ever all right to steal. Not ever!"

"Why, son?" Zach asked, going to Cody and kneeling in front of him. "Do you know where we can find some of these pills?"

"Sure. Doc Mulligan keeps all kinds of 'em in the little white cabinet at his office. 'Member, Mom? When I had the strep throat? He just opened up his cabinet and got out a bottle of penicillin. He has lots of antibiotics in there."

Zach looked at Jane. Cody looked at Jane.

"No." She shook her head firmly. They were still looking at her. "No, we're not doing it. Isn't it bad enough we have the whole town thinking I'm having—" She bit her lip. "We're not going to convince them I'm a master burglar and a drug addict, as well."

"We could leave money to pay for the pills, Mom. So it wouldn't *really* be stealing."

"Cody Nicholas Fortune, I do not want to hear one more word about this. Do you understand? Not one word. No one in this house is stealing *anything, anywhere, anytime.* Got it?"

Cody's chin fell to his chest. "Yeah."

"Good. Now...lunch is ready. Come on downstairs, the both of you."

She sailed out of the room, and they followed.

"Perhaps," she heard Zach saying, "I could convince this good doctor to give me some of the pills. If I were to see him, I mean."

"He's smart," Cody replied. "He always knows if you're faking it."

"Well, maybe if I spoke to him. Where did you say his office was, Cody?"

Jane turned and glared at Zach, but Cody was already giving him detailed directions to Doc Mulligan's office. She couldn't put it off any longer. She had to talk to Zach, tell him why he couldn't go through with this. And she had to do it soon. Tonight, after Cody went to sleep.

Five

Zach needed rest. Jane had made up a spare bedroom for him to sleep in. He hadn't taken advantage of it yet, though every muscle in his body was aching to do just that. He was fairly certain he was running a fever. He felt slow and a bit groggy at times. But then, at other times, he felt perfectly fine. The symptoms did not seem to be easing as quickly as he had expected they would. Hopefully the research he was doing while he waited for the device to recharge would give him the answers he needed to avoid this kind of illness hitting him on the return trip.

The device. It sat on Cody's desk beside his computer, and Zach picked it up, held it in his palm. Hard to imagine that something this small could mean the difference between life and death for his son. Already it was beginning to recharge. It might even be strong enough to open the doorway now, though if it wasn't at full power, there would be something different awaiting him on the other side. He might go back farther than he'd intended, which wouldn't be too terrible. Then again, he might not get back far enough. And that would be disastrous. No use risking it. He didn't have the drug yet, anyway. Two more days. The device would be at full power, and it would send him back to the precise moment whence he'd come. And he'd save Benjamin's life.

He was glad that the time travel hadn't seemed to affect his intelligence. He'd picked up Cody's computer lessons very quickly, and spent half the night "inputting data," as the boy called it. Transferring all his notes and calculations onto the computer. With the boy's help, he'd contacted a physicist in Detroit, and "downloaded" some "software" that enabled the computer to perform the tasks Zach needed it to. It was amazing. Utterly amazing.

He'd nearly finished filling this thing with all his notes. Cody had fallen asleep on his child-size bed. Zach felt bad for having the light on and clicking the keys while the child tried to sleep. It was time for a break, anyway. His eyes were beginning to glaze over.

He went to the bed, bent over it and gently slipped his arms beneath the sleeping child. When he picked him up, he was painfully reminded of Benjamin, so weak he could barely get out of bed anymore without Zach's help. Cody was heavy by comparison, and the age difference wasn't solely responsible for that, as Zach knew all too well.

He looked down at Cody's freckle-spattered face and red curls. And his heart squeezed tight. Lowering his head, he kissed the child's forehead. Zach wondered whether Cody's father were truly dead, or whether he'd simply abandoned his child the way Claudia had abandoned Benjamin. If he had, Zach thought grimly, he was a fool. To have a son like Cody and a woman like Jane... Any sane man would kill to keep them. Not walk away.

He stepped into the hallway, carried Cody to the guest room Jane had made up for him, then lowered him gently into that bed. He'd sleep more soundly here, without the light and the clicking keys. He tucked Cody in, and the boy stirred, opened his eyes and peered up at Zach.

"I wish," he said, his voice slurred with sleepiness, "I could have a dad like you."

Zach blinked the inexplicable burning that sprang into his eyes. "If I could, my boy, I'd make you my own." Cody smiled and fell back into a deep sleep. But Zach only stood there, shocked at the words that had just fallen from his lips. Make Cody his own? And Jane, as well? Good Lord, what kind of foolish fancy had come over him just now? For just an instant, though, the thought had occurred to him, and now he couldn't get it out of his mind. The thought that he could take them both back with him when he opened that doorway the day after tomorrow. Make his son well, and give him the mother he'd been wishing for. And an older brother to boot. That he could keep Jane Fortune, that incredible mixture of modern woman and old-fashioned girl, by his side, make her a part of his life, for always...

Ridiculous. Not only did he have no use for a woman in his life, he had no delusions that Jane would agree to such a scheme. To leave her modern conveniences, her microwave, her automobile? To take Cody from his computers and Nintendo games? Half of what the child had learned in his life wasn't even known in Zach's time. No, it was a foolish notion, and one best left unexplored. He had his son, and his work. And that was all he needed. All he'd ever needed.

He returned to Cody's computer screen, working some more, waiting, as he'd been waiting all night, for the sound of Jane's footsteps as she walked past on her way to bed. He glanced down at the note he'd made earlier, when he asked Cody if he knew the name of the drug that would cure quinaria. And, of course, the boy genius had readily supplied it. Tryptonine. He had everything he needed to proceed, but he couldn't do a damned thing until Jane was asleep. A glimpse at his watch told him it was after eleven, and she still hadn't retired. What was she waiting for?

The door opened, and Jane stood there, a cup of fragrant coffee in her hand. "I saw the light was still on," she said. "Thought you could use sustenance." When she came in, he saw the plate of cookies in her other hand. And his stomach growled a welcome.

"Thank you, Jane."

"Are you going to stay at this all night?"

"I want to be ready. When the device has recharged, I need to be ready to use it. If I can find an explanation for these side effects before then, all the better."

She nodded. "I know that, but Zach, you won't do Benjamin any good at all if you work yourself until you collapse." She lifted the cup, and he took it, his hand touching hers. Jane frowned, quickly looking down at his hand. Then she came closer, pressed a palm to his forehead, and then to his cheek.

He liked her this close to him. He liked her touching him.

"You're burning up!"

"You're exaggerating. It's only a slight fever."

Her brows rose, twin arches over beautiful eyes that he could have spent a very long time looking into. "So what is it? Are you coming down with quinaria fever, too?"

"No. I had it as a child and somehow survived, so I'm immune. This is just...another side effect, I suppose."

She set the plate of cookies on the table and left the room, returning seconds later with a pair of small white tablets, which she gave to him. "Take these. They'll help with the fever."

He did. And then he snatched up a cookie and dunked it.

"Zach, have you thought about what's going to happen to you when you go back through that...that portal of yours? If you don't find a way to avoid the side effects, I mean?"

He averted his eyes. "No way of telling. I've been trying to understand exactly what it was about the portal that caused these reactions, but so far, I just don't know."

"You don't look any better than you did when you arrived. Worse, in fact."

He shook his head. "No, it's no worse. Not much better, but a little. Perhaps I'll build up a tolerance, so that when I go back the side effects will be less pronounced."

"Or maybe it will get worse every time, and you'll arrive back there barely able to function."

"That's not a consideration, Jane. As long as I get the drug back to Benjamin, I really don't care what ill effects I suffer."

"I know." She closed her eyes very briefly. Bit her lip, as if there were something there, about to jump out. A second later, her eyes opened again, and she drew a shaky breath. "But there are some other side effects—repercussions to what you're planning to do—that you haven't considered, Zach. And I think it's time you did."

Zach frowned down at her. "Something's bothering you about all of this. I knew that this morning. But, Jane, my son is dying. What else could possibly matter?"

Jane lowered her head, and Zach caught her chin, lifted it, searched her beautiful eyes. "You don't want me to go back. Why, Jane?"

She parted her lips, but closed them again.

"It's all right. I think I know why." And then, very slowly, he lowered his head, and touched her lips with his. They trembled against his mouth, and the desire he'd felt for her all along came flooding back, swamping him, shaking him to the core. He slipped his arms around her slender waist and pulled her close to him, tight to his body. His mouth fed on hers as her lips parted. A tremulous sigh escaped her, and he inhaled it, relished it, as her arms crept around him. Her hands clasped his shoulders, and she arched against him.

Dazed and aroused beyond reason, Zach lifted his head. "I want you, Jane. I want you to the point of distraction."

He lifted one hand to thread his fingers in her hair, while the other remained at the small of her back, holding her tight to him.

"I..." she breathed, and then stiffened, her eyes widening as she stared up at him. "No," she said softly, and there was no mistaking what he saw in those eyes. It was fear. "No, I won't fall...not again."

And then she turned and ran from the bedroom. Something compelled Zach to move. He lunged for the door and watched her run down the hall to her own room. Watched her go through the door, closing it hard behind her. And then he heard the gentle sounds of her bedsprings creaking as she lay down. He closed his eyes and told his imagination to behave itself. And while he was at it, he told his heart to go back to sleep, where it had been for the past six years, and to stop yearning for things it could never have.

God, he must be suffering mental, as well as physical, exhaustion for these thoughts to keep creeping in. He needed to sleep.

But not just yet. He had a mission tonight, and nothing, not even Jane and the fearful yearning in her eyes, was going to stop him from accomplishing it.

He was not the man she'd been wishing for. Not the father she'd longed for Cody to have and not the man of her dreams. He was a womanizer, dubbed the Don Juan of his time in one of the books she'd read. And even if that was an exaggeration, one fact could not be overlooked. He was going to leave her. Just as Greg had. She would not give in to the feelings that kept creeping in, like slow-moving waves eroding a sandy shore. She would not let her heart be broken again.

She wouldn't.

And yet she lay awake for hours, wishing that there was some way...

God, she hadn't even told him why he couldn't go ahead with his plan. And even when he realized how impossible it was, he'd still want to go back to his son, to be with him at the end. The thought brought tears to Jane's eyes. He'd hate her for what she had to tell him. Hate her for being the one to make him realize that it was his son's destiny to die, and thereby save countless lives. Hate her. He'd hate her.

And it was going to kill her to see that emotion in his eyes when she told him.

She couldn't sleep. She felt sick to her stomach, and after tossing and turning restlessly she got up, intending to go downstairs, maybe do some pacing, and rehearse the words she would use to deliver the blow that might very well destroy Zachariah Bolton.

She tiptoed down the hall, but when she came to the door of the bedroom where Zach was sleeping, she found her feet wouldn't go any farther. It was stupid. He was asleep by now. No light came from beneath the closed door. But she couldn't go past without at least peeking in, just glancing at him as he lay there, drinking in the sight of him and wishing things could be different.

How had the man managed to get under her skin so thoroughly in so short a time?

She closed her hand around the doorknob, opened it gently. But the bed was empty. She stepped into the room, snapping on the light, but Zach wasn't there. And a gnawing sensation in the pit of her stomach told her he wasn't anywhere else in the house, either. She had a damned good idea of where he had gone.

After she'd expressly told him not to. To Dr. Mulligan's office, a few miles away. Probably on foot.

Jane closed her eyes and pressed her fingertips to her forehead. Damn him. He had no business being out alone, trying to break and enter, in the condition he was in. No business at all. He could collapse in the street, and then what would happen? Suppose he woke up with no memory again and started rambling on about 1897 and Aunt Hattie's credenza? They'd toss him into a mental ward, for God's sake.

She searched the ground floor, all the same, even though she knew full well she wouldn't find him there. Then she paced the living room. She should go after him. She really should. He could be hurt or sick or delirious somewhere. Or in jail. Oh, for heaven's sake, and what was she supposed to say when she found him? How was she going to explain that she'd known he'd gone out? Was she going to confess that she'd been lonely and restless and unable to sleep? Was she going to admit that she'd slipped out of bed and tiptoed down the hallway in the dead of night, and that she'd quietly eased the bedroom door open so that she could look at him as he slept?

No way in hell.

But she couldn't very well leave Cody alone to go after him, either. And she couldn't wake her son up, or the little mischief-maker would want to go along on Zach's crime spree. He'd want to...

An odd little feeling rippled up her spine and into the back of her neck. A feeling only another mother would understand. Frowning, she tilted her head, narrowed her eyes. Cody...

She hurried up to the guest room where Cody had been sleeping and slipped inside, and then she had what felt distinctly like heart palpitations.

Cody's bed was empty.

"Zach, look out!"

Zach dropped to his knees automatically at the harsh whisper. And then he turned, squinting through the darkness at the small body that had landed there beside him. An automobile passed, its headlamps brushing the bushes in front of them with white light, then fading in the distance.

Zach gripped Cody's shoulders, staring into his freckled face in stark disbelief. "What in the name of heaven are you doing here?"

"I followed you, Zach. Thought I could help. Did you get it?"

Zach pushed a hand through his hair. "If your mother finds out—"

"Did you get it?" Cody asked again, urgency in his tone.

"Yes. I got it."

"How?" Cody shook Zach's arm. "How, Zach?"

"I broke a window, reached through and unlocked the door. The cabinet was right where you told m—"

"You shoulda waited for me!" Cody rasped. "Darn it all, Zach, there's an alarm on that door. Doc has to punch in a code, even though he has a key. If you don't . . . I think the sheriff . . ."

"Let's get out of here." Taking Cody's arm, Zach raced around the building, through the damp grass.

He crossed the road, in the darkness. His breaths made little puffs of steam.

"We'll never make it, Zach. That alarm probably went off as soon as you opened the darn door. Man, we shoulda brought my bike."

"Oh, sweet Jesus," Zach said, glancing at a vehicle in the distance with flashing red lights on the top. "Is that—?"

"Yeah, that's Sheriff O'Donnell. Boy, are we in trouble! My mom's gonna *kill* us." Cody turned in a circle, then paused, at the sight of another vehicle approaching rapidly from the opposite direction. "Look, Zach! I think it's... Yeah! It's Mom! C'mon!"

Gripping Zach's hand, Cody raced toward the approaching vehicle, and away from the one with the red lights. It was dark, and the sheriff's headlamps hadn't yet fallen on them. Zach didn't think the sheriff had seen them. Yet.

"She'll be mad as all get-out," Cody panted, still running and clinging to Zach's hand. "But at least she'll keep us outta jail!"

She couldn't believe it. She could not believe what she was seeing. Her son. Her ten-year-old genius son, running away from a police car in the middle of the night, like some kind of fugitive. She gunned the accelerator, sped up beside them and skidded to a stop.

Cody yanked the back door open, and the two of them dived into the back seat just as Quigly O'Donnell's cruiser pulled up beside Jane's car.

"Sit there and look innocent," she ordered. She rolled her window down as Quigly sauntered across the street, looking serious.

"Hello, Sheriff," she said, and tried to sound cheerful, which was difficult, given the fact that she was grating her teeth behind her smile.

"Well, now, Jane Fortune! What in the world are you doing driving around town this time of the night?" He braced his hands on the driver's door and leaned closer.

"Couldn't sleep," she blurted.

Quigly frowned. "Ayuh. And they couldn't, either?" He nodded to the two in the back seat.

"Oh... well, no. None of us could. You see, my, uh... my cat disappeared today, and we were worried. So we decided to drive around and see if we could find her." It was, she thought, the perfect answer. Quigly O'Donnell was a known animal lover. She caught Cody's smirk in the rearview mirror and realized he'd caught her lying again. Fine example of motherhood she was turning out to be.

"That's too bad," the sheriff said, rubbing his chin with one hand. "And here I didn't even know you *had* a cat. Any sign of her?"

"No, not yet."

"Well, now, don't you worry. Just give me a description, and I'll keep an eye out."

"Uh... sure. She's, um..."

"Black," Cody helpfully supplied. Unfortunately, he blurted it out at the same moment his mother said, "White" and Zach said, "Cinnamon."

Jane shot the two bigmouths a glare, then turned to the sheriff again, smiling. "Calico."

"I see. She wearin' a collar?"

"Shouldn't this wait for another time, Sheriff? I don't want to keep you. You were obviously on business." She nodded toward the still-flashing lights.

"Ayuh, but nothing too urgent. Doc Mulligan's alarm went off again. Third time this month. I have to head over there and check it out, but I do believe he has a critter living in his office. Sets off the motion detector when it crosses the beam, you know. Squirrel or a mouse or something. Say, why did you pull over out here? Did you see something?"

"Uh . . . no. I mean . . . just your lights. I thought it was the law, you know, pulling over when . . ."

"Well, not when you're headin' the opposite direction."

"Oh."

He stuck his head right in her window. "You must be Bolton. I heard you were, er . . . staying with *Miss* Fortune."

"Renting a room, actually. Good to meet you, Sheriff." Zach thrust one hand over the seat to shake Quigly's.

"Renting a room, eh?" It was obvious the man doubted that little ploy. "Well, it's a pleasure, Bolton. I'd best be on my way, take a look around the doc's place." He touched the brim of his hat. "I'll keep an eye out for that cat of yours, Jane."

"Night," she said, and pulled the car into gear.

She paced. Back and forth across the sizable living room, crossing between Zach's easy chair and the red-orange glow in the fireplace, again and again. And he watched, waited, feeling a bit the way he had when

Headmistress Landon had caught him smuggling that pet mouse into primary school so long ago. Although Miss Landon had never looked quite as attractive as Jane did right now. She was even prettier in her anger, and that struck him as unusual in a woman. Her eyes sparkled with it. Her smooth cheeks had taken on a cherry gleam, and her lips were slightly parted.

Cody had wisely chosen to obey without question when she sent him straight up to bed. The little hellion got him in all sorts of hot water and then skinned out at the first opportunity, leaving Zach to face the music alone.

Smart boy.

Oh, well. At least it had given him the chance to see Jane this way. It wasn't a sight he'd forget anytime soon.

She paused in her pacing and looked at him. He decided to face the music, cleared his throat and said, "I had no idea Cody was following me."

She rolled her eyes, shook her head.

"I slipped out very quietly, Jane. I thought you were both sound asleep. I wouldn't involve the boy in a theft. You must believe that."

Her eyes narrowed.

"I have a son of my own, Jane. I'm a parent, too."

That soft chin came down, the clenched jaw eased a little, and air rushed from her lips in a sigh. "I know. Okay, Zach, I believe you. But I told you not to—"

"Try to imagine yourself in my place, just for a moment."

Jane's thickly lashed eyes slammed closed, as if, perhaps, she didn't want to imagine any such thing. But, perhaps, was doing so anyway.

"Your son—your Cody—lies dying of the fever. And a mile from you, under lock and key, is a drug that can save him. Would you go after it?" He got to his feet and went to her, cradled her chin in his palm and lifted it, very gently, so that he could look into those stunning eyes. "Would you, Jane, even though some very beautiful, very wise person had advised against it?"

She held his gaze. "You know I would."

He smiled, nodding as his hand fell to his side again. "And I knew you'd answer honestly. I have it now, Jane." He took the small plastic pill bottle from his pocket, set it on the coffee table and stared at it, barely able to contain his joy. "I can save my Benjamin. If I can just get back to him, I can—"

"No, Zach," she whispered. "No, you can't."

He frowned and felt his smile slowly die. "Of course I can."

"Zach..." She shook her head as if in frustration. "Look, there's something I haven't told you. I thought it could wait until you were feeling better, stronger— No, that's a lie. I was waiting because I didn't want to tell you. I couldn't find the words, and I don't want to see the hatred in your eyes when I—" She bit her lip.

"Jane." She stopped her rambling, looked at him, and to Zach's surprise there were tears standing in her eyes. His own reflection shimmered in them. The sight of those tears alarmed him beyond all common sense. So much so that he found himself gripping her shoulders, searching her face. "My God, Jane, what is it?"

She sniffed once, and then seemed to draw herself up. "Quinaria fever was cured because of Benjamin's death," she told him. "When you disappeared, Zach, your colleagues, Waterson and Bausch, came together. Instead of competing against one another, they worked together to develop a cure, and they did. They did it in tribute to you, Zach, and to your loss. The loss of all those other lives was never enough to inspire them the way the loss of a man they considered to be the finest scientific mind of their time did. They thought you'd gone insane when Benjamin died, and you disappeared. They blamed it on the fever."

Zach blinked down at her, shaking his head in disbelief.

"It's all here," she said as she turned from him to pick up the large book that laid on the table. "Zach, if you save your son, those men won't find a cure. Maybe no one will. If you change the past that way—" she shook her head slowly "—then what becomes of the present? How many hundreds of people will die? And how many thousands of their descendants will never be born? What about—"

"Stop!" Zach turned away from her, pressing his hands to his ears. Because he couldn't bear to hear her, and know she was right. So right, and yet she hadn't even touched on the magnitude of the implications. The way the life—or the death—of one little boy could change the world as she knew it. The succession of other research that had likely sprung from what science learned in curing one disease had probably led to cures for several others. All of that might be lost. And the victims those diseases took....some of them might turn out to be today's most influential figures. What would Jane's world look like if they'd never been born, because their ancestors had died of something that should have been cured?

Soft hands came to his shoulders from behind. They squeezed, and then Jane's head lowered to rest lightly against his back. "I'm sorry."

"I can't..." he said, then had to pause to clear his throat. "I can't simply give up, Jane. There has to be a way."

"You can't change history without impacting the present...and the future. Anything you do in the past is going to have repercussions, Zach. It's like throwing a pebble into still water. The ripples go on and on."

He turned around, facing her. "I will not allow my child to die when I have the means to save him."

"I know it's—"

"I can't, Jane. And I *won't.*"

"You're a scientist. Think about what could happen, Zach, think about mankind."

"I don't give a damn about mankind!" he shouted. "I want my son!" And then his knees seemed to buckle beneath him, and he found himself on the floor, one fisted hand on the easy chair to keep himself upright. He closed his eyes and let his chin fall, because he couldn't bear for this strong woman to see him cry. "I just want my son," he whispered once more.

Before he saw her move, she was kneeling there with him, facing him. Her arms slipped around his waist, silk-wrapped steel. She drew him closer, like a mother cradling her child, and she held him to her breast, rocking slowly as her palms made soothing patterns over his back and shoulders. "I know," she whispered. "I know, Zach, I know."

His cheeks were damp, but he wasn't certain whether the tears were hers or his own. "I can't give up on him, Jane. Sweet Jesus forgive me, but I can't." He twisted his arms around her, clinging to her as if to salvation.

"Maybe there *is* a way." She turned her face to his, kissed his mouth, drank their mingled tears from his lips. She lifted her head, searching his eyes. "I've been going crazy trying to think of some way... and if there is, Zach, we'll find it. I promise you that. But if there isn't..."

"There has to be!" He held her tighter.

Her sob was wrenched from her breast, and she buried her face in his neck. They knelt like that for a long moment, clinging to each other as Jane cried softly. Finally she sniffed, and straightened. "For now, Zach, just for now, rest. You're sick and exhausted and half out of your mind. Rest."

Zach lifted his head to stare into Jane's eyes. He couldn't hate her, couldn't even be angry with her for what she'd pointed out. It was nothing less than the truth. Her tear-dampened eyes met his, clung to them as if in a spiritual embrace. She got to her feet then and, bending low, she took his hands and drew him up, as well. Taking three steps backward, Jane stopped when she stood beside the sofa, still not letting go. So Zach let his numb legs carry him where she led. He sat down when she guided his body to do so.

He felt dazed, shocked. His mind swirled as he sought a solution, but he was too devastated to see one.

She knelt in front of him and took off his shoes, peeled the socks away. "Put your feet up, Zachariah. Go on."

He did as she said. His mind buzzed. What if he— No, that wouldn't work. Jane seemed to melt away, only to return a second later with pills in her palm. She tucked them between his lips. Her fingers tasted salty and cool. He took the drink she offered, swallowed the tablets, his mind still awash in possibilities. Seemed Jane Fortune had a pill for everything. But not one to cure this nightmare. Maybe nothing could.

Jane sat on the end of the sofa, and she caught his shoulders, drawing him downward until his head rested in her lap. And he thought very briefly of the silken thighs beneath his cheek, and the way he'd like to touch them . . . kiss them. Anything to forget this awful pain.

She pressed her forefingers to his temples and began rubbing tiny circles there. Sleep came slowly, as he stared up at her looking down at him. Her face became the face of an angel, and then blurred and dissolved into nothingness.

Cody sat at the top of the stairs, and he tried not to cry like a baby, the way the grown-ups had. All his life, all he'd wanted was a little brother. Someone he could watch out for, and play with, and teach. And since Zach had come here, he'd begun to feel like he really had one. Little Benjamin, just a few years younger, sick and needing help. Sure, he was far away, out of reach, but Cody still felt close to him. He'd felt like a big brother as he helped Zach find a way to save little Ben. And then those stupid grown-ups had to go and ruin it with all their "good of mankind" talk.

A kid was dying, for crying out loud! There would be enough time to think about the good of mankind later. Right now...that little guy back in 1897 needed someone. And right now, it seemed like Cody was the only someone Benjamin had.

No. He wasn't going to just sit around and let the grown-ups decide what was best. They didn't understand. They just...they just didn't get it.

Cody slipped down the stairs, quiet as a mouse. He sneaked to the coffee table, and he reached out, keeping his eyes on his mom just about the whole time. Zach wouldn't wake. He was out cold, and snoring like a chain saw. Mom might, though. She was a light sleeper most of the time. But she'd dozed off, too, and she didn't stir as he crept forward. Cody's hand closed around the brown plastic bottle. He drew his arm to his side, and sneaked away, up the stairs, and finally into his room. He only sighed in relief when the door was closed behind him.

Phew. That was the hard part. The rest, he decided, would be easy as pie. He went to the table, and picked up Zach's remote-control box. Pretty simple. Two knobs.

He turned one of them.

Six

Something woke Jane up. It might have been the fact that Zachariah Bolton now lay facedown in her lap. Her dorm shirt had somehow bunched up around her hips, and his face rested against her naked thighs and silk panties. She felt every whisker as his soft snores blew warm breath in places that hadn't been breathed on in ages. Places that came to life and let Jane know they resented the neglect they'd suffered of late. She automatically shifted, trying to extricate herself from the awkward position, but her movements only made matters worse. Zach stirred. The change in his breathing patterns told her he was awake. But he took his time about sitting up. And when he finally did, she almost wished he hadn't, because the look in his dark eyes when they met hers made her stomach twist.

She half expected a smart remark. But he didn't smirk as he stared up at her. The sun was just beginning to rise, and the deep orange blush painted his face and glinted in his eyes.

"I've never been so afraid in my life," he told her.

"Neither have I." She lifted one hand to brush his sable hair away from his forehead.

"You?" His brows went up. "Why, Jane?"

She swallowed hard, deciding she had to tell him

the rest. All of it. "I didn't tell you everything last night, Zach."

He closed his eyes. "Then don't do it now. Damnation, Jane, I don't think I could stand much more."

"You have to."

He sat up slowly, facing her. "Coffee first," he said, and as he did, he ran the backs of his fingers down one side of her face, stroking it as if he were deriving some sort of pleasure from doing so. "At least let me wake up thoroughly before you give me any more to worry about. I'm still a little dazzled by the dream I was having." His gaze dipped to caress her thighs once more, and she hastily got to her feet, yanking the dorm shirt down where it belonged. "Besides, I'm still not over the shock of how much undergarments have changed in the past century," he went on slowly. "I like those you're wearing. Silk, are they? They felt like it against my face."

She'd have shot him down with a cutting reply, if not for the pain she could still see in his eyes. He was only avoiding the subject at hand. She knew that. He was afraid to discuss it just yet, afraid of the time when he'd be forced to admit that he couldn't take the drug back to save his son. And so he was putting it off. Delaying what he must realize was inevitable.

"I'll make that coffee," she said, turning for the kitchen.

"I'm acting like an ass," he muttered, and he followed her. "And it's doing me no good. You're obviously not a woman who melts at pretty words."

"I'm not a woman interested in petty affairs, either."

He tilted his head, narrowed his eyes. "And yet you're lonely, aren't you, Jane? I'm sure I've never met a woman as lonely as you."

She averted her eyes, because his words were like blades that drove through to the bone. "Don't be ridiculous. I have Cody."

"And I have Benjamin. A boy I love more than...than life itself. But that doesn't mean I'm not lonely."

She blinked, and swung her gaze up to meet his. "You?"

"You're right about petty affairs, Jane Fortune. They only leave you more empty than before."

Shaking her head in confusion, Jane turned away from him. She yanked the carafe from the coffee maker and held it under the faucet, filling it with water. But when she turned, he was there, lounging against the counter, watching her with something speculative and curious in his eyes.

"Why don't you tell me about Cody's father?"

"Why do you want to know?" She continued what she was doing, pouring the water into the coffee maker, then removing the basket and reaching for the filters.

"It was unusual, in my time at least, for a woman to bear a child out of wedlock, raise him on her own, and still manage to hold the respect of her neighbors. Yet the people here seem to hold you in high regard."

"Yeah, well, they did until you showed up." She couldn't get a single filter separated from the rest of the stack, though she kept trying. "More has changed in the past century than underwear, Zach."

He smiled at her, but it was a sad smile. They both knew what they were doing. Making small talk. Avoiding the issue. With his tousled hair and rumpled clothes, he looked like a little boy. Well, maybe not quite. Still, he seemed vulnerable—enough so that she was having trouble working up to telling him the rest of it.

He came a step closer, and reached past her to take the stack of coffee filters from her hands. Deftly he peeled one from the pile, handed it to her, then returned the rest to their spot in the cupboard. "Tell me," he said, "about Cody's father."

Sighing, Jane wondered why it was so difficult to break free of his gaze when he looked at her that way. So intently. As if she were the very center of the universe. No wonder the women of his time had fallen at his feet. She tucked the filter into the basket, opened the coffee canister and fished out the scoop. "I was young, and gullible. He was a smooth-talking lady-killer in sheep's clothing. A lot like you, actually."

"Like me?" His brows went up.

Jane had to focus hard to keep track of how many scoops of coffee she'd dumped into the basket. She slid it into the coffee maker and switched the machine on.

"Were you in love with him, Jane?"

She shrugged. "I thought so at the time. He said he loved me, but it was just a line."

"A line," he repeated.

"Just a phrase he used to get me into bed." She turned to face him, leaning back against the counter. His eyes widened a little—probably, she figured, at what she'd said. No doubt the ladies of his time hadn't used such straightforward terms about sex. "He pretended to be an idealist. He was a musician, with a band, and they wrote songs about the troubles of our times, moral bankruptcy, war, that kind of thing. And I fell for it, hook, line and sinker." She shrugged her shoulders. "I told him I was pregnant about the same time he and his band were offered a lot of money to sign with a record producer. He said he couldn't put his career on hold, not when it was just taking off. He hopped a plane, leaving me and all those sterling ideas of his in the dust."

Zach tilted his head. "He left you, alone and carrying his son?" Jane nodded, and Zach's jaw twitched. "He was not only an irresponsible dog, Jane, but a fool."

She drew a breath and sighed. "You're right, he was a fool. Cody is a miracle. Greg never realized he was turning up his nose at the greatest gift he'd ever receive."

"You speak of him in the past tense."

She licked her lips. "His band was a one-hit wonder. They recorded an album that didn't sell, went on a tour that ended up being canceled. The band flopped, and he couldn't take it. Died of a drug overdose within a few months."

Zach's lips thinned. "He wasn't worthy of a son like Cody," he said, and he reached out, closing his hand around hers, squeezing gently. "Or of a woman like you, Jane."

"At least he taught me a valuable lesson," she said, drawing her hand away, though reluctantly.

"Never to trust a man again?"

The coffee gurgled into the pot and spread its aroma throughout the kitchen. Jane shook her head. "I know better than to let myself care for a man who's going to walk out on me in the end," she told him. And then, lowering her head, she added, "Or... I thought I did."

He leaned forward, bracing his hands on the countertop on either side of her. His lips brushed over the top of her head, and then his arms came around her to hold her, very gently. "I thought I'd learned a lot of things, too, Jane. But you're testing every one of them."

Blinking in surprise, she looked up quickly. His face was very close to hers, and his body only a hairsbreadth away. Every cell in her urged her to press closer, just a little. Just enough so she could really feel him there. She clenched her jaw and closed her eyes. "I can't do this, Zach," she whispered. "It'll kill me when you go." And then she blinked, and desire was replaced by heartache for what she had to tell him. What she knew it would do to him. "If you go," she went on. "Once I explain..."

She felt him move away from her before she opened her eyes. He stood two feet from her now, staring at her, shaking his head. "*If?* I *have* to go. Dammit, Jane, I'm trying to save my son's life."

"And I'm trying to save mine."

He frowned at her. "I don't understand."

"I've been thinking about this all night, Zach. And even if you do go back, even if you give that drug to your son, I can't see how it will work. If Benjamin is saved, your colleagues won't be moved to work together to find a cure for the fever. Maybe no one else will be successful. Maybe there will be no cure, and if there isn't, then it couldn't have been in Doc's office for you to steal. It couldn't have been here for you to take back to Benjamin. You'll lose him anyway. Don't you see? Everything you do will cancel out everything you've done. It can't work."

Zach turned in a slow circle, shaking his head. "No. No, you have it wrong. Those men were meant to develop the drug, and they will still do it."

"But what if they don't?"

"Then someone else will."

"Maybe. But maybe not. And then—"

"It won't matter. Once I give the drug to Benjamin, he'll be well. It won't reverse itself—I'm sure of it, Jane. I can save him."

Jane licked her lips, drew in a steadying breath. "And what about what I said to you last night, Zach? What about all the people who have been sick with the fever since then? What becomes of them, if the cure isn't developed?"

"The hell with them!" he shouted, pushing both hands back through his hair. The look of torment on his face was almost more than she could bear.

Jane moved forward, and put her hand on his shoulder. She didn't want to do this. Wished she could avoid it with everything in her. But she couldn't. "You don't mean that."

"I do. I can't—"

"Zach, when Cody was two years old, I nearly lost him. He was so sick I didn't think he'd pull through. And it—"

"No..." He took a step away from her, staring down in horror. "Don't, Jane...."

She bit her lip to stop its trembling, but there was nothing she could do to prevent the tears that filled her eyes. "Yes. It was quinaria. And if it hadn't been for that drug, Cody would have died." She lowered her head, biting back a sob that managed to escape anyway, and suddenly his arms came around her, drawing her closer, holding her to his chest, and she felt him shaking. "I know it's selfish, Zach, but I'm so afraid. If you go back, if you save your son, I might just lose mine."

Zach cradled her against him, held her tight, as if trying to shield her, and himself, from this horrible dilemma. The nightmare was beyond them, outside the circle of his arms, and as long as he didn't let her go, it couldn't get in. She cried softly, her tears wetting her cheeks, so that when she tipped her head up, when he kissed her, he tasted their salt, as well as her sweetness. He drank the misery from her mouth, and she fed on his in exchange. They clung, tears mingling, two strangers sharing one nightmare. And he couldn't stop kissing her. Wouldn't stop. Because when he did, when this tiny interlude that was serving as a refuge ended, he'd have to face reality again. And he couldn't. He couldn't.

His mouth never leaving hers, he moved backward until he reached the swinging doors that separated kitchen from living room. One hand groped, found a wooden spoon, and deftly slid it into place, linking the two door handles together so that no one could walk in. And then he returned his hands to her hair, burying his fingers deeply, twisting them in the satin of it. He bent over her, arching her backward, sliding his tongue between her lips to taste her.

He felt her heart pounding, felt the way she arched against him. And sensed her desperation, knew it, because it was his own, as well. She clung to him as if to life, to sanity, to hope. And when his mouth moved down over her throat, her hands slid into his hair, to draw him even closer.

He slipped his hands down her body, tracing the swells of her breasts, the curve of her waist. He moved over her hips to her thighs, until he met bare skin, and then he gathered the nightshirt she wore and lifted it. Kept lifting it as his caress skimmed upward again, his palms tingling over her warm flesh, and finally tugging the garment over her head. He dropped it to the floor and stared down at her, naked now, aside from the silk underwear. At her breasts, bare and beautiful and perfect. He touched them, closed his hands over them, and then closed his eyes and moaned deep in his throat. This desperation had become desire, so potent and strong he thought it would kill him if he didn't sate it soon. He grasped her legs, lifted them up and around him, and moved forward until her buttocks slid over the countertop. His hands pushing her panties down before he stepped between her parted thighs. She arched backward, offering what he craved, and he dipped his head, taking the very tip of one luscious breast into his mouth, nursing at it with ever-growing hunger, devouring and pulling at her nipple until she panted and cried. He was so hard, so in need of her it was painful, and while he worried her other breast, he slipped one hand between her legs, parting and testing the slick heat there. And then teasing the core of her desire until her hands came to his trousers, frantically working the buttons free, shoving them downward. She gripped his buttocks with both hands and pulled him forward, plunging him into her so fast and so deep that he groaned aloud.

He found her mouth again, took it, savored it as he moved with her. The pace of his thrusts gained speed, and force, but still he wanted more of her. More of her. He'd never have enough. He gripped her hips and lifted her off the counter, pulling her down farther, her own weight driving him deeper inside her. And she linked her arms and her legs around him, and began to move up and down, her hands tugging at his hair as her mouth became the voracious one that fed from his.

His knees buckled as every other part of him seemed to twist into tight little knots of pleasure so intense it was almost pain. And when he exploded inside her, he felt her climax adding to his, enhancing it. The rippling convulsions of her, milking him, drawing what felt like the very soul from his body along with his seed. And capturing it in her own.

He mouthed words he'd never uttered to a woman in his life. But not a sound emerged. They clung, and shuddered, and trembled with the aftershocks of that incredible lovemaking for a long time.

And then she lifted her head, and she kissed his mouth, and she gently lowered herself until she was standing on her feet again. And . . . and she was crying.

He wanted to take away her pain, and didn't know how. But all he could say was "There has to be a way.

We'll find a way. We can save them both, Jane. We must."

She stared deeply into his eyes, her tears brimming and burning holes through his heart. "You're going through with this? Even though it might cost my son his life?"

"*Might* cost his life, Jane." He stroked her hair, kissed her again. And again. Held her naked, trembling body in his arms and wished with everything in him that he'd never have to let go. "But I have no doubt that my son *will* lose his life if I don't. I have to try."

Trailing her hand down his damp cheek, she whispered, "I'm sorry, Zach. But I won't let you. I can't let you do this."

And they stood there, aching for each other, and for themselves. Each willing to do whatever it took to protect their child. They just stared, and he knew this was destroying her as surely as it was destroying him. He couldn't even be angry with her for what she'd said, what she'd no doubt try to do.

Shaking his head with regret, he reached past her, picked up her nightshirt and, with exquisite tenderness, put it over her head. She tucked her arms into one sleeve, then the other, as he held them for her. And he lowered the garment until its hem brushed her thighs, as before.

A loud knock at the door made her whirl. Zach saw the sheriff from the night before, Quigly O'Donnell, standing there with a ball of fur cradled in his arms.

Jane's eyes shot to Zach's, wide, and he knew she was wondering how long the sheriff had been standing there, peering through the glass into the kitchen.

Zach shook his head. "I would have seen him, Jane. He wasn't there."

With a sigh of relief, she moved forward and opened the door.

"Found your cat," the sheriff said, thrusting the multicolored beast into her arms. "Don't think she likes riding much. Clawed my upholstery up like you wouldn't believe."

Jane blinked down at the animal, but said only, "Thank you."

God, her voice sounded dead.

"Mornin', Bolton," Quigly offered.

"Good morning."

"Say, Jane, what in the name of all hell is that boy of yours up to?"

Jane frowned, and Zach came to stand very close beside her, alert. "Cody's still sleeping," Jane said. "Why?"

Quigly chuckled and shook his head. "Ayuh. Now, maybe. But I'm thinking you ought to sneak on upstairs and look in on him all the same, Jane. Judgin' by the flash of light I saw coming from his bedroom window when I drove past here a few hours ago, I'd say he short-circuited his computer or something."

"Flash of..." Jane's eyes widened, and she looked at Zach. He knew the panic that was surging in her, because he was feeling it, too.

"Keep tabs on that cat now, you hear?" Sheriff O'Donnell turned from the door and sauntered back to his cruiser.

Jane's knees started to buckle. Zach saw the way she sagged, and he gripped her shoulders, steadied her. She was shaking like a leaf, and whiter than chalk, but she stiffened and started through the kitchen, the cat still cradled in her arms. Her steps quickened as she moved, and Zach kept pace. By the time she reached the foot of the stairs, she was running.

"Cody!" she called. "Cody, answer me!"

She burst through the doorway at the top of the stairs. But the room was empty. Jane swung her head this way and that, scanning the entire room, whispering Cody's name once more in what came out as a hopeless gasp. And then she went still. Zach followed her gaze to the device, lying in the very center of the floor. Its back cover had popped off, and wires sprung from inside.

Slowly Zach moved past her to stand at the spot in the center of the room. He felt the static electricity teasing the hairs at his nape, sensed the remaining charge in the air here. A low yowl came from the frightened cat, and it leaped from Jane's arms and ran from the room.

"The doorway's been opened," he said slowly. "Within the last few hours."

"No."

He bent to pick up the device, examined it, and swore under his breath.

"Is it..."

"Broken all to hell." He met her stricken eyes. "Looks as if Cody dropped it before he went through."

"Went...through?"

He held her gaze steadily, seeing the horror, the panic, the sickening feeling of helplessness, that he knew only too well. She shook her head in denial, tore her gaze from his and ran from the room. He heard her steps, her agonized cries, as she went from room to room, searching for her son. "Cody!" she shouted. "Cody, where are you? Answer me! Cody!"

Zach lowered his head in anguish. Two children, now, instead of one. And both of them might well be beyond his reach. Almighty God, the device hadn't even been up to full power when Cody used it. He might not have gone back to the moment Zach had left, but to sometime even earlier. He wasn't even certain he'd be able to find the child. Harsh breaths from the doorway drew his gaze upward, and he saw Jane there, her face already streaked with tears. He lifted a hand, took a step toward her.

"Fix it," she told him, and he stopped in his tracks. "Fix it now, Zach."

"I'm..." He looked into her eyes and couldn't complete the sentence. He'd been about to tell her he wasn't certain he could fix the device, but the words wouldn't come. "I will," he heard himself say instead, though he knew there was a strong chance it was a lie. He turned from the hope in her eyes, unable to face it and know he might fail. He cleared a spot on the desk where Cody's computer stood, set the device down, then bent to retrieve his tools from his carpetbag. Pulling his spectacles from his shirt pocket, he slipped them on, sat down and began dismantling the small box.

"The pills are gone," Jane whispered.

Zach's head came up.

"They were on the coffee table, by the sofa. But they're gone. Cody must have heard us talking last night...must have heard *me* talking." She closed her eyes. "He's wanted a brother so badly."

"I know."

She paced to the window, parted the curtains to look outside. Then stiffened and turned to him again. "What if he's sick? God, you were so sick when you came through! It will be worse for him... Zach, what if—?"

He shot to his feet and went to her, gripping her shoulders hard. "Stop it."

"Zach, what if we can't get him back? God, what if I've lost him?" Sobs tore through her body, wracking her slender frame, and he pulled her closer. "Damn you and your stupid inventions, Zach Bolton! Damn you for coming here!"

He grimaced at the condemnation in her voice. She was so right. If he hadn't come here... Ah, but what choice had he been given? And yet, even as she railed at him, she pressed closer. "Hold me," she whispered.

"I am holding you."

"I can't feel it."

Zach's arms around her closed tighter, and hers came around his waist, just as desperately, just as forcefully. Her anguish brought his own to the surface, though he'd thought he'd battled it into submission. All the fears that he might not win this skirmish against fate, all the uncertainties, all the doubts, came rushing back, because they were so keenly reflected in her grief.

"I'm his mother," she sobbed. "I'm not supposed to let anything happen to him."

"I know."

"When he's hurt or upset . . . I can always make it better, Zach. Always. It isn't supposed to be this way."

She lifted her head to search his face, and he pushed the hair out of her eyes. "This is how you felt before you came here, isn't it?"

"Yes, Jane. It's how I still feel."

"I'm sorry . . . I'm so sorry I tried to stop you. . . . I was—"

"You were protecting your child. I'd have done the same."

She sniffed, and Zach brushed her tears from her cheeks with the tips of his fingers. "Nothing's changed," she said. "You know that."

She was wrong about that, he thought. Something had changed. He felt it right to the core of his being. But now was not the time to try to understand just what that something was.

"We could still cause unthinkable trouble by trying to alter the past."

"We can't afford to focus on that right now," he told her. "All we can do now is concentrate on getting back there, finding our sons, keeping them safe. The repercussions of our actions . . ." He shook his head. "Those we'll think about later."

She blinked away fresh tears, looking doubtful.

"And we will, Jane," he told her, and he tried hard to inject certainty into his tone, because he knew just how badly she needed to hear it there. "We'll weigh every move we make before we take action. I promise you that.''

She nodded hard. "All right." Glancing past him, toward the table, where the crippled device lay in pieces, she whispered, ''What can I do to help?''

Seven

Cody picked himself up off the floor and brushed at the knees of his jeans. Then he froze and stared down at his hands. The box! Where was the box? Realizing he must have dropped it, he quickly scanned the room, the floor around and behind him. But there was no sign of it there, and the blinding white hole he'd come through had vanished.

"Oh, no," he muttered. He quickly checked his pockets and found the bottle of pills he'd brought along. Thank goodness he hadn't dropped those, too. He breathed a sigh of relief and, for the first time, examined his surroundings.

His bedroom... or it had been up until a minute ago. Now it was different. And the most noticeable difference was the sickly little boy all tucked into the big bed over there, and the three strangers who stood around him, all of them slowly turning shocked glances on Cody.

Cody cleared his throat, took a single backward step, smiled and said, "Uh... hi." A couple of oil lamps threw off about enough light to see by, and not a drop more. But there was enough to know that those three were none too pleased to see him there.

Moving as one, they came toward him, surrounding him, three stunned faces blinking down at him. A fat man with gray whiskers, and a taller, skinny man with black ones. Both wore old-fashioned suits and ties. The lady was older, with silvery hair and a crinkly face. She took one look at him and fell backward. Both of the men grabbed hold of her, one fanning her face until she blinked and got herself upright again.

"Don't drop her, Eli. For the love of God, you're dropping her!"

"I'm not dropping her! I have her. For God's sake, get the chair, Wilhelm."

Eli? Wilhelm? Cody stared at the men, too shocked to move. Holy cow, he was standing in the same room with Eli Waterson and Wilhelm Bausch!

One pulled a chair over, tucked it under the lady and then fanned her face. After a moment, her eyes fluttered open, and she smiled weakly at the two men, then gaped at Cody. "Land sakes, child! You nearly frightened me out of my life! What *was* that flash of light? And where on God's earth did you come from?"

"Who are you, boy? How did you get in here?" The younger of the two mustached men leaned forward as he spoke. "Where is Mr. Bolton?"

Cody figured he'd better not say too much. They'd think he was nuts, and God only knew what they did with crazy little boys in the 1890s. So he just shrugged. "I dunno."

"None of that matters, Eli," said the older man. "We really must get this child off the premises in all haste."

"No way," Cody said, crossing his arms. "I came to see Ben, and I'm not leavin' till I do." He craned his neck to see past them, to the boy in the bed. The light wasn't that bright, but Cody didn't think the kid looked very good.

The lady blinked as if she were going to cry, and ran one hand over Cody's hair. He smiled at her, because it had always worked on Grandma Kate. "You dear, sweet child," she said. "Are you a friend of Benjamin's?"

"Yes, ma'am. And I think he'll feel better if I visit him." Cody stuck a hand in his jeans pocket and closed it around the pill bottle. He had to get these three out of here. Get them to leave him alone with the kid for a few minutes, and then he could get the first pill down him.

"Oh, dear," she said.

"Young man," said Wilhelm, hunkering down on his haunches, "I'm sorry to tell you that Benjamin is quite ill. He can't have visitors."

"But I'm already here," Cody countered. "So you might as well just give me a few minutes to—"

"Mrs. Haversham, do you know this child?"

"No," she replied. Then, to Cody, she said, "I know it's hard to understand, but truly, it's for your own good, dear."

"Oh, I understand just fine. You think I'll catch the fever if I go near Ben. But I already had it, a long time ago, so I'm immune. Honest."

The two finest scientists since Louis Pasteur exchanged glances. One pulled his glasses down to the bridge of his nose and peered over the tops of them at Cody. "What does a boy of your age know about contagions and immunity?"

Cody only shrugged.

"How did you get into this bedroom, young man?" the man asked yet again.

"I told you, I came to see Benjamin. Just started trying doors, and here I am."

The other man pursed his lips, shook his head slowly. "And is Mr. Bolton aware of your presence in his home, young man?"

"Sure," Cody said, having a brainstorm.

"Impossible," the man returned, looking pleased with himself. "He's gone into town to fetch the doctor."

"He's gone, all right, but you don't have a clue—"

"Mrs. Haversham, send one of the servants for a constable. We shall find this lad's parents and get to the bottom of this."

"Very well, sir," she said, with a remorseful glance at Cody and a click of her tongue. She moved to the door, opened it. One of the men reached out, as if to grab Cody's arm, but he was quicker than both of them. He ducked the grab, and shot between them, under Mrs. Haversham's beefy arm, and into the hall, straight out to the stairway. They spun around, shouting and chasing after him, but he leaped onto the banister with the ease of practice, slid to the bottom and jumped to the floor. He heard their feet pounding down the stairs, heard one of them saying, "Stop him! He might be carrying the fever!"

Cody raced through the kitchen, and straight out the door.

Zach wasn't so involved in tinkering with the small, dismantled box that he didn't notice Jane. In fact, he came very close to asking her to leave the room. Having her here, so close, made it difficult to stop noticing her, to stop remembering what it had felt like to be...with her. It was the first time in his life a woman had managed to shake him so thoroughly, or to touch him on such a deep level. Or to distract him from his work. Oh, there had been women. God, had there been women. But none had come anywhere close to breaking his concentration this way.

Only Jane.

And his thoughts were anything but lascivious. That he could have understood. But this...this constant glancing over his shoulder at her, with some kind of gut-deep worry gnawing at him...this was beyond his experience. And his understanding. Women had no place in his life, aside from the bedroom. That was the way it had to be for him. He'd made that decision long ago, when selfish, society-conscious Claudia drove a blade into his young heart. But he'd healed. And then he'd enclosed that vulnerable organ within its own custom-made suit of armor, and vowed he would never leave it so exposed again.

And it was a vow he'd kept...until now.

Jane sat with her legs curled beneath her on Cody's bed. Strewn about her were open books, a notepad and a couple of pencils. She'd asked what she might do to help, and he'd suggested she put her penchant for history to use. She was reading all the information she could find on his two colleagues and their development of tryptonine. Once they returned to the past, Zach was hoping, they'd find a way to save both the boys and still not interfere with the subsequent development of the drug.

Meanwhile, Zach tinkered with the device itself. All her information would be utterly useless unless he could repair the damage and make the thing operable. He'd already figured out how to get to the exact point in time where Cody had gone. According to the figures he'd keyed into Cody's computer machine, with two days' worth of recharged power, Cody would have gone back to one day before Zach left the past. He and Jane would try to go back that far, as well, though there might be complications to doing so. He'd worry about that when the time came. He didn't want to allow time for anything to happen to Cody.

He set his mess aside and again scrolled the information he and Cody had spent hours keying into the boy's computer, but wound up sighing in frustration.

Bedsprings creaked, and in a second Jane's hands closed on his shoulders and began massaging him. It startled him that she'd be so kind to him, despite their being of opposing points of view in this crisis. It also confused him. Mainly because her touch brought desire for her rushing back into his loins, and because she smelled so damned good.

"We've been at it for hours," she said. "Time for a short break."

Her voice was hoarse from all the crying she'd done earlier, and Zach experienced another stab of concern for her. She was half out of her mind with worry for her son. He knew. God, how well he knew. Her thumbs pressed into the backs of his shoulders while her fingers kneaded and rubbed the front. He arched his back, closed his eyes. What she was doing felt wonderful.

"It's not the time bending over the worktable that's getting me," he told her as he let his head drop forward. "I'm used to that. It's the frustration."

Her hands stilled. Crying shame, that.

"Then you aren't getting anywhere?"

"Actually, I am. But I know I'd be getting there a lot faster if I were making the most of this... computer of Cody's." He shook his head, frowning at the screen. "I considered myself a genius in my own time," he said. "Now I feel like an ignorant fool."

Her hands began working their magic once more. "You're no fool, Zach."

"No? Even a small child knows more about science today than I. I'm baffled by your televisions and microwaves and aeroplanes. By today's standards, Jane, I'm not fit to graduate primary school."

"You're forgetting one thing," she said, working up and down the back of his neck, and making him curious as to what other magic her hands could perform.

"What's that?" he asked.

"Not even the most accomplished physicist has managed to travel through time, Zach. Not with the help of high-powered computers, or even data gathered from outer space. Yet you did, with tools considered primitive by our standards. You did what they all still believe is impossible."

He turned to look up at her. "I did, at that, didn't I?"

She nodded. "Yes. Which is why I know you're going to find a solution to this disaster." Her eyes were deadly serious. "You have to, Zach. I'm counting on it."

He lowered his eyes. God, but he didn't want to let her down. Having a woman counting on him, believing in him, for any reason, was such an unusual feeling that he wasn't quite sure what to make of it.

"Those circles under your eyes are coming back," she told him. "Look, I'm as eager as you are to solve this thing, but I think you'll work better if you rest for a few minutes. Get something to eat. I think we should stop for a sandwich, and a few minutes to rest our eyes."

He managed to conjure up a gentle smile, and he stroked her hair, something he was growing ridiculously fond of doing. "We're going to get your Cody back, Jane. I promise."

She tried to avert her face before he saw her tears, but didn't quite succeed. He was too astute, or perhaps just too focused on every aspect of her, to miss one so vital. "You must think I'm the most selfish person alive. I was so against all of this when it suited me. And now I'm..."

He surged to his feet, capturing her pretty face between his palms, caressing it with his eyes. "Now you're a mother, Jane. And like any mother, you'll do whatever it takes to protect your child. I don't find that selfish at all.... In fact, it..."

Shaking her head slowly, she whispered, "It what?"

Zach dipped his head, unable to look into her eyes just then. But when he brought his gaze level, he found himself drowning in hers all over again. "It makes you even more beautiful to me, Jane. And no, don't accuse me of using what you refer to as a line. It's true, and every bit as unbelievable to me as it probably seems to you. I've never in my life noticed much about any woman, aside from the way she filled out her bloomers. But with you..." He didn't finish the sentence, didn't even know how, really.

She searched his face. "I hope to God Cody is all right."

"Cody is nothing less than brilliant. With his wit, he'll manage just fine until we get to him."

She nodded. "I know he will."

"So, how about some sandwiches?"

For some reason she couldn't have named, Jane believed every word that smooth-talking ladies' man Zachariah Bolton said. He told her everything would be all right, and heaven help her, she accepted it as gospel. Had she lost her mind?

No. No, that wasn't it at all, she thought as she made a pair of sandwiches and laid them on paper plates. She believed the man because she was fairly certain there wasn't much he set his mind to doing that didn't get done.

That thought niggled at her a little, because it seemed Zach had also set his mind to sweet-talking his way into her heart. Intentionally or not, that was what he was chipping away at, and had been since the day he stepped out of time and into her life. He was...he was mischievous and brilliant, and sexy, and she could fall for him fast and hard. Seemed she hadn't learned as much from the past as she thought she had. Keeping her heart immune to the considerable charms of Zachariah Bolton was a matter of self-preservation. He'd be leaving soon. Very soon. She'd find a way to bring Cody back here, and he'd return to the past and try to cure his own son. And that was where he would stay. In the past. Jane couldn't afford to go forming any attachments to Zach.

But she did have utmost confidence in his ability to pull this off. He'd travelled a hundred years forward in time, she told herself. It stood to reason that he could do just about anything. Rescuing one little boy wouldn't be all that much harder.

Two little boys, she corrected herself with a pang of guilt. Two. Cody, and Benjamin. His son. She'd thought she understood what drove him before, and she'd thought her own practical point of view was the correct one. Now she knew she'd have done the same thing if she was in his shoes and she had the means. Nature couldn't be completely overpowered. Any parent alive would damn the world to save his or her own child. It was simply the way it was.

She opened the cupboard, saw Cody's New York Giants mug, felt her knees try to buckle. But she stiffened them by sheer force of will, blinked her eyes dry. She'd have her Cody back.

Something warm brushed her leg, and she glanced down to see the stray cat, rubbing against her. "I suppose you might as well stay," she said, reaching down to scratch its ears. "You'll be a nice surprise for Cody, when he gets back." She straightened, frowning. Then returned to the cupboards for a couple of cans of tuna and a pair of bowls. She emptied the fish into one bowl and filled the other with water, placing both on the floor. "Just in case I have to leave," she said, stroking the feline's head as it dove into the food with relish.

She opened the back door just slightly, so the cat could get out should the need arise.

"Jane!" Zach bellowed from upstairs. "I have something!"

Gripping a plate in each hand, Jane raced for the stairs.

She half expected to see a wormhole straight out of a science-fiction film hovering in the air in the center of the room. What she saw instead, as she burst through the bedroom door, was Zach bending over the computer, peering through his specs at the screen.

"What is it?" she said, crossing the room and setting one of the plates on the desk in front of him.

"The side effects. I'm almost certain Cody won't suffer from them. Look at this." He pointed at the screen. "I hadn't completed my testing when I came through. Mainly because...I was running out of time. But I had done some, and Cody and I transferred all of the data to this machine. This program he... uh...downfed—"

"Downloaded," Jane corrected him.

"It's amazing. It finds correlations I wouldn't even have thought to look for."

"Break it down for me, Zach. Cut to the chase."

He frowned up at her, but went on. "To put it simply, Jane, the larger the object, the greater the side effects. I suffered pronounced ill effects, but Cody is a lot smaller than I am. If these calculations are correct, then it stands to reason—"

"He isn't sick."

"No. No, I don't think he is."

Jane closed her eyes as every muscle in her body seemed to uncoil in relief. "If he isn't sick, then he'll be fine until we get to him. I know he will."

Zach nodded, but she noticed that his smile was less than sincere. Sadness and worry clouded his eyes. "You're thinking you wish you could be so certain about Benjamin, aren't you?"

"Are you a mind reader, Jane?"

She pushed his plate closer to him, then gently reached up to remove the glasses from his face. "Eat, Zach. Rest your eyes. And tell me about your Benjamin."

He closed his eyes. "If I lose him..."

Her hand cupped his cheek. "You're not going to lose him," she said, repeating his earlier reassuring words to him, almost verbatim. "I promise."

Zach covered her hand with his own and drew it around to his mouth, so that he could press his lips to her palm. "You're a treasure, Jane Fortune."

"Eat," she said.

So he did.

Eight

Cody hid out in a sagging, creaking barn a few miles down the road from his house...er, Zach's house. Whatever. He wasn't sure what had happened to the barn, but he knew it was no longer standing in 1997. And it didn't surprise him. The way the building leaned to one side and drooped in the middle, and the amount of wind managing to find its groaning way through the cracks, were enough to tell him the thing wasn't exactly new, even now. It wasn't ready to fall down around him or anything—he hoped—but the barn was *old*. And if it was old now, in 1897, then it must be *really* old. Maybe even as old as the Revolutionary War. Imagine that!

He didn't have as much time to think about the wonder of it as he would have liked. Later, he told himself. For now, he had something even more important to think about.

The bottle of pills in his pocket jiggled every time he moved, and Cody bit his lip as the sound reminded him sharply of the responsibility he'd taken on. It was a heavy burden weighing on him. But one he wouldn't turn away from. He'd come here to help Benjamin. It was up to him, and only him, to save that little guy's life. And now he couldn't do it, because of those crabby scientists at the house. Was he going to let that stop him? Well, if he did, then the boy he'd already begun to think of as the closest thing to a little brother he would ever have was going to die. Maybe he'd die soon. Maybe he was dying right now.

Cody knew that he was putting his own life at risk by trying to save Benjamin. But he didn't have a doubt that he'd be all right, somehow. Mom was always saying that kids his age believe themselves to be immortal. Maybe she was right. All Cody knew for sure was that helping Ben was the right thing to do. Ben even had the same name as Cody's great grandfather. If that wasn't a sign that he was meant to be part of Cody's family, then he didn't know what was. Benjamin Bolton was going to be Cody's brother. He knew that beyond any doubt, though it made no sense to feel this strongly about it. It wasn't logical or scientific. It was just there, a gut-deep certainty that he couldn't convince himself to doubt. He had to help Benjamin. But how?

Cody closed his eyes and bit his lip. "Mom, what should I do? What should I do?" he whispered into the darkness.

Be smart, Cody. Use your head.

Cody's eyes flashed open, and he looked around him, half expecting to see his pretty mom standing nearby. She wasn't, of course. He was all alone in a big, empty, dark barn, with nothing but the groaning and whistling of the wind in his ears, its cold caress reaching in to chill him through all those cracks, and the musty, sour smell of old hay. Only…he didn't *feel* quite as all alone as he had before.

* * *

It was supposed to have been a brief five-minute rest. When Jane consented to lean back against the headboard, and Zach settled down next to her, barely able to keep his eyes opened, they'd agreed to a quick, short break. Then right back to work. He didn't know when her eyes had fallen closed or how she could have managed to fall asleep at all, as worried as she was about her son. But she had. She'd drifted off as he was talking through his theory about why he was able to move through time. Boring to her, he supposed. If it had occurred to him that he could bore her into getting a bit of rest, he'd have attempted it sooner. The poor woman was on the verge of collapse, her exhaustion more emotional than physical, he knew. And now, though he ought to be working on the device, he simply didn't have the heart to wake her. And if he moved at all, he'd probably do just that. Because timid Jane Fortune was virtually twined around him. A situation he'd fantasized about several times since making the lady's acquaintance, but made come true only once. And once, Zach mused, fell a great deal short of being enough.

He let his eyes roam her relaxed face. A hundred times wouldn't be enough, he realized with a shiver of alarm tickling up his spine. Now what was it about her that made her so attractive to him, that drew him like the lure of the sirens? If only things were different. If only he had the time to find out.

She'd slid lower in the bed, until her head rested in the crook of his neck. Her arms had crept around his waist, and one leg, bent at the knee, held his thigh captive beneath it.

The entire situation worried Zach. Because he wasn't responding the way he normally would. He wasn't sitting here devising seemingly innocent methods of touching her. Or of arousing her enough in her sleep to leave her pliant and willing when she awoke. Though his skills at both tricks were up to the challenge, he felt oddly reluctant to use them. Instead, he found himself content to simply hold her, look at her. Smell her. Feel her warmth seeping into him wherever she touched him. And know that she was getting some much-needed relief from the horror of the nightmare they seemed to be trapped within, together.

He tilted his head as he considered that. Here, wrapped in his arms—in a bed, no less—was a woman he wanted. Quite possibly—no, most certainly—more than he'd ever wanted another. And here he was doing nothing to capitalize on the predicament. It was damned unlike him. Yes, the situation was dire, but he'd never been one to let that interfere before. A bit of physical exertion would do his stress level a world of good, he thought rather sardonically.

Moving very slowly and carefully, he reached for the device, and the screwdriver, and his notes, spreading all of them upon the bed, where they wouldn't interfere with her rest. He grabbed for his spectacles lastly, and perched them on his nose. And then he began to work, reattaching the broken bits to the device, one by one.

Jane sighed, and shifted lower. Her head slipped down to his lap, her hand settling on his hip. Zach pulled his spectacles down onto his nose and peered over the tops of them at her, curled up and sleeping peacefully there, facedown in his... Lord have mercy. If his reaction to *that* didn't wake her, he didn't think anything would.

Something hard was pressing into her cheek. Jane grumbled in her sleep, doubling up her fist to punch the lump out of her pillow and refusing to open her eyes. A hand closed over hers before she could carry out the plan. "Uh-uh, none of that."

"Hmm?" She opened her eyes, lifted her head a little and saw what she'd been lying on. Her eyes widened, and she looked up fast, into a pair of twinkling dark brown eyes. *"Zach."*

"What? You're the one with your face nestled in my..." He let his eyes finish the sentence for him. Then reached out to stroke a gentle hand over her hair, and there was something besides lust in his eyes. Something that made her stomach turn over. "You'll never know how much I wish I had more time, Jane. You'll never, never know...."

She didn't know how to respond to that. So she said nothing. Just held his eyes with hers, and wished she could see what he was thinking. Wished... But wait. What did he mean? He sounded as if... Her gaze darted to the device on the bed beside him.

"Zach?"

He nodded, and picked up the black box. "Look at this," he whispered. He pointed the thing, pressed a button, and the tiny pinprick of light appeared in the center of the bedroom.

"My God," she whispered, her heart leaping in her chest. "My God, it's working. You fixed it."

"I think so."

"What do you mean, you think so?" She sat up, got to her feet and took a step closer to the light. "You're not sure?"

"No, I'm not at all sure."

"Then—"

"Wait." He adjusted the dial, and the light grew larger, brighter. Zach got up, gripped her arm and pulled her away as the sphere of illumination took up more and more space in the room. When it extended beyond the ceiling, and through the floor, the light began to take on distinctive shades, and forms hovered on the other side of a swirling mist. The sphere became a mirror, reflecting the room back at them, minus the modern furniture and new wallpaper and electric fixtures. It was the same room, a hundred years ago.

"Look," Zach whispered. "The calendar, there on the wall."

He pointed, and Jane saw the page, with each date methodically crossed off as it passed. "I believe we've done it. We've found the doorway to the exact day before I left. And I'm certain this is where Cody came through."

Jane blinked, shaking her head. "But... but if it's *before* you left, then—then you're there? *And* here? You... There are two of you? Zach, what if—"

"I don't know. I don't know if the past me will be there or not, Jane. I should be all right as long as I don't confront him... er, me." He clasped her shoulders, turned her toward him. "Jane, I have to go now." And, to her surprise, his eyes seemed damp. "Saying goodbye to you... saying goodbye..." He shook his head, apparently giving up on words. Instead of speaking, he pulled her tight to his chest, and kissed her. He kissed her slowly, tenderly, for a very long time. And Jane found herself kissing him back, slipping her hands up to his shoulders and parting her lips in invitation, and pressing her body tight to his. Before, they'd had passion, desperation, desire. This... this was different. This was emotion... so much emotion that it took her breath away.

Could it be that he... ?

He lifted his head away, turning toward the light. Jane gave herself a mental shake, trying desperately to swim her way to the surface of the pool of feeling she'd nearly drowned in just now. She blinked twice, and cleared her throat, but her voice was hoarse all the same. "I don't know what you're thinking, Bolton, but you can think again. My son is back there. I'm going with you."

He shook his head. "The side effects..."

"I'm a little more than half your weight, Zach. I'll be fine. Besides, as you told me earlier, that's not a consideration."

"It's not safe. Not even necessary. Jane, I'll take care of Cody as if he were my own, you know I will. I love the boy." He frowned after he said that, as if the words had surprised him. But then his brow cleared, and he nodded once. "I love the boy. He'll be safe with me, and as soon as the device recharges, I'll send him back to you."

"I'm going with you."

He searched her face, shook his head. "I can't let you risk it."

"It isn't your decision." Jane pulled from his strong grip so suddenly that he was taken by surprise. She didn't waste a second, just spun around and ran directly into the light. There was the sensation of being squeezed until she felt like a turtle under a truck tire, and then sudden relief as she hit the floor. Or the floor hit her. Like a two-by-four in the face, swung by a giant.

Zach landed beside her with a crash, and lay there on his side, hands pressed to his head, face twisted in a grimace of anguish. The box hit the floor beside him, and then the light blinked out.

Jane tried to stand, and was surprised when a wave of dizziness washed over her, sending her right back to her knees again. Her brain sloshed as if she'd been drinking too much. Her vision was spotty, and her balance way off kilter. Lord, what a frightening sensation!

But Zach...Zach was still on the floor. He'd rolled onto his back now, and lay there, eyes squeezed tight, palms pressing the sides of his head.

"Zach?" Jane knelt beside him, battling her own reactions, because his were obviously far worse. "Hang on, Zach. Hang on, okay? Zach?"

His eyes opened, focused on her without recognition. Blank. Utterly blank. His brows came together, and he stared at her. "I know you," he said weakly, blinking his vision into focus, and taking in the surroundings. His gaze fell upon the box on the floor, and narrowed as he struggled to sit up. But then he was looking at her again. He reached for her, touched her hair as his eyes probed hers. "I know you," he repeated. "I know your face, and your scent and the taste of your lips. And I know there's no other woman in the world quite like you. Wait..."

"Jane, I'm Jane," she said, but her voice was a bit breathless, in reaction to those words. She gave herself a mental kick. He was confused, disoriented. "Come on, Zach, I need you now."

"Jane," he muttered, lying back down as if for a little nap. She quite understood the feeling. She shared it. Exhaustion. Jet lag to the tenth power. "Come back to bed, Jane."

She took his face between her hands, slapping his cheeks several times. "Zach, come on. Wake up, this is an emergency."

He opened his eyes. "Darling, you're insatiable...."

"Benjamin, Zach. Cody. Remember?"

"Benja—" He blinked, and the dazed expression left his face. "Benjamin. My son!" He sat up, paused to give his head a shake, then gripped her outstretched hand and struggled to his feet. He paused, blinking down at his hand, still surrounding hers. "Jane...yes..." He lifted his gaze to hers. "I'm sorry."

"It's the portal. It does something to your mind, Zach. It isn't your fault."

"We're a day early," he whispered. "Jane, I can't run into...into the other Zach—if he exists. I can't. I've no idea what would happen if I did."

"Well...think, Zach. Where were you at—" she glanced around the room, found the mantel clock and went on "—5:30 p.m., on the night before..."

"The night before my son slipped into a coma?" Zach finished for her. "I was at his bedside. Nothing could make me leave."

And as he said it, the two of them turned, gazes falling on the tiny, sleeping child in the big bed, and the empty chair beside him. "Well, something apparently made you leave tonight," she whispered.

He staggered away from her, to the bedside, bent over and brushed his lips over his son's forehead. Benjamin slept soundly, not even stirring. And Jane's eyes burned as she moved closer and looked down at his pale face and red curly hair, at the freckles scattered across his nose. Just like Cody.

Zach straightened up, his eyes moist, his jaw taut. "Come on. An earlier version of me is liable to show up at any moment. Help me..." He put his arm around her shoulders, bracing himself against her as if he'd fall down without her help. "Get me to my...your..." He lifted his brows. "Our bedroom. No one will bother us there, and we can plot our next move."

She nodded and helped him into the hall.

Cody waited until it was late enough that he figured everyone would be asleep. And then he went back to the house. He had several advantages, and he'd spent his time listing them, one by one, to build up his confidence. One was that he was a lot smarter than just about anyone else in this century. Nothing to be vain about, just that he came from a more enlightened time. So he ought to be able to outwit every last one of them, right down to Eli Waterson and Wilhelm Bausch. That thought made him smile a little. Imagine outwitting two genius scientists.

Another advantage was that he knew the house like the back of his hand. He'd explored it thoroughly since he and his mom had moved in. And he knew how to get in, even if it was locked up tight. He also knew which room was Ben's. And he had his penlight. Perfect. Advantage number four was that no one was expecting him. So he had the element of surprise on his side.

Now, he also had a couple of things working against him, the main one being that the medication was supposed to be taken over a period of several days, every four hours. If he gave Ben a dose now, and then missed one later, the whole treatment would have to start over, and he only had enough pills to do this once. So there was no way he could leave Ben in that house. He had to get him out of there. And he had to do it tonight.

Cody plotted and planned until the wee hours. And then he gathered up every bit of courage he had, and he tiptoed out of the barn and back to the deserted road.

The road was in worse shape than ever. No hint of pavement, no fresh gravel. Just packed dirt. It wasn't wide enough for two cars to pass safely, and there was only one sign on the whole thing, as far as he could see. A wooden board nailed to a post. Someone had painted Rockwell on the sign, and one end had been sawed off to a point. Cody picked up his pace. He thought that if he squinted until his eyes went out of focus, and didn't pay too much attention to details, it was just like being back home. Only... it truly wasn't. It felt different. Even the air seemed different.

Something clattered and clunked, and Cody went stiff. Then he kicked himself into high gear, and dived into the bushes along the roadside, crouching there and watching the road behind him, as bright as day beneath the moon.

The sounds grew louder, and then the thing making them came into view. A horse, wearing blinders and all kinds of straps. A big black horse, pulling a big, wobbling buggy behind it, and it was headed toward Rockwell. Cody shook his head in stark wonder as the wooden wheels, trimmed in metal, rolled and squeaked past him. The seat inside looked like soft brown velvet, with little buttons all over it. A man and a lady rode on that seat, the lady wearing a striped dress and a hat that almost made Cody laugh out loud. So did the man's long, curled mustache, which was so well waxed it gleamed in the moon's reflection. His bowler hat was almost as good.

Cody bit back his grin and shook his head in wonder. He really had traveled a century into the past, hadn't he? Gosh. It was unbelievable, but he'd done it.

And now he had to do something even harder. Save a little boy who had no hope left except for him.

Unlike Zach, Cody hadn't suffered any ill effects from coming through. He'd had a slight headache that lasted a couple of hours, nothing else.

He felt just fine now. So when the buggy had passed, he clambered right back onto the road, and headed for the house, faster this time. He was getting antsy, and he wanted this over with. There was only one light on, and he knew well enough that it was in Ben's room. He walked around the house, just as quiet as he could, looked around once, and then bent to the hatchway door that led into the cellar. Mom kept this door padlocked, but it seemed like locks weren't as necessary in this past. The door opened, creaked loud, making Cody grate his teeth. Then he ducked inside, lowering the door behind him and pulling out his penlight.

He didn't intend to take time to look around. The place was creepy, anyway. Dark and unfinished. Dirt floor, instead of the cement he was used to. No lights. No washer and dryer in the corner. No boxy metal furnace to keep the place warm. There was a giant hulking iron thing, with an orange-red glow spilling from its every crevice, of which there were many. And a pile of what looked like coal sitting beside it.

Shining his penlight ahead of him, Cody made his way to the stairs, and tiptoed up them. The door at the top had a hook and eye for a lock. It did in his time, anyway. He hoped that was the case here, because if it was he could open it. He'd played around trying to once, when he and some friends played hide and seek down here. At the top of the cellar stairs, Cody listened, heard no one. Then he pulled his library card from his jeans pocket, and slid it into the crack between the door and the frame. Slowly he moved the card upward, and soon he felt the resistance of the hook. He lifted it, jiggled the card a little and smiled when he heard the pinging sound as the hook fell against the door on the other side. Then he turned the knob and pushed the door open.

Pitch-dark in the kitchen. Good thing he knew his way around. He slipped through, clicking off his penlight and sticking it back into his pocket. He got through the dining room, too, and then the living room, where he went even more slowly as he approached the stairs. He thought he heard someone moving around up there, but when he went still and quiet, he decided it had only been his imagination.

Silently he moved up the stairs, and turned toward Ben's room. But then he stiffened, because voices were coming from beyond the door. And then footsteps. Cody almost passed out from fear, and then he slipped farther down the hall and ducked into the hall closet.

Jane swallowed hard as she stood silently in the bedroom, staring down at the small, pale-faced little boy. Benjamin, his breathing labored, dark circles ringing his thickly lashed eyes, laid sleeping, his hand clasped in a larger, fleshier one. The woman had fallen asleep in the hard wooden chair beside the bed. Jane could see only the back of her bowed head, her plump, slumped shoulders. And then, as she stood there, wondering how in the world she would handle it when the woman turned and looked at her, she stiffened, straightened in the chair and did just that.

"What—who are you? How did you get—?"

Jane held up a hand to calm the startled woman. "It's all right, Mrs. Haversham. I'm a friend...of Zachariah's. Is he here?"

The woman rose, smoothing her dress's long, rumpled skirts, blinking the sleep haze from her eyes. "No. No, and I've no idea where he's gone."

Jane frowned. Neither she nor Zach had known what to expect. The prospect of meeting another Zach, one who didn't know her, had been so absurd it made her dizzy. "Are you certain? This is very important. I have to know—"

"If Zachariah were here, don't you think he'd be at his son's side? When we've barely been able to pry him from this room long enough to eat or to sleep? No, miss. Zachariah seems to have vanished without a trace, and I'm worried to death about him." The woman's lower lip trembled, and she clutched at her apron, wringing it in her hands.

Jane stepped closer, her throat tightening, and put a hand on the woman's shoulder. "It's all right. It's going to be all right. But I need your help, Mrs. Haversham. I'm looking for my son, Cody. He's missing, and I—"

"Your son?" the woman repeated, and it seemed she calmed considerably. "Young boy...looks enough like Benjamin to be his twin, only older and a good deal healthier?"

"Yes! Then he's here?"

"No, I'm afraid not. He was, of course, but that was earlier, and— Land sakes, the boy never made it home?"

Jane closed her eyes as tears threatened. "No."

"Lord," the woman muttered, shaking her head. "The lad was upset that we couldn't let him see Benjamin. Lit out of here like a bandit, and heaven only knows where he got himself off to. But don't you worry, missy, I'm sure he'll find his way home." Then she tilted her head and frowned at Jane, eyeing her jeans and T-shirt with a puzzled expression. "And where is your home, if you don't mind my asking?"

"Far away," Jane said. She fought the bitter disappointment that made her want to sink to her knees and cry. She battled the worry over Cody, tried not to let herself panic at the thought of him out there, alone in the night somewhere. She cleared her throat and brought her focus back to the questions that needed to be asked. If there were two Zachariah Boltons running around this house right now, and they happened to run into each other, God only knew what the results might be. "I need to know, ma'am, when did you discover Zach was missing?"

The pale blue eyes welled up with tears. "An hour ago, miss. When I came in to check on Benjamin and saw this chair empty. I knew something was wrong. Zachariah hasn't left his son's side in days, except to go and fetch Doc Baker when things look bad." Her eyes turned pleading. "I searched the house through, but there was no sign of Zachariah anywhere, and no one saw him leave. Please, miss, if you know where he is..."

"I'm here, Mrs. Haversham."

The bedroom door stood open, and Zach stepped through it. Jane gasped as she whirled around and saw him there, uncertain which Zach this man might be. He met her gaze, nodded once. "Hello again, Jane."

Her breath escaped her in a rush, and her muscles seemed to go limp in relief.

"Merciful heavens, Zachariah. I've been frightened to death!"

"I'm sorry I worried you," Zach told the woman. "But I'm here now. Why don't you go on back to bed? You need your rest, you know."

Mrs. Haversham looked worriedly at Benjamin, who was still sleeping soundly. "I'll go," she said. "But call if you need me."

"Of course I will." Zach hugged the woman briefly, and then she left them. His gaze shifted to his son, and he closed his eyes.

She wanted to go to him, touch him. She wanted to feel his arms around her, and hear his strong, confident voice telling her that Cody would be all right, that they'd find him. But his confident air was nowhere in sight right now. When he looked at his dying child, he was the one who needed comforting.

"Cody?" he asked, not taking his eyes from his son.

"He was here," Jane told him. "But he ran away. Zach, where could he be?"

Zach closed his eyes, moved toward the chair. "I don't know."

He turned as if to sit, but Jane caught his arm and pulled. "No, Zach. You're not going to slip right back into your role of sitting here watching your son fade away. I'm not going to let you. We have to find Cody."

"My son is dying," he muttered, pulling free of her.

"And mine has the drug that will cure him."

He blinked at her as if he'd gone blank for a moment. Gave his head a shake. "You're right." The words came out on a deep sigh. "Of course, you're right."

Jane shook her head, pacing the room. "I don't get this. We came back here on the day before you left, didn't we? I mean, you seemed so sure. But if that's the case, then why isn't there another you, sitting here? Why—?" She turned to face him, pushing both hands through her hair. "This is so confusing."

"It seems to me that it would be physically impossible for a man to exist in two places at the same time. I couldn't be in the room down the hall, and here, in this room, at once. It simply could not happen."

"Then where did . . . the other one . . . go?"

Zach got up and walked to the window, parting the curtains to stare at something outside. "I don't know, Jane. But I do know we came back farther, if only by a day. That's certain."

Jane came to stand beside him, following his gaze. "How can you be so sure?"

"There was a thunderstorm on the night before I went forward. Lightning struck that barn, the one you can see in the distance. A little after 9:00 p.m." He pointed, and she saw the decrepit-looking building. "It burned to the ground within an hour, Jane."

She bit her lip, nodded. "Okay. All right, then we know we're here a day earlier, and we know the other Zach vaporized or something when we came through."

"No. I think . . . I think I somehow merged with him . . . with me. It's odd, Jane—I remember everything about my trip to the future, but I also remember being here by my son's bedside an hour ago, holding his hand and praying for a miracle."

A cold shiver worked up Jane's spine.

"Father?"

The weak voice coming from the bed made them both turn quickly. Zach rushed forward and bent over the bed, gathering his son into his arms. "I'm sorry, Benjamin. Did we wake you?"

"No," he said. Jane winced at the thinness of his arms, the whiteness of his skin. "My head hurts. That's what woke me up, I think."

"Well, then, I'll get you something for it," Zach said, standing again, running gentle, soothing hands over his son's head. "And I'll put it in some warm chocolate, since I know how you hate the taste."

The boy smiled and leaned back on the pillows. "I love you, Father."

"And I you, Benjamin. More than you know."

Then those curious green eyes landed on Jane, narrowed briefly, then widened. "Are you her? Are you?"

Jane frowned sending a questioning glance to Zach. He only lifted his brows, shook his head slightly, obviously having no more idea than she did what the boy was talking about. "Am I who, sweetheart?"

"The mother! The one I wished for when I saw the shooting stars! I knew you'd come. Oh, I knew you would. You're just as pretty as I wished you'd be. And—" His words were interrupted by a bout of coughing that racked his reed-thin body.

Jane's heart broke into bits, and she pulled the little boy more upright in the bed, holding him gently and rubbing his back until the spasm eased. And when it did, the little arms encircled her neck. "I'll be a good son, Mother. I promise."

Jane couldn't let him go for a long moment. The tears that were streaming down her face as she held him there were not anything such a sick little angel needed to see or to be worrying about. Zach saw them, though, and his own eyes were red-rimmed and brimming when they met hers. She held Benjamin in her arms until she could get her tears under control, and then she carefully wiped at her cheeks before straightening away from him.

"You can go and get my cocoa now," he said softly, closing his eyes and lying down. "I'll be fine. I know I will, now."

When Zach nodded at her and inclined his head toward the door, Jane walked slowly away from Benjamin's bedside, and she knew beyond any doubt that there had to be a way to save this child, and hers, too. There had to be. And she'd find it or die trying.

She followed Zach down the stairs and into the kitchen, where he set a kettle on a wood-burning stove, and then chucked a couple of bits of wood on the grate. He stood there for a moment, head bowed, back to her.

And she went to him, compelled to do so. She slipped her arms around his waist from behind, and lowered her head against his back. "We'll make him all right, Zach. I swear to you, we'll make him well again."

He turned and wrapped his arms around her, pulled her tight and lowered his face into her hair. She felt the tears, understood them all too well. "We have to," he whispered.

Nine

Cody waited until he heard the muted footsteps fade. Whoever had been in the room had left, gone down the stairs. Now was his chance. He slipped out of the closet, hurried back down the hallway to Benjamin's room and ducked inside, closing the door behind him.

Benjamin sat up, blinking at him. It looked like he was awfully tired. But he smiled at Cody all the same.

"Hi, Ben," Cody said, coming forward and feeling uncomfortable as all heck. He wasn't sure exactly what to say, how to act. "I'm—"

"My second wish?" The little guy blinked at him.

"Cody Fortune." Cody thrust out a hand, and moved closer to the bed.

Ben looked at Cody's hand, and slowly shook his head. "You better not. I'm sick, you know."

"I know." Cody sat down in the big chair. "But I had it already. You can only catch it once."

"Really?"

"Uh-huh."

"You had it?" Ben sat up a little straighter in the bed. "But you're okay now?"

"Sure."

Ben shook his head slowly. "My dad had it once,

and he got better, too. But . . . that's almost unheard-of. I heard them say so."

"They don't know it," Cody said, glancing quickly at the door, and then back at the boy in the bed. "Nobody here knows about it but me, but there's a medicine, and it works."

Ben closed his eyes. "I wish it were true," he said softly. "I'm so tired of feeling bad all the time."

"It is true," Cody said, and he fished the small brown bottle of pills from his jeans pocket and held it up. "This is the stuff, right here. I brought it for you. I tried to get in earlier, but that lady wouldn't let me."

"They don't let anybody see me, except the doctors and my dad, and Mrs. Haversham, of course. I haven't seen anyone except for grown-ups in weeks." He eyed the bottle, and tilted his head. "My third wish," he whispered, then looked at Cody, his eyes round and trusting. "It really will make me well again?"

"Yeah, but you have to take it right way. Every four hours, Ben, and you can't miss a single pill, or they'll all be wasted."

Ben blinked, chewed his lip. "I sleep a lot," he said. "I'd probably sleep right through a dose or two. Maybe if we told the grown-ups—"

"No way. Listen, Ben, they wouldn't believe me. They'd say I was a liar. And there's no way I can sneak in here every four hours to give you a pill. Heck, when I tried to get in before, they threatened to call the boys-in-blue on me."

"Boys-in-blue?"

"Er...the sheriff." Ben frowned and tilted his head. "Look, Ben, I've been trying to figure this out for a while now, and as far as I can see, there's only one way we can do it."

"How, Cody? I'd do anything to get better again."

"You have to run away," Cody said, deciding not to beat around the bush. Who knew when someone would walk in and haul him away by his earlobe? "Right now, tonight. I found a place where we can hide out. I'll take care of you, and make sure you get the pills on time."

Ben's eyes widened. He took a breath, shook his head. "I don't know, Cody. How long will we have to stay?"

"Just a couple of days," Cody said. "You'll have to take the pills for longer, but after two days you oughta be so much better that they'll have to believe us. At least well enough to take them on your own, without my help."

"If I was that much better, they'd let you stay," Ben said, and Cody thought he was thinking out loud. "My dad will be real worried if I up and leave, though."

"Yeah, but think how happy he'll be when you turn up healthy and strong."

Ben smiled a little. "Yeah, that would be something."

"We have to hurry, Ben. Before someone comes in."

Ben frowned. "I'm not very strong."

"I'll carry you piggyback if I have to. Come on, you'll need some warm clothes. And we'll take a blanket, too." As Cody spoke, he shook out a capsule, then put the cover back on the bottle and stuck it in his pocket. He handed the capsule to Ben. "Better take the first one now. Just wash it down with some water." As he said it, he poured water from the pitcher on the bedside stand, into the glass beside it. He handed the glass to Ben, and the boy obediently popped the pill into his mouth. It took him three tries, and he almost choked on it, but he finally swallowed it. Then he swung his legs over the edge of the bed.

"My clothes are in there." He pointed, and Cody opened the giant wardrobe and pulled out a heavy wool sweater and a pair of pants. Ben dressed, but he was clumsy and slow, and when he was finished he sank onto the bed, head hanging down, breathing hard.

"You really are weak," Cody said. He knelt and pushed a pair of socks onto the younger boy's feet. Then shoved on a pair of odd-looking button-up shoes and went back to the closet for a coat.

"There. You're all set now."

"Take another sweater, Cody," Ben said, lifting his head long enough to speak. "You don't have a coat on. I have one in there that's way too big. It will fit you."

Cody found the sweater Ben was referring to, and then balled up a blanket and tucked it under his arm. "You ready?"

"I guess so," Ben said. He got to his feet, but swayed and almost fell down. Cody moved to his side and pulled Ben's arm around his shoulders.

"Let's go. Don't worry, Ben, this is gonna work."

Ben nodded, and Cody opened the door and led him through the hallway, away from the stairs the other two had descended. He knew the house well, and he knew there was a set of back stairs that led straight to the rear of the house and the back door. It was slow going. Ben could barely walk, but soon they emerged into the chilly, starry night.

Ben leaned on Cody, and took a deep breath. "Gosh, it's been so long since I've been outdoors."

"I bet."

"Where is our hideout, Cody?"

"The barn up the road. I was there earlier, and no one was around. It will be safe, I think. And there are plenty of places to hide if anyone should come snooping."

Ben lifted his head and stared off at the barn in the distance. "I don't think . . . I can make it that far."

"You have to, Ben. Come on, I know it's hard, but—"

"No, wait," Ben argued. "Listen, I have a pony. In the shed, over there."

Cody looked, and blinked in surprise. There was no shed in the yard in 1997. But one stood there now, right where the garage ought to be. Man, this was like the "Twilight Zone" or something. Nodding, he helped Ben make it across the lawn, eased him onto a bale of hay and opened the shed door.

A soft brown Shetland pony greeted him with a soft nicker and a toss of his shaggy head. Cody gripped the pony's halter and led him outside. And the animal went, stopping beside the hay where Ben sat and nudging the boy with his nose. Big brown eyes seemed to say that he knew exactly what was going on. And the animal stood perfectly still as Cody helped Ben onto his back.

"Good pony," Cody said, taking the halter again and stroking the animal's muzzle.

"His name's Pete," Ben informed him.

"I always wanted a pony."

"Me too," Ben said. "But I've been too sick to ride him for a long time."

"Well, then, you oughta enjoy this." Cody unbunched the blanket and draped it around Ben's shoulders, tying a knot to hold it there. "Hang on, Ben, and holler if you need to stop." He turned and led the pony and the boy across the back lawn and onto the road. Then he started down it toward the barn, and whispered a silent prayer that he wouldn't run into any horse-and-buggy travelers before he got Ben under cover.

Zach opened the door quietly, in case Benjamin had fallen asleep again. It had been a while, by the time he stoked the fire and heated the milk, and melted the chocolate and added the sugar. Nothing like the two-minute hot chocolate from Jane's time. But Ben was used to this. He knew how long hot chocolate took. Zach tiptoed into the room, the teacup brimming with chocolate in his hand. And then he froze, because the oil lamp on the table spilled its light onto an empty bed.

"Benjamin," he called softly, scanning the room as his heart thumped harder in his chest. "Benjamin, where are you?"

Jane came in behind him, and he heard her swift intake of breath. "Zach?"

Zach turned to her, searching her eyes as if looking for an answer, though he knew she had no way of knowing where his son had gone. "He was too weak to get out of that bed," he told her. He set the cup down and dropped to his knees, searching under the bed, seeing nothing.

"Zach, the wardrobe..."

He turned and saw the door of his son's wardrobe hanging open. He pulled it farther, lifting the oil lamp and scanning the inside. "By God, his coat is gone!" Real fear was gripping him now. This made no sense. No sense at all.

Jane's hands came to Zach's shoulders, and he felt the warmth and the comfort of her touch, the calming energies she sent through him as if by magic. "Maybe he just got sick of lying in bed," she whispered, and her soft voice conveyed the same soothing as her hands. "He could have decided to go outside, get some fresh air."

"He could barely walk on his own, Jane." He felt her tense as he got to his feet, turned toward the door.

"Look, I'll search this floor. You go and check all the rooms downstairs. If we don't find him—"

"If we don't find him, I'll lose him," Zach said, and his voice was barely audible for its coarseness.

"You're not going to lose him."

Zach looked down into her warm, wide eyes, and tried very hard to believe her. The panic in his chest seemed to still when she looked at him, spoke to him, when she touched him. Unfortunately, the second he was away from her, searching the ground floor of his home for his dying son, the panic returned. Jane Fortune ought to be pint-size, so he could carry her with him, wear her like a charm around his neck. When she was with him, he could be confident and optimistic, but as soon as she left his side he felt that gut-deep fear he'd been living with for so many months cast its dark shadow over his soul once more. When he'd searched every room without success, he raced outside and began searching the grounds. And when that was done, he searched the guest house, and then the shed.

He stood there, in the shed's open doorway, and a chill night wind buffeted him, tugging his hair into chaos and trying to drive the big wooden door from his hands. Pete, Ben's pony, had vanished, as well. And it seemed all the strength in Zach's body left him as he scanned the horizon, the deserted, dark road unrolling to his left and then the forested hillsides to his right. Ben could be anywhere. He let go of the door, and the wind slammed it back against the wood, then drew it away and slammed it again. It became a rhythm, a hopeless, steady rhythm.

"Hold on, Zachariah," she said, and her voice was strong and firm. "We'll find him. I promise."

That voice was like steel coated with velvet, and it was one he was beginning to think of as belonging to his guardian angel. It came from close to his ear, and Zach managed to pull himself to his feet again. Jane's arms came around him, and he held her the way a drowning man would cling to a bit of driftwood. "His pony's gone. God, Jane, he wasn't strong enough to ride for long. What if he took to the woods? What if he fainted and fell off? He could be lying out there somewhere, alone and afraid."

"I don't think he's alone," she told him, stroking his hair. "I have a feeling he's with Cody."

Zach's head came up sharply, and he stared down into her eyes. Hope surged in his chest. If Ben was with Cody... "What makes you think that?"

"Well, you just said he was too weak to walk very far on his own. I can't imagine him having the strength to come all the way out here and climb onto that pony's back, can you?"

He blinked, then shook his head. She made it sound so logical, so simple. "No. No, I can't," he said.

"And who else do you suppose would have helped him? Zach, we already know that Cody overheard us arguing about this the other night. That's why he came back here, because he thought we might not. I know my son. He's trying to save Ben, because he thinks he's the only one who can. He took the pills when he left. It's obvious he intended to give them to Benjamin. And that's probably precisely what he's doing, even as we speak."

Zach gazed past her, out into the pitch-black night, and he shivered at another gust of that cold wind. "But that's all conjecture, Jane. You can't know—"

"Call it mother's intuition. I'm ninety-nine percent certain."

Zach closed his eyes. The panic ebbed, now that he had Jane's explanation to cling to. He envisioned Benjamin warm and snug, unafraid because he was in the company of Cody Fortune, already beginning to feel the effects of the drug Cody would, no doubt, have given him by now.

Thank God for Jane.

The wind picked up still-greater force, bringing doubt along with it. "It's so damned cold tonight."

Then he opened his eyes again at the sounds of voices coming from the house, and when he looked, he saw the glow of oil lamps in nearly every window. "What's—?"

"I woke Mrs. Haversham, and the other maid. One of them woke the groundskeeper, and he's heading into town to get more help. We'll have a search party formed within the hour, Zach. We'll find them both, no doubt safe and sound somewhere, and probably feeling bad for worrying us all so much."

He sighed involuntarily. "You're a wonder, Jane. An absolute wonder."

She took his arm and drew it around her shoulders as they started back toward the house.

Thunder rumbled in the distance, and the wind held steady, blowing her hair into a riot of silken curls that caressed his face. "Damn," he said. "That storm is moving in already. We have to hurry, Jane—it's going to be a brutal one." He knew, having witnessed its force once already. The thought of his son exposed to such powerful, elemental forces scared the hell out of him. Jane trembled, and he knew she was frightened right to the soul of her for the safety of the two boys, as well. But she wouldn't admit it, would she? Not now, when things were so uncertain.

"We should have thought to bring a lamp." Ben huddled beneath the heavy blanket in his bed of hay. Cody sat close by, but he didn't dare lie down. He had to be awake when it was time for the next dose of Ben's medicine. He wasn't going to let himself fall asleep and miss it. There were only enough pills to do this once, and if he didn't do it right...

Well, he wasn't going to think about that right now. "We don't need any old lamp," he said, making a conscious effort to sound cheerful. He knew Ben was scared to death right now, and he didn't blame the kid. "Look, I have something even better." Cody pulled the penlight out of his pocket, and clicked it on.

"Wow!" Ben whispered, drawing the word out. "What *is* it?"

"A flashlight," Cody explained, handing his treasure over without hesitation. At least now Ben wasn't lying there listening to that thunderstorm outside and shaking like a leaf.

"How does it work?"

"Electricity," Cody said. "The power is generated by a little battery inside. When it gets light enough out, I'll show you."

"You will?"

"Sure. You can even take it apart, if you want."

Ben smiled broadly for the first time. The flashlight's small glow illuminated his face and his missing front teeth. The pony, who had been munching peacefully on some of their bed, lifted his head and blew through his nostrils.

"Pete's scared of it," Ben said. He played around until he'd switched the light off.

"It's best we don't waste the battery, anyway," Cody told him. "Save it for when we need it."

Ben settled back under the blanket, holding the flashlight to his chest, as if it were a diamond or something.

"Yeah, you'd better get some sleep now."

Thunder crashed, so loud it sounded as if it were in the barn with them. Ben's hand shot out and closed on Cody's arm. "You...won't leave me, will you, Cody?"

"No way," Cody said. "I'm not going anywhere. You know something, Ben? All my life I've been wishing I had a little brother."

"You have?" Ben's voice sounded sleepy, and his grip on Cody's arm relaxed a little, but he didn't let go. "That's funny."

"Why?"

"'Cause I've been wishing I had a *big* brother." Ben rolled onto his side. "Do you have a pocket-knife on you, Cody?"

Cody did, but he had a pretty good idea what Ben was thinking, so he didn't say so. "Why?"

"Well, some of the kids, they cut their fingers, and rub them together, and swear an oath, and then they're blood brothers."

"That's what I thought you meant," Cody said, and he chewed his lip, thinking hard. He didn't think it was a very good idea for a kid as sick as Ben was to be cutting himself with a germy old jackknife. "They do that where I come from, too. But some of them do it differently."

"How?"

"Why? You wanna be brothers, Ben?"

Ben looked up at Cody in the darkness. "Yeah. I mean...I do if you do."

"Well, I just told you I'd always wanted a little brother, didn't I?" He could see the white flash of Ben's gap-toothed smile in the night. "So here's how we do it. First, you spit on your palm," Cody instructed. Ben did, and then Cody did the same. "Now we shake hands," Cody said. They groped in the darkness for a moment, but then they connected, and Cody closed his hand tight around Ben's. "And then we say the vow. I, Cody Fortune, do solemnly vow that from this day forward Benjamin Bolton is my very own little brother, and that we'll stick together no matter what." Cody said the words very seriously, making them up as he went along. "Now you say it, Benjamin."

Ben sat up a little. "I, Benjamin Bolton, do solemnly vow that . . ."

Cody cued him. "From this day forward."

"From this day forward, Cody Fortune is my . . . my very own big brother. And that we'll stick together . . . no matter what."

It sounded to Cody as if Ben were choking up a little at the end. And he'd never have admitted it to anyone in the world, but his own throat felt a little tight. "There," he said. "That's all there is to it. We're real, true brothers."

"Honest?"

"Honest. We swore an oath. That's even more than natural-born brothers ever do."

Ben settled deeper into the hay, but he still held Cody's hand. "And you won't leave me?"

"No way. Brothers have to stick together, no matter what, just like we said in the vow. Go to sleep now. I promise, I'll be right here when you wake up."

"Thanks, Cody."

Ben was quiet after that. Soon Cody heard his raspy but steady breathing, and knew he'd fallen asleep. He put his hand into his pocket, closed it around the bottle of pills and squeezed hard. Grating his teeth and closing his eyes tight, he whispered, "You'd better work, you hear me? You'd just better make him well again."

The soggy searchers regrouped at the house. Water dripped from hat brims, and rain slickers glistened in the lamplight as the men filed inside for a cup of coffee and a bit of warmth from the fire. Hours of combing the woods and the ditches along the roadside, and even of canvassing the town, had turned up nothing. No clue as to where the boys might be. And then the storm had unleashed its fury, and the men had gradually worked their way back here, all of them grim-faced and soaked to the bone. None of them ready to give up.

Zach's face was bleak as he listened to one after another of the searchers tell him of their lack of progress. He was soaking-wet, too, and while Mrs. Haversham poured coffee from the metal pot on the cookstove and doled out a cup to each chilled volunteer, Jane took Zach's arm and led him into the living room, urging him into a chair near the roaring fire.

"Just take a minute," she whispered, pressing a hot mug of the steaming brew into his chilled hands. "Here's a dry coat. Come on—"

"There's no time for this," he said, not meeting her eyes. His gaze was riveted to the leaping flames, his attention seemingly focused on the hiss and snap of resin in the hearth.

"You won't do Benjamin any good if you collapse in this rainstorm somewhere. It's only a short break,

Zach. Warm yourself, drink your coffee. Then we'll go right back out.''

He drew his gaze away from the flames then, locked it with hers. ''By rights, you should be falling apart by now. I know full well you're as afraid for Cody as I am for Ben.''

''I'll fall apart later, when they're both safe.''

His eyes narrowed as he studied her face. ''You're not like any woman I've ever known, Jane Fortune. I know, I'm repeating myself. But I want you to believe it. I mean what I say. You're different from the rest.''

She lowered her head. ''And you've known a lot of them, haven't you?''

''Dozens.''

It hurt to hear him say it out loud, though she'd already known. And she had no idea why the thought of him with all those other women should bother her at all, but... Oh, who was she kidding? Of course she knew why it bothered her.

''Why?'' she heard herself ask.

''Why what? Why do I take my pleasure wherever I wish? It's simple, really. A physical need that I assuage when I can. Nothing complicated about it.''

''But there are no feelings involved? Not with any of them?''

''No. Not ever. Not until—''

''What about...what about your wife? Benjamin's mother?''

He averted his face very quickly, fast enough that she knew she'd hit on something.

''You loved her, didn't you?''

He cleared his throat. "Claudia, Benjamin's mother, was never my wife."

Jane blinked in surprise, and then in disappointment. God, was he so much like Greg, then? That he'd got a woman pregnant and then...and then...

"She had a husband. An old, impotent, very rich husband. I was young enough and foolish enough to be flattered by her attentions, and to believe she wanted more of me than a pleasant diversion."

Jane tilted her head. "Then...you did love her."

"I thought I did. But I was a flighty youth with more book learning than common sense. I had no money or social standing. She had plenty of both. I was no more than a romp to her. When she found herself with child, Christian woman that she was, she went abroad to visit an aunt, or so the story went. She gave birth with no one in her estimable social circle any the wiser. Even her husband had no clue. The child arrived on my doorstep with a note stating that she never wished to see me or hear from me again, and that if I was to breathe a word suggesting the child was hers, she'd see me ruined. She had enough power to make it a valid threat."

While there was bitterness in his voice, she saw the real hurt in his eyes. "She broke your heart, didn't she, Zach?"

He only shrugged. "It was a painful lesson, but a valuable one. She's been widowed recently. Perhaps being alone will teach her something, as well."

"I don't think she taught you a thing. You became what she was. You closed off your heart and made yourself into a person who's only interested in meaningless flings with strangers." Was that all she had been to him, she wondered? Just one more round of mutual satisfaction between two consenting adults? No, she knew better than to believe that. What had happened between the two of them wasn't based on physical lust, but on emotional turmoil. Shared grief. They'd had no one to turn to except each other, and so they had.

"At least I didn't lock myself away from the world, the way you did, Jane."

"I thought I had," she said softly, and she lifted her face to stare into his eyes and, somehow, swallowed the lump in her throat. "But you got in, all the same."

He blinked up at her, as if she'd shocked him speechless. Then he got to his feet, and set the cup down. His hands rose to settle on her shoulders. "Jane—"

He stopped as the front door was flung open and a dripping-wet, raggedy-looking man stumbled through it. Beyond him, the dark clouds were churning with renewed vigor, as the already horrible storm steadily worsened.

"I seen somethin'!" the man shouted as he swept back the hood of his raincoat. "An odd-lookin' bit of light, in the old Thomas barn."

Zach went utterly rigid, eyes widening. "The old Thomas—" His head swung around, his eyes fixing on the pendulum clock ticking loudly on the mantel. It read 9:08 p.m. "No," he whispered. "Any minute now, that barn is going to—"

A blinding flash split the night, and Zach raced to the door, knocking the man aside as he moved out into the pouring rain. Jane rushed out beside him, and followed his gaze to the old barn, some three miles away. Even as she stared, the tiny tongues of flame began licking up at the black sky from the barn's roof.

"God, no..." Zach whispered.

Jane's calm was shattered. She could no longer hold the mask in place. Her piercing scream shattered the night, and she dropped to her knees in the pounding rain, heedless of the cold, or of the puddle in which she knelt. "Cody!" she sobbed. "God, don't take my baby!"

Ten

Jane's blood turned to ice when she realized that the barn in the distance was the same one Zach had told her about. According to Zach's tale, it would burn to the ground within a frighteningly short period of time. As old and dried-out as the building's wood had seemed when he pointed it out to her earlier, she could understand why. And right now, her son—and Zach's—might very well be inside. Perhaps asleep. Unaware of the danger. Trapped, maybe.

She could only stand in the pouring rain, watching helplessly, as Zach snatched the reins of his dripping-wet horse and leaped onto the startled animal's back. He kicked the horse into a gallop, nearly running an approaching buggy off the narrow road as he passed it. Then he vanished into the blackness of the storm-tossed night.

The buggy rocked to a halt and a woman clambered down, swinging her head around in the direction Zach had taken before hurrying up the steps to the stoop where Jane stood. She was nearly knocked back down them by the rush of searchers surging out of the house as they realized what was happening. Men raced to their horses, and the sound of pounding hooves as they galloped away rivaled the sound of the storm that enveloped them.

"What's going on?" the woman asked. And when Jane didn't reply, she gripped her shoulders, shaking her slightly. The sounds of the horses galloping away slowly faded, until it joined with the howl of the wind and the unending rumble of the thunder. "I asked you what's going on? The entire town is astir. They say the boy is missing, and—" She stopped there, closed her eyes and bit her lower lip.

And for the first time, Jane looked at her. Her blond ringlets hung damply around her face from beneath the hood of the dark blue cloak she wore. She was beautiful. And she was very, very frightened right now. Frightened . . . and hiding it.

"You're her, aren't you?" Jane whispered. "You're the one. . . ."

The woman's eyes widened, and her lips parted on a soft gasp. "I . . . I've no idea what you're talking about. I'm simply a concerned neighbor." Her gaze dipped, taking in Jane's wet jeans and T-shirt. "And who in the world are you?"

Jane shook her head. God, no wonder Zach had fallen for this beauty. She had the cheekbones of a goddess. Full, moist lips, and large green eyes that could swallow a person whole. Part of her resented the woman for hurting Zach and abandoning her own child. Another part was insanely jealous. This woman had held Zach's heart in her hands. He'd loved her. Maybe. . .maybe, deep down inside, he still did. Jane had been trying not to think too deeply about her suspicions, but they flooded into her mind now. He'd loved her. She'd hurt him. He'd never allowed himself to love again. It stood to reason that that might very well be because he'd never gotten over her.

Part of Jane wanted to tell this woman, this Claudia, what she thought of her. But the largest part of Jane was the mother in her. And that part of her knew and understood the fear in the other woman's eyes. It was a mother's fear for the life of her own child. Even if it was a child she'd never held, never wanted, perhaps never even loved...the biological bond was there, somewhere. Even one as weak as hers must be. It was the mother in Jane that reached out, took the woman's gloved hand. "My son is missing, as well," she said softly. "And we have reason to believe the two boys are in...in that barn." With her free hand, she pointed, and the woman looked.

"But...but it's *burning!*"

Jane choked on a sob, and averted her eyes. "I have to go to my son," she said hoarsely. "Let me take your buggy."

The other woman nodded mutely, turning and starting down the steps beside Jane. "I'm coming with you," she said, sounding dazed.

Jane didn't argue.

Zach drove the horse relentlessly, digging his heels into the beast's flanks even when he knew they were already running at top speed. The road had turned to muck, and still more rain pounded down, making it slick and deadly. Not enough rain to quench those flames, though. He wished he could get the image of that burning barn out of his mind. But he couldn't. He'd stood in his son's bedroom and watched as the flames devoured the entire structure, so quickly it seemed impossible. He knew how little time he had to reach Benjamin and Cody. He knew, and the knowing was killing him.

The wind blew icy droplets that cut his face like razors. He could barely see the muddy road in front of him, and likely wouldn't have seen it even in daylight. His gaze was riveted to that awful light in the distance. The flames spread rapidly across the roof of the structure, reaching to the heavens as if they'd devour the sky itself, and working lower, down the aged, tinder-dry boards. Great pieces of flaming debris fell through the darkness, only to land on the ground and begin licking their way up the sides of the building again.

Zach thought of Benjamin inside. Perhaps just waking to the knowledge that the building was aflame. Perhaps still unaware. Soon he'd be trapped. Soon there would be no escape. Soon...

No!

Zach kicked the horse harder, leaning forward over the sleek, rain-wet neck and feeling the heat that rose from that black hide. "C'mon, Demon. Faster, dammit!"

The horse stretched his legs, lunging even more rapidly than before. Mud and water splashed with every impact of those flying feet, soaking both Zach and the animal. Finally the barn loomed before them like a giant torch illuminating the night and cutting through the blackness of the storm. Rain pounded uselessly down, doing little more than adding a sizzle to the roar of the flames. The horse skidded to a halt and reared up, shrieking in terror. Zach was flung from the animal's back to land hard in the mud. The impact jarred him, but he surged to his feet, heading for the blazing barn even as the horse turned and fled from the terrifying spectacle of it.

Shielding his face with one arm, Zach went closer, until the heat seared his skin right through his clothes, and the roar overwhelmed every other sound. It was deafening. The flames were impassable walls, and he skirted them, circling the inferno as he sought an opening. A way in. There must be one. And at last, eyes stinging from the smoke, he found it. A gap in one side. Like a lopsided ring of fire from some dog-and-pony show. Without a second's hesitation, Zach plunged through the opening, in a desperate dive. He landed rolling in the musty hay inside.

The darkness was relieved only by occasional flashes of flame, springing to life as they found new fuel to feed them. The stench of burning wood and smouldering hay weighted the smoky air, so that it burned his lungs as he got to his feet. He was coughing before he'd gone three steps from the opening. Lifting the lapel of his jacket to his nose and mouth in an effort to filter the air, he shouted, "Boys! Where are you? Benjamin! Cody!"

He could see nothing but thick, deadly smoke and occasional flashes of firelight. He could hear nothing but the roaring and snapping, which was like a living being. A monster intent on devouring them all. A sudden movement made him spin to the side. Then he was mowed down by Ben's pony as it bolted past him in absolute panic. Zach's head cracked against a beam as he went down, and one shod hoof slammed down on his shin as the frightened animal flew toward the opening. At least the poor thing was headed in the right direction. Gripping a beam to pull himself up again, Zach moved toward the area the pony had been coming from. His shouts and coughing all mingled together.

And then he tripped and fell again. But this time, it was a body that caused him to stumble.

When the buggy bounced to a halt in the mud near the barn, Jane cried out in anguish. She lunged from the seat, jumped to the soupy ground and raced forward, and only the firm hands of one of the searchers kept her from running headlong into the flames. "Easy, missy. Stand back now, and let the men handle this. We're doin' all we can."

She shook her head, and rainwater flew from her hair as she struggled against the hands that held her shoulders. "Let me go! My son is in there! Cody! Cody!"

But there was no give in the man's grip. He held her firm, despite the pouring rain and all her struggles, and she stopped fighting as her knees gave out. She sank to the muddy ground in anguish, sobbing, unable to take her eyes from the fire.

Men had formed a brigade; a crooked line of bodies leading to a nearby stream, where the roiling water reflected the red-orange horror like a mirror. Buckets were filled and passed, hurled on the fire and passed back down. She had no clue where the buckets had come from. Nor did she care.

"This spot. Here, where Zachariah went in!" someone shouted. "Douse this, men, so he can get back out alive!"

Zach was inside? God, all three of them, trapped in that hell of heat and smoke?

In the buggy, the woman who'd driven Jane out here sat stone-still. Paralyzed, in shock, perhaps. She didn't cry out or sob, as Jane was doing. Only sat there, staring, and the light of the fire was reflected in those huge, dazed eyes.

Jane looked at her for just a moment, before her gaze was drawn back to the burning barn that might be devouring her child even as she sat here, safe and helpless. The man holding her eased his grip as she listened for Cody's screams. She didn't hear them.

Then she surged to her feet, free, and raced around the side of the building, slipping in the mud, fighting for footing and then lunging onward. The place the men were soaking in water was a charred oval. Gray smoke spiraled from its blackened edges. And Jane aimed for that opening, with every intention of rushing through it.

A small form stopped her just before she reached the hole. A small, precious, oh-so-familiar shape that stumbled out of the death trap and slammed into her. Small, strong arms snagged her waist, and a grimy face pressed to her belly.

"Cody!" Jane fell to her knees again, in relief this time, sobbing anew, holding him tight.

"Mom... Mom, I was so scared!"

She cradled her son to her, unable to let him go even if she'd wanted to. But her gaze returned to that gaping black hole as she waited, holding her breath.

Seconds ticked by like hours. But finally Zach stumbled through, his son cradled in his arms. Kneeling, Jane stared up into his eyes. And he stared down into hers, his face sooty, his hair singed. He shifted Benjamin to one side, freeing a hand to reach down to Jane. She took it, and Zach pulled her to her feet, turned her and quickly drew her and Cody away from the building. Not stopping until they reached the road.

"Doc Baker!" he shouted. "Someone find the doctor!"

"I'm here, Zachariah. Right here." An elderly man elbowed his way through the crowd and gently took Benjamin from Zach's arms. "I'll see to him, son. There, now. He's alive. He's alive, Zach. Don't go fainting like a woman on me."

"I wasn't planning to."

Doc handed the boy off to someone else. "Get him into my buggy. This one, as well," he said, nodding to Cody.

Cody clung to Jane's hand, hard enough to break the bones, she thought, as he stared at the unconscious younger boy. He turned to Zach, who stood on the other side of her. "Ben's going to be okay," he told Zach. "I've given him two doses already, and in a little while it'll be time for—" As he spoke, Cody dug his hand into the pocket of his jeans. Then he froze, eyes going wide as saucers. "The pills! Oh, no, the pills are gone! They must have fallen out of my pocket when we—"

"Zach, no!" Jane cried, but it was no use. Zach was already bolting back toward the burning barn, leaping through the hole, which was once again ringed in fire.

The doctor swore. Cody cried. The men who surrounded them shouted. But it was too late—Zach was gone.

"Mom..."

Jane shook her head, hugging Cody once more. "I want you to go back to the house with the doctor, Cody."

"But Zach—"

"There's nothing more you can do here, sweetheart. Please. Go with him. You need to get warm and dry, or you'll end up as sick as Benjamin is. Besides, he might need you when he wakes up."

Cody shuddered and stared for a long moment at the blazing barn. "Mom, I don't want Zach to die. I didn't mean for any of this to happen. I only wanted to help Benjamin...." He hugged her hard, clung to her in the pouring rain.

"He's not going to die. I promise. And none of this is your fault, Cody." She bent down and kissed his soot-streaked face. "Please, go, so you'll be safe. Take care of Benjamin. That's what Zach would want you to do."

Cody sniffed and stiffened his spine. "Okay. I'll go. Promise you won't go in after him, Mom."

"I promise."

Cody nodded, hugged her once more, and then climbed into Doc's waiting buggy. Benjamin was lying on the seat, so Cody sat on its edge, and took Ben's hand in his. "You're gonna be all right, Ben," he told him. Doc gave her a nod. "I'll take good care of your boy, ma'am. You see they bring Zachariah along the second they get him out. You hear?"

"I will."

"If I get the lads settled in before you bring him back, I'll return here. Though I sadly fear that if it takes that long, all will be lost." He studied her through narrowed eyes. "What is this 'medicine' the boy lost in there?"

She lowered her chin, shook her head. "I... It's experimental, Doctor. That's really all I know."

"Funny Zachariah didn't mention it to me before," the man muttered, turning to his buggy and climbing aboard. He gave the reins a snap, and the vehicle rolled away. Jane moved forward.

The bucket brigade was going full force again. Two men had gone inside after Zach, and Jane waited, praying silently, as tears slid down her face. "Be all right, Zach," she whispered. "Please, for the love of God, be all right."

There was a crash as the roof gave way. Flaming boards fell to the ground, sending showers of glowing embers into the night. Men jumped back, one of them pulling Jane with him. As the barn caved in on itself, she saw three dim outlines near the opening. And then they were gone.

The sparks whispered to the ground, and the flames that had leaped skyward lowered again, carrying what remained of the building with them. Jane raced forward to where she'd seen the three—or thought she'd seen them—hopping over flaming bits of debris. Two of the men were already struggling to their feet, crying out in pain as they beat their smoldering clothes, and then staggering away. The third remained where he was, half buried in rubble. And Jane went to him, frantically throwing charred wood from his back, burning her hands and not caring.

"Help me!" she screamed, and only then did several others surge forward to finish the job and lift Zach's still body from the mud and rubble. They carried him to the road, laid him on his back there. One bent over him for a moment as Jane joined them there.

Then he straightened, looking at all of them, slowly shaking his head. "It's no use. He's dead."

Eleven

"**No!**" Jane screamed the word, pushing past the men who surrounded Zach's still body. Her hair was stuck to her face, and dripping wet, her jeans muddy to the knees, her shirt soaked. Her running shoes were caked in mud, and she imagined she looked like some kind of crazy woman to most of them. But she didn't care. "Get out of the way! Let me through!"

"I'm sorry, ma'am. We all cared for him, but it's no use. He's gone."

Jane fell to her knees beside Zach as the rain pummelled her back and shoulders and pounded down on him, rinsing away the mud and soot from his still face, beading on his face and pooling in the corners of his closed eyes. She pressed her fingers to his throat, but felt no pulse. She laid her face against his lips, but felt no breath. Then she slipped one palm beneath his nape, lifting slightly, and she tipped his chin back with her other hand. She pinched his nose and covered his mouth with hers, and she blew air into his lungs.

"Land sakes, woman, you oughtn't be kissing on a dead man thataway!"

"He's gone, ma'am. Best to let him be, now."

She lifted her head briefly, then blew again. And

then again. Someone touched her shoulder, as if to pull her away.

"Leave her alone!" a strong female voice said. And Jane knew it was the woman who'd come here with her. Benjamin's mother. And the tone of anguish in her voice left no doubt in Jane's mind. She still cared for Zach. "Can't you see she's trying to help him?"

Jane ignored all of them and positioned her hands over Zach's chest. Counting silently, she pressed down, once, twice, over and over. Then she breathed into his mouth. And then she pumped again.

"Get her off him!" a man shouted. "It's unnatural, what she's doing!"

Again hands came to her shoulders, tugging her back this time. And again that female voice, the one she knew belonged to the woman Zach had loved, interfered.

"Get your hands off her, or I'll shoot."

Startled, Jane turned, and saw that beautiful, fragile-looking woman, standing there in the firelit night, with rain dripping from her velvet hood, pointing a tiny pistol at the man nearest Jane.

"All of you, back off. Now!"

Slowly the men backed away, shaking their heads and muttering. "She's plumb lost her mind," one man said. "They both have."

Jane didn't waste a second. She bent over Zach again and continued the CPR. She pumped until her arms screamed for relief, and then still longer. "Please, Zach," she muttered. "Please. We need you, dammit."

Finally she felt a soft beat against her hand when she laid it over his heart. She lowered her head to Zach's chest and dissolved in tears of relief.

Zach drew a raspy breath, then another, and then he coughed. His hands came up, found her head there, and his fingers wound in her hair, holding her to him.

The group of bystanders had gone utterly still. Some crossed themselves, while others swore aloud, and still others only gaped.

"Jane," Zach whispered.

She lifted her head to stare down into his eyes. He licked his lips, tried to swallow. Jane pressed her palms to his cheeks, and kissed him gently, slowly. Her tears dampened his lips, and when she lifted her head away, he licked them again.

"I got them," he rasped. "I got the pills."

She closed her eyes. "I never doubted you would," she told him.

"Let's get him back to the house," someone said, and it seemed the words jerked the others back from their stunned state of confusion.

Jane rose, allowing them to lift Zach bodily.

"Put him in my buggy," Claudia ordered, and the men obeyed her as if they might be quite used to doing so.

Jane followed, climbing in without an invitation. And Claudia came in after her. She took the reins, shook them, and the wheels rolled to life. The buggy bounded and bounced over the muddy road, making sucking sounds and splashing its way back toward the house as the rain pattered down on its top. Jane sat beside Zach, clinging to his hand.

She wondered what on earth she'd done, how she'd let it happen. She hadn't realized the truth until she was bending over him, realizing he might very well die there in the mud. She'd fallen in love with another man who would leave her alone in the end. A man who thought of women the way he thought of a good meal. Something he enjoyed while he could and then thought no more about. At least ... that was the way he thought of most women. With one notable exception, she thought, with a sidelong glance at Claudia. Jane had lowered her guard, somehow, and let a sweet-talking womanizer waltz out of the past and straight into her heart.

And she knew, without a doubt, that when he waltzed back out again, he'd leave nothing behind but shattered bits.

There was something soft petting him like a cherished pet. Over and over it smoothed through his hair, across his face. Slowly, hypnotically. Zach inhaled, half expecting to get a lungful of acrid smoke for his trouble. Instead, though, he breathed the sweetest perfume this side of heaven.

The feminine scent of Jane Fortune.

Jane? Stroking him like *that?*

Very cautiously, Zach opened his eyes, just a crack. Enough to peek out and see her without letting her know he was awake just yet. And what he saw surprised him. She was sitting in a chair beside him—he was, apparently, in his own bed. But she looked so ... soft. Vulnerable. There was an ache, a longing, in her eyes, utterly unveiled. No masks right now. Not when she thought no one could see. It was all right there, on her face. And it rocked him, because he'd never seen it quite this clearly before. Probably because she kept it so well hidden.

Tenderness. Caring. Need. And, God, the loneliness.

He turned toward her, reaching out, compelled to do so, before he gave it a second thought. Jane's reaction was to stiffen, and draw away. A mask slammed down over her face in the blink of an eye, hiding that caring, heartsick Jane away behind it. Probably for her own protection, he thought. Dear God, for a moment there, she'd been looking at him as if...

No. That was impossible. Perhaps he'd been hallucinating.

"Jane," he whispered, searching her face even as she averted it and tried to swipe her tears away without him seeing. He smiled at the effort. So he hadn't imagined it, then. "Too late, Jane," he said, though his voice was coarse as tree bark. "I already saw you crying."

"I'm not crying," she told him.

"No. And you haven't been sitting here, touching me and stroking my head, either, have you?"

"Of course not. You're delirious." She got out of the chair, her movements jerky and quick, and poured a glass of water from a pitcher. "Here. You're probably thirsty."

"Thank you, Jane." He took the glass, drank deeply, and watched her watching him. Her eyes focused on his throat as he gulped the water down. When he was finished, he set the glass on the nightstand. He absently licked his lips, and then froze as her eyes flared wider. She quickly looked away as her face went red.

He glanced past her at the window, and was surprised to see no droplets beading the pane. Just darkness, stark and unrelieved. "What time is it?"

"I don't know. Well after midnight, at least." She scanned his puzzled face and went on. "You were unconscious for a few hours, Zach. I think it was a combination of the side effects you were already suffering from and the smoke of that fire."

"I've slept that long?"

Smiling slightly, she nodded.

"And how are the boys?" he went on.

"Cody's okay. Tired, but okay. I set up a cot for him in Benjamin's room. He didn't want to leave him."

Zach shook his head slowly. "That's one special boy you have there, Jane." Then he frowned, and swallowed hard. "And what about Benjamin? How is my son?"

"The same," Jane told him. "I've given him another dose of tryptonine, but it's too soon to see any real improvement yet. Tomorrow, though, he'll start to feel better."

Zach grinned, unable to help himself. "Everything is going to work out. It will—you'll see." She looked doubtful, but Zach couldn't rid himself of the feeling of optimism that had decided to overwhelm him. Not only was his son going to be fine, but Miss Jane Fortune was showing signs of...caring. And that, for some reason, made him feel almost giddy. "And where is everyone now, Jane?"

Her brows rose. "Asleep, of course."

"Of course," he repeated. "Asleep. All except for you. You hold a vigil at my bedside, devoted as a lovesick young wife would be."

"Don't be stupid, Bolton."

"Don't be stubborn, Jane," he replied. "At least admit the truth. Why is it so difficult for you to say it? You care about me, Jane. And you want me, too. Every bit as much as I want you. You know you do. You haven't stopped thinking about what it was like . . . what it could be like again, if we—"

She lifted her gaze, locked it with his. "Unlike some lower life forms I could name, I do not act on every physical craving."

He smiled at her, sitting up. "You . . . you'd call it a craving? You *crave* me, Jane?"

"Go to hell, Zach." She whirled to stomp away, but Zach caught her wrist, and slowly drew her back around until she faced him. He pulled her nearer, until her thighs touched the mattress, and then kept pulling, until she had no choice but to sit down on its edge.

He scanned her face, wishing he knew why she denied her feelings so vehemently. "Do you hate me, Jane?" he whispered, searching those blue eyes.

"Of course not."

He couldn't have told it from her tone, or the look in her eyes, though. He lowered his head, suddenly, and began to cough. He coughed until he doubled over, until he fell back against his pillows in exhaustion. Until his skin was coated in a thin sheen of sweat and his lungs felt as though they would burst.

And she was leaning over him, swiping his forehead and neck with a cool cloth, pushing her fingers through his hair. "Zach, easy. Relax. That's it."

Weakly he looked up at her. Now she looked as if she cared again. A second ago she'd looked at him like an assassin. Now her eyes were wide with concern, and her touch was as tender as a lover's. "I don't understand you," he managed to whisper.

"So who said you had to understand me?" She dabbed at his brow again. "Dammit, Zach, are you all right?"

He closed his eyes, nodded.

"I don't believe you. Twice through the damned twilight zone, and then nearly killed in a fire. How much more do you think your body can take?"

He lifted a hand, cupped her nape and drew her closer. Gently he brushed a kiss across her lips, and he knew she didn't object to it when her eyes fell closed. "Climb into this bed with me, Jane, and we'll find out," he whispered, and then pressed his lips to hers again.

Only this time she jerked away so fast she almost yanked him out of the bed and onto the floor. Her eyes flew open wide, and flashed with an anger so hot it nearly seared him. "Damn you, Zachariah Bolton!"

"What?" He blinked in total confusion. What was her problem, anyway?

"I was not one of your one-night stands, that's what! What happened between us . . ." She balled up the washcloth in her fist, and hurled it at him. "It wasn't just sex—at least it wasn't for me. So stop treating me like one of your giggling sluts, Zach, because it meant something to me. It meant something, even though I didn't want it to. And now I find myself in a place where I said I'd never be again.''

He shook his head quickly, scanning her face. "It meant something to me, too, Jane. And what place is it you're talking about, the place you swore you'd never be again?''

She closed her eyes. "Heartbreak, Zach. Its name is heartbreak.'' Then she spun on her heel and walked slowly away. Leaving Zachariah to wonder where he'd gone wrong. Dammit, didn't she know how he felt about her? How she touched his heart in a way no woman ever had? Hadn't he made that clear to her? He'd never wanted another woman the way he wanted her. Never... never *felt* for another woman the way he felt for her. No, he realized with newfound clarity, not even Claudia.

But then again, Jane Fortune was not any other woman. Far from it, in fact.

He blinked as he considered his unusual feelings for her—the ones she apparently had no clue about—and then he froze, blinking in shock. By God, he hadn't gone and fallen in love with her, had he?

Lord, what if he had?

Well, he supposed there was one way to find out. He'd simply have to sit down and analyze his feelings, the way he would perform any other experiment. Meanwhile, though, enough was enough. He did not deserve her being this angry with him. And he didn't want her living in what she referred to as heartbreak. He'd talk to her. She was going to sit down and explain to him exactly what she was feeling, and she was going to do it now. He got out of the bed, steadied himself, and started for the door. Maybe...maybe he could ask her to stay, after all.... Maybe...

Jane closed Zach's bedroom door and turned from it, only to run smack into Claudia. The woman was the very picture of elegance in her high-necked, lace-trimmed dress. Her blond-gold ringlets framing her delicate face. Her button-up shoes peeking from the frilly hem of her dress. Jane felt like a slob in her filthy jeans and shirt.

Claudia eyed her, then the door through which she'd just come, and then her again, brows lifting this time. "Well," she asked, not even bothering to hide her meaning, "how is he?"

"I thought you were the expert on that, Claudia."

The woman blinked as if in surprise. "You're a very strange woman," she said. "Candid in your speech, foreign in your mannerisms. And your clothes..."

"You have a problem with my clothes?" Jane asked.

"Of course not. I'm not the one who has to wear them."

Jane glared at her.

"Oh, come now, surely we can be friends." Claudia hurried on. "In fact, I feel that I can do you a favor, if you'll let me."

"Oh, really? And just what would that be, Claudia? You going to teach me how to breathe with my waist cinched down to thirteen inches, just so I can impress some male? Sorry. I'm not interested."

Claudia's smile was one of bewilderment, but she shook her head and went on with the conversation all the same. "I can warn you about Zachariah. Don't fall in love with him, Jane. He'll never care for any woman the way he cares for me. If you pin your hopes on winning his heart, you'll only be disappointed. He'll never give me up for you."

"I'd never ask him to."

"He can't love any woman the way he loves me, Jane. And you already guessed the reason. I'm the mother of his child."

"You're right," Jane whispered. "And I have the feeling you're counting on that, aren't you?"

Claudia blinked, and averted her eyes.

"What's the matter, Claudia? Truth hurt? What the hell are you doing here, anyway? Do you want him back? Is that it? Do you think you can abandon him, break his heart, deny your own child, and then just waltz in one day, wanting to take it all back, just because you've fallen on hard times?"

"Yes!" she cried, and she squeezed her eyes shut tight, and made her small hands into fists on either side of her head. "Yes, that's exactly what I want. Now that my husband is gone, there is nothing to stop me. I need a husband to provide for me, Jane. And I'm not going to let some odd little bird like you stop me."

Jane closed her eyes, shook her head slowly. "Fine," she whispered. "If he's stupid enough to fall for the same bull twice, then he deserves you. But you know, I really don't think he is." She waved a hand toward Zach's door. "Be my guest, Claudia. Knock yourself out." And with that, Jane turned and paced away down the hall, to the room that had been assigned to her. On her way, she opened Benjamin's door to check on the boys. Cody slept in the cot she'd set up for him in Ben's room. Both were sleeping soundly, but she didn't like the sound of Ben's wheezing. Damn, he should be improving at least a little bit by now, shouldn't he?

Well. Maybe in the morning he'd seem better. She pulled the boy's door closed, and as she did, she heard Zach's open. Heard soft footsteps creeping inside, and heard the door close again. Her heart twisted into a hard little knot.

Lifting her chin, Jane moved on to her own room. She left the door open, though, and then tried to tell herself it wasn't so that she could see when the little tramp left Zach's room. Or... if she left.

And then she wished she hadn't. Because after she'd bathed, and dressed in a borrowed nightgown, and brushed her hair, Claudia still hadn't left. And then she lay awake all the rest of the night, twisting and turning and unable to sleep. Because it was dawn, now, and Claudia hadn't come out. Not at all. She'd spent the night where Jane had wanted to. Wrapped up tight in Zachariah Bolton's arms.

Jane wanted to claw the witch's eyes out.

She'd talked herself silly. Talked about all the reasons she'd had for doing what she did to him and Benjamin. Zach hadn't wanted to hear any of it, of course. All he'd wanted to do was get hold of Jane and make her explain herself to him. But Claudia had been insistent and Zach had been weak. So he'd listened to her excuses and her explanations and her apologies. And then her incredibly generous offer to be a wife to him and a mother to Benjamin now that her wealthy husband had died.

Zach had glanced at her, lifted one brow and said simply, "No."

"What?"

"No, Claudia. I don't know how I can put it any plainer than that. I don't want you. Neither does my son. I find it intriguing how you didn't want me when I was poor and had no standing, but now that I'm wealthy and respected, and you're the penniless widow, you've suddenly developed tender feelings for me. As for Benjamin, you've known for months he was dying. You could have spent time with him, if you'd wanted to. But you didn't. Now, when he's reduced to perhaps another day or two of life, you show up. No. We're not interested. Now, please, get out of my room." He yawned, laid his head back on the pillows, closed his eyes.

"It's her, isn't it? That strange woman you brought here from God knows where! It's her. I know it is. You're in love with her, aren't you?"

"Don't be ridiculous," he said softly. But then his eyes popped open and refused to close. All this time, he'd been lying here pondering Jane's feelings for him. God, perhaps he should have been pondering his for her.

"It's true," Claudia whined. "I see it in your eyes when you look at her. And it's even more obvious in hers. The way she stares at you when she thinks no one's looking. The way she touched you when she sat here beside you, the things she whispered. Even her voice changes slightly when she's speaking to you. She's in love with you!"

Zach lay still, staring thoughtfully up at the ceiling. "What an intensely interesting theory," he muttered, and he closed his eyes.

He didn't intend to fall asleep, but he did. With a stupid grin on his face, and an empty feeling in his chest. And when he woke, he was astonished to see Claudia still there. Pacing the floor, peering out of the window, waiting as if for daylight.

"Dammit, woman, what are you still doing here?"

"Leaving," she said very simply. She opened his door, stepped into the hall, and then, for some reason he could not have explained if his life depended on it, she blew him a kiss and said, "I love you, too, darling. Goodbye, for now."

She left, but didn't close the door.

Frowning in confusion, Zach got to his feet and went to do so himself. But he froze when he reached the doorway, because he saw, just two doors down, Jane standing frozen in her own. And the hurt he saw in her eyes was almost more than he could bear.

He opened his mouth, but she spoke first. "I'm glad you're up," she said softly. "Your son has his medication, and you're obviously fine. I think it's time for Cody and me to go . . . home."

"But—"

"Ten minutes," she said, and her words fell like stones clattering from an unreachable peak. "I'll meet you in the workroom."

Twelve

Zach felt as if she'd slapped him when she closed the bedroom door in his face. Immediately he gripped the knob, shoving the door open again and stomping into the bedroom. She stood with her back to him, near the window. He was encouraged that at least she hadn't locked him out. But then he told himself that might not mean a thing.

"You can't leave, Jane. Not yet." He closed his eyes and congratulated himself on the stupidest argument he'd ever put forth. "What I mean to say is that it's too soon. We don't know yet what... what..." Blinking, he studied her back, her shoulders, the barely noticeable tremor there. The soft, almost inaudible sound of her uneven breathing. He swallowed hard and stepped nearer.

"Go away, Zach," she said, her voice unusually deep and very soft.

He didn't go away. He moved closer, and he clasped her shoulder with one hand to turn her around to face him. She refused to budge. So he tried harder, and he managed to move her this time. Then all he could do was stare down at her damp cheeks in shock. "You're crying," he said, no less astonished than he'd been when he first suspected it. "I can't believe it. You're—"

"I asked you to leave."

"I can't leave." He shook his head, continuing his search of her beautiful face, her glistening eyes. Dear God, had he been blind all along? Could it be true, what Claudia had said? He couldn't believe it. She couldn't be crying for him, or because of what she'd seen just now. She couldn't care that much for him. Could she? "Is it Cody?" he asked her. "Is it all the worry, Jane? Are you homesick?" He touched her face, laid his palm against her cheek and tilted her head so that he could see her better. And when he did, she closed her eyes, as if against her will. And he knew.

"My God," he murmured, taking a startled step away from her. "All this because of Claudia? That's it, isn't it?" She met his eyes, averted hers, and he took another involuntary step backward. He couldn't seem to help himself. It was as if she'd shoved him bodily. The idea that she might...might truly...love him ... Frankly, it scared the hell out of him.

She narrowed her eyes. Then her chin fell and she shook her head slowly. "What if it were? It wouldn't matter, would it, Zach? The very thought of it sends you running scared, just like—" She bit her lip, shook her head. "Well, you don't need to panic, Bolton. It's true enough, I fell for the Don Juan routine. You got me into bed. Hell, you even had me believing you might actually..." Lifting her chin, she licked her lips. "Don't worry. I'm taking my son and I'm leaving."

"But I..." He let the protest trail off, unable to find the words, not even sure what it was he wanted to say.

"You see? You can't even tell me you don't want me to go, can you?"

"Dammit, Jane, why are you so angry with me?"

"I'm angry with myself," she whispered, turning from him, pulling her freshly laundered jeans and sweatshirt from the back of the chair. "Hell, I shouldn't be. I ought to be congratulating you, wishing you well. It's a fairy-tale ending, isn't it? You and Benjamin and his mother, finally together. A real family. It's storybook-perfect."

"Dammit, Jane, you think just because she spent the night in my room that I intend to—"

"Don't you pull that love-'em-and-leave-'em routine out of your hat now, Zach. Not now. It's different when you're in love with the woman."

He tilted his head, skimming her from head to toe with his eyes. "Maybe you're right about that."

"And we both know there's only one woman you'll ever love, don't we?"

He turned his gaze inward, frowning hard. "Yes. But I'm only just beginning to realize it."

She swallowed hard. He heard the gulping sound, saw her rapid blinking as she turned away yet again. By God, the woman actually cared for him. It was beyond Zach's ability to understand, but it was obviously true.

"I wish you well, then," she said. "I hope you'll be—"

"Jane," he said softly, again stepping in front of her, tipping her chin up with his forefinger, getting lost in her swimming eyes. "We're going to work this out. I don't know how, but we'll find a way. But first, sweet Jane, you have to know that nothing has—"

"Mom! Zach! Come quick!"

Zach stiffened in surprise, then turned to the doorway, where Cody stood in a nightshirt, breathless and wide-eyed. "What's—"

"It's Ben! Hurry!"

Zach's body went rigid, and utterly immobile. "No," he whispered. "Please, no, not now..."

Jane started to rush past him, but turned when she realized he wasn't following. The anger that had been in her eyes before was utterly gone now. Now there was only compassion. Empathy. She knew exactly what he was feeling right now and, whether he deserved it or not, she cared. Though she fully believed he'd spent the night in the arms of another woman, she could still feel compassion for him.

"Stop it," she told him. And when he only stood there, she stood close to him, gripped his shoulders, shook him slightly. "Stop thinking the worst. Snap out of it. Your son needs you."

He blinked at the strength in her tone, the flash of passion in her eyes. He stiffened his spine, nodded once. Jane turned again, but this time she slipped her hand into his as she did so, drawing him along at her side.

The fear of what he would find when he walked into his son's bedroom gnawed at his stomach like a corrosive. And he knew that if not for the warmth of the small, trembling hand tucked into his own, he'd never be able to put one foot in front of the other. To walk down the hallway, and then to step across the threshold of the open door. With an effort, he settled his gaze on his son. And then his muscles turned limp with relief. Benjamin wasn't dead. He lay there, sleeping peacefully. As peacefully as Zach had ever seen him sleep. But only sleeping. His little chest rose and fell in rhythm.

Sighing in relief, Zach crossed to the bedside, and gathered Benjamin's hand into his own. He closed his eyes and sank into the chair beside the bed, kissing that tiny hand, battling tears of relief.

"Cody, you scared us half to death," Jane was saying. "What were you thinking of, saying that—"

"I can't wake him up, Mom."

Just like that. Five little words, each one hitting Zach in the chest like a bullet. His jaw clenched painfully, and he lifted his head, turned his gaze to lock with Jane's.

Her blue eyes had widened in shock and fear. "I don't understand," she whispered. "The pills were supposed—"

"He hasn't missed a single dose, Mom. I'm sure of it. He should be getting better, not—"

"Benjamin." Zach bent over the bed, gripped the boy's shoulders. "Benjamin, wake up. Wake up now, son."

There was no response. Zach was vaguely aware of Cody moving to the opposite side of the bed, clinging to Benjamin's other hand. And vaguely aware of Jane moving around the bedroom, the sounds of pills rattling as she shook them from the bottle.

And then her voice, sounding dead. "Cody," she said. "Close the door."

Zach looked up, saw Cody frowning at his mother, but obeying all the same. Then he turned to Jane. "Today...is the day he slips into the coma. But I thought, with the pills, he might..."

She held a capsule, one end in the fingertips of each hand. And as he stared, she twisted, and she pulled, until the thing came apart. She turned the ends, looked inside, shook her head. And when she met Zach's stare, she swallowed hard. "There's nothing inside, Zach. You brought back a drug that hasn't been invented yet. It just...it just doesn't exist in this time."

Zach's stomach knotted, and a feeling of dread slowly chilled every part of his body. "My God...my God, Jane, you were right." And then his gaze turned to Cody. "Dammit, what have I done? What if my coming back here altered history, as you feared it would? Maybe now that I've returned the cure will never be found." Lowering his own son's hand to the bed, Zach walked slowly to Cody, searching his face, fear filling his heart. "How do you feel, son? Are you sick at all? Feverish?" He pressed his palm to Cody's forehead, and heard Jane's pain-filled gasp when she realized what he suspected.

"Just a little tired is all," Cody said. "It's Ben we have to worry about. Why won't he wake up, Zach?"

"Is your throat sore?"

Cody nodded. "Yeah. From all that smoke last night."

Zach's eyes met Jane's over Cody's head. And he knew they were both hoping to God that it was the smoke, and not something far deadlier.

Jane came to her son, slipped her arms around him and slid one hand, very casually, over his forehead. And she felt the heightened warmth of him, just as Zach had. He saw it in her widening eyes, saw the agony, the fear.

"We have to get back to our own time, Zach," Jane said, as she sank to her knees and wrapped her arms around her son. "We have to. And if you want to save your son, you have to come with us. Bring him along."

"And if I'm right? If I've changed the course of things, and my esteemed colleagues didn't find the cure after all? If we return to your time, only to find that the miracle drug known as tryptonine doesn't even exist?"

Jane blinked as moisture filled her eyes at the very possibility of losing her son. Then her gaze turned inward and she gnawed her lower lip. "Bausch and Waterson find the cure because they believe your son died, and that you, their good friend, a brilliant scientist, lost your mind with grief. That's what drives them."

He turned to stare through pooling tears at Benjamin. "He's slipped into a coma now. It won't be much longer before those very things occur."

"You have to make them believe it's *already* occurred."

He swung his head around sharply.

"It's the only way, Zach. You have to convince them all that Benjamin is…is gone. Let them see your grief. And then disappear, never to be seen or heard from again. Everything has to happen exactly as it's supposed to, exactly as it's recorded as having happened in those books I read about you. Don't you see?"

He nodded slowly. "You're right. It…it might just work."

"You won't be able to come back here, Zach. Not ever again. You'll be abandoning your work. Your life, your friends. And . . . and Claudia."

His brows came together fast as he searched her face in confusion. And then he recalled that she'd somehow come to the conclusion that selfish, grasping Claudia was the love of his life. She must think him a shallow fool. "Do you think I'd trade my son's life for my own happiness? Even if I really did care for—"

"We're going to have to be very careful," she said quickly, and he had no doubt that the interruption was deliberate. "Plan every single step." She sent a worried look to Benjamin's still form, and to Cody, who'd returned to the bed and was whispering to the comatose child, stroking his head. "And we're going to have to hurry."

Jane stepped into the hallway and pulled Benjamin's bedroom door closed behind her, just as Mrs. Haversham and the doctor came bustling toward the room. She heard Zach turn the lock behind her. She'd already hustled Cody into Zach's workroom, down the hall. No one knew he was in there, waiting.

Ben was worsening by the minute, and they had no time to lose.

Lifting her chin, drawing a deep breath, she met first one pair of eyes and then the other.

"Benjamin . . . has passed," she told them.

Mrs. Haversham bit her lip, crossed herself. "He's no longer suffering," she said softly. "At peace now, sweet lamb."

"And Zach?" Dr. Baker asked.

Jane lowered her eyes and shook her head. "Not good, Doctor. He's locked himself in with the boy, says he won't let anyone take him."

"Oh, my!" the plump housekeeper gasped.

"I think," Jane added, feeling guilty as hell, but knowing she did what she did to save the child's life. "If we just give him some time alone, to come to grips..."

"Yes, I agree." Doc Baker nodded hard as he spoke. "Let's go downstairs. Leave him be with his boy for a while."

Jane cleared her throat. "Where is Claudia? I think she ought to know."

Mrs. Haversham sniffed. "That one left before anyone was astir this morning. I saw her for just a moment, and she would only say she was off on a cruise to the Continent and to give everyone her goodbyes. Some handsome fellow in a fancy carriage picked her up at the door."

Jane blinked in shock. Had Claudia found herself a bigger fish to sink her hook into? "But she knew..." It was beyond Jane's realm of understanding how a woman could set off on a trip while her own flesh and blood lay sick and dying. But, obviously, Claudia's interests had been in the boy's father, not in her own son. Zach might spend the rest of his life pining away for her, never realizing what a narrow escape he'd had.

She linked arms with the doctor and led them both down the stairs, knowing Zach needed a bit more time to accomplish what needed to be done. No one else was left upstairs. Just Zach, Benjamin and Cody. Jane's job was distraction. So she brewed some tea, and made plenty of noise. And an hour later, when the groundskeeper returned with Eli Waterson and Wilhelm Bausch, whom he'd fetched at Dr. Baker's suggestion, everyone insisted it was time to go back upstairs. Eli and Wilhelm would be able to talk some sense into Zachariah, they all concurred. Jane hoped to God everything was ready.

Doc rapped gently on the bedroom door. "Zachariah. It's Aaron Baker. It's time to open the door, Zach."

There was, of course, no answer.

"I have your friends here with me, Zachariah. Eli and Wilhelm. They'd like to talk to you."

"Yes, Zach, please, let us in," Eli called.

Doc tried the doorknob and found it unlocked, as planned. He twisted it, pushed it open, stepped inside... and then froze in place. Mrs. Haversham gasped. The bed stood empty, covers thrown back, sheets crinkled and barren. A breeze stirred the curtains in the open bedroom window. The doctor rushed forward to push them aside, and they all saw the rope that hung over the sill.

"By God!" Doc shouted. He leaned out the window, scanning the horizon, but of course he saw no sign of Zach.

"Land sakes, he's taken Benjamin away!" Mrs. Haversham cried.

"Look," Jane said. "There's a note."

Eli Waterson spied the paper on the bed, snatched it up and read it, shaking his head as he did. "Poor Zachariah. Lord, he's gone out of his mind with grief. Says he's taking the boy into the wilderness, where no one can come for him."

"Lord have mercy, Zachariah's lost his mind," Mrs. Haversham breathed, and she sank onto the bed, hugging herself.

"I've seen it before," said Wilhelm Bausch. "But never in a man as intelligent as Bolton."

"Gentlemen, shouldn't we be forming a search party? Surely we can find Zach and Benjamin...bring them home...?"

"Yes, yes, of course," Dr. Baker said. "I'll see to that. I'll go right now."

"Perhaps you ought to give Mrs. Haversham a...er...a sleeping powder or something," Jane suggested, leaning forward and speaking low. "She's very distraught."

The doctor nodded. "Where is your boy, ma'am? Is he accounted for?"

"Still sleeping. I didn't want to wake him with this awful news, but now I suppose I'll have to. And...well, I'll stay with Mrs. Haversham until she falls asleep, of course, but then I'd like to take my son home. He's going to be terribly upset by all of this."

"That's probably for the best," Doc said. He crossed to the bed and took Mrs. Haversham's arm. "Come with me, dear woman." Jane drew a breath, crossed her fingers and whispered a prayer. This just might work.

Please, God, let it work.

"We'll come along, Dr. Baker," Bausch said, stomping into the hallway and down the stairs. "If we find him, we might be able to pull Zachariah out of this. The sooner we begin the search, the better."

* * *

Zach cradled Benjamin, wrapped in a blanket and all but lifeless. So small, so thin. The illness had ravaged his body until there was little left between his skin and his bones. His drawn face lay still and quiet. Pale as a wraith, except for the purplish wells that housed his eyes. Cody sat nearby, steadfast and quiet. But Zach knew full well it was all the child could do to contain his tears. He was trying, valiantly, to behave the way he thought a man should behave. And doing a sight better at it at the ripe old age of ten than Zach was doing at thirty-five.

There was a tap at the workroom door that brought Zach's head up sharply. He sat still, silent, and held one hand up to tell Cody to do the same. He needn't have. The boy knew the plan as well as he did. After a brief pause, there were two more knocks on the door. Zach nodded at Cody, and the boy crossed the room to unlock it.

Jane came inside, looking slightly ill. Lying about the death of an innocent child, he supposed, wasn't likely to have agreed with her. She was nothing if not honest. Brutally so, at times.

And strong, he mused as she stepped quietly inside, closing the door behind her. Strong, when he so needed strength. He'd never have expected to find a wellspring of it embodied in one petite female. Looks, he decided, could certainly be deceiving.

"It's done," she said softly.

"We're alone in the house?"

"Doc's gone into town to form a search party. Bausch and Waterson are with him. I made him give Mrs. Haversham a sedative before he left, and she's sound asleep now."

"Good. Let's get on with this, then, before someone else shows up." He stood, cradling Ben in his arms, and they all walked into the hallway, and down it, to Benjamin's room. Jane kept one arm around Cody, and closed the door after they entered.

Zach didn't waste any time. He laid Benjamin carefully on his bed. Then he took the little black box from his pocket, pointed it toward the room's center. "Are you ready?"

Jane nodded firmly. "The question is, are you? You're giving up an awful lot, Zach."

He scowled at her and flicked the button. Immediately the pinprick of light appeared in the room's center. Zach turned the dial slowly, and the light grew bigger and brighter. Silvery mists swirled like a tempest inside, then gradually cleared until the sphere shone like a mirror, reflecting the room back at them . . . from a hundred years into the future.

"You're going to be sick again, Zach."

"But my son will be well," he said. He tucked the device firmly into his pocket, then gathered Benjamin into his arms again. "Jane?" Shifting Benjamin to one side, he reached for Jane's hand with his free one.

She took it, pulling Cody tight to her other side.

Zach stepped through the glimmering doorway, and the impact this time was more like being hit by a truck than a post.

Thirteen

As she pulled herself to her feet, Jane battled dizziness and terrible nausea. She gripped the foot of Cody's bed to keep from falling to her knees again, then paused and blinked at it. Cody's bed. And beside it was Cody's desk, and his computer, and his stack of books.

She turned quickly, and saw her son, picking himself up off the floor and looking a little stunned. And then her gaze found Zach, lying still, his arms wrapped tightly around Benjamin, who wasn't stirring a bit. Staggering a little, she went to them, knelt beside their embracing forms.

"Zach? Zach, are you all right?"

His eyes blinked open when she touched his face. His lips moved, but no words came out. Very gently, she eased his arms from around his son, and gathered Benjamin into her own. She heard his slow, labored breathing as she carried him to Cody's bed and carefully laid him down.

"He oughta be in a hospital, Mom."

She nodded, turning to Cody. "You're right, as usual, kiddo. How about you? Are you okay?"

"That time traveling packs one heck of a wallop, but yeah, I'm okay." He frowned up at her, seeming older than he had any right to. "You don't look so good, though."

She waved a dismissive hand at him. "What about your sore throat?"

Cody tilted his head, ran his fingertips over his Adam's apple. "That's odd."

"What, honey?" Jane would have sworn every cell in her body froze as she awaited his answer.

"It's gone."

"Gone," she whispered, closing her eyes. She nearly went limp with relief, hoping, praying, that this meant what she thought it did. She touched Cody's forehead, laid her palm on his cheek, but he didn't seem feverish now, though he had only seconds ago. Please, she thought, please let it be okay.

"Mom, we'd better hurry. You want me to call an ambulance?"

"What? Oh, yes, I guess you'd better."

Cody raced from the room, and she heard his feet pounding down the stairs to the only telephone in the house. Jane bent over Benjamin, stroked his hair away from his face. "You hold on a bit longer, little one. We're going to take care of you. I promise."

"Jane?"

She turned at the strained sound of Zach's voice. He'd pulled himself into a sitting position, one palm pressed to his forehead, eyes squeezed tight. She went to him, knelt beside him. "It's all right, Zach. We made it back, and there's an ambulance on the way."

He lifted his head, searched her eyes. "Benjamin?"

"He's hanging in there."

He brought one hand up to cup her face, stared into her eyes. "And you, Jane? What about you?"

My heart's breaking, you idiot.

"I'm fine."

But she wasn't. All along, she'd resisted her feelings for Zach, because she'd known he'd leave her in the end, to return to his own time, a century in the past. Now he was here to stay. But his heart remained back there, with a woman who wasn't even worthy of a passing glance from a man like him. She'd been foolish, but there was no help for it. She'd gone and let herself fall in love with the jerk.

"Then..." His thumb brushed across her cheek, "Why are there tears in your eyes?"

She tried to blink the alleged tears away. "When the ambulance arrives, Zach, you ought to let them take you to the hospital, too."

"I'll go, Jane, but not as a patient. I need to be with my son."

She nodded, understanding that perfectly. "What if you have another memory lapse, like last time?"

"You'll be with me...won't you, Jane?" His eyes probed hers so deeply she felt their touch on her very soul.

"Of course I will."

He smiled weakly. "Good. If my memory does fail me again, you'll be able to handle it. I have no doubt about that."

"That's me," she whispered. "Solid, dependable Jane."

Zach frowned, and tilted his head. "And just what is that supposed to mean?"

"Nothing. Nothing at all."

* * *

Jane said her head felt a little clearer by the time the ambulance—a motorcar painted white, with flashing lights and a screaming noise to it—arrived. So she and Cody followed in her auto. Zach climbed into the back of the noisy machine to ride with his son, all the while answering the questions of the fellow who rode back there with him.

"Any history of allergies?"

"Uh . . . no. But he hasn't been exposed to much in the way of modern drugs." The man looked at Zach strangely. "We've been living in remote areas, in, uh, India." He hoped to God there were still remote areas in India.

"I see. So, is he up-to-date on his immunizations?"

"Probably not," Zach confessed, and he winced as a needle with a rubberized tube attached was inserted into his son's forearm. "What's that?"

"Just fluids. We get the IV started now, and it'll be easier to administer whatever drugs he needs at the hospital."

Zach studied the tubing, and the liquid-filled bag attached. Ringers Lactate, it read. "Ingenious."

"And what makes you think this is quinaria fever?"

Zach blinked, hoping he was giving all the right answers. If ever he'd needed Jane by his side, it was now. Then again, it seemed he felt that way whenever he was away from her. He didn't just need her now, but always. "He was exposed," he said to the attendant. "There was an outbreak in the village where we were staying."

"Damn. I thought that disease was pretty well eradicated by now."

"Then . . . then there is a cure?"

The younger man looked at Zach as if he were insane. "Man, that must have been one isolated village. There's been a cure for almost a hundred years now. Don't know how you could spend a day in Rockwell and not know about it. It's our town's one and only claim to fame."

He kept on talking while he worked on Benjamin, and Zach listened, bouncing with the rhythm of the speeding vehicle as it raced toward the hospital, to the story of Zachariah Bolton, the brilliant scientist who'd lost his mind with grief at the death of his son. And of his two colleagues, who'd joined forces to develop a cure, in honor of their lost friend.

Zach couldn't stop the tears of relief that flowed unchecked as he heard the tale, unchanged from the way Jane had told it to him only a few days ago. *Unchanged.* And the medic only looked at him oddly as he closed his eyes and whispered, "It worked, Jane. We did it."

The young man's hand fell onto Zach's shoulder. "If he makes it to the hospital, pal, they'll be able to pull him through. You hang tough, okay?"

Jane sipped the stale, machine-generated coffee, grimaced and set it on the vinyl table beside the vinyl chair in which she sat. Cody had fallen asleep in the seat beside her. Zach was still pacing. He hadn't stopped since they'd arrived here, in time to see him being firmly told he had to stay in the waiting room while Benjamin was being treated. He'd argued, naturally. It wasn't like Zach to give up without a fight. Jane had intervened, though, guiding him to this bustling waiting area, and he'd been pacing ever since. The fear and worry on his face were more than she could stand.

She got up, took his hand. "Sit down, Zach. You're exhausted, and dizzy, and all this pacing isn't going to do Benjamin any good."

He stopped walking, but didn't sit. He just stared down at her, gripping her hand tightly. "What if he doesn't make it, Jane? What if—?"

"He'll make it. He can't give up now, not after all we've gone through. I can't believe we made it this far only to lose him, Zach. I won't believe it."

"It's been so long. Two hours now." Zach turned toward the double doors with the mesh-lined windows. "I have to know what's happening in there."

"Zach—"

He pulled free of her restraining hand, and headed for the doors. But before he reached them, Dr. Mulligan emerged and held up his hands. Zach came to a wobbly stop, and Jane hurried up beside him. She slid her arm around his waist, since he was none too steady on his feet.

"How is my son?" His voice, when he said it, was little more than a coarse whisper.

"We've stabilized him."

"Then he's all right?"

"Not yet. He's still in a coma, but we've started an IV with tryptonine. Once the drug begins to take effect, we're hoping he'll come around."

"Hoping?"

"Mr...." The doctor paused, glanced down at the chart in his hands and looked up at Zach again. "Bolton," he went on. "We can't be sure of anything at this point. If your son can hold on long enough for the medicine to take effect, we'll be able to pull him through, but there's still a great chance that he won't. I have to be honest with you about that. You should prepare yourself."

Jane felt the jolt that went through Zach's body, and she held him tighter. His arm came around her shoulders, as if he were clinging to her for survival. "Go on," he said, when he could speak again.

The doctor lowered his head. "Even if he survives, there's a possibility of brain damage. His fever was very high when he was brought in. We have no way of knowing how, or even if, that affected him. We'll only know when he comes around. He might be just fine, Mr. Bolton. But there's a slim chance his motor skills and cognitive abilities could be impaired for the rest of his life. We just can't tell at this point."

"I see."

"We should know something by morning."

Zach nodded. Then as the doctor turned to go, he brought his head up sharply. "Can I see him?"

"Of course. We'll be moving him to his room shortly, so you'll have to keep it brief."

Zach started forward, his arm still anchored around Jane.

"Only family," the doctor said softly.

"Jane *is* family," Zach replied, and kept right on going.

"Go home, Jane. You need rest."

She didn't, though. She came the rest of the way

into the stark white room, with its wondrous beeping and blinking machines. She came all the way to the chair where Zach had been sitting for what seemed like years, and she gently took his son's limp hand from his much larger one, enclosing it lovingly in her own. "I've been home. I brought you a change of clothes and something to eat," she said softly, her gaze pinned to the face of his son.

She smelled good. Fresh and clean. She'd changed clothes herself, though it didn't look to Zach as if she'd taken the time to get any sleep. Knowing Jane, he'd say she'd rushed home and back for his sake more than her own. She laid Benjamin's hand down atop the bedsheet, and then opened the small bag that hung from her shoulder. She pulled a container from it, and then a plastic-wrapped spoon. "Here. Yogurt. It's good for you. I've got some cookies, and a few—"

"Where is Cody? Not still sleeping on that horrendous excuse for a chair in the waiting room, I hope."

Smiling slightly, Jane shook her head. "A nurse took pity and let me lay him in a vacant bed in the next room. I just hope I don't get billed for it."

She said it in jest, he knew, but the thought of bills and such made him wince. He'd been a man of means in his time. Now . . . now he had no clue how he'd begin to make his way. But he couldn't worry over that now. He couldn't think of anything else, except his son, lying here in this strange bed, perhaps at the brink of . . .

"Father?"

The yogurt cup fell to the floor from nerveless fingers as Zach's heart swelled to bursting. Eyes wide, he turned his head slowly. But Benjamin wasn't focused on him. Instead, he was blinking up at Jane, as if he were seeing an angel. She stroked his hair away from his forehead and leaned low to place a tender kiss there. Then she stepped away, making room for Zach at his son's bedside.

"Benjamin," he whispered, tears choking him. Ben tried to sit up, lifting his arms to his father, and Zach responded by wrapping his arms around his son's thin frame and holding him very close. "You're awake. Thank God, my son, you're awake." His words deteriorated to grateful mutters as he buried his face in his son's red curls and closed his eyes to hide his tears.

"It was Cody's medicine, Father. He said it would make me well again, and..." Ben backed up a little, staring up at his father. "Is it true? Am I really going to be well, Father?"

Stroking those riotous curls, Zach nodded. "It's true."

"It was my wish, you know. The shooting stars... I knew it wasn't very scientific, Father, but when I saw them from my bedroom window, I wished on them. And my wishes came true. All three of them really came true!" He lay back on the pillows, sighing, and Zach knew he was still easily tired. But, by God, there were healthy splashes of color in his cheeks now. And his eyes had regained some of their former shine.

"Three wishes?"

"Oh, yes! My first wish was to be well again. That came true. And then I wished for a big brother, and Cody came. He promised he'd be..." Benjamin blinked and looked around the room, and Zach did the same. "But . . . he didn't leave me, did he?"

"No, son. Cody is taking a nap in the next room." And, apparently, his mother had decided to join him there. She must have slipped out to give him time alone with his son.

"Oh." Benjamin frowned, tilting his head. "We're not home, are we, Father?"

"No, son, we're in a hospital, a long ways from home."

Squinting at the overhead light fixture, Benjamin said, "We must be where Cody comes from, huh?"

Now how in the world could he know that? No matter. "Tell me about the rest of your wishes, Benjamin. What else did you wish for? Whatever it is, I'll get it for you, I swear."

Benjamin grinned, and Zach fully expected to hear a request for a new toy or a puppy or some such. Instead, he heard, "Oh…well, like I said, I wished for a big brother. I've been wanting one for ever so long, Father. But you don't need to get one for me. Cody is my brother now."

"He is?"

"Uh-huh. We swore an oath. Those were my first two wishes, and they both came true. And there's only one more to go. And I think it's come true, too."

Swallowing hard, Zach whispered, "What's the third wish, Ben?"

"I want a mother," Benjamin whispered, closing his eyes and smiling softly. "I want a real mother, who will live with us and who will love me for always." He tilted his head, and looked at his father. "I know you've been looking for one for a long time,

Father, but you never find any really good ones. Anyway, it doesn't matter now, because I have her all picked out.''

"You do, do you?"

Benjamin nodded firmly, then looked toward the door, his eyes lighting up. Jane stood there, and Zach was left with no doubt about the identity of the woman his son had chosen. And then Cody crowded past her, and raced to the opposite side of the bed. The two boys chattered excitedly, seemingly forgetting the presence of the adults in the room. Jane took Zach's arm and gently led him into the hallway.

"You look worried. Zach, you ought to be relieved. He looks so much better."

Searching her face, Zach saw the telltale traces of tearstains. "I'll never get over how deeply you feel things, Jane Fortune," he whispered, tracing those marks on her cheeks with his fingertips.

"What is it you're worrying about?" she persisted.

He shook his head. "A hundred things. A thousand. My son is well, though, so what right do I have to complain? I'd live in the streets and be happy."

"Is that it? You're wondering where you'll live when he's released? Zach, you know you're welcome to stay with Cody and me for as long as—"

Shaking his head, Zach turned away from her. "And how long would that be, Jane? How long do you suppose it will take a man like me to find a means to earn a living in this time? I don't even know where to begin."

She placed a hand on his shoulder. "Zach, you're a genius."

"No. I was a genius. Surrounded by modern technology, I'm a bumbling fool." He sighed hard, and began to pace. "I'm back where I began. A man with little wealth and no social standing. No security. Nothing to offer a woman—" He bit his lip, and broke off.

"A woman?" Jane repeated. "Zach, I know you miss Claudia, but you can't possibly be thinking of going back there and bringing her—"

"Can't that brain of yours think about anything but Claudia?" he snapped. She blinked hard at his harsh tone, and Zach instantly regretted it. But the woman was so frustrating! Ah, but who did he have to blame for her misconceptions? No one but himself. "I'm simply trying to illustrate how ill-equipped I am to make a living for myself, much less anyone else, amid the modern technology of today's society." He hoped that covered his slip, as well as his bad manners. He was too tired to think this through right now, and too frustrated to be this close to her without touching her. He recalled her telling him that her family was one of the wealthiest in the country. Good God, he felt as if he'd gone backward in time all over again.

"Modern technology, my foot," she snapped, and then she spun him around to face her, with more force than he'd expected. "You traveled through time, Zachariah Bolton. No other scientist has managed to do that, not with the help of every scrap of modern technology available today. Not one. You're still a genius. And you'll find a way to apply that brain of yours in today's world. I know you will."

He swallowed hard, but nodded. "Perhaps..."

"I'll help you," she told him. And he knew perfectly well she meant it.

"Why, Jane?" he whispered. "Why are you so good to me?"

Lowering her chin, she shook her head slowly. "We've been through hell together, Zach. I . . . like to think we're . . . friends. And besides, you'd do the same for me."

I'd cut out my heart for you, he wanted to tell her. But, of course, he couldn't. Not now. Especially not now. In fact, maybe it was better that she go on believing he was pining away for selfish little Claudia.

It wasn't what he wanted her to think. Not at all. He wanted to tell her . . . to tell her that he had done what he'd never in his life believed himself capable of doing. That he'd fallen in love with her. He wanted . . . good God, he wanted to ask Jane Fortune to marry him. Ben loved her. And, dammit, so did he.

But how could he ask that of her? He knew she was trying to get by without her fortune, but it was there, all the same. It was there. And what would she want with a man who was only steps away from being a pauper? She couldn't be expected to continue giving to him and Ben. He couldn't ask it of her. Nor of himself.

He looked at her, everything in him aching to tell her that it was her he loved, not Claudia. But instead, he clamped his jaw, and said nothing.

Fourteen

Dammit, why did men have to be such utter fools? She'd had it with them. Or... Well, she'd thought she'd had it with them. Until now. Now she'd made up her mind that no man would ever figure anything out unless a woman drew him a picture. Oh, she had her pride. And pride was all well and good, but facts were facts. And the fact was that more than her heart would be broken when Zachariah Bolton marched out of her life. Cody would be shattered, as well. He loved Zach madly, and had claimed little Benjamin as his very own brother. It would kill him to lose those two. And Benjamin was just as enamored of Cody. Not only that, but the boy seemed to have become attached to her. And, God, how she had fallen in love with that little tyke. Those carrot curls and those big blue eyes and that mischievous grin. He'd been home from the hospital for a week now, and he'd dug himself a permanent place in Jane's heart. She loved him so much she felt as if she'd given birth to him. And she was not going to let him go. Not without a fight.

That damn thickheaded Zachariah Bolton had been brooding for days, heartsick, no doubt, over losing the selfish little witch he'd fancied himself in love with. And when he wasn't moon-eyed over his lost love, he was scheming and plotting ways to earn a decent living in the 1990's. There was no doubt whatsoever in Jane's mind that the second he got his hands on a dependable income, he'd take his son and march straight out of her life. Which was why she hadn't told him what she'd discovered when she finally got into that old safe that was stored in the attic. If she told him, she'd lose him. She'd been waiting, hoping against hope that he'd realize he belonged with her. Maybe even begin to love her a little bit.

But the jerk hadn't come around, even after a week, and she was beginning to think he never would. Time to change tactics.

Besides, she couldn't keep the information from him much longer. But she'd made up her mind that when she told him about that, she was going to tell him everything else, as well. Might as well lay it on the line and go for broke. Her delaying tactics certainly hadn't been effective.

So she was going to tell him, flat out, tonight. She'd had all she could stand of watching him pine for another woman, and not even notice her. Enough was enough. More than enough, thank you very much.

It was driving him insane, living with her! Dammit, she seemed to go out of her way to be near him, tormenting him with her presence until he thought he'd go mad with wanting her. Must she wear those formfitting jeans all the time? Must she always leave her hair loose and flowing, for God's sake? Couldn't she bundle it up, spinster-style, just once? And for the love of God, why did she have to *smell* so good? Why did she have to sing in the shower? Why did she have to be so blasted loving and caring to his son that it melted his heart each time he saw it. Why?

He wanted her. Not just in his bed, but right to the base of his soul, he wanted her. He'd thought he'd loved once, but with every day that passed, he realized more and more how dim his young yearnings for Claudia had been in comparison with the real thing. But he hadn't told Jane. He had his pride, dammit, and right now he had nothing to offer her. Nothing at all. He'd been slowly growing more and more frustrated as he sought to find his place in this new world, to understand where he fit in, to find a way to earn a living, for heaven's sake. But he hadn't. Not yet.

But he would. He'd find his way and he'd make Jane his own. It was the waiting that was driving him to distraction.

"Zachariah?"

He turned to see the object of his every waking thought, standing in the doorway of his workroom. He caught her unaware, and in that instant before she felt his gaze, he saw her pain, etched into the porcelain features of her face. Pain he'd caused. Hell, she cared for him. And he'd been a fool to let her go on believing he didn't feel the same. In that moment, he changed his mind. He couldn't wait any longer. To hell with his pride. To hell with his income, or lack thereof. He'd deal with that later. It was important, yes, but not as important as what he felt for this woman. Nothing was as important as that.

Jane had moved Cody to another bedroom, worried about prolonged exposure to the time warp that existed, invisible, here in this one. Benjamin had the room beside Cody's, though they spent most of their time together in one place or the other. Usually wherever the Nintendo machine was set up at the time. Zach had set up a cot in here.

Jane was not smiling when she met his eyes. Lord, he'd done something to make her angry. Well, he deserved her anger for allowing her to doubt him so long. And he couldn't blame her, could he?

"We have to talk," she said.

"Yes, we do," he said. "It's long overdue."

"Not here. I don't want to wake the boys. Downstairs, okay?" And without another word, she backed out into the hall, closing the door behind her.

Zach drew a fortifying breath, and got to his feet, closing the journal where he'd been recording his thoughts. Jane had suggested he try his hand at writing, and he'd begun with the life story of the town's most famous resident—himself. He'd have to write the ending as if it were fiction, though he knew full well it was not. Jane had assured him the project would sell and earn him a substantial amount, but it was a long process, and he needed something in the meantime.

He'd been impatient, thinking he couldn't wait. That he needed an income before he could tell Jane how he truly felt, and knowing he could not, *would not,* wait much longer to make Jane his. If she'd have him, that is.

Shaking his head, he walked downstairs, preparing himself for the worst.

Jane's loins were girded. She stood in a rigid posture when Zach entered the living room, and vowed she wasn't going to take pity on his poor broken heart.

"Coffee?" she said, when he took a seat on the sofa.

"No."

"All right then. I guess I should come right to the point."

"If you don't mind, Jane, I'd like to go first."

She blinked at him, her pretty eyes puzzled. "You would?"

Zach nodded.

"Actually, yes, I do mind. I've been rehearsing this in my mind for hours, and if I don't get it out right now, I never will." Jane paced the length of the living room, walking away from him in brisk strides, her luscious hips swaying as she moved.

Zach pursed his lips. "All right, if you insist. I must admit, you've piqued my curiosity. Whatever could you have to say to me that would require so much preparation?"

She whirled on him. "Damn you, Zachariah Bolton, you have to be the most hardheaded, utterly *dense* man I've ever known."

"Now, wait a minute!" Zach jumped to his feet, intercepting her as she paced back the other way, catching her shoulders in his hands and staring down into her blazing eyes. "I know I've made you angry with me, Jane, and I'm sorry."

"Angry? Zach, you've made me more than angry. This is beyond anger. I want to slap you. The way you've been walking around as if there's a dark cloud over your head ever since you left the last century. I'm sick and tired of watching you pining away for that brainless, air-headed, vapid, overly made-up, self-centered bitch.''

He frowned down at her. She was breathless now, but he could see she was only warming up. ''I'm sorry. I'm sorry I let you go on believing I was still pining over Claudia. It was unforgivable, Jane.''

''Yes, dammit, it was! When are you going to wake up and see her for what she is . . . was, I mean. Zach, she walked out on her own flesh and blood. Not once, but twice. The second time when she had every reason to believe he was on his death bed. How in the name of God can a man as intelligent as you are think he's in love with a woman like that?''

He shrugged. ''I don't, Jane I never really did.''

''Well, I'm sick and tired of seeing it, and that's all. I've been waiting and waiting for you to wake up, Zach, because I don't want you to leave me . . . us. But dammit, I can't stand watching this anymore. I'm twice the woman that Claudia ever was and it's high time you realized it.''

''Ten times, easily.''

''I don't want to . . . what?'' Jane stopped yelling, drew a breath, and stared up at him.

''I said you're ten times the woman Claudia is. More than that. Perhaps a hundred times, Jane. And I haven't been pining away for her at all. In fact I haven't given her a second thought since we came back here.''

Jane blinked. ''You haven't?''

''No, I haven't.''

''Well, then . . . why have you been . . . so . . .''

''Depressed? Ah, Jane, it has nothing to do with Claudia. Nothing at all, I promise you that.'' He let his hands fall upon her shoulders, met her eyes fully, so that she could see the sincerity in his own. He didn't want her doubting him. Not ever again. "In fact, there's something you should know. That night, that night she spent in my room. Nothing happened between us, Jane. She wanted it to, but I... I found I simply wasn't interested anymore."

"You weren't?"

He smiled and looked at her. "You sound so amazed, Jane. Did you really believe me that gullible? I knew perfectly well she only came to me because my wealth and standing had suddenly made me desirable in her eyes. And because her wealthy husband died, and left most of his fortune to his nephews. You're right, she's utterly selfish. Her heart is made of solid stone... if she even has one."

"But I don't understand. All this brooding you've been doing—"

"The source was purely financial. I hate being a burden on you and Cody."

"Burden," she snapped, rolling her eyes. "You know better."

He nodded. "I guess I do. It's more than that. Jane, I've been feeling so low because I've been having trouble dealing with the fact that I have nothing to offer you."

"Nothing to..."

"But I've decided to swallow my pride, Jane, because I can't wait any longer to tell you how I feel."

She blinked up at him. "H-how?"

Zach smiled very slightly. "Utterly, madly, completely in love with you," he said softly. "And irrevocably devoted to your son. And determined to make the both of you mine." Her lips parted, but no words escaped. "I know I'm in dire straights right now, Jane, but I won't be. I'm a reasonably intelligent man with a strong back. I'll find a way. I'll dig ditches if I have to, darling, but..."

"I'm so sorry," she whispered. And for a moment, his heart stopped, because he thought she was going to turn him down. "Zach, I'm not sure you're going to forgive me for this...but..."

"But what? You don't feel the same? Jane, you do. I know you do, I see it in your eyes and I feel it when..." He let his words trail off, because there were no words powerful enough to show her that they were meant to be together. He pulled her closer to him, tight and hard against his body, and he bowed his head, capturing her pliant lips beneath his, kissing her so deeply and so passionately that she couldn't possibly doubt the truth. Heat grew and sizzled in his veins when their tongues met and twined, and her hands threaded into his hair, and she fed hungrily from his mouth.

And at last he lifted his head, met her blazing eyes. "Don't tell me you don't feel anything for me, Jane," he whispered.

"I...I wasn't going to," she replied, a bit breathlessly. She stiffened her spine, and gently extricated herself from his grip. "I'll never tell you that, Zach. But there's something you need to know."

At her insistence, he released her, but reluctantly.

She went to the coffee table and picked up a stack of aged-looking papers, and when she straightened, she handed them to him. "Here. These belong to you."

"What . . ." Frowning, Zach took them.

"I found these in the safe that was stored in the attic. The safe itself was an antique, but worthless unless it was usable, of course, so I called a locksmith, when we first moved in. I found these things inside, and tucked them away and forgot about them. I didn't even think of them again until you and Ben came here to stay."

Zach sorted through the papers, nodding in recognition. They belonged to him, all of them. Stocks, savings bonds, investment certificates and the like. "I really don't see what difference is makes, Jane. These are over a century out-of-date, worthless and—"

"They're probably worth a fortune, Zach." She lowered her head, eyes focused on the floor.

"What?"

"Well, most of those banks on the notes are still thriving. Some of those companies you invested in then are multimillion-dollar conglomerates today. Take my word for it, Zach, I know about these things. A century's worth of interest adds up to quite a hefty sum."

Zach shook his head slowly as the information sank in. He held in his hands the very thing he'd been agonizing over for days now. "Jane, for God's sake, why didn't you tell me about this?"

Biting her trembling lower lip, she lifted her gaze to meet his. "Because I didn't want you to leave."

"You—"

"I didn't want to lose you, Zach. I kept telling myself that if I could just keep you here long enough, maybe you'd start to feel for me, what I . . . what I feel for you."

"What you feel for me?" He realized then, that she still hadn't told him what she did feel for him. And he waited, though far from patiently.

She closed her eyes. "I was afraid you'd take Benjamin and leave when you realized you had the means. And, well, I love him, too, Zach."

"*Too?*"

"Yeah," she whispered. "Too."

Zach shook his head. She swallowed hard, so hard he heard it, saw the motion of the muscles in her throat as she looked up at him and nodded.

"I've been slowly going insane with wanting you, needing you...*loving* you, Jane Fortune...but I convinced myself I couldn't ask you until I had something to offer—"

"You could've come to me with nothing but the clothes on your back, Zachariah. Don't you realize—" She blinked fast, took a breath. "Ask me what?"

"To be my wife, Jane. To be the mother Benjamin has never had, the one he's been wishing for. To let me be a father to Cody. To let me love you for the rest of my life. Will you, Jane?"

He saw her lips tremble, saw her eyes well with tears.

"Say yes!" two voices shouted in unison.

Zach swung around at the same moment Jane did, to see the two small forms perched on the stairs, watching them. Ben and Cody came the rest of the way down, hesitating at the foot of the stairway, arm in arm. Two curly heads of red hair, two pairs of big green eyes, two freckled faces. Two strong, healthy bodies, one a bit bigger than the other. They were brothers to their souls. They stood grinning, awaiting Jane's reply as breathlessly as Zach was.

"Say yes, Jane," Zach whispered, hooking her chin with a forefinger and drawing her gaze to his once more.

"Yes," she said.

The two boys broke into whoops of triumph and ran to them, shouldering their way between them and forcing them apart. "A dad!" Cody said, rushing into Zach's arms and hugging him hard. "I really have a dad!"

Zach had to swallow past a lump in his throat, and then it became impassable when he glanced up to see Benjamin, his arms linked around Jane's neck as she held him tight. "Can I call you Mommy?" Ben whispered loudly in her ear.

"You'd better," she told him, and her tears flowed unchecked down her cheeks. She met Zach's eyes over the heads of the boys. And he knew his own were probably tearing up, too, but there was no helping it. He gently moved Cody aside, his eyes locked with Jane's as he moved toward her. She set Benjamin down on the floor and came to him. They met, and his arms went around her. He kissed her then, the way he'd been longing to do for so long it seemed like forever.

"Did I mention that I love you, Jane?" he asked her, unsure whether she heard over the joyous shouts of the boys.

"It never hurts to say it again," she told him.

Epilogue

"Well now, Sterling, dear," Kate Fortune said, her eyes twinkling, "Didn't I tell you Jane was going to find her heart's desire in that house? Didn't I?"

"Kate, you know perfectly well you were referring to the antique shop and the old-fashioned atmosphere, not that time-hopping inventor."

"Don't be so sure," she chided.

"Now, Kate, there's no way you could have known all of this would happen," Sterling said softly.

"Don't forget, dear, I lived in that house for a time."

Sterling only gaped for a long moment as Kate waggled her eyebrows. "Are you saying...that you knew...about that doorway through time?"

She only shrugged and moved away. "I'm very, very worried about Natalie, Sterling. I have a feeling she needs me." She tilted her head. "Let's go check on her."

"Kate..." Shaking his head, Sterling began to pace. "Kate, the entire idea is to keep you away from your family. But you insist on hopping from one grandchild to the next like some kind of fairy godmother! I'm trying to keep you alive, dear."

"But I'm having so much fun being dead!" She winked. "Besides, I've never had so much freedom to meddle without getting caught. It's wonderful, darling. Now come here. Sit down with me and let's make some travel plans. I do believe my darling granddaughter Natalie Fortune has been responsible, reliable, and *lonely,* for just about long enough."

"Perhaps I should send her an anonymous note warning her of the whirlwind that's about to descend on her docile life."

"But it's much more fun when it's a surprise, don't you think?"

"You never fail to surprise me, Kate."

"That's good, Sterling. I only hope I never will."

*   *   *   *   *

FORTUNE'S CHILDREN

continues with

WIFE WANTED

by Christine Rimmer

Available in February

Here's an exciting preview....

WIFE WANTED

Rick Dalton pulled up in front of a two-story house with touches of gingerbread trim in the eaves. Rose trees lined the pebbled walk to the front porch—a deep, inviting porch, furnished with wicker armchairs and love seats. There was even a swing.

"It's perfect," Rick said to his son, Toby.

And just then someone inside decided it was time for rock and roll. *Loud* rock and roll.

Rick couldn't help grinning. "So much for perfection." He recognized the song—"Piece of My Heart."

Rick glanced at Toby, and found his blue eyes just like his own watching him.

"Stay here. I'll see what's going on." Rick had to raise his voice to compete with the tortured wails.

Toby granted his father a tiny nod.

From the house, competing with Janis Joplin's agonized moans, came a dog's howl.

What the hell was going on?

By the time he rang the bell, the dog was yowling as loud and as hard as Janis. And Rick thought he heard another voice, human and female, wailing along. Of course, there was no answer. No one could hear anything over the racket.

The door was unlocked. Stepping inside, Rick moved toward the sound. He halted on the threshold of an old-fashioned front parlor.

He immediately saw a St. Bernard dog, its massive head tipped back, its throat working enthusiastically to produce an earsplitting approximation of doggy harmony.

Between the door where Rick stood and where the dog yowled, a shapely brunette in a forties spangled cocktail dress and gaudy platform shoes wiggled and wailed. Rick leaned in the doorway, wondering with amusement what she'd do when discovered.

It took a few minutes to find out. The brunette was too involved to realize she'd attracted an audience. But the dog noticed Rick right away. It lowered its huge head. It loped over to Rick and nuzzled him with a large, wet nose. Rick granted the animal a quick scratch.

The woman went right on singing her heart out. Though he'd yet to see her face, she looked great from behind. She shimmied around, no doubt wondering where the dog had gone. She froze in mid-screech when she caught sight of Rick.

"Oh!" Her creamy skin flooded with agonized color. "How long have you been here?" She had to shout to be heard.

Rick did his best to stop grinning. "Long enough," he yelled back.

She made a pained face. "I was afraid you'd say that."

"I rang, but..."

She waved a hand. "Never mind. I understand." She went to turn off the stereo.

"You must be my prospective tenant. Excuse us. We just . . . well, Bernie begged me to play Janis, so I did."

"Bernie," Rick echoed. "That would be the dog?"

"Mm-hmm."

"The dog can talk?"

"Not exactly. But when he wants Janis, he brings me the CD."

"A bright dog."

"Extremely."

Neither of them paid attention as the dog in question wandered out. The woman drew her shoulders back and closed the distance between them, holding out her hand.

"I'm Natalie Fortune."

Rick took her hand. It was soft, a little hot from all that dancing—and a nice fit in his. She smelled of clean sweat and soap and flowers. He introduced himself.

"And there's a little boy, right?"

"Right."

She looked down at their hands and he realized that the handshaking was finished. He released her. She stepped back and gazed at him. She had the most gorgeous brown eyes he'd ever seen. "I, um, thought you'd be here at two."

He glanced at his watch. "I guess I'm a few minutes early."

She smiled. "And I let the time get away from me." Her smile became tender. "Hello."

Rick turned to see Toby hovering inside the door, his mouth quirking upward in response to Natalie's greeting, his hand resting in the ruff of the St. Bernard.

Rick was stunned. His son had actually smiled!

"I see you've met Bernie," she said.

Toby nodded.

"I'm Natalie. What's your name?"

"Toby. His name's Toby," Rick supplied quickly.

Toby reached out and touched one of the bangles on Natalie's dress. A silvery laugh escaped her. "You like?" Taking Toby by the hand, she rose.

At one end of the sofa lay a huge steamer trunk, its lid flung back, various articles of clothing spilling out. Natalie led Toby to it.

"This trunk was my Grandma Kate's," she announced. "I found this fabulous dress in there." She gave Rick a wink.

Kneeling by the trunk, she pulled out a flowered scarf, a wide-brimmed pink hat and a black patent-leather clutch purse, all of which she set on the floor.

She chatted away to Toby and he watched her, his small face rapt.

Then Natalie began dressing the St. Bernard. She slanted the hat just so on the dog's head, tied the scarf around his neck and stuck the purse in his mouth. Then she clapped her hands in delight and declared, "He looks great, don't you think?"

Toby actually nodded. The dog thumped his tail.

Natalie looked up and caught Rick watching. She flashed him a grin, then rose and advised Toby, "Go ahead. Bernie loves to play dress-up." Bernie managed to bark in agreement without dropping the purse. "I'm going to show your father the house."

She moved toward Rick. "Ready for the tour?"

Captivated, Rick heard himself say, "Sure."

She marched past him in her silly shoes. He fell behind her, but couldn't resist one backward glance at his son, who was trying on a helmet and ducking Bernie's tongue.

Natalie led Rick to the foyer and up the stairs first, explaining the finer points of the house as they moved along. Then she stopped near the top of the stairs.

Her brow furrowed. "Is Toby all right?"

Rick tensed. "What do you mean?"

She leaned against the banister. "I mean, is something bothering him? He seems...too quiet. He didn't say a word."

Rick looked away. He'd been in this woman's house for ten minutes, max. She was a stranger. But she didn't *feel* like a stranger. She drew him. And in ten minutes she'd already accomplished the impossible: she'd made his son smile.

He met her eyes. "Toby's mother died several months ago. Toby was in the car when it happened. He hasn't spoken since the accident."

"Oh. I'm so sorry."

"His mother and I were divorced. And I...hadn't seen Toby in a while. That's why I'm interested in this place. We need a little time together, just Toby and me, where he can learn to trust me and I can get to know him better. Does that make sense?"

Those big eyes were full of understanding. "Yes, it does. Perfect sense. Let me show you the rest of the house."

He thought that he could stand here talking to her forever, but all he said was, "Yes, that's a good idea."

Later they trooped out behind the house and down to the lake. Natalie took Rick out onto a wide dock and into the attached boathouse where a fifty-six-foot houseboat, the *Lady Kate,* was moored.

"This was my grandpa Ben's," Natalie explained fondly, patting the hull of the boat. "She'll be at your disposal during the time you stay here." For a moment those enormous eyes met his.

And he couldn't help thinking that he'd like more than the boat to be at his disposal.

In the tradition of
Anne Rice comes a
daring, darkly sensual
vampire novel by

MAGGIE SHAYNE

BORN IN TWILIGHT

Rendezvous hails bestselling Maggie Shayne's vampire
romance series, WINGS IN THE NIGHT, as
"powerful...riveting...unique...intensely romantic."

Don't miss it, this March, available
wherever Silhouette books are sold.

The spirit of the holidays...
The magic of romance...
They both come together in

You're invited as Merline Lovelace and Carole Buck—
two of your favorite authors from two of your favorite
lines—capture your hearts with five joyous love stories
celebrating the excitement that happens when you
combine holidays and weddings!

Beginning in October, watch for

HALLOWEEN HONEYMOON by Merline Lovelace
(Desire #1030, 10/96)

Thanksgiving—
WRONG BRIDE, RIGHT GROOM by Merline Lovelace
(Desire #1037, 11/96)

Christmas—
A BRIDE FOR SAINT NICK by Carole Buck
(Intimate Moments #752, 12/96)

New Year's Day—
RESOLVED TO (RE)MARRY by Carole Buck
(Desire #1049, 1/97)

Valentine's Day—
THE 14TH...AND FOREVER by Merline Lovelace
(Intimate Moments #764, 2/97)

HH

At last the wait is over...
In March
New York Times bestselling author

NORA ROBERTS

will bring us the latest from the Stanislaskis as
Natasha's now very grown-up stepdaughter,
Freddie, and Rachel's very sexy brother-in-law
Nick discover that love is worth waiting for in

WAITING FOR NICK
Silhouette Special Edition #1088

and in April
visit Natasha and Rachel again—or meet them
for the first time—in

The Stanislaski Sisters

containing TAMING NATASHA
and FALLING FOR RACHEL

Available wherever Silhouette books are sold.

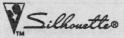

Take 4 bestselling love stories FREE

Plus get a FREE surprise gift!

Special Limited-time Offer

Mail to Silhouette Reader Service™

3010 Walden Avenue
P.O. Box 1867
Buffalo, N.Y. 14240-1867

YES! Please send me 4 free Silhouette Intimate Moments® novels and my free surprise gift. Then send me 6 brand-new novels every month, which I will receive months before they appear in bookstores. Bill me at the low price of $3.34 each plus 25¢ delivery and applicable sales tax, if any.* That's the complete price and a savings of over 10% off the cover prices—quite a bargain! I understand that accepting the books and gift places me under no obligation ever to buy any books. I can always return a shipment and cancel at any time. Even if I never buy another book from Silhouette, the 4 free books and the surprise gift are mine to keep forever.

245 BPA A3UW

Name	(PLEASE PRINT)	
Address	Apt. No.	
City	State	Zip

This offer is limited to one order per household and not valid to present Silhouette Intimate Moments® subscribers. *Terms and prices are subject to change without notice. Sales tax applicable in N.Y.

UMOM-696   ©1990 Harlequin Enterprises Limited

Harlequin and Silhouette celebrate
Black History Month with seven terrific titles,
featuring the all-new *Fever Rising*
by Maggie Ferguson
(Harlequin Intrigue #408) and
A Family Wedding by Angela Benson
(Silhouette Special Edition #1085)!

Also available are:
Looks Are Deceiving by Maggie Ferguson
Crime of Passion by Maggie Ferguson
Adam and Eva by Sandra Kitt
Unforgivable by Joyce McGill
Blood Sympathy by Reginald Hill

On sale in January at your favorite
Harlequin and Silhouette retail outlet.

You're About to Become a

Privileged Woman

Reap the rewards of fabulous free gifts and
benefits with proofs-of-purchase from
Silhouette and Harlequin books

Pages & Privileges™

It's our way of thanking you for
buying our books at your
favorite retail stores.

**PROOF OF
PURCHASE**
FC-PP21
Offer expires March 31, 1997

Pages
& Privileges ™

Harlequin and Silhouette—
the most privileged readers in the world!

For more information about Harlequin and
Silhouette's PAGES & PRIVILEGES program call the
Pages & Privileges Benefits Desk: 1-503-794-2499

Silhouette®

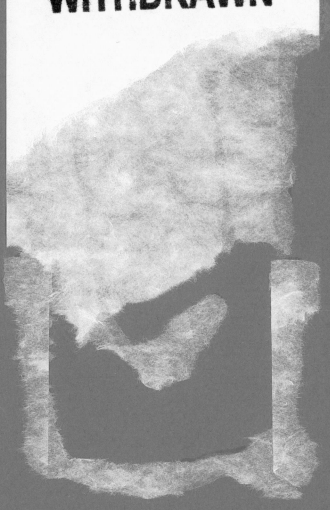

WAVE ENERGY
A Design Challenge

ELLIS HORWOOD ENERGY AND FUEL SCIENCE SERIES

Series Editors: **I. Bousted** and **G. F. Hancock**, Faculty of Technology, The Open University.

HANDBOOK OF INDUSTRIAL ENERGY ANALYSIS
I. BOUSTEAD and G. F. HANCOCK, Faculty of Technology, The Open University

ENERGY AND PACKAGING
I. BOUSTEAD and G. F. HANCOCK, Faculty of Technology, The Open University

PROCESSING OF NORTH SEA OIL
P. LEWIS, Lecturer in Materials Science, The Open University

LIQUEFIED PETROLEUM GASES
Guide to Properties, Applications and Uses: Second Revised Edition
A. F. WILLIAMS, Esso Research Centre, Abingdon, and W. L. LOM, formerly Esso Research Centre, and Technical Advisor on Energy to the European Investment Bank, Luxembourg

WAVE ENERGY

A Design Challenge

R. SHAW, B.Eng.
Senior Lecturer
Department of Mechanical Engineering
University of Liverpool

ELLIS HORWOOD LIMITED
Publishers · Chichester

Halsted Press: a division of
JOHN WILEY & SONS
New York · Brisbane · Chichester · Toronto

First published in 1982 by

ELLIS HORWOOD LIMITED
Market Cross House, Cooper Street, Chichester, West Sussex, PO

The publisher's colophon is reproduced from James Gillison's drawing of the ancient Market Cross, Chichester.

Distributors:

Australia, New Zealand, South-east Asia:
Jacaranda-Wiley Ltd., Jacaranda Press,
JOHN WILEY & SONS INC.,
G.P.O. Box 859, Brisbane, Queensland 40001, Australia

Canada:
JOHN WILEY & SONS CANADA LIMITED
22 Worcester Road, Rexdale, Ontario, Canada.

Europe, Africa:
JOHN WILEY & SONS LIMITED
Baffins Lane, Chichester, West Sussex, England.

North and South America and the rest of the world:
Halsted Press: a division of
JOHN WILEY & SONS
605 Third Avenue, New York, N.Y. 10016, U.S.A.

© 1982 R. Shaw/Ellis Horwood Ltd.

British Library Cataloguing in Publication Data
Shaw, R.
Wave Energy – A design challenge. – (Ellis Horwood series in energy and fuel science)
1. Ocean wave power
I. Title
621.31'2134   TC147

Library of Congress Card No. 82–11780

ISBN 0–85312–382–9 (Ellis Horwood Ltd. – Library Edn.)
ISBN 0–85312–504–X (Ellis Horwood Ltd. – Student Edn.)
ISBN 0–470–27539–1 (Halsted Press)

Typeset in Press Roman by Ellis Horwood Ltd.
Printed in Great Britain by Butler & Tanner, Frome, Somerset.

Table of Contents

6   **Contents**

Foreword

Like most new developments, wave energy was at first 'technology lead'. Now increasingly the theoretical work is catching up and providing explanations and insight where previously we had experiments and 'feel'.

In a fast-moving technological development anything printed and bound must be to some extent out-of-date at a detailed level. The underlying physical principles are constant however and this book will provide students with a sound basis from which to develop their ideas. To support these fundamentals Mr. Shaw has included the most up-to-date pictures and descriptions which are available.

To all those technologists who now seek to pursue this fascinating subject I recommend one of the fundamental laws of wave energy conversion: almost any well designed wave energy converter (WEC) will 'work' in the sense of generating electricity. The trick is to do it cost-effectively.

For all involved in wave energy development there is likewise a fundamental law: in research you are backing people, and therefore the decision makers (be they individuals or committees) must always listen directly to the people doing the work.

To those who will manage the research, V. A. Thompson's comments are important: 'Innovation is a by-product of freedom – a true freedom in which the individual has such a sense of personal security that he is not afraid to make choices'.

It gives me great pleasure to commend Mr. Shaw's book to those who seek to follow us on the stormy seas ahead. Let us hope that wave energy research will be allowed to continue for we are sure it could contribute to the World's energy needs.

Clive O. J. Grove-Palmer
Programme Manager
Wave Energy
ETSU, Harwell
April 1982

Author's Preface

The realization that fossil fuel resources are seriously limited at present rates of consumption has naturally promoted the study of alternative energy resources. Wave energy which is both relatively abundant and benign, has received much attention in those industrial countries with appropriate coastlines and the extent to which this resource is exploited is dependent on the completion of the relevant research and development programmes. The aim of this book is to present the necessary background information for engineers and scientists, who are involved with energy supply and utilization and for students of engineering who will eventually have to make informed judgements concerning energy resources.

The introductory chapter deals briefly with future energy supply and demand projections, the efficiency of energy conversion processes and the various renewable energy sources. A review of wave energy conversion devices is presented together with an assessment of unit costs. To facilitate an understanding of the behaviour of the various devices, Chapter 2 presents the essential background on the characteristics of sea waves. The primary conversion processes from wave energy to mechanical energy are then discussed in Chapter 3, whilst Chapter 4 deals with the final conversion processes to other usable forms of energy, such as electricity. Chapter 5 describes the construction and mooring of the devices, whilst Chapter 6 deals with the environmental and social implications.

I acknowledge gratefully the opportunity presented by the University of Liverpool to enable me to write this book, especially the experience of teaching an energy course and supervising wave energy projects. I also express my thanks to Ms. Pauline Shaw for producing the diagrams, to Mr. David Shaw for checking the manuscript and to Ms. Anne Shaw and Ms. Marie Hemingway for their patience and care in typing the manuscript. Ms. Amanda Shaw is thanked for her help with the proof reading.

R. SHAW,
Liverpool
1982

Notation

A	area	m^2
	arbitrary constant	—
a	area	m^2
	radius of cylinder or sphere	m
	amplitude of wave	m
	added mass per unit length	kg/m
B	arbitrary constant	—
	magnetic flux density	tesla
b	breadth	m
	damping coefficient	kg/s
C	added mass coefficient	—
	capacitance	farad
	arbitrary constant	—
C_c	contraction coefficient	—
C_D	viscous drag coefficient	—
C_f	solid friction coefficient	—
C_S	slip coefficient	—
c	arbitrary constant	—
	phase velocity or celerity	m/s
	absolute velocity	m/s
c_i	ideal velocity	m/s
c_r	radial velocity	m/s
c_x	axial velocity	m/s
c_θ	tangential velocity	m/s
D	damping coefficient	kg/s
	diameter	m
	duration of record	s
d	spacing between devices	m
e	electromotive force (e.m.f.)	V
F	force	N
Fr	Froude number $= V/\sqrt{gL}$	—

f	frequency	Hz
fo	spectral peak frequency	—
g	gravitational acceleration	m/s^2
H	head	m
	height of wave	m
	inertia time constant	s
H_s	significant wave height	m
h	depth of water	m
I	electric current	A
	moment of inertia	$kg\,m^2$
	wave momentum per metre of crest	kg/s
I_p	phase current	A
i	$\sqrt{-1}$	—
J	Bessel function	—
j	$\sqrt{-1}$ for electrical applications	—
K	arbitrary constant	—
	multiplying factor	—
k	wave number $= 2\pi/L$	m^{-1}
L	inductance	henry
	length of air column	m
	wavelength	m
l	cylinder depth	m
	length of channel	m
M	moment	Nm
M_n	nth spectral moment	$m^2(Hz)^n$
m	mass	kg
N	Newton number $= F/\rho V^2 L^2$	—
	number of turns	—
	rotational speed	rev/min
n	distance in normal direction	m
	number	—
	ratio of duct width to wavelength	—
P	power	W
	real power (electrical)	W
p	pressure	Pa or N/m^2
Q	quantity (volumetric)	m^3
	reactive power	VA_r
	volume flow rate	m^3/s
q	interaction factor	—
	resultant velocity	m/s
R	electrical resistance	Ω
	radius	m
	Reynolds number $= \rho L V/\mu$	—

Re	real part	—
r	equivalent gear ratio	—
	radius	m
S	apparent power	VA
	restoring force coefficient	N/m
	Sommerfeld number $= \mu N/p$	—
	surface	m^2
$S(f)$	power spectral density function	m^2/Hz
s	attenuation factor	m^{-1}
	distance	m
T	period	s
	temperature	K
	tension	N
	torque	Nm
T_e	energy period	s
T_z	zero-crossing period	s
t	time	s
U	blade speed	m/s
	wind speed	m/s
u	velocity component in x direction	m/s
V	variable	(various)
	voltage	V
V_p	phase voltage	V
v	velocity component in y direction	m/s
w	relative velocity	m/s
	velocity component in z direction	m/s
	weight per unit length	N/m
X	reactance	Ω
X_j	exciting force (or moment) amplitude	N (or Nm)
x	distance in direction of wave propagation	m
y	distance perpendicular to still water surface	m
Z	complex number (transformed plane)	—
	impedance $= R + jX$	Ω
z	complex number	—
z_b	heaving displacement of buoy	m
α	angle	rad. or degree
	arbitrary constant	—
	displacement in x direction	m
$\bar{\alpha}$	energy extraction coefficient or damping rate	Nms
β	angle of relative flow velocity	rad. or degree
	arbitrary constant	—
	displacement in y direction	m
γ	angle	rad. or degree

Δ	damping ratio	—
	non-dimensional diameter	—
δ	directionality factor	—
	phase angle	rad. or degree
ϵ	infinitessimal radius	m
	phase angle	rad. or degree
ζ	displacement	m
η	efficiency	—
	free surface ordinate	m
$\bar{\eta}_{i}$	area averaged displacement of internal free surface	m
Θ	angular deflection	rad. or degree
θ	angle	rad. or degree
κ	hydrodynamic damping coefficient	Nms
μ	dynamic viscosity	Pas
ν	kinematic viscosity $= \mu/\rho$	m^2/s
	specific speed	—
	wave number $= 2\pi a/L$	—
Π	dimensionless power	—
	product (mathematical operator)	—
π	3.14159	—
ρ	density	kg/m^3
Σ	summation (mathematical operator)	—
σ	angular velocity	rad/s
	root mean square water level	m
Φ	magnetic flux linkage	wb
	velocity potential	m^2/s
ϕ	angle of precession	rad. of degree
	flow coefficient	—
	electrical phase angle	rad. or degree
	velocity potential	m^2/s
ψ	dimensionless head	—
	energy coefficient	—
	pressure coefficient	—
	stream function	m^2/s
Ω	angular velocity	rad/s
	angular velocity of precession	rad/s
	radian specific speed	rad
ω	angular velocity	rad/s

Superscripts

derivative with respect to time
second derivative with respect to time

$^-$	average value
$\rightarrow$	vector quantity with direction

Subscripts

a	air
	atmospheric
c	correction
	contraction coefficient
d	damped
e	energy
	energy extraction
f	friction
i	ideal
	incident
	instantaneous
L	loss
o	centre of particle orbit
	natural
	overall
	principal direction
	resonant
	tuned
p	phase
r	radiated
	reflected
s	significant
t	transmitted
x	in x direction
z	zero-crossing
θ	tangential
∞	infinity

Special notation

GW(e)   electrical power in GW

GW(th) thermal power in GW

$\dfrac{\mathrm{d}W}{\mathrm{d}t}$ work rate (indicating an inexact differential)

CHAPTER 1

Introduction

Before any study of an alternative energy resource is undertaken in detail, it is pertinent to consider the recent trends in energy supply and demand and to evaluate possible future requirements, so that the potential value of the new resource can be assessed correctly. The first section of this chapter therefore deals briefly with global energy prospects through to the early part of the next century. For further detail the various references must be consulted. The chapter continues with an essential review of energy conversion processes and a comparison of energy resources and conversion costs. An historical review of wave energy is then followed by a description of recent research and development, and finally the estimated cost of electrical generation from ocean waves is presented.

1.1 ENERGY SUPPLY AND DEMAND

World energy consumption has increased significantly since 1950 and the extra demand has been provided primarily by fossil fuels, as shown in Fig. 1.1. In the

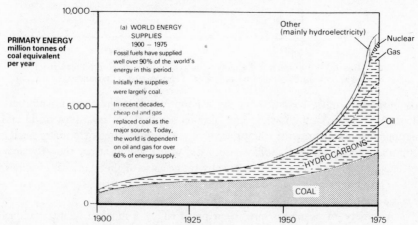

Fig. 1.1 – World energy consumption 1900–1975. Reproduced from [41] by permission of the Controller of Her Majesty's Stationery Office.

years 1950 to 1975 this increased demand was satisfied by an almost sixfold
increase in the use of oil and natural gas. By the early 1970s however, an aware-
ness that these resources would be seriously depleted within two or three decades
caused considerable concern, especially in industrialised nations, and from 1973
a significant rise in oil prices in real 1973 value currency. In spite of the temporary
effects of recession, increased energy demands must be anticipated in order to
sustain the desired increase in the gross national product (GNP) of the industrialised
nations and the ever-increasing requirements of the developing countries.

Under these conditions of increasing real price of oil and increasing energy
demand, it became vital for governments to formulate appropriate national
policies, especially as the time to bring new energy-production technologies from
research and development through to final application can be long (~ 20 years).
Various energy advisory groups have therefore attempted to identify possible
future energy demands and supplies in order to formulate the necessary strategies
for the remainder of this century and the early part of the next. Fig. 1.2 shows
one such projection to the year 2050. These different but plausible futures,

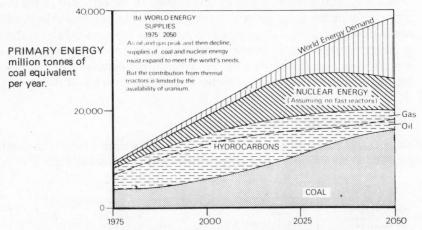

Fig. 1.2 – Future world energy supply and demand. Reproduced from
[41] by permission of the Controller of Her Majesty's Stationery Office.

or 'scenarios', must be based on the assumptions that there are no political,
economic or physical disasters and also on assumptions regarding world and
national economic growths, the price of oil and other forms of primary energy
and the various national policy responses, which would affect the efficiency
of energy use for a given economic activity. Because of the many assumptions,
these scenarios cannot be considered as predictions or forecasts and must be
revised continuously.

A variety of scenarios have been prepared by a number of international
research groups such as the Workshop on Alternative Energy Strategies (WAES),
directed by Wilson at the Massachusetts Insititute of Technology in the United

States, the Energy Research Group (ERG) lead by Eden at the University of Cambridge in the United Kingdom and the International Energy Agency (IEA). These scenarios were based on the assumptions of world economic growth rates as shown in Table 1.1.

Table 1.1 – Assumed world economic growth rates (GWP % p.a.).

Author(s)	Date(s)	References(s)	Growth Rates
WAES	1976	[145]	3.5% and 6% (to 1985)
	1977	[146]	3% (1985–2000)
ERG	1977	[147]	3% and 4.1%
IEA	1974	[72]	4%
EDEN	1981	[47]	3% to 3.2%
ESSO	1981	[49]	3%

The economic growth rates for individual nations would vary significantly, but they would integrate to give the world figure. For example WAES assumed that Mexico (6% and 7.5%) and Japan (4.5% and 8%) would have high national economic growth rates relative to the low (3.5%) and high (6%) world figures given in Table 1.1, whereas the UK would have lower rates of 1.8% and 3.1% respectively.

The scenario assumptions for the price of primary energy varied considerably, with WAES even considering a decreasing real price of oil as shown in Table 1.2.

Table 1.2.

Assumed variations in world oil price to 1985 (based on the 1975 US dollar price per barrel of Arabian light crude oil FOB Persian Gulf).

   (1) Constant price of $11.50 per barrel.
   (2) Price falling linearly from $11.50 in 1976 to $7.66 per barrel in 1985.
   (3) Price rising linearly from $11.50 in 1976 to $17.25 per barrel in 1985.

Assumed variations in world energy price to 2000.

   (1) Constant price equivalent to $11.50 per barrel.
   (2) Rising price equivalent to $17.25 per barrel.

By comparison ERG assumed that the world energy price would increase in real values by a factor of between 1.7 and 2.2 in the period 1972 to 2020, whereas the UK Department of Energy [41] assumed that the price of oil would

double in real terms in the period from 1977 to 2000 and increase by a further 50% by 2020 (Fig. 1.3).

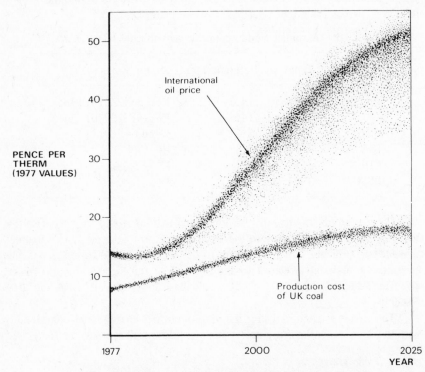

Fig. 1.3 – Future oil and coal prices. Reproduced from [41] by permission of the Controller of Her Majesty's Stationery Office.

The assumptions regarding national policy response are difficult to express numerically and have been described subjectively by WAES as "restrained" and "vigorous". Government action however can affect both conservation and supply and the former is eventually defined by the energy ratio (that is, the total consumption of primary energy per unit of gross world or domestic product in real values). The Digest of United Kingdom Energy Statistics 1981 [63] indicates that for the UK this ratio has decreased by 6.8% in the five years to 1980, whilst the Statistical Abstract of the United States 1980 [135] shows a decrease of 8% in the USA in the five years to 1979. Early studies generally assumed very little fall in energy ratio, but now it appears reasonable to assume that by the year 2000, this ratio may have fallen by 20% to 32% (Eden [47]).

Other scenario variables relate to the longer term studies and include the rate at which oil reserves are increased each year by the discovery of new fields, the production limits which might be set by the OPEC countries because of their inability to absorb further revenues, and the rate at which oil is replaced by

alternative fuels or by renewable resources. In 1977 WAES assumed that the
ratio of oil to total energy consumption would fall from 54% in 1972 to between
39% and 42% by 2000. The figures now assumed to be more likely are 37%
to 39%.

The unpredictability of the scenario variables is demonstrated by the 1980
oil price rise, which was responsible for the 50% increase in the price of heavy
fuel oil to UK industry in real terms between 1979 and 1981 [44], resulting in
decreased demand and a surplus of supply. Although future energy requirements
are therefore very difficult to assess with confidence, Table 1.3 lists the range of
estimates made by WAES, IEA, ERG and the UK Department of Energy (DOE)
whilst Fig. 1.2 gives the DOE projections in graphical form. Future energy
supply projections by ERG are given in Table 1.4 and by DOE in Fig. 1.2.

Table 1.3 — **Future energy demand estimates in exajoules/year (that is, 10^{18} joules/
year).**

Author	Area	1972	1985	2000	2020
WAES	WOCA	176	251–271	352–455	—
IEA	World–CCPA	—	395	—	—
	USSR	—	97	—	—
	WOCA	—	298	—	—
ERG	World	269	349–392	519–689	839–1323
	USSR	55	72–84	119–162	213–319
	CCPA	23	32–38	45–67	73–148
	WOCA	191	245–270	355–460	553–856
DOE	World	—	399	586	835

WOCA = World outside communist areas.
CCPA = China and centrally-planned Asia.
USSR = USSR and East Europe.

Table 1.4 — **Future energy supply projections
in exajoules/year for the world (ERG).**

1985	2000	2020
350–420	580–680	820–1010

It is clear that some scenarios suggest that there will be problems in matching
supply and demand early in the next century. Furthermore since the real cost of
primary energy will almost certainly rise, it follows that some current uneconomic
sources of energy may become viable.

Another important consideration in the planning of energy strategies concerns the form in which the energy in eventually consumed. The energy may ultimately be utilised as 'high-grade' electrical energy or as 'low-grade' thermal energy at a variety of temperatures to suit different requirements (see section 1.2 for the distinction between energy 'grades'). The US Department of Commerce [135] indicated that the percentage of world consumption of primary energy used for electricity generation rose from 26% in 1972 to 30.1% in 1978. Because of the low conversion efficiency from fossil fuel to electrical energy ($\sim$33%), this implies that the electricity actually generated is now about 10% of the total primary energy consumption worldwide. ERG [147] assume that the world demand for electricity will cause this electrical energy ratio to increase from 10% to 20% by the year 2020, so that electricity generation from resources other than fossil fuels will become increasingly attractive. 25% of the world consumption of primary energy is consumed, mainly as liquid fuel, for transporation purposes, whilst the remainder is used, either in the industrial sector ($\sim$25%) or in the residential and commercial sectors ($\sim$20%), mainly for low-temperature heating. These heating requirements might be met by the use of coal in those countries with the necessary indigenous reserves (Australia, Canada, China, UK, USA and USSR).

Thus in order to meet these demands for energy, especially electrical energy, the need to increase nuclear generation to provide about 80% of the electricity demand by 2025 is generally assumed. However, political pressure from environmental groups and public concern and fear of nuclear power processes and products may limit the increase in the number of power stations using fissile fuel. Alternative forms of energy conversion to electrical power, which can make significant contributions to the projected demands shown in Table 1.5, must obviously be investigated and developed as either supplementary or insurance technologies.

Table 1.5 – Electricity demand for 1972 and projections for 1985.

Region	1972		1985	
	Electrical power GW(e)	Percentage of primary energy	Electrical power GW(e)	Percentage of primary energy
Japan	36.5	8	56–78	8
Norway	6.3	19	9–10	19
Sweden	7.3	12	14–17	15
UK	23.5	8	32–38	10
USA	175.7	7	232–336(370)[†]	9
WOCA	410	7	722–1423	9–10
WORLD	650[†]	9		

Taken from [145] except where marked †, these are from [135].

This requires an increased commitment by engineers and scientists to energy studies and to research and development programmes initiated and supported by appropriate governmental departments. Wave energy, which can make a significant contribution to the energy requirements of many countries with ocean coastlines, has recently received considerable attention in the UK, the US, Japan, Norway and Sweden. The technological developments, supported more recently by detailed mathematical analyses, must therefore command the attention of all engineering students and those professional engineers involved with energy supply and utilisation.

In the UK, the governmental action, to ensure that the country had the technical ability to meet its energy requirements economically, was initiated by the Department of Energy (DOE) with appropriate guidance from the Energy Technology Support Unit (ETSU) located at Harwell. Although this location is more widely known in connection with the development of nuclear power, ETSU is involved with research, development and demonstration (RD & D) in all the various energy technologies, including wave power.

In the US, the energy programme was initiated by the DOE, with wave power investigations supported through the Office of Naval Research. In Japan, the Science and Technology Agency is responsible for wave energy research at the Japan Marine Science and Technology Center. Norwegian wave-energy development is supported by the Royal Ministry of Petroleum and Energy and the Norwegian Water Resources and Electricty Board, and in Sweden research is sponsored by the National Swedish Board of Energy Sources Development.

1.2 ENERGY CONVERSION PROCESSES

Before considering specific alternative technologies, it is necessary to recall the efficiencies of conversion from one form of energy to another. In particular, the efficiency limitation imposed by the Second Law of Thermodynamics on all thermal power stations must be appreciated. In such power plants, the chemical energy of fossil fuels or the nuclear energy of fissile fuels is first released as thermal energy, before being converted in an engine by means of a thermodynamic cycle to mechanical and eventually electrical energy.

The Second Law of Thermodynamics, as stated in the Kelvin-Planck form, requires that an engine, operating cyclically, must experience heat transfers with *two* energy reservoirs, one at high temperature T_1 and the other at a low temperature T_2. Reference to any standard text on thermodynamics will confirm that a corollary of this law requires that the maximum possible efficiency of conversion of the heat transfer from the hot reservoir to work transfer at the output shaft of an ideal engine is $(T_1 - T_2)/T_1$, with temperatures T_1 and T_2 expressed in (absolute) degrees Kelvin. The temperature of the cold reservoir is normally close to atmospheric temperature (~ 300K) whilst the upper temperature is limited by the properties of the materials of the engine. For the steam

turbine of a fossil-fuel power station T_1 is slightly higher than 800K, so that the maximum ideal efficiency would be about 63%. Such ideal (Carnot cycle) engines are impossible to create as factors, such as friction and heat transfer through finite temperature differences, cause losses in performance. The best actual steam-turbine-cycle efficiency would be about 45% and after allowing for boiler and generator efficiencies, the average overall efficiency (fuel to electricity) for UK steam stations (excluding nuclear) in 1978/79 was 32%.

The Second Law limitation becomes more important when considering low-grade thermal energy sources for which the temperature of the hot reservoir is much lower than in the previous example. This applies to geothermal, solar and ocean thermal sources and in some cases it might be more appropriate to use the low-grade thermal energy for direct heating purposes (for example, solar-heated water) especially as 50% of primary energy consumption is used for heating. Alternatively a low conversion efficiency to mechanical energy might be accepted because the source of thermal energy is plentiful; but only if it is also cheap to exploit.

The Second Law limitations is only applicable to the thermal to mechanical energy conversion and other energy conversions are achieved with much higher efficiencies. Combustion processes are affected only by incomplete combustion and dissociation and are generally about 98% efficient. The heat transfer between hot combustion products and a working fluid, such as steam in a boiler, incurs some loss due to incomplete energy transfer and hence loss from the chimney. Boiler efficiencies of 80%–90% are therefore typical. Mechanical to electrical energy conversion is also very efficient with small mechanical losses due to bearing friction, small heating effect losses due to current flow in conductors and magnetic circuit (iron) losses. Efficiencies of 98% are typical. Electrical to mechanical conversion is also achieved with high efficiency, typically 92%. Battery and fuel cell conversions of chemical to electrical energy have efficiencies of 70%–75%, and avoid the thermal to mechanical energy conversion with the Second Law limitation. Likewise direct photovoltaic conversion of solar to electrical energy using 'solar cells' is attractive, but the efficiency of these devices is still too low to be viable ($\sim 11\%$).

Because the conversion of thermal energy to mechanical and subsequent electrical energy involves the restriction of the Carnot cycle efficiency, it is common practice to refer to thermal energy as low grade energy and mechanical and hence electrical energy as high grade energy.[†] This may not necessarily imply however that electricity should not be used for heating purposes if the application process itself requires much less energy. For example, heat pumps effectively reverse the thermodynamic cycle and but for the accumulated dissipative losses would return the thermal energy expended. Again microwave and induction

---

† The distinction between the two grades of energy is indicated in the text by (th) for low-grade thermal energy and (e) for high-grade electrical energy.

heating processes transfer the energy to the core of the material to be heated in a more efficient way than by surface heat transfer, so that this may counter the inefficiency of the original thermodynamic cycle.

1.3 COMPARISON OF ENERGY RESOURCES AND CONVERSION COSTS

For the purpose of comparison of the various energy resources the following factors should be considered:

(i) The extent and availability of the energy source.
(ii) The effects on the environment.
(iii) The cost per unit of energy to the consumer. The cost to the consumer essentially depends on:

(a) The cost of the fuel.
(b) The capital cost of the conversion plant accounted for as depreciation.
(c) Repairs, maintenance and operating costs.
(d) The efficiency of the conversion process.
(e) Transmission costs.
(f) Administration costs, etc.

The importance of each item contributing to the total cost will vary markedly between different energy conversion systems, but for reference, the 1979/80 accounts of the Central Electricty Generating Board (CEGB) [21] indicate that out of a total expenditure of 4.7G£, fuel cost amounted to 2.8G£; repairs, maintenance and operating costs were 0.5G£, whilst depreciation accounted for 0.3G£. For the renewable energy resources fuel costs are nil (unless auxiliary power is required), whilst the capital cost and maintenance become all-important, and the former is dependent on the size and complexity of the plant and the materials, energy and labour costs of manufacture. These contributory factors to capital cost are themselves dependent on the extent of technological knowledge and experience and might be expected to fall rapidly as an embryo technology is developed.

Existing fossil fuels, having been created over millions of years, are not renewable at present rates of consumption, and hence oil, gas and coal are limited in the extent of the resource. Fig. 1.2 based on Energy Paper No. 39 [41] shows the probable decline in the use of gas and oil after the turn of the century and although coal will be an important resource for two or three centuries, alternative energy sources must be found eventually. Nuclear energy is shown to increase in importance to 2020, but will be limited by the extent of the supply of uranium, unless fast 'breeder' reactors or fusion processes are developed. The shortfall in primary energy supply below the predicted world demand early in the next century will require the employment of fast or fusion reactors or the use of renewable energy resources.

Although debate on the environmental effects of the nuclear energy programme will be finely balanced, a serious nuclear accident could cause a sudden
and dramatic change of public opinion. The near-serious accident at the Three
Mile Island Nuclear Power Station at Harrisburg, Pennsylvania in the USA on
28th March, 1979, emphasises this point and justifies and encourages the research
and development on the various renewable resources. Coal will probably provide
a significant part of the primary energy demand for some considerable time, as
indicated in Fig. 1.2, but its effect on the environment should not be overlooked.
The sulphur content of the coal oxidises to produce sulphur dioxide which in
turn combines with water to produce sulphurous acid, which can then be deposited
on land surfaces during rain showers, with harmful effects on crops and buildings.
The climatic effect of excessive carbon dioxide production is uncertain, but
might be serious, and it must also be accepted that coal is an important chemical
raw material for the production of methanol and ammonia and it should not be
consumed for its energy content, if this can be avoided.

Although the foregoing comments have justified attention to renewable
energy sources, the extent of the commitment in the UK is limited. This may be
assessed by comparing the 1.3M£ spent in 1977/78 on all renewable energy
resources compared with 250M£ total expenditure on energy RD & D, including
136M£ on nuclear energy alone. The increased expenditure on 'renewables'
to 36.1M£ by June 1981 does however indicate some small increase in the
commitment to these resources.

1.4 RENEWABLE ENERGY SOURCES

Of the alternative sources, geothermal energy is extensive, but not strictly
renewable. It is viable, especially for those parts of the world where geological
faults occur in the earth's crust, as long the western coast of the Americas, in
Iceland, Italy and New Zealand. Boreholes to tap the steam generated in such
areas and the associated steam-turbine power plant call only on established
technology and many geothermal power stations exist. In the UK pilot schemes
have been initiated in Cornwall and 13.2M£ allocated in June 1981.

Wind energy, a renewable source resulting from different solar radiation
over the earth's surface, also received a modest RD & D budget of 1M£ in June
1978. The technology for building 2 MW units has been developed in the USA
and Denmark particularly, but the size to power ratio is unattractive, the 2 MW
units being 54 m in diameter. The power developed is proportional to the effective
area of the aerodynamic absorber and the cube of the wind speed which is of
course very variable. Furthermore fluid momentum considerations limit the
conversion efficiency to 59.3% maximum and typically a good practical efficiency
would be 30%. Only 2.3M£ has been committed to wind energy development in
the UK at June 1981.

Tidal energy, resulting from sun–moon gravitational interaction on the seas, fared little better in 1978 with a budget of 1.7M£. The UK is fortunate to have a favourable site in the Severn Estuary, and here the extent of the resource is about 2GW(e) or 8% of the total UK demand. Capital costs estimated at 3G£, a construction period of 20 years and the obvious commitment to the complete system are unattractive, but the technology exists and a 240MW scheme has been in operation in the Rance Estuary in northern France since 1968. A total of 2.5M£ has been allocated in June 1981.

Solar energy RD & D received a larger share (3.6M£) of the 1978 allocation of funds from the DOE. This sum was divided between solar water heating, solar space heating and biofuel development, and did not cover research into photovoltaic conversion, which was funded to the extent of 2.6M£ by other government departments. It is estimated that by the year 2000, solar water heating will provide less than 3GW(th) and solar space heating less than 1GW(th). Biofuels, fuels from crops and organic wastes, already exist as a significant resource and could be extended to provide 25GW(th) by the year 2000.

The largest allocation of funds in 1978 was made to Wave Energy RD & D and amounted to 5.4M£. This has been increased to 13.1M£ by June 1981. Wave energy is derived from the winds as they blow across the oceans and this energy transfer provides a convenient and natural concentration of the wind energy in the water near the free surface. Once created, waves are attenuated only over considerable distances and hence waves created on the American side of the Atlantic will reach the western coast of the British Isles. Thus on average about 80kW of wave energy pass from various directions over a circle of 1m diameter in the location of Ocean Weather Ship *India*, some 710km to the west of the Hebrides (Fig. 1.4(a)). Nearer the coastline this average energy intensity falls to about 50kW/m and to an effective 32kW/m when a fixed direction is selected. After allowing a 50% efficiency for both wave energy capture by the device and for the power chain system, a final figure of 8kW(e)/m could be anticipated. The 700km of sea space available from the Shetland Isles to the southern end of the Hebrides could therefore produce over 5GW(e) or 20% of the total UK demand if fully used. This resource is therefore sufficiently extensive to be attractive, but for the first generation of wave energy devices, the estimated cost to the consumer of between 20p and 50p/kWh was far too expensive compared with about 2p/kWh for electricity generated by conventional fossil-fuel power stations. A second generation of devices, assessed in 1980, suggested costs of less than 5p/kWh, and warranted the increase to nearly 4M£ per annum in the allocation of funds to wave energy research and development.

It is therefore apparent that wave energy could contribute to the UK energy supply towards the end of the present century, either for local communities on the islands to the north-west of Scotland, where electricity is relatively expensive even today, or for the nation as a whole, as improved wave power designs lead to further reductions in cost, whilst the real cost of fossil fuels rises.

The interest in wave energy shown by many other maritime countries can be anticipated from Fig. 1.4(b) which shows the estimated wave-energy levels around some selected coastlines of the world. Although these energy intensities do not quite reach those to the north-west of Scotland, they are still sufficiently high to be attractive, especially to those countries which are net energy importers (particularly Japan, USA, Canada and other western European countries).

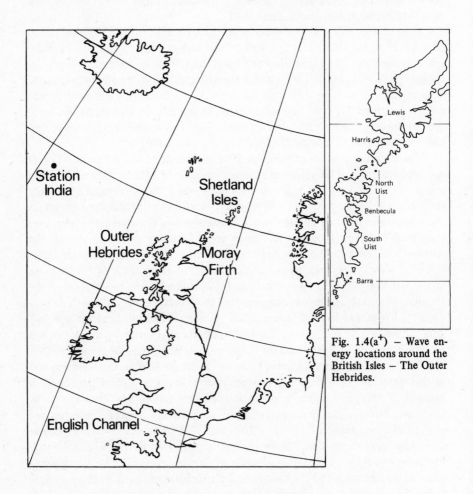

Fig. 1.4(a^+) — Wave energy locations around the British Isles — The Outer Hebrides.

Fig. 1.4(a) — Wave energy locations around the British Isles.

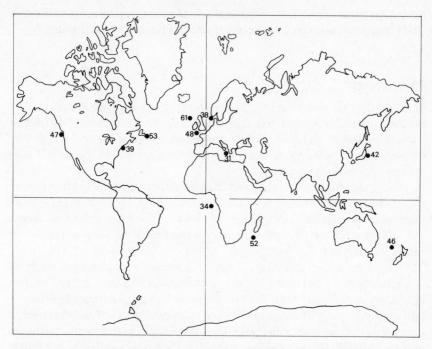

Fig. 1.4(b) – Annual average wave power from selected sites (kW/m).

Whereas it was estimated (above) that for the UK the actual power brought ashore would be about 8kW(e)/m, a figure of about 5kW(e)/m might be more appropriate for these other possible sites. Thus, if the full coastline was used in each case, the contributions to national electricity demand would be as shown in Table 1.6.

Table 1.6 – Contributions to various national electricity demands.

Country	Wave power GW(e)	Percentage of projected electricity demand in 1985
Japan	11	15%
Norway	5	50%
UK	5	15%
USA	23	7%

The value of wave energy to Japan, a highly industrialised country with

limited indigenous coal and oil resources, is apparent. Japanese expenditure of 22M£ over seven years on wave energy research is therefore understandable.

1.5 HISTORICAL SURVEY

Probably the first ever patent for a wave energy device was filed in Paris in 1799 by the Girards, father and son. The translation by A. E. Hidden of Queen's University, Belfast, indicated that they envisaged a 'ship of the line' attached by a gigantic lever to the shore, with the oscillatory motion of the lever driving machinery directly or via pumps.

Leishman and Scobie [81] have carefully documented the development of wave-powered devices from the first British patent in 1855 up to 1973, when there were already 340 patents. A brief review of the more significant devices will now be given and, if further details are required, the appropriate references should be consulted.

One of the earliest and most informative papers on wave power was presented at a meeting of the American Society of Mechanical Engineers at San Francisco in 1892 by A. W. Stahl [128]. The first sentence of his paper warrants repetition — "An intelligent study of the possibility and practicability of utilizing the power of ocean waves presupposes a thorough knowledge of the geometry and mechanics of wave motion". He then demonstrated that the trochoidal theory (see Stoker [129]) practically satisfied the conditions of 'dynamical equilibrium' (the equation of motion), the condition of continuity, and the boundary conditions. Many wave energy devices were then described, although they were limited to floating structures or vertical flat vanes whose motions were transferred by ropes, levers, and racks and pinions to the "pumping or other suitable machinery". One device however consisted of a pair of floats whose relative angular motion was employed to operate a ratchet wheel, from which the power was transmitted to "any suitable mechanism". This idea was subsequently further developed by Masuda in Japan and by Wavepower Limited in the UK, as described later.

An early practical application of wave power in 1910 at Royan, near Bordeaux, France is described by Palme [114]. M. Bochaux-Praceique supplied his house with 1kW of light and power from a turbine, driven by air which was pumped by the oscillations of the sea water in a vertical bore hole in a cliff. This is claimed to be the first form of the device developed by Masuda in Japan from 1965 onwards and by the National Engineering Laboratory more recently as a part of the present UK wave energy programme.

In 1947, Y. Masuda [94] developed a three float system at the Oceanographic Unit of the Japanese Defence Department. This utilised the relative angular motion between three floats, which has an overall length of one wavelength. The device produced 200W of power, but tests were abandoned after it had been overturned by a large wave. This device has recently been further developed by

Wavepower Limited at Southampton, under the direction of Sir Christopher Cockerell, the inventor of the Hovercraft, and the principle is illustrated in Fig. 1.5.

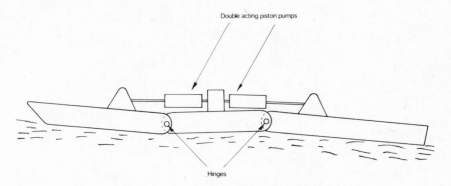

Fig. 1.5 – The three-raft system of Wavepower Ltd.

In 1959 Walton Bott *et al.* [137] devised a scheme for the island of Mauritius in the Indian Ocean which made use of existing coral reefs. Breakers would fill the low-head reservoir formed by the extended reefs and turbo-ram pumps would deliver the water to a high-head reservoir and hence to the 5 MW power station. The scheme was abandoned in 1966 as the price of oil decreased, but reviewed in 1976, when a 20 MW scheme appeared to be most viable. Further developments are now considered possible.

In 1962, the AVCO Corporation, Research & Development Division [126], carried out tests at Buzzard's Bay, Massachusetts on a buoy with taut-line mooring and an internal diaphragm which was deflected by the fluctuating pressure within the waves. The diaphragm operated a hydraulic piston and eventually about 1 watt was produced. The diaphragm was however ruptured during a hurricane.

By 1965, Masuda [94] had invented and the Ryokuseisha Corporation of Japan had patented and manufactured air-turbine buoys with an output of 60 W. More than six hundred of these wave-powered navigation buoys have been in operation off Japan, USA, Canada, the Persian Gulf and the British Isles. Fig. 1.6 illustrates the principle of operation of this device. A container, open at the bottom is partially immersed in the water so that air is trapped in the upper part. The water in the container rises as a wave crest passes and causes air to be forced through valves at the top. The air passes through a turbine and so produces power. As the level of water falls in a trough, air is drawn through another set of valves and passes through the turbine in the original direction so continuing to develop power.

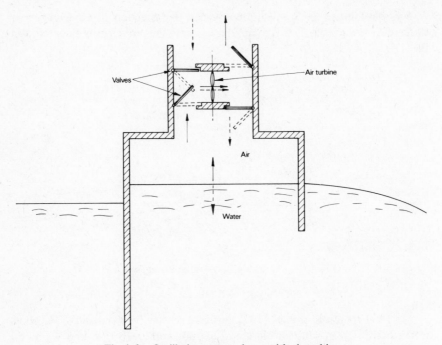

Fig. 1.6 – Oscillating water column with air turbine.

At EXPO 1970 at Osaka in Japan, Masuda [94] demonstrated 500W air-turbine generator units. Also in 1970, the Power Systems Company [4] of Boston, Massachusetts, USA successfully completed tests on a small-scale sea-bed device consisiting of diaphragms in concrete troughs. The pressure fluctuations caused hydraulic fluid to be pumped to an accumulator on the adjacent shoreline.

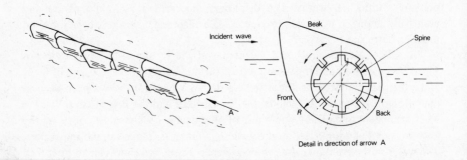

Fig. 1.7 – Nodding Duck – original concept.

In 1973, S. Salter [121] of the Department of Mechanical Engineering at the University of Edinburgh initiated a series of experiments, first on a hinged plate and then on an oscillating cam-shaped device usually referred to as a 'Nodding Duck'. The high efficiency of these ducks in model tests in the laboratory, combined with Stephen Salter's considerable engineering ability and conviction, undoubtedly played an important role in the formulation of recent UK policy (discussed in section 1.5.1). Originally the duck oscillated back and forth about a 'spine', so that internal splines on the duck interacted with external splines on the spine to pump fluid which then drove hydraulic motors coupled to generators (Fig. 1.7). In more recent designs gyroscopes are employed in the 'beak' of the duck instead of the spline-pump system (Fig. 1.8).

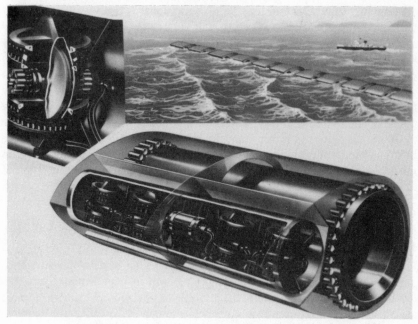

Fig. 1.8 – Latest design of the Nodding Duck. Reproduced from
a photograph supplied by Mr. C. O. J. Grove-Palmer by courtesy
of the Energy Technology Support Unit.

1.5.1 The Recent UK Government Programme

Energy Paper Number 42 [42] describes the development of the UK programme and indicates the government interest in wave energy began formally in 1974 with the publication by the Central Policy Review Staff of a report entitled *Energy Conservation* [22]. The recommendation in that report was for a full technological and economic appraisal to be put in hand. This preliminary evaluation was initiated in February 1974 at the National Engineering Laboratory (NEL)

at East Kilbride, Scotland by the newly-formed DOE, and resulted in the report by Leishman & Scobie [81] which assessed the situation up to February 1975. Following this detailed study, the government announced, in April 1976, the start of a two-year study costing about 1M£ to establish the feasibility of the large scale extraction of wave power and to provide information to enable the cost of further development to be estimated. Four conversion devices (described in section 1.6) were chosen initially for this two year programme, whilst research into a number of problems common to all devices was undertaken. This included the collection and analysis of wave data, the effects of wave forces on structures, the methods of anchoring and mooring, and power generation and transmission, as well as environmental effects.

By April 1977 encouraging progress persuaded the government to increase the funding to 2.5M£ and in June 1978 an additional 2.9M£ was allocated, so as to allow development work at 1/10th scale in open water and the testing of vital components at a larger scale. In September 1980, the Minister with responsibility for renewable energy announced in a Press Notice [43], that 3M£ had been spent on wave energy in the previous year and that the allocation for this present year would be 3.5 to 4M£. New contracts were awarded to Edinburgh University for work on spines and tank operation, to Vickers Limited for work on oscillating water columns, to Sea Energy Associates and Lanchester Polytechnic for work on spines and mooring systems and to Sir Robert McAlpines for work on the Bristol Cylinder device. As these new contracts indicated, further work on fundamental problems was required as well as work on the new generation of devices.

1.6 RECENT RESEARCH AND DEVELOPMENT IN THE UK AND ABROAD

1.6.1 Devices

Further details of the various wave energy devices under development will be given in Chapter 3. In order to complete the chronological presentation, however, it is appropriate to discuss briefly the principle of operation of the devices which are currently receiving attention.

After the success of Masuda's air-turbine buoys, the Japan Marine Science and Technology Center initiated further studies in 1974 on large-scale wave power generation using the oscillating water column principle; Masuda himself being the Chief Scientist of the Marine Technology Department. In 1976, a prototype wave power machine, KAIMEI, was constructed. This long ship-like structure was chosen for ease of construction and safety of mooring, and in 1977 three turbine-generator units, constructed by the Fuji Electric Company, were installed, and the first sea tests completed between July 1978 and April 1979 [95]. Each impulse-type turbine was 1.4 m in diameter and the a.c. generators were rated at 125 kW at 900 rev/min. Peak outputs of 260 kW were achieved, but average values were reported to be lower (~ 40 kW). In 1979

the UK, with Canada, Eire and the USA, accepted an offer by the Japanese to participate in a joint programme of tests under the auspices of the International Energy Agency. Eventually seven Japanese units and one UK unit were installed and Miyazaki and Masuda [106] reported the results of these latest tests, which indicated that generator number 9 (Japanese) recorded a maximum output of 291 kW, exceeding all expectations. The UK turbine rotor is shown in Fig. 1.9.

Fig. 1.9 – Turbine rotor. Reproduced from a photograph supplied by Mr. C. O. J. Grove-Palmer by courtesy of the Energy Technology Support Unit.

Salter's work at Edinburgh University, already mentioned in section 1.5, received governmental approval first as an award from the Mechanical Engineering & Machine Tools Requirements Board and later, in 1976, as one of the four first-generation devices of the UK programme supported by the Department of Energy. Dr. N. W. Bellamy [8] Lanchester Polytechnic, Coventry carried out preliminary trials on a string of model Salter Ducks at 1/50th scale on Draycote Reservoir, Coventry, and then in 1977 was involved with the NEL in the manufacture of a modified Edinburgh design at 1/10th scale for tests on Loch Ness. Although there were many teething troubles, requiring several modifications, the device weighing 25 tonnes and measuring 50m long was returned to the loch in September 1978 for testing. Meanwhile, Salter [123] was more concerned with "small-scale laboratory tests with increasing levels of hydrodynamic realism". To this end a new wide tank was completed at Edinburgh by the end of 1977 [123]. The tank is 27m × 11m and has 89 independently-controlled wavemakers along one of the longer sides. Suitable programming allows the creation of a variety of wave conditions closely representing real sea states. Since the start of 1979, Salter has also been concerned with the problems of full-scale design. Gyroscopes, in the beak of the duck, now absorb the torque and the precession motions of these gyros drive ring-cam pumps which pressurise oil, which in turn

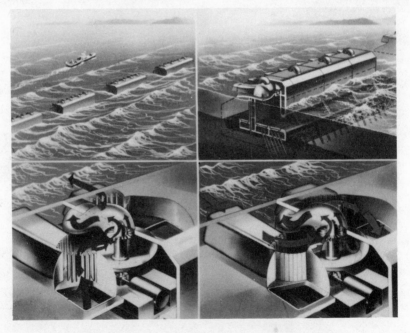

Fig. 1.10 — Oscillating water column — artist's impression. Reproduced from a photograph supplied by Mr. C. O. J. Grove-Palmer by courtesy of the Energy Technology Support Unit.

drives a swash-plate motor coupled to the electrical generator (Fig. 1.8). This system not only provides a completely sealed power unit, but, by using contra-rotating gyros, torques can be cancelled and the loading of the spine reduced.

The second of the first-generation devices supported by the DOE in 1976 was the Oscillating Water Column (OWC) unit, developed by the National Engineering Laboratory (NEL), East Kilbride, Scotland. Initial experiments described by Meir [102] were concerned with achieving the optimum shape and size, comparing two- and three-dimensional devices, and assessing the performance of fixed and floating systems. Consideration was also given to the type of air turbine required and a Francis type recommended. In a later report, Moody [107] explained that a free-floating concrete structure (Fig. 1.10) was selected in 1978 because of its low material cost even though some slight loss of hydrodynamic performance compared with a steel structure resulted. The Francis turbine would drive an a.c. generator, but, after transforming and rectifying, transmission ashore would be via a high voltage d.c. link. Moody also indicated that a seabed mounted OWC in shallow water ($\sim 15\,\text{m}$) was possible. These NEL devices were arranged in line to face the oncoming waves and were classified as 'terminators'. An alternative arrangement in line and perpendicular to the line of the wave crests and with side openings has also been designed and tested as a model in the Edinburgh wave tank. This device, classified as an 'attenuator', would be at least 1.5 wavelengths long for cost effectiveness and productivity.

The third of the first generation of devices was the wave-contouring raft developed by Sir Christopher Cockerell [25] since 1971. Early experimental work in 1974 by his company Wavepower Limited, indicated that high efficiencies could be obtained and in 1976 the DOE provided financial support. Although early models had up to seven sections with six hinge lines, it was soon found that there was little gain in power from having more than two hinge lines. In 1978, trials with a three-raft system at 1/10th scale were conducted in the Solent (Fig. 1.11) with the centre raft of the three fully instrumented to measure the loads on the structure. An oil hydraulic system was employed with double-acting rams mounted above the hinges. The pressurised oil operated a piston-type motor which drove an automotive alternator. Based on the initial testing and experience a full-size system was designed. This consisted of a rear section 50m wide with two separate front sections each 25m wide connected along a single hinge line (Fig. 1.12). The pump, extending fully across the raft and forming an integral part of the structure, was a double-acting oscillating vane type, with appropriate flap valves to allow sea water to be pumped to a reservoir on the rear raft section. The water then flowed from the reservoir through an axial-flow Kaplan-type turbine and discharged to sea below the raft. The generator was rim-mounted to the turbine, although it was also possible to use a bulb-type unit. Two materials were considered for the rafts, steel and concrete, with the latter more durable, and with a better corrosion resistance, but heavier. In their paper of 1978, Cockerell, Platts & Comyns-Carr [25] suggested a pro-

Fig. 1.11 — One-tenth scale Cockerell Raft in force 6–7 conditions in the Solent, UK. Reproduced from a photograph by courtesy of Wavepower Ltd.

gramme of manufacture commencing in 1990 with 50 rafts per year, and rising to 300 rafts per year in 1995. This programme would ensure a final installed capacity of about 19GW by 2020. However, the estimated cost of electricity produced by rafts has not yet been demonstrated to be competitive, so that future development by Wavepower Limited continues as a private enterprise.

Fig. 1.12 – Latest design of Cockerell Raft. Reproduced from a photograph supplied by Mr. C. O. J. Grove-Palmer by courtesy of the Energy Technology Support Unit.

The fourth first-generation device was the HRS Rectifier, initiated at the Hydraulics Research Station by R. C. H. Russell in 1975 and described by Rance [119]. The Hydrualics Research Station had first been involved with wave power in the late 1950s with the Mauritius scheme mentioned in section 1.5. The Rectifier is a large rectangular hollow caisson with a series of narrow compartments (<10m wide) as shown in Fig. 1.13. The narrow front faces of alternative compartments are fitted with non-return flap valves, allowing water entry under the pressure of wave crests, whilst the intervening compartments have flap valves which open to allow discharge into a wave trough. To avoid valve closure due to wave reflections from the rear face of the device the front-to-back dimension must be $\lessdot 1/4$ wavelength (~ 25 to 50m). To avoid problems with torsional strength, buoyancy and mooring, a sea-bed location in about 30m of water was selected. Water flowed from the higher level in the inlet compart-

ments through a Kaplan turbine to the outflow compartments. To inhibit the intrusion of sediment a new design was considered with a 1 in 3 ramp leading to the inlet chambers. This device was to be located in 15m of water and use a bulb-turbine. The difficulties in aligning the device to face the oncoming waves because of the sea-bed contours near the Hebrides and the size and hence cost per unit output have resulted in this scheme falling from favour.

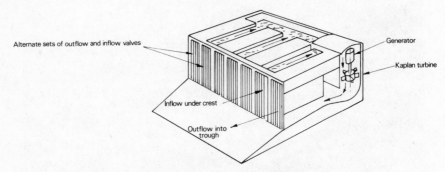

Fig. 1.13 – Hydraulics Research Station Rectifier.

With the realisation in 1978 that the first generation of devices were costly, ETSU considered a number of second-generation devices and three of these received support from the DOE.

One promising device, created by Professor French [58,59], at Lancaster University was funded initially by the Science Research Council and consisted of a long beam of prestressed concrete aligned perpendicular to the wave crests, and kept afloat by flexible air bags attached along the top of the beam (Fig. 1.14). As a wave crest rises round a bag, the air is forced through non-return valves into a high pressure duct, from which it flows through a turbine and then back during a wave trough to the bag, via non-return valves and a low-pressure duct. This device was found to be close to cost competitiveness – less than 5p/kWh generated at 1980 prices compared with 2p/kWh for conventional means – and is now being developed by Lancaster University and by Wavepower Limited with DOE funding. The original design dimensions were 190m long, 6m beam and 8m deep, but a shorter length is now considered more economical. The air bags, made of flexible material 8mm thick were arranged in two groups, either side of the central turbine housing; each group being formed by dividing the continuous outer cover into about 10 separate bags by transverse membranes of the same material. Two single-stage air turbines with adjustable nozzle blades were employed; the nozzle blades being closed for high waves to give a low reaction stage and opened to give about 50% reaction for low waves. Fig. 1.15 gives an artist's impression of the device.

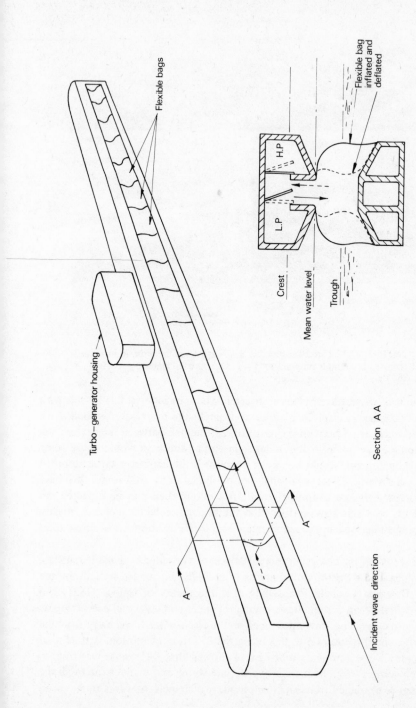

Flexible bags

Turbo–generator housing

A

A

Incident wave direction

Crest

Mean water level

Trough

H.P

L.P

Flexible bag inflated and deflated

Section A A

Fig. 1.14 – The Lancaster Flexible Bag energy converter.

Fig. 1.15 – The Lancaster Flexible Bag – artist's impression. Reproduced from a photograph supplied by Mr. C. O. J. Grove-Palmer by courtesy of the Energy Technology Support Unit.

Several of these Wave Energy Converters would be moored side-by-side with sufficient spacing to clear each other even under the most adverse conditions. Although waves would obviously pass through the gap between the devices, the absorption of energy from the water adjacent to the bags would cause some refraction and energy would be drawn in towards the converter to be absorbed towards the stern. Theoretical analyses by Budal [16] and Ambli [3] have indicated that this interaction between a row of absorbers may be expected and experiments by Budal have verified that the interaction factor increases linearly with the absorber spacing-to-wavelength ratio (d/L) up to π as d/L approaches unity.

The second of the new generation of devices was invented by a mathematician, Dr. D. V. Evans of Bristol University early in 1978 and funded initially by the Science Research Council. Evans [51] used the theory of Ogilvie [112], who predicted that when a submerged circular cylinder rotates on an eccentric axis parallel to its own, the waves produced on the free surface travel away from the cylinder in one direction only; this being the direction of motion of the top of the cylinder at the top of its orbit. Evans showed that the reverse was true, so that by loading the cylinder with appropriate spring and damper forces all the energy can be extracted from small amplitude regular incident waves, under tuned

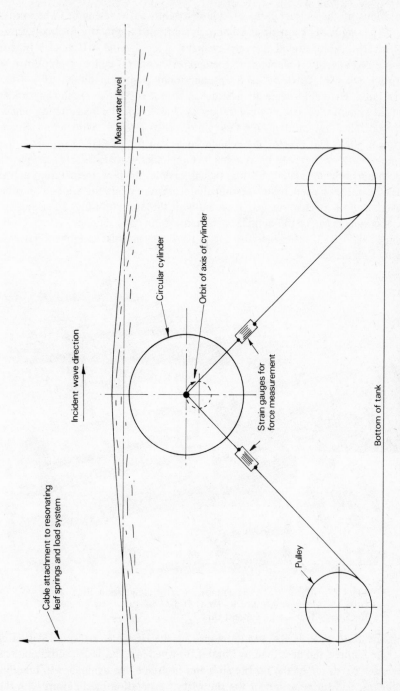

Fig. 1.16 – Submerged circular cylinder converter.

conditions of the correct ratio of cylinder radius to wavelength. Experiments
[51, 53] using Salter's test rig at Edinburgh confirmed the theory for small waves
and clearly demonstrated the achievement of acceptable efficiencies over a
reasonable range of wavelengths. In these experiments, the cylinder was positively
buoyant and held down by cables passing round pulleys at the bottom of the
wave tank. The cables were then attached to leaf springs above the surface so
that the system resonated at wave frequency (Fig. 1.16). The load on the cylinder
was controlled by printed armature motors with integral tachometers. Strain
gauges in the cables near to the cylinder measured the oscillating forces on the
cylinder and together with measurements of cylinder velocity enabled the power
absorption to be evaluated. In the original scheme, for power generation in real
seas, the cables passed round torsionally-loaded drums at the sea bed and the
power take-off mechanism was included with the drum housing. Subsequently
the mooring lines for the cylinder actuated a spring and damper system which
pumped fluid to a turbogenerator. Fig. 1.17 shows an artist's impression of this
Bristol Cylinder device.

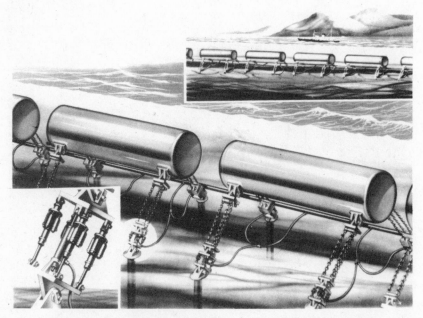

Fig. 1.17 – The Bristol Cylinder device – artist's impression. Reproduced
from a photograph supplied by Mr. C. O. J. Grove-Palmer by courtesy of
the Energy Technology Support Unit.

The third new device was developed by the Design & Projects Division of
Vickers Limited and described by Chester-Browne [24]. The design considerations
were the avoidance of the hostile air/water interface, the avoidance of mooring
problems, and the selection of the simplest of generation mechanisms with the

minimum of moving parts. The operating principle involved the use of a resonant oscillating water column, as suggested by Professor Sir James Lighthill [84], with flow rectification achieved by allowing some of the water in the column to overflow, at the top of each oscillation, into a reservoir which included a trapped air volume (Fig. 1.18). The pressurised air then forced a controlled flow of the overspill water through a low-head hydraulic turbine which drove the generator.

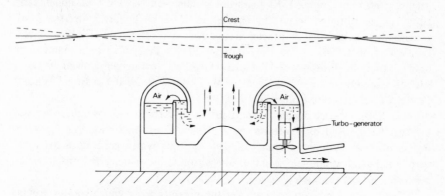

Fig. 1.18 – Submerged resonant duct.

Fig. 1.19 – Submerged resonant duct – artist's impression. Reproduced from a photograph supplied by Mr. C. O. J. Grove-Palmer by courtesy of the Energy Technology Support Unit.

The device was located on the sea bed to meet the first two design conditions and had an upward facing inlet close enough to the surface to capture most of the wave energy. A model of the device was tested in a small wave tank at Lancaster University and at the resonant frequency had an efficiency of 93%. An artist's impression of the device is shown in Fig. 1.19.

Additional research and development in the UK has been supported by the Science Research Council (SRC) and has included an isolated hydro-pneumatic buoy system initiated by A. E. Hidden in 1973 at Belfast University [86], a stationary cylindrical converter developed by Professor J. O. Flower and Dr. G. F. Knott [56] at the University of Sussex in 1977, a twin-chamber air buoy devised by Professor J. G. Morley [108] at Nottingham University and a triplate converter created by Dr. F. J. M. Farley [54, 2] at the Royal Military College of Science, Shrivenham in 1977.

The Belfast device, which is essentially an air-turbine buoy, is unique because the turbine, devised by Professor A. A. Wells, is self-rectifying. The blades of the turbine are symmetrical uncambered aerofoils which generate a lift force with a forward component whether the absolute air velocity is from above or below the axis of symmetry.

The Sussex converter depends on the pressure wave which rotates around the circumference of a stationary immersed cylinder in synchronism with the regular incident waves. The original device consisted of a deformable layer of fluid-filled bags completely surrounding the cylinder, but eventually discrete pulsating sources and sinks were used, in the form of pistons fitted to two of three cylindrical openings arranged at 120° to each other and perpendicular to the main cylinder axis.

The Nottingham device, consisting of a twin-chamber air buoy, was an interesting development of the Masuda air buoy, because the two chambers were designed to resonate at different frequencies, whilst pitching and heaving occurred at still different frequencies. It was thereby proposed to accommodate the range of frequencies encountered in a real sea.

The Triplate Converter employed the horizontal component of the wave motion. The two rear plates are fixed rigidly together half a wavelength apart and, as a result of a resonant wave between them, they do not move horizontally. The front plate, in three separate sections, was located one quarter wavelength in front of the rear pair, at the point of maximum horizontal motion, caused by the full reflection from the stationary rear pair. This horizontal motion has an amplitude of oscillation twice that of the incident wave, but by suitable loading of the front plate the amplitude can be restored to that of the incident wave, with full energy absorption. In 1980, Dr. Farley [55] proposed a Flexible Resonant Raft device, "Porpoise", consisting of a long slender flexible raft floating on the water and aligned with the direction of wave propagation. The thin elastic structure was designed to oscillate with waves and an internal pumping mechanism was proposed for power generation.

Another new device is the 'Clam', devised by Dr. Bellamy [9] at Lanchester Polytechnic and developed by Sea Energy Associates, a consortium led by the Ready Mixed Concrete and Cawood groups and including Fairclough Construction whose associated company Howard Doris has built concrete structures for the offshore oil industry.

The 'Clam' wave energy converter is a spine-based pneumatic terminator, as is the Salter Duck. Such devices have high capture efficiency and relatively low mooring forces. The Clam uses air as the working fluid and is illustrated in Fig. 1.20. It consists of flaps attached at the bottom to a floating concrete spine with flexible air bags located between the two parts. Waves impinge on the flaps and the resultant oscillatory motion forces the entrapped air through self-rectifying turbines. The air is contained in a closed circuit and returns to the bags when the flaps move out in wave troughs.

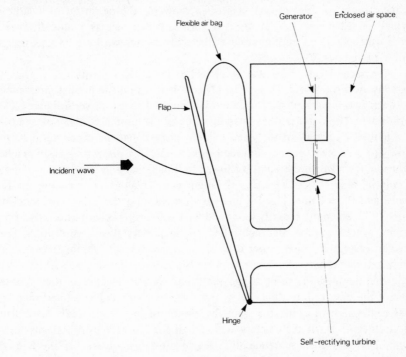

Fig. 1.20 – The Lanchester Clam wave energy converter.

In the original concept a 10 MW generator unit consisted of 10 clam elements each 30 m long, with the rectangular spine 15 m deep by 10 m wide. A 2.5 MW unit, 180 m × 10 m × 8 m, and displacing 18,000 tonnes could be built initially at a cost of 10 M£ and eventually it is envisaged that 320 units each 275 m long could generate 2 GW.

Recent inventions in the US include the Dam-Atoll device evolved at the Lockheed Rye Canyon Research Laboratory, Saugus, California in 1973 and demonstrated successfully as a 1/100th scale model in 1977. This device was patented by L. S. Wirt [143] of Lockheed Corporation and is described in a Lockheed Report [85] and in Solar Energy Digest [5]. The principle employed is that of wave refraction caused by change of water depth. Waves travel slower in shallower water, so that the direction of propagation (the ray path) is bent towards the shallower water. This phenomenon has long been observed with natural atolls where unidirectional waves bend around to approach the beaches of the atoll radially from all directions. Furthermore as the water becomes shallower, the waves steepen and eventually break. Provided that the beach is correctly designed, the breakers are of the surger type and all the wave energy is converted to kinetic energy. In the Dam-Atoll, guide vanes direct this irregular radial motion of the breakers tangentially towards the perimeter of a vertical cylindrical chamber. This produces a vortex, which acts as a fluid flywheel, from which energy is continuously and steadily withdrawn by a turbine, which drives a generator.

The second US device was developed at the Scripps Institution of Oceanography by Professor J. D. Isaacs [73] and depends on the inertial interaction between two integrated systems, a buoy connected to a long vertical pipe filled with water. The water is accelerated upwards by the motion of the buoy and the low natural frequency of the water column ensures that the water continues to flow upwards, even as the buoy and pipe drop. This pressurizes an hydraulic reservoir, from which the water is allowed to flow steadily to a turbine.

In Norway at the University of Trondheim a small group, including Mr. K. Budal and Dr. J. Falnes [17, 18], have studied wave power devices theoretically since 1973, and more recently have conducted supporting experiments on heaving buoys, whose motion was controlled for maximum power absorption. For regular waves, maximum power is obtained at resonance, when the force on the buoy and its velocity are always in phase. Experimentally this was achieved by adjusting the mass of the buoy and the counter-weight located on the opposite side of the power absorption pulley. For irregular waves, enhanced performance was achieved by locking the buoy by means of an electronically-controlled electromagnet when the velocity was zero at the lowest and highest positions. The buoy was then subsequently released after one quarter of the natural period, which was arranged to be slightly less than the wave period. The buoy velocity was then in phase with the heave excitation force and approximately fulfilled the conditions for maximum power absorption. Budal et al. [18] also experimentally confirmed the theoretical prediction of a beneficial interaction between point absorbers in a linear row. They defined an interaction factor q as the maximum power absorption, with interaction, divided by the maximum power absorption of an isolated buoy and showed that this increased linearly with the ratio of the spacing of the buoys to the wavelength (d/L) up to $q = \pi$

as d/L approached unity. They also demonstrated that 50% of the incident wave power may be absorbed by a single row of heaving buoys, whilst 100% capture efficiency can be achieved when a reflector is placed behind the buoys.

This work at Trondheim was supported by the Norwegian government to the extent of 0.4M£ in 1980, whilst a further 1M£ was provided for work on the focusing of ocean swells by Dr. E. Mehlum and Mr. J. Stamnes [100] at the Central Institute for Industrial Research in Oslo.

Work in other European countries and in Canada has also been described in the Proceedings of the First Symposium on Wave Energy Utilization held at Chalmers University of Technology, Gothenburg, Sweden in October–November 1979.

1.6.2 Generic Research

From the description of the various devices for harnessing wave energy in section 1.6.1, it is apparent that, although the possible solutions are original and diverse, there are difficulties and problems which are common to all devices. These common problem areas were identified in Energy Paper No. 42 [42] and have received appropriate attention and government support.

The first generic problem is the shortage of wave data, especially close to shore. The required information includes the record of wave height with time and the directional properties of the waves.

The second general problem relates to the effect of the wave forces on the structures of the devices. A device which absorbs or reflects wave energy must also absorb or reflect momentum and be subject to a mean horizontal force. This force must be balanced by an opposing force provided by fixing the device to the sea bed, and/or by arranging for opposing forces to be exerted by the sea on other parts of the device. Fixing to the sea-bed by cables obviously introduces anchoring and mooring problems, whilst forces which are not balanced at a point provide a bending moment on the structure which may be difficult to accommodate.

The third problem concerns the power generation from the slow irregular motion of the waves to the steady high-speed rotary motion normally required for electrical machines. The transmission of this power ashore may also be difficult if flexible cables are required.

The fourth common problem relates to the effects of the devices on the environment. Changes in the wave climate caused by the wave energy converters could affect the local shore-line. Fish feeding and spawning could be affected by the devices, which would also present some hazard to shipping.

These generic problems will be considered in some detail in the subsequent chapters.

1.6.3 Analytical Treatment

The mathematical analyses of Evans [50] and Lighthill [84] in the UK and of Budal & Falnes [17] in Norway have already been mentioned in section 1.6.1.

In the last few years further attention has been given to analytical studies. In the UK, Count [28], Evans [52] and Jefferys [74] have analysed the interaction between waves and energy absorbing devices, as have Budal [16] and Budal & Falnes [17] in Norway. In the US, mathematical methods have been developed at the Massachusetts Institute of Technology, relating to the performance of the Salter Duck by Mynett *et al.* [110], Mei & Newman [101] and Greenhow [65], and relating to the performance of wave-contouring rafts by Haren & Mei [67]. In the UK, Count [28] and Glendenning [62] have also predicted the performance of the Salter Duck, whilst French [57] has produced an analytical method appropriate to the flexible bag device.

1.7 ECONOMIC ASSESSMENT OF THE LATEST DESIGNS

Cost estimates for wave-energy devices must obviously be related to the costs for conventional power stations presently under construction, which range from 2.6p/kWh in the case of the nuclear station Dungeness B to 7.1p/kWh for the oil-fired station Ince B. Expensive oil-fired stations would not be used continuously however, but would only be brought into service to deal with peak demands.

By comparison with these figures, the 1979 estimates for wave-energy devices (by consulting engineers Rendel Palmer and Tritton) and the latest design-team estimates (given by Cottrill [26]) are shown in Table 1.7.

Table 1.7.

Device	1979 estimate p/kWh	1981 estimate p/kWh
Lancaster Flexible Bag	6	3.5–4.7
Salter Duck	10	4.5–5.6
Bristol Cylinder	14	5–10
Vickers Twin Oscillating Water Column	15	6
Vickers Chamber	–	6
Lanchester Clam	–	6
Belfast Buoy	12	8
Cockerell Raft	12	9
NEL Oscillating Water Column	13	10–11

The closeness of these latest estimates to the costs of between 3 and 4p/kWh for most 'based-load' power stations greatly encourages the design teams and

ensures that wave energy remains as a most promising source of energy to meet the future demands of all countries with ocean coastlines.

Although there is a degree of commercial confidentiality attached to some of the cost estimates, figures have been published showing the breakdown of the costs for the Cockerell Raft and for the Lanchester Clam.

Woolley & Tricklebank [144] have considered the mass production of concrete wave energy devices and although their report relates primarily to Cockerell Rafts, their conclusions have general validity. A feasible method for mass production of large concrete cellular structures is described and this method is significantly cheaper than the conventional method, by virtue of the highly mechanised and repetitive production processes employed. However research and development of the fabrication techniques is required in order to achieve the necessary fatigue strength of the reinforcement cages. For a capital-intensive flow-line facility it is estimated that, for a concrete hull of 13500 tonnes, the cost of the structure would be about £100 per tonne.

Woolley and Tricklebank also gave a breakdown of the unit cost for the case of the Cockerell Raft as shown in Table 1.8.

Table 1.8.

Hull	30%	
Maintenance	22%	
Power take off	22%	of the
Mooring and anchors		total
(at sea work)	15%	cost
Sundries	8%	p/kWh
Electrical transmission	3%	

Taylor [131] confirmed that maintenance has a first order effect on the cost of wave energy and estimated that for a generalised wave energy device, the maintenance cost would be in the range 2–3p/kWh[†]. For a spine-type device with a manifold power system, the maintenance costs would be 0.8–1.5p/kWh[†] and for a fixed device would be $\leqslant$0.5p/kWh[†]. The assumptions made in making these estimates were that all components were of modular construction and built with present day materials and technology. It was also assumed that remote diagnosis of all equipment failures was possible and that the average annual output of a 2GW rated system would be 0.5GW.

For the spine-based Clam, a mean figure of 1.2p/kWh for maintenance costs would represent 20% of the total estimated cost of 6p/kWh. The breakdown of the unit cost for the Clam would then be as shown in Table 1.9 (based on Bellamy's capital cost figures [9]).

---

† Revised figures presented at the Conference [131].

Table 1.9.

Structure	40%	
Maintenance	20%	of the
Power plant	11%	total
Transmission	9%	cost
Moorings	7%	p/kWh
Contingencies	7%	
Sundries	6%	

CHAPTER 2

Characteristics of sea waves

An understanding of the geometry and mechanics of wave motion, as suggested by Stahl in 1892 (see section 1.5), is an essential requirement for any study of wave energy converters, in order to conceive appropriate methods for extracting the energy from the waves and also to design devices capable of withstanding the very significant forces involved. Therefore this chapter is devoted to a statement of the various physical relations and properties of waves, together with the appropriate derived equations. The more essential mathematics is presented in Appendix A, whilst even further analytical treatment can be found in the many references listed throughout the chapter.

Fortunately the water may be considered to be incompressible and inviscid and the motion irrotational and generally two-dimensional. Considerable simplification results, although the motion is obviously periodic and hence unsteady. One of the boundary conditions unfortunately involves a non-linear term and the equation of motion also results in the non-linear kinetic energy term (q^2). Fortunately for waves of modest steepness these non-linear terms can be neglected without significant error and the analysis simplified by 'linearisation'.

2.1 PHYSICAL PROPERTIES OF WATER WAVES

A water wave whose crest moves in a direction perpendicular to the line of the crest is called a travelling or progressive wave, as illustrated in Fig. 2.1.

The points where the free surface crosses the still water line are the zero crossing points ($y = \eta = 0$). These zero crossing points, like the crests and the troughs, move in the x direction, with a velocity called the phase velocity or phase speed or sometimes the celerity, c.

After a time $\Delta t = T$, the wave form will reproduce the full line shown, but will of course be displaced by one wavelength L. The phase velocity $c = L/T$ where T is the period.

Another type of wave, called a standing wave, is illustrated in Fig. 2.2. In this case the crest does not progress longitudinally but, at the fixed value of x, becomes sequentially still water, a trough, still water again, and a crest again.

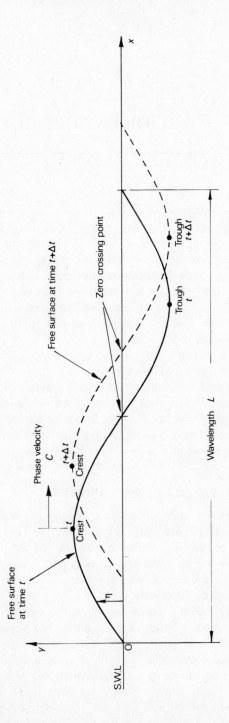

Fig. 2.1 – A progressive wave.

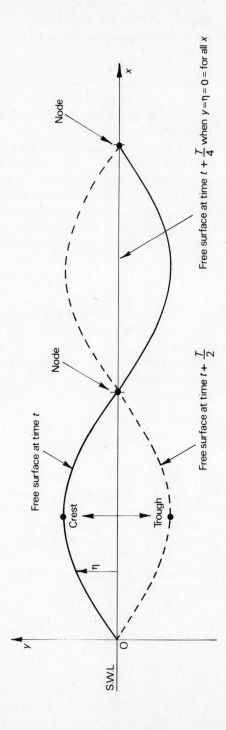

Fig. 2.2 – A standing wave.

This part of a standing wave is called the loop. During the same period, the point at which the free surface crosses the still water line, called the node, remains on the still water line.

Waves on the open sea are progressive waves and their physical properties are therefore of the greatest importance. However when a progressive wave encounters a flat vertical wall it is reflected and a standing wave results. The properties of standing waves must also be appreciated, as some reflection from wave energy converters must generally be expected.

The physical behaviour of water waves can be interpreted from mathematical analysis, provided all assumptions and approximations are clearly validated by observation or proof. Although there are hydrostatic pressure gradients and temperature and salinity gradients in the oceans, these variations may be considered to have negligible effect on the density within the surface layers of interest. Hence the water may be considered to be homogenous and incompressible and thus the density ρ constant. The continuity equation therefore simplifies to

$$\text{div}\,\mathbf{q} = 0 \tag{2.1}$$

where $\mathbf{q}$ is the resultant velocity vector with components u, v and w. Equation (2.1) indicates that the volume flow rates into and from a fixed elemental 'control volume' are balanced.

Furthermore it is reasonable to assume that waves are two-dimensional (that is, constant properties along lines parallel to the wave crests, so that partial derivatives with respect to z are zero). Thus the continuity equation becomes

$$\frac{\partial u}{\partial x} + \frac{\partial v}{\partial y} = 0 \tag{2.2}$$

The motion of fluid particles under the influence of the waves leads to other relevant equations. When fluid particles move, even on curved paths, they may do so without rotation about their own axes, as illustrated in Fig. 2.3.

This condition of irrotationality is valid, if the original motion of the particle was generated from rest by normal forces and the viscosity of the water can be ignored. Except near the sea bed, the inviscid assumption is valid and the wave motion is generated mainly by normal pressure forces. The motion can therefore be considered irrotational, so that

$$\text{curl}\,\mathbf{q} = 0 \tag{2.3}$$

For the x-y plane of interest this becomes

$$\left(\frac{\partial v}{\partial x} - \frac{\partial u}{\partial y}\right) = 0 \tag{2.4}$$

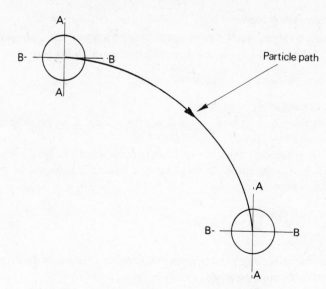

Fig. 2.3 — Fluid particle movement without rotation.

Although the velocities u and v, in the x and y directions respectively, are obviously vector quantities, it is possible to define a scalar quantity to simultaneously satisfy the condition of irrotationality *and* simplify the equation of continuity. This scalar quantity, called the **velocity potential**, ϕ, which is a function of x, y and t is defined as:

$$u = \frac{\partial \phi}{\partial x} \quad \text{and} \quad v = \frac{\partial \phi}{\partial y} \qquad (2.5(a) \text{ and } (b))$$

(that is, the gradient of ϕ in a particular direction is the velocity in that direction.)
Obviously

$$\frac{\partial u}{\partial y} = \frac{\partial}{\partial y} \frac{\partial \phi}{\partial x} = \frac{\partial^2 \phi}{\partial y \partial x}$$

and

$$\frac{\partial v}{\partial x} = \frac{\partial}{\partial x} \frac{\partial \phi}{\partial y} = \frac{\partial^2 \phi}{\partial x \partial y}$$

Since the order of differentiation for the second derivatives is optional it follows that (2.4) is satisfied. Furthermore (2.2) becomes

$$\frac{\partial^2 \phi}{\partial x^2} + \frac{\partial^2 \phi}{\partial y^2} = 0 \qquad (2.6)$$

2.1.1 Progressive Waves

Equation (2.6) is Laplace's Equation for $\phi(x, y, t)$, which has a progressive wave solution, easily verified by appropriate differentiation, of the form

$$\phi = A \cosh k\,(y + h) \cos \{k(x - ct)\} \tag{2.7}$$

where A, k, h and c are constants.

Obviously ϕ and its two partial derivatives u and v are periodic in x and t and hyperbolic in y.

The other relevant equation is the dynamical equation, which describes the conservation of momentum. In its integrated form, this becomes the non-steady Bernoulli Equation

$$\frac{p}{\rho} + \frac{1}{2}q^2 + gy + \frac{\partial \phi}{\partial t} = 0 \tag{2.8}$$

where the $\partial \phi / \partial t$ term originates from the 'local' accelerations $\partial u / \partial t$ and $\partial v / \partial t$, which would of course be absent in steady flow.

The properties of the water ϕ, u and v and the particle displacements α and β in the x and y directions respectively, may be found from (2.7), once the constants A, k, h and c are determined. Then the pressure p can be found from (2.8).

The constant k is readily determined from the periodicity with respect to x. Obviously $\cos kx$ must be equal to $\cos \{k(x + L)\}$, which implies that

$$kL = 2\pi \quad \text{or} \quad k = 2\pi/L \tag{2.9}$$

The other three constants are determined from the three boundary conditions:

(1) No water particles can cross the sea bed.
(2) No water particles can cross the free surface.
(3) The pressure at the free surface is zero (gauge), since surface tension is negligible for all but very small capilliary waves.

At a horizontal sea bed the first condition is satisfied by

$$v = \left. \frac{\partial \phi}{\partial y} = 0 \right|_{y \text{ at sea bed}} \tag{2.10}$$

whilst the free-surface condition, simplified by removal of the non-linear term, which is the product of small quantities, is

$$\frac{\partial \eta}{\partial t} = \left. \frac{\partial \phi}{\partial y} \right|_{y=\eta} \approx \left. \frac{\partial \phi}{\partial y} \right|_{y=0} \tag{2.11}$$

The Bernoulli Equation (2.8) at the free surface is simplified because $p = 0$ and also because it is reasonable to assume, since velocities are small, that q^2 is negligible. Hence

$$\frac{\partial \phi}{\partial t} + g\eta = 0 \bigg|_{y=\eta} \qquad (2.12)$$

Partial differentiation of 2.12 with respect to t and combination with 2.11 give the **surface boundary condition**

$$\frac{\partial^2 \phi}{\partial t^2} + g\frac{\partial \phi}{\partial y} = 0 \bigg|_{y=\eta \approx 0} \qquad (2.13)$$

Inserting the appropriate partial derivatives from (2.7) into (2.13) gives

$$c^2 = \frac{g}{k} \tanh kh \qquad (2.14)$$

whilst the sea-bed condition (2.10) establishes that the constant h is the depth of the sea-bed below the still water line.

The ordinate η of the free surface is found from (2.12) after inserting the appropriate expression for $\partial \phi / \partial t$ from (2.7).

$$\eta = a \sin \{k(x - ct)\} \qquad (2.15)$$

where a = amplitude = $-A/c \sinh kh$ and for reproduction of the waveform every period $kcT = 2\pi$.

The velocity potential ϕ becomes

$$\phi = -ac\frac{\cosh k(y + h)}{\sinh kh} \cos \{k(x - ct)\} \qquad (2.16)$$

2.1.2 Standing Waves

For standing waves the same fundamental equations and boundary conditions apply but now the phase velocity $c = 0$ and the local amplitude is periodic in time. The appropriate solution of the Laplace Equation (2.6) is now

$$\phi = A \cosh k(y + h) \sin kx \sin \sigma t \qquad (2.17)$$

where $\sigma = 2\pi/T$.

Thus

$$\eta = a \cos \sigma t \sin kx \qquad (2.18)$$

and

$$\phi = -\frac{a\sigma}{k}\frac{\cosh k(y + h)}{\sinh kh} \sin kx \sin \sigma t \qquad (2.19)$$

2.1.3 Particle Motion and Water Pressure in the Presence of Progressive Waves

The velocity components u and v of the water particle at the point P(Fig. 2.4(a)) can be obtained from the velocity potential ϕ, and since the displacement α and β are small for waves of modest steepness, a first order approximation yields the relation

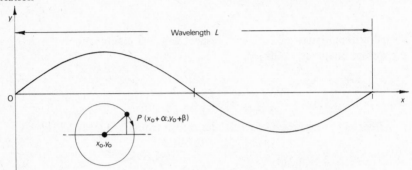

Fig. 2.4(a) – Particle motion in the presence of progressive waves.

$$\frac{\alpha^2}{\dfrac{a^2 \cosh^2 k(y_0 + h)}{\sinh^2 kh}} + \frac{\beta^2}{\dfrac{a^2 \sinh^2 k(y_0 + h)}{\sinh^2 kh}} = 1 \tag{2.20}$$

which is the equation to an ellipse, with an eccentricity which depends on the depth h. As $h \to \infty$ for very deep water, so the denominators tend to the same value $(a \exp(ky_0))^2$ and the equation becomes that of a circle $\alpha^2 + \beta^2 = r^2$ with radius $r = a \exp(ky_0)$. Since y_0 cannot be positive, it follows that this radius is a maximum at the surface when $r = a$ and decreases exponentially with depth.

In shallower water, at the sea-bed when $y_0 = -h$, $\cosh k(y_0 + h) = 1$ and $\sinh k(y_0 + h) = 0$. Thus β becomes zero and α varies periodically between $\pm a/\sinh kh$.

The particle orbits for varying depth of water are shown in Fig. 2.4(b) and indicate that the motion of the water is significant near the surface.

The cyclic variation of pressure beneath the waves is readily determined from the non-steady Bernoulli Equation once the velocity potential and hence $\partial\phi/\partial t$ are known. Assuming that the kinetic energy term $(q^2/2)$ is negligible, it follows that the cyclic pressure variation

$$\Delta p = \frac{2\rho \, ac^2 k \cosh k(y + h)}{\sinh kh} \tag{2.21}$$

which for deep water becomes

$$\Delta p = 2\rho g a \exp(2\pi y/L) \tag{2.22}$$

Again, since y is not positive, the maximum pressure variation occurs at the surface and the variation decays exponentially with depth.

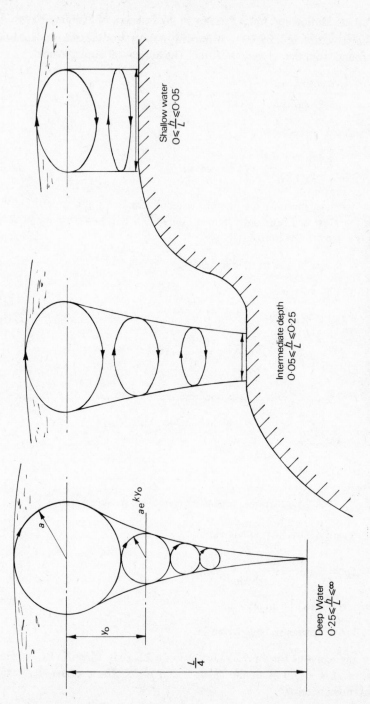

Fig. 2.4(b) – Particle orbits for different depths.

2.1.4 Particle Motion and Water Pressure in the Presence of Standing Waves

Again the velocities and, by integration with respect to time, the displacements may be found from the velocity potential. The horizontal displacement

$$\alpha = \frac{a \cosh k(y_o + h)}{\sinh kh} \cos kx_o \cos \sigma t \tag{2.23}$$

and the vertical displacement

$$\beta = \frac{a \sinh k(y + h)}{\sinh kh} \sin kx_o \cos \sigma t \tag{2.24}$$

The particle motions are therefore rectilinear, with the motion vertical beneath the crest and horizontal beneath the nodes. Between crest and node the motion is angled to the horizontal by

$$\theta = \tan^{-1} \{\tanh k(y_o + h) \tan kx_o\} \tag{2.25}$$

as shown in Fig. 2.5.

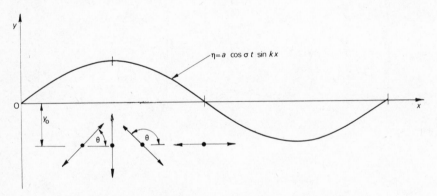

Fig. 2.5 – Particle motion in the presence of standing waves.

In this case the cyclic pressure variation

$$\Delta p = 2\rho ga \frac{\cosh k(y_o + h)}{\cosh kh} \sin kx_o \tag{2.26}$$

which for deep water becomes

$$\Delta p = 2\rho ga \exp(2\pi y_o/L) \sin kx_o \tag{2.27}$$

which is the same as for a progressive wave (2.22) *only* when $\sin kx_o = \pm 1$ or when $x_o = L/4$ or $3L/4$ at the *crests and troughs*. The pressure fluctuation beneath a node is zero.

2.1.5 Mass, Momentum and Energy Transfer by Progressive Waves

In view of the closed orbital motion predicted by linear theory, it is not imme-diately obvious that mass, momentum and energy are transferred by progressive waves. However, both the rate of mass and momentum transfer across a vertical plane perpendicular to the direction of wave propagation can be determined by restricted use of the results of linear theory and by the retention of some second order terms.

The wave momentum I_x in the x direction, equal to the mass flux $\dot{m}_x$ in that direction, due to the waves, is

$$I_x = \dot{m}_x = \rho \overline{\int_{-h}^{\eta} u \, dy} \qquad (2.28)$$

where the overbar indicates an average over the waves (either over one wavelength or one period). The velocity u may be obtained from the velocity potential ϕ (2.16) by partial differentiation with respect to x and then integrated with respect to y as suggested by (2.28) to give

$$\dot{m}_x = \rho ac \left[\sinh ky \coth kh + \cosh ky \right]_{-h}^{\eta} \sin \{k(x-ct)\} \qquad (2.29)$$

At the lower limit the hyperbolic terms evaluate to give zero, whilst the upper limit gives, to a first order approximation, $[k\eta \coth kh + 1]$ where η according to linear theory is given by (2.15) as $\eta = a \sin \{k(x-ct)\}$. Whereas averaging the simply periodic term over the waves, gives zero, the average of the $\sin^2 \{k(x-ct)\}$ term is $1/2$, and then by making use of (2.14).

$$I_x = \dot{m}_x = \frac{1}{2} \rho a^2 g/c \qquad (2.30)$$

To determine the forces on floating or submerged objects Longuet-Higgins [89] considered the flux of horizontal momentum, across a vertical plane $x =$ constant, less the corresponding flux in the absence of the waves, due to the hydrostatic pressure $p_o = -\rho gy$. Thus the excess flux of momentum due to the waves is

$$\int_{-h}^{\eta} (p + \rho u^2) \, dy - \int_{-h}^{o} p_o \, dy \qquad (2.31)$$

In the absence of a reflected wave and change in the time-averaged water level, this resultant flux is defined as the radiation stress (Longuet-Higgins and Stewart [91]). However, when allowance is made for the small, second-order displacement of the mean surface level on either side of the object the resultant force per unit width is

$$F = \frac{1}{4}\rho g(a_i^2 + a_r^2 - a_t^2)\left(1 + \frac{2kh}{\sinh kh}\right) \qquad (2.32)$$

where a_i = the amplitude of the incident wave; a_r = the amplitude of the reflected wave; a_t = the amplitude of the transmitted wave.

The change in the mean surface level across the object is

$$\Delta\bar{\eta} = -\frac{1}{4}(a_i^2 + a_r^2 - a_t^2)\left(\frac{2k}{\sinh kh}\right) \qquad (2.33)$$

In deep water, $h \to \infty$ and so $\sinh kh \to \infty$. There is then no change in mean surface level across the object and the force becomes

$$F = \frac{1}{4}\rho g(a_i^2 + a_r^2 - a_t^2) \text{ per unit width} \qquad (2.34)$$

This analytical prediction was checked experimentally for a wave raft and a nodding duck and found to be in good agreement for low wave amplitudes. For breaking waves acting on the duck however the forces were less than predicted.

Experiments by Salter *et al.* [125] on a circular cylinder indicated that the mean force was quite small for non-breaking waves, as expected from the linearised non-viscous theory of Dean [39] Ursell [133] and Ogilvie [112]. For higher wave amplitudes however the horizontal force changed to act in a direction reverse to the direction of wave propagation. Longuet-Higgins concluded that this strange behaviour was in part due to the presence of an appreciable second harmonic in the transmitted waves. For breaking waves however the negative forces were attributed to the change in the local mean water level $\bar{\eta}$, by the phenomenon known as wave 'set-up'. Wave geometry changes as the depth of water changes as shown in Fig. 2.6(a). In particular the wave amplitude reduces slightly for water of intermediate depth and then rises significantly for shallow water. Upon breaking the waves lose amplitude again, and the resultant changes in radiation stress and static pressure cause a dramatic rise in *mean* water level. For wavelengths which are not small compared to the diameter of the cylinder, this wave 'set-up' is unsymmetrically down-wave and causes the reverse force as shown in Fig. 2.6(b). For the prediction of the forces on floating or submerged objects under differing conditions further reference should be made to the paper by Longuet-Higgins [89]. The effect of a mainstream flow, such as the Gulf Stream, interacting with waves affects the momentum transfer. Crapper [32] has derived the appropriate equations of continuity and momentum conservation.

The energy transfer across a vertical plane at $x = x_0$ in an elemental interval of time δt is determined by considering the movement of an elemental fluid particle $\delta x \delta y$ as shown in Fig. 2.7.

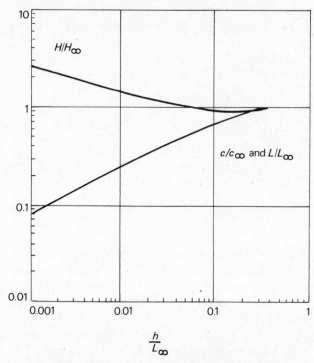

Fig. 2.6(a) – Variation in wave characteristics as function of ratio of water depth h to deep water wavelength L_∞. H = wave height, c = phase velocity, L = wavelength, subscript ∞ = deep water. From data by Wiegel, [138], reference 8, appendix 1.

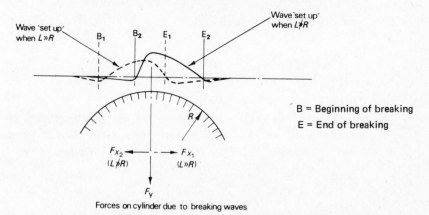

Forces on cylinder due to breaking waves

Fig. 2.6(b) – Forces on a submerged cylinder due to unsymmetrical changes of mean water level when waves break. From [89] by courtesy of M. S. Longuet-Higgins and The Royal Society.

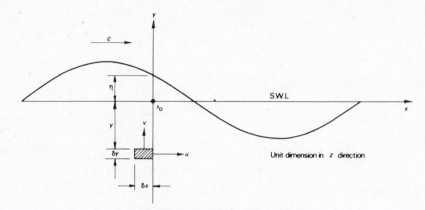

Fig. 2.7 – Energy transfer across a vertical plane at $x = x_0$.

If δx is chosen so that the whole fluid particle crosses the plane $x = x_0$ in time δt, then since the horizontal velocity is u, evidently $\delta x = u\delta t$. The fluid particle transports kinetic energy at a rate $(\rho \delta x \delta y) [(u^2 + v^2)/2]/\delta t$ and potential energy at a rate $(\rho \delta x \delta y) gy/\delta t$ whilst displacement work is done by the force due to the pressure at a rate $(p\delta y) \delta x/\delta t$.

Writing $q^2 = u^2 + v^2$ and $\delta x/\delta t = u$ and integrating with respect to y gives the rate of energy transfer or power per unit width in z direction

$$P = \int_{-h}^{\eta} \rho u \left(\frac{q^2}{2} + gy + \frac{p}{\rho}\right) dy \qquad (2.35)$$

Using (2.5(a)) and (2.8) this becomes

$$P = \int_{-h}^{\eta} \rho \left(\frac{\partial \phi}{\partial x}\right) \left(-\frac{\partial \phi}{\partial t}\right) dy \qquad (2.36)$$

The occurrence of sin $\{k(x - ct)\}$ in both the terms in brackets in the integrand means that the average over the waves (wavelength or period) involves $\sin^2 \{k(x - ct)\}$ which gives $1/2$. Thus when (2.14) is used the mean power is found to be

$$P = \frac{1}{4} \rho a^2 gc \left\{1 + \frac{2kh}{\sinh 2kh}\right\} \qquad (2.37)$$

which simplifies for deep water ($h \to \infty$ and thus $\sinh 2kh \to \infty$) to

$$P = \frac{1}{4}\rho a^2 g c = \frac{\rho a^2 g^2 T}{8\pi} \tag{2.38}$$

watts per metre length along the wave crest.

This expression for power is valid for monochromatic waves found in many experimental wave tanks but requires some modification for real seas (see section 2.3).

2.1.6 Mass, Momentum and Energy Transfer by Standing Waves

A standing wave can be created by the summation of two progressive waves of equal amplitude but opposed directions of propagation, so that

$$\eta = \eta_1 + \eta_2 = a \sin(kx - \sigma t) + a \sin(kx + \sigma t)$$
$$= 2a \sin kx \cos \sigma t \tag{2.39}$$

Equation (2.39) represents a standing wave of twice the amplitude of the two constituent progressive waves. It therefore follows that there is no mass, momentum or energy transfer *averaged over the wave* for a standing wave.

There is however a reversing flow within a quarter wavelength either side of a node as indicated by the streamlines in Fig. 2.8.

There is also a force on an object placed vertically in the water, so as to cause a standing wave by complete reflection of an incident progressive wave. This force has a normal hydrostatic component and a periodic component and may be derived from the integration over the depth of the pressure derived from (2.8) neglecting the non-linear ($q^2/2$) term, that is,

$$p = -\rho g y - \rho \frac{\partial \phi}{\partial t} \tag{2.40}$$

Thus for a sea-wall, with the loop or antinode formed at the wall, integration over the wetted surface per unit width of wall gives the force

$$F = -\underbrace{\frac{2\rho g a}{k} \frac{\sinh k(y + \eta)}{\cosh kh} \sin \sigma t}_{\text{periodic component}} - \underbrace{\frac{\rho g}{2}(\eta^2 - h^2)}_{\substack{\text{hydrostatic} \\ \text{component}}} \tag{2.41}$$

To evaluate the forces on structures of finite geometry located in a progressive wave environment, reference should be made to Wiegel [138] (Chapter 11).

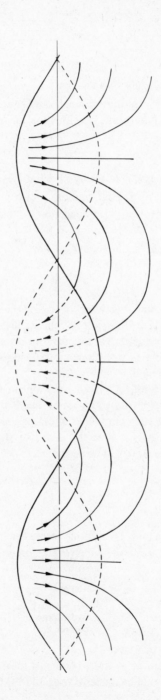

Fig. 2.8 – Streamlines below a standing wave.

2.2 RANGE OF APPLICABILITY OF THE LINEAR PROGRESSIVE WAVE THEORY

The linearised progressive wave theory summarised in section 2.1 was originally developed by Airy [1] (1845) and was limited to waves of small steepness (that is, small amplitude a compared with the wavelength L). The limits to this theory are shown in Fig. 2.9, which also shows the limit of wave steepness above

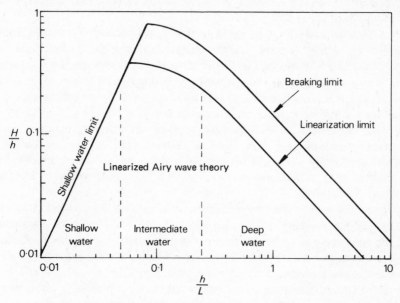

Fig. 2.9 – Range of applicability of linear progressive wave theory.

which the waves would 'break'. This breaking limit was derived by Miche [103] as

$$\left(\frac{H}{L}\right)_{breaking} = 0.140 \tanh\left(\frac{2\pi h}{L}\right) \tag{2.42}$$

and although Madsen [93] showed errors in this derivation, nevertheless the experiments of Danel [35] provided supporting evidence for this limit. Well before this breaking limit, however, the neglected non-linear terms in the Airy theory become significant. In the Bernoulli Equation (2.8) comparison of the kinetic energy term ($q^2/2$) with the potential energy term (gy) at the free surface suggests that it is necessary for

$$\frac{H}{L} \ll \frac{2}{\pi} \tanh\left(\frac{2\pi h}{L}\right) \tag{2.43}$$

If the error, which has only a small periodic ripple on an otherwise constant value, is limited to just below 10% then a convenient limit becomes

$$\frac{H}{L} \leqslant \frac{1}{16} \tanh\left(\frac{2\pi h}{L}\right) \qquad\qquad (2.44)$$

Under these conditions the error caused by neglecting the non-linear term in the kinematic boundary condition at the free surface (2.11) is fully periodic with an amplitude of about 20%.

A shallow water limit to the Airy theory, first defined by Stokes [130] requires that L^2H/h^3 is small. Longuet-Higgins [88] gave the limiting value as $32\pi^2/3$ and this is shown on Fig. 2.9. The steeper, shallow-water waves outside this limit are described as **Cnoidal waves** with sharp crests separated by wide troughs and eventually in even shallower water the waves become solitary waves. Even for the inshore wave-energy site to the west of the South Uist in Scotland for which wave data has recently been acquired and where the depth is 15 m, values of $h/L < 0.06$ are unlikely to be encountered. In the circumstances neither cnoidal nor solitary waves will be discussed in this book and readers are referred to standard texts on water waves such as by Stoker [129] and to papers by Laitone [79] and Munk [109].

It is also unlikely that waves between the limit of linearisation given by (2.44) and the 'breaking' limit (2.42) will frequently occur and again discussion of the wave theories applicable in this region is omitted from this book and readers referred to the report by Dean [38] in which a detailed evaluation of the various theories is presented. In wave-tank experiments this region is also affected by an instability identified by Benjamin and Feir [11]. In such cases, steep periodic waves generated in deep water lose their regular periodic shape after travelling 10 to 20 wavelengths down the tank. The wave form is then variable in both amplitude and period.

2.3 CHARACTERISTICS OF WAVES IN REAL SEAS

Although discussion so far has related to monochromatic waves, the real sea conditions create a whole spectrum of waves of different heights, periods and directions. This situation arises because waves, once created, dissipate very little energy and, unless they encounter head-winds, they continue over considerable distances (perhaps thousands of miles) for long times (perhaps several days). Any given location may therefore receive waves which have been generated at many different places by winds blowing in many different directions. Waves generated by distant storms are referred to as 'swell', whilst waves generated by relatively local winds acting over short distances ('fetches'), of around 100 km, are called 'sea', and have relatively short wavelengths compared with swell.

2.3.1 Wave Height Variations

A typical wave record is shown in Fig. 2.10 and for such a random variation,

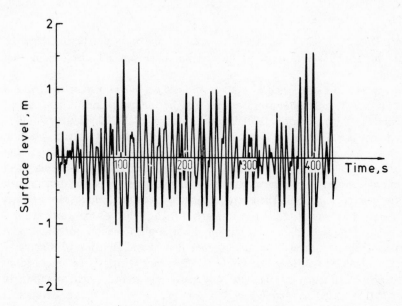

Fig. 2.10 – Wave height – time record. From
[42] by courtesy of HMSO and the DOE.

some form of statistical representation is required. A simple approach is to
define a representative wave height and a representative frequency or period.
Traditionally a 'significant height' was defined as the average height of the
highest one-third of the waves ($H_{1/3}$) with an associated 'significant period'
defined as the average period of those waves ($T_{1/3}$).

$H_{1/3}$ and $T_{1/3}$ are not now considered satisfactory and a more convenient
representation of the height is the root mean square value of the water level
relative to the mean water level (Dawson [37])

$$\sigma = \sqrt{\dfrac{\displaystyle\sum_{i=1}^{n} y_i^2}{n}} \tag{2.45}$$

where y_i is the water level at instant i relative to the mean water level. The
'significant height' H_S is then defined as

$$H_S = 4\sigma \tag{2.46}$$

A convenient period is the 'zero-crossing period' T_z defined as

$$T_z = \frac{D}{n_z} \tag{2.47}$$

where D = duration of the record in seconds, and n_z = number of times the water surface moves through its mean level in an upward direction in that duration.

However this simple representation of a real sea by two parameters (H_S and T_z) is not really adequate, because there may be wide variations in both height and period, which are not indicated by these average values. Longuet-Higgins [87] has shown the relationship between the various wave height statistics, such as H_{max} and $H_{r.m.s.}$, for waves within a narrow frequency band. Cartwright and Longuet-Higgins [20] have extended these comparisons to any frequency band width, whilst Putz [118] has produced curves relating wave period distributions to the mean wave periods. These relationships between the various wave statistics are reported by Wiegel [138] and Komar [76]. The height of the waves in a real sea is an example of data for a random physical phenomenon, for which each particular observation will be unique. (See Bendat and Piersol [10], Chapter 1 for a complete discussion). Therefore the data cannot strictly be described by an explicit mathematical relation. Any particular record, such as shown in Fig. 2.10 is called a 'sample function' (or 'sample record', if the duration is finite). The collection of sample functions is called the 'ensemble'. If the mean value (and the autocorrelation function) of the random process can be computed at time t_1 by taking the mean value of each sample function of the ensemble, the process is said to be stationary. Furthermore, if the ensemble average is also equal to the time-averaged value for individual specific sample functions of the ensemble, the process is said to be 'ergodic'. It is usually assumed that wave records are stationary and ergodic, so that meaningful values can be obtained from single records. With such an assumption, the best representation of a real sea is by means of the 'power spectral density function' $S(f)$ defined as

$$S(f) = \lim_{\Delta f \to 0} \lim_{T \to 0} \frac{1}{(\Delta f)T} \int_0^T y^2(t, f, \Delta f) \, dt \tag{2.48}$$

where the function is defined for a small frequency interval Δf at frequency f. The function $S(f)$ may be measured by suitable filtering of the electrical analogue signal, using band-pass filters with sharp cut-off characteristics, or it may be evaluated from the autocorrelation function by means of a Fourier transform (see [10], page 22, with alternative notation $G_x(f)$).

If $y(t)$ is measured from an arbitrary datum $S(f)$ will exist at $f = 0$ and there will be a static component or mean value of $y(t)$. However, if $y(t)$ is measured relative to the mean value, then the mean square value of $y(t)$ is given by

$$\sigma^2 = \int_0^\infty S(f)\,\mathrm{d}f \tag{2.49}$$

The spectrum derived from Fig. 2.10 is shown in Fig. 2.11 as a plot of

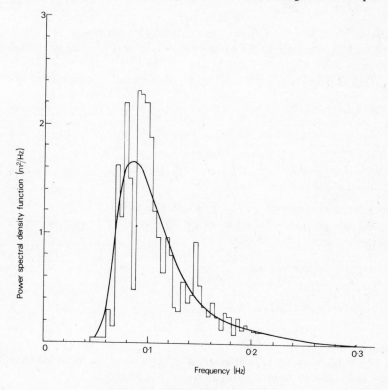

Fig. 2.11 – Power Spectrum. From [42]
by courtesy of HMSO and the DOE.

$S(f)$ against f. Inspection of (2.48) indicates that the dimensions of $S(f)$ are (length)^2/frequency (for example, m^2/Hz). Using a computer and digitised wave data other representative quantities can be evaluated from Fig. 2.10 by defining spectral moments

$$M_n = \int_0^\infty f^n S(f)\,\mathrm{d}f \tag{2.50}$$

where M_n is the nth spectral moment taken about the vertical axis ($f = 0$). Thus when $n = 0$, $M_0 = \sigma^2$ and hence the 'significant wave height' from (2.46) is

$$H_S = 4\sigma = 4\sqrt{M_0} \tag{2.51}$$

when $n = 2$, the dimensions of M_2 are (length)^2 $\times$ (frequency)^2 or (length/period)^2. Thus a mean zero crossing period can be defined by

$$T_z = \sqrt{M_0/M_2} \tag{2.52}$$

when $n = -1$, the dimensions of M_{-1} are (length)^2/frequency or (length)^2 $\times$ period which when multiplied by the dimensions of ρg^2 would give power per unit width of wave, as seen from (2.38).

Thus an 'energy period' (or strictly a 'power period') can be defined as

$$T_e = M_{-1}/M_0 \tag{2.53}$$

The power per unit width of wave, from (2.38), may be written as

$$P = \frac{\rho g^2}{8\pi}a^2 T = \frac{\rho g^2}{4\pi}\sigma^2 T = \frac{\rho g^2}{64\pi}H_S^2 T_e \tag{2.54}$$

(since the mean square $\sigma^2 = a^2/2$ for a simple sine wave).

For a typical density of sea water $\rho = 1025$ kg/m^3, the power per unit width of wave becomes

$$P = 490.6\,H_S^2 T_e \ \ [\text{W/m}] \tag{2.55}$$

For most seas $T_e \sim 1.12\,T_z$ so that

$$P = 549.5\,H_S^2 T_z \ \ [\text{W/m}] \tag{2.56}$$

Although obvious, experimenters with fresh water are reminded to reduce these values for the normal density of water ($\rho = 1000$kg/m^3).

2.3.2 Directional Variations

Longuet-Higgins *et al.* [90] studied the directional characteristics of some 1955/56 wave records from west of Portugal and south west of Ireland, and concluded that the angular distribution was best represented by a cosine-power law. Mitsuyasu *et al.* [105] analysed the wave data from records taken in 1971 and 1973 in Japanese waters, in both the open sea and a bay, and modified the one-dimensional wave spectrum by this cosine-power law to give a directional spectrum. Dawson [37] has described this modifying factor as the 'spreading function', which distributes the energy at each frequency over a range of directions. A typical function is given as

$$f(\theta) = \cos^S \left\{ \frac{1}{2}(\theta - \theta_o) \right\} \tag{2.57}$$

where $S = 15.85 \, (f/fo)^5$ for $f \leqslant fo$; $S = 15.85 \, (fo/f)^{2.5}$ for $f > fo$;
fo = spectral peak frequency; θ_o = principal wave direction.

This method is applicable to a single peak power spectrum (as shown in Fig. 2.11) and must be modified as suggested by Dawson [37] for the double-peaked spectrum typical of the sea off South Uist.

The directional variations of the waves are most easily described by means of a 'directionality factor'. In Fig. 2.12, the power $p(\theta)$ crossing a vertical cylindrical surface of one metre diameter in the sea is shown to vary with angle θ.

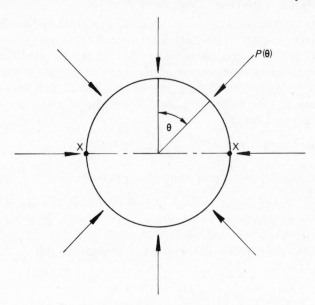

Fig. 2.12 – Directionality of power transfer.

The total power transmitted across the cylindrical boundary is

$$p = \int_{-\pi}^{+\pi} p(\theta) \, d\theta \quad [\text{W/m}] \tag{2.58}$$

whilst the power transmitted across a diameter (XX) in one direction ($\theta = 0$)

$$p_o = \int_{-\pi/2}^{+\pi/2} p(\theta) \cos \theta \, d\theta \quad [\text{W/m}] \tag{2.59}$$

The directionality factor δ is then defined as

$$\delta = \frac{p_0}{p} \qquad\qquad (2.60)$$

Winter [142] has suggested typical values of the directionality factor for the UK as follows:

north-west coast ~ 0.8
south-west coast ~ 0.7
north-east coast ~ 0.45

2.3.3 Prediction of the Power Spectrum

Using dimensional analysis, Pierson and Moskowitz [115] plotted the data for the spectrums of fully developed wind seas as the dimensionless power spectrum $S(f)\, g^3/U^5$ against dimensionless frequency Uf/g. As the wind speed U was actually measured by anemometers on the weather ships at 19.6m above the surface, so the resultant prediction must be used with care, as wind speeds are usually given at 10m above the surface. The predicted power spectral density function can be written as

$$S(f) = (5 \times 10^{-4})f^{-5} \exp{(-4.4/f^4 U^4)} \ [\text{m}^2/\text{Hz}] \qquad (2.61\text{a})$$

where f = frequency in Hz; U = wind speed at 19.6 m in m/s.

This prediction applies to 'seas' created by a wind blowing in a constant direction for sufficient time for the waves to have ceased to grow and would not apply to a mixture of 'sea' and 'swell'.

For wave power studies Glendenning [60] suggests that it is more convenient to express (2.60) as

$$S(f) = Af^{-5} \exp{(-Bf^{-4})} \qquad\qquad (2.61\text{b})$$

where $A = H_S^2/4\pi T_z^4$ and $B = 1/\pi T_z^4$.

2.4 METHODS OF WAVE MEASUREMENT AND ANALYSIS AND PRESENTATION OF RESULTS

2.4.1 Measurement

The Institute of Oceanographic Sciences make the wave measurements in UK waters and employ both shipborne wave recorders and Waverider buoys (Crabb [29]). An accelerometer is used to measure the vertical acceleration of the ship or buoy and an electronic integrator performs the double integration necessary to obtain the vertical displacement. The buoys which are spheres of 0.7m diameter, also contain telemetry equipment for transmission of the digitised data

to a nearby fixed or floating receiving station, by a VHF radio link. Typically, data is acquired every 0.5s, for a period of 1044s, every three hours, and is transmitted over distances between 25km and 50km depending on the sensitivity of the aerial arrangement.

Directional measurements have been made by a buoy equipped with sensors which respond to pitch and roll angles as well as heave (Longuet-Higgins *et al.* [90]). UK Data Buoy 1 now installed about 300km WSW of Land's End provides pitch-roll-heave information without an attendant parent ship. New techniques being developed include viewing the surface by means of an airborne radar system, or a satellite system. To be selective such systems may have to operate at wavelengths of the same order as the gravity waves of interest, in order to eliminate the effects of the short (centimetre) capilliary waves which are also usually present.

2.4.2 Analysis and Presentation

The 'power spectral density function' (see section 2.3) is calculated for each of the records of wave height against time, using a fast Fourier transform routine, and then the various spectral moments are calculated to obtain:

the significant wave height H_S
the zero-crossing period T_z
the energy period T_e

The data is usually collected and analysed for at least a year to obtain reliable characteristics. With records taken every three hours, nearly 3000 values are obtained and these are usually plotted as the number of occurrences in parts per thousand of H_S in half-metre intervals against T_e in half-second intervals, as shown in Fig. 2.13. This diagram is called a 'scatter diagram' and also shows contours of constant power per unit length of crest, ranging from less than 10kW/m to more than 300kW/m.

Directional data can be presented either as a directionality factor ((2.58), (2.59) and (2.60)) or as a histogram of number of occurrences per $10°$ interval, as shown in Fig. 2.14 (Crabb and Fortnum [30]).

2.5 WAVE DATA COLLECTION AND ESTIMATED POWER AVAILABLE

Initial wave measurements were made at Ocean Weather Ship *India*, 710 km west of the Outer Hebrides. From this data Leishman and Scobie [81] calculated an annual mean power intensity of 80kW/m.

In 1976, the Institute of Oceanographic Sciences installed a waverider buoy 16km west of South Uist in 42m of water. Subsequent analysis of this data suggested an annual mean power intensity of 48kW/m with approximately 2/3 of this power attributable to 'swell', which had a predominant west to east

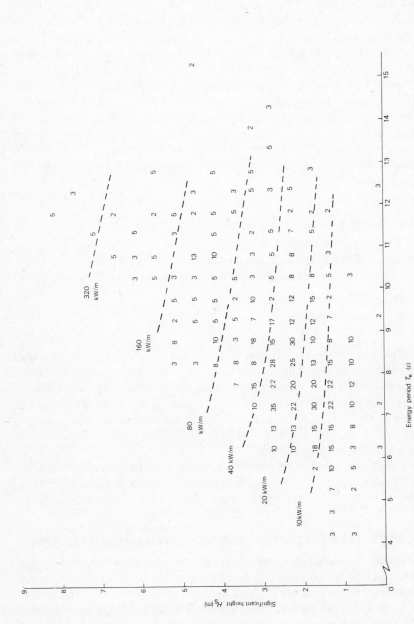

Fig. 2.13 — Scatter diagram for South Uist during year 1976–77 (occurrence in parts per 1000). From [42] by courtesy of HMSO and the DOE.

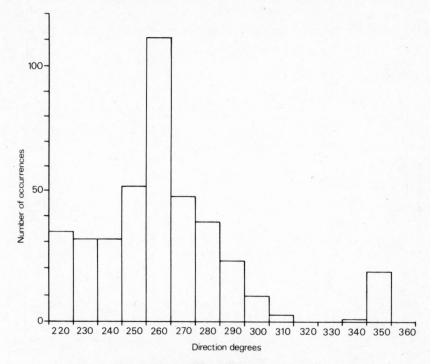

Fig. 2.14 – Distribution of selected set swell directions. From [30] by
courtesy of J. A. Crabb and B. C. H. Fortnum (work funded by DOE).

direction (Crabb [29]). In 1978 a second buoy was installed 5 km west of South
Uist in 15 m of water and initial results indicated a reduction in mean power
intensity to about 20kW/m.

At the location 16 km offshore, the power available to a directionally sensitive
device would be reduced by the directionality factor to about 40kW/m and if
the capture efficiency of the device was only 50% and the power transmission
efficiency was also 50%, then about 10kW/m would eventually be delivered to
shore. Thus if wave power devices were located, with suitable gaps for shipping,
between Islay and Shetland, over a catchment length of 600km, then 6GW
would be delivered ashore, thus providing more than 20% of the total UK
demand at the present time.

Capture efficiency and transmission efficiency will be dealt with in Chapters
3 and 4. It is however pertinent to reiterate here that there is an interaction
between point absorbers in a row, as demonstrated analytically by Budal [16]
and proved exprimentally by Budal *et al.* [18]. The interaction factor q, defined
as the maximum power absorption with interaction divided by the maximum
power absorption of an isolated buoy, increases linearly with the ratio of the
spacing of the buoys to wavelength (d/L) up to $q = \pi$ as d/L approaches unity,

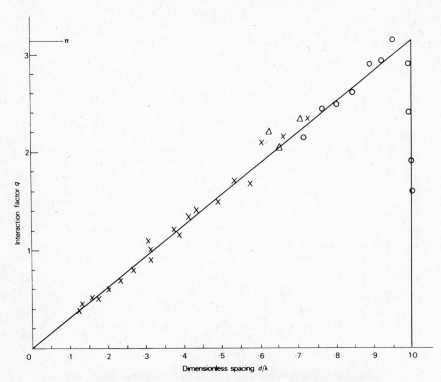

Fig. 2.15 – Interaction factor as function of buoy spacing.
From [18] by courtesy of The Group of Wave Energy Research,
Chalmers University of Technology, Gothenburg.

as shown in Fig. 2.15. Since it is also theoretically possible for a single point absorber, operating under optimised conditions, to absorb power equal to that contained in a wave frontage of $L/2\pi$ (where L is the wavelength) then it follows that a single row of interacting point absorbers can capture power over a frontage of $L/2$ or $d/2$ (since $L/d = 1$ when $q = \pi$), even though the spacing is nearly seven times the diameter of the buoys. When a reflector is placed behind the row of buoys, the capture efficiency theoretically becomes 100%.

CHAPTER 3

Wave energy conversion to mechanical energy

The primary conversion process may be considered as that which produces the mechanical energy of relative motion of solid body mechanisms from the energy of the waves. This chapter will deal with such processes. Utilisation of this mechanical energy, including secondary conversion to electrical energy or chemical energy, will be discussed in Chapter 4.

3.1 INTERACTION BETWEEN WAVES AND ENERGY ABSORBING DEVICES

As well as the physical properties of water waves, presented in Chapter 2, it is important to consider the motion of wave energy converters and also *their interaction* with the waves. These interactions are complex and command the attention of applied mathematicians, especially as the motion of a floating body as a function of time involves a 'convolution integral', which describes the continuing influence of previous body motions on the present motion. (Count [28], Evans [52], and Jefferys [74]). However, for simple harmonic motions at the fundamental frequency there are simpler solutions which are appropriate to this text. These solutions will be presented in this chapter, but as necessary, reference will be made to more advanced analysis and the underlying principles and main conclusions described. The designer of a wave energy converter must certainly be aware of these theoretical conclusions, which have generally been verified by experiment, as enhanced performance of the converter beyond that predicted by the simpler theory can frequently be expected.

3.2 RESPONSE OF DEVICES TO INCIDENT WAVES

The motion of a wave energy device and the fluid which may be within it obviously both depend on the amplitude and period (or angular frequency ω) of the incident wave, which produce a periodic disturbing force of the form

$F \cos \omega t$ (or $\mathrm{Re}.F \exp(i\omega t)^{\dagger}$). The motion (Fig. 3.1) will also be controlled by

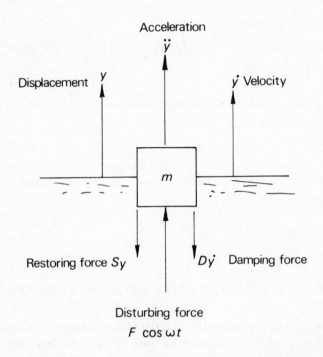

Fig. 3.1 — Forces acting on a wave energy device.

a restoring force, produced by changing buoyancy and proportional to the displacement, and by a damping force caused by friction, energy extraction, and radiation (see later). This force is generally assumed to be linearly related to the velocity of motion of the device or the fluid.

Under the action of these forces, the device or the fluid will be accelerated (and decelerated) and the classical equation for forced, damped oscillation is obtained as follows:

---

† $\mathrm{Re}.F \exp(i\omega t)$ indicates the real part of $F \exp(i\omega t)$ and is more easily manipulated than the trigonometric form.

   Now a complex number $z = x + iy$ can be represented in polar form $z = r(\cos\theta + i\sin\theta)$ with the modulus of $z = |z| = r = \sqrt{x^2 + y^2}$ and the argument of $z = \theta = \tan^{-1}(y/x)$. Thus $z = |z|\exp(i\theta)$ since $(\cos\theta + i\sin\theta) = \exp(i\theta)$. If F is complex, then $F = |F|\exp(i\theta)$ where $\theta = \arg F$. Thus $\mathrm{Re}.F\exp(i\omega t) = \mathrm{Re}|F|\exp[i(\omega t + \theta)] = |F|\cos(\omega t + \theta)$.

$$F \cos \omega t - D\dot{y} - Sy = m\ddot{y} \qquad (3.1)$$

applied   damping restoring   mass × acceleration
force   force   force

opposing applied
force

Hence

$$m\ddot{y} + D\dot{y} + Sy = F \cos \omega t \text{ or } \operatorname{Re}.F \exp(i\omega t) \qquad (3.2)$$

Before solving (3.2), it is worthwhile to simplify the problem by considering natural, undamped oscillation for which $D = F = 0$.
Thus

$$m\ddot{y} + Sy = 0 \qquad (3.3)$$

The fact that the two terms on the left hand side must cancel suggests a solution of the form $y = \cos \omega_0 t$ or $y = A \exp(i\omega_0 t)$ so that (3.3) becomes

$$mA(i\omega_0)^2 \exp(i\omega_0 t) + SA \exp(i\omega_0 t) = 0$$

or

$$-m\omega_0^2 + S = 0$$

or

$$\omega_0 = \sqrt{\frac{S}{m}} \qquad (3.4)$$

where ω_0 is referred to as the natural or resonant angular frequency.

Upon reintroducing the damping term, the solution for y must be such as to equate the left hand side of (3.2) to $F \cos \omega t$, but may also include terms which satisfy

$$m\ddot{y} + D\dot{y} + Sy = 0 \qquad (3.5)$$

Again an exponential solution of the form $y = A \exp(\alpha t)$ is apparent, although α may now be real or imaginary, positive or negative. Thus, upon inserting y and its differentials in (3.5) and cancelling $A \exp(\alpha t)$ throughout

$$m\alpha^2 + D\alpha + S = 0 \qquad (3.6)$$

so that

$$\alpha = \frac{-D \pm \sqrt{D^2 - 4mS}}{2m} \qquad (3.7)$$

Unless $D^2 - 4mS < 0$, α is real and negative and the displacement decreases to zero asymptotically with time without periodic motion. This overdamped situation is not relevant to wave energy devices and so the solution of interest is

$$y = \exp(-Dt/2m)[A_1 \exp(i\omega_d t) + A_2 \exp(-i\omega_d t)] \qquad (3.8)$$

where

$$\omega_d = \sqrt{\frac{S}{m} - \frac{D^2}{4m^2}} \tag{3.9}$$

Putting $A_1 = A(\cos\delta + \sin\delta)/2$ and $A_2 = A(\cos\delta - \sin\delta)/2$ in (3.8) gives

$$y = \exp(-Dt/2m)\, A\,[(\cos\delta + \sin\delta)\exp(i\omega_d t)/2$$
$$+ (\cos\delta - \sin\delta)\exp(-i\omega_d t)/2]$$

or

$$y = A\exp(-Dt/2m)\,[\cos\delta\,\cos\omega_d t + \sin\delta\,\sin\omega_d t]$$

or

$$y = A\exp(-Dt/2m)\cos(\omega_d t - \delta) \tag{3.10}$$

Finally to satisfy the right-hand side of (3.2) a solution involving the disturbing frequency ω must be expected of the form

$$y = B\exp(i\omega t) \tag{3.11}$$

Substitution of y and its derivatives in (3.2) then gives

$$-m\omega^2 B + iD\omega B + SB = F \tag{3.12}$$

So that

$$B = \frac{F}{(S - m\omega^2) + iD\omega} \tag{3.13}$$

Again using the properties of complex numbers (see footnote on page 84) the denominator can be written as

$$\{\sqrt{(S - m\omega^2)^2 + D^2\omega^2}\}\exp(i\alpha) \tag{3.14}$$

where

$$\alpha = \tan^{-1}\{D\omega/(S - m\omega^2)\} \tag{3.15}$$

So that if F is complex $F = |F|\exp(i\theta)$ and

$$y = \frac{|F|\exp(i\theta)\exp(-i\alpha)}{\sqrt{(S - m\omega^2)^2 + D^2 m^2}}\exp(i\omega t) = \frac{|F|\exp[i(\omega t + \epsilon)]}{\sqrt{(S - m\omega^2)^2 + D^2\omega^2}} \tag{3.16}$$

where $\epsilon = (\theta - \alpha)$.

Because of the exponential decay with time t in (3.10) that part of the solution soon becomes negligible and hence (3.16) becomes the significant solution.

The oscillatory motion of buoys and other floating devices will be governed by an equation of the form of (3.2), whilst the oscillatory motion of water columns within various devices will also be governed by a similar equation. The solution given by (3.15) and (3.16) will therefore be used extensively in subsequent analysis of the behaviour of various wave energy converters. However, the

coefficients of (3.2) and the magnitude of the force F each require special consideration, and mostly depend upon some form of experimental evaluation.

3.2.1 Evaluation of Coefficients in the Equation of Motion

Fortunately the restoring force coefficient S is readily determined as the change in buoyancy force per unit vertical movement. Fig. 3.2 shows a cylindrical-

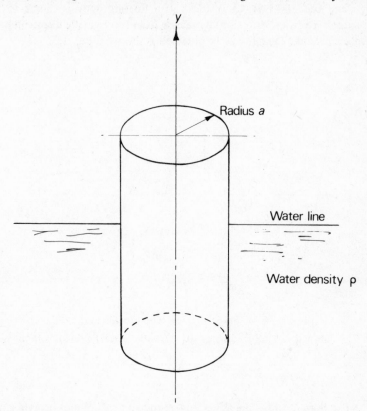

Fig. 3.2 – Cylindrical shaped floating body.

shaped floating body with a horizontal cross-section area

$$A = \pi a^2$$

For a vertical displacement y the change in buoyancy force is $\rho g(Ay)$ and so the restoring force coefficient

$$S = \rho g A = \rho g \pi a^2 \tag{3.17}$$

Obviously the area A must be modified for other water-line cross sections and the linearity of (3.2) would be destroyed if this area was a function of y.

To evaluate the mass m to be used in (3.2) and subsequent equations, the mass of the floating body must be augmented by a mass of water which is influenced by the motion of the body. This so-called 'added mass' has been predicted by hydrodynamic theory and is related by an 'added-mass' coefficient to the mass of water displaced by the body. The total equivalent mass can also be found, together with the damping coefficient D, from free vibration experiments and use of (3.5), (3.7), (3.9). If a floating body is caused to 'heave' (oscillate in a vertical direction) by release from an originally displaced position, a displacement-time graph may be obtained as shown in Fig. 3.3.

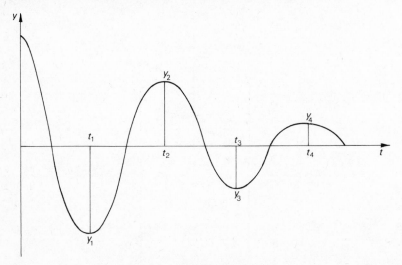

Fig. 3.3 – Displacement-time graph.

The damped natural frequency ω_d can then be determined from the observed period $T = t_3 - t_1$ as

$$\omega_d = 2\pi/(t_3 - t_1) \tag{3.18}$$

Since both D and m are as yet undetermined (3.9) cannot be used alone and (3.10) must be used together with the measurements of y_1 and y_3. Thus,

$$\frac{y_1}{y_3} = \frac{\exp(-Dt_1/2m)}{\exp(-Dt_3/2m)} = \exp[D(t_3 - t_1)/2m] = \exp(2\pi D/2m\omega_d) \tag{3.19}$$

For convenience, the damping ratio Δ is introduced and defined as the ratio of the actual damping coefficient D to the critical damping coefficient when $\omega_d = 0$ and $D = 2\sqrt{mS}$ from (3.9). Thus,

$$\Delta = \frac{D}{2\sqrt{mS}} = \frac{D}{2m\sqrt{S/m}} = \frac{D}{2m\omega_o} \tag{3.20}$$

from (3.4) and (3.19) becomes

$$y_1/y_3 = \exp(2\pi\Delta\omega_o/\omega_d) \tag{3.21}$$

But (3.9) may now be written as

or
$$\omega_d = \sqrt{S/m}\sqrt{1-D^2/4mS}$$
$$\omega_d = \omega_o\sqrt{1-\Delta^2} \tag{3.22}$$

and (3.21) becomes

$$y_1/y_3 = \exp(2\pi\Delta/\sqrt{1-\Delta^2}) \tag{3.23}$$

Thus from the measurements y_1 and y_3, Δ is found from the rearranged (3.23)

$$\frac{2\pi\Delta}{\sqrt{1-\Delta^2}} = ln\left(\frac{y_1}{y_3}\right)$$

or
$$\Delta = \frac{ln(y_1/y_3)}{\sqrt{4\pi^2 + (ln\,y_1/y_3)^2}} \tag{3.24}$$

With ω_d already determined from (3.18), ω_o can now be found from (3.22) and hence m from the rearranged (3.4) $m = S/\omega_o^2$. Since Δ is usually small ($\Delta^2 \ll 1$), it is frequently adequate to assume that $\omega_o = \omega_d$ and evaluate m directly from (3.4).

Values for added mass have been determined by Lewis [82], Lamb [80] and Havelock [69] for rectangular shapes, cylinders and spheres respectively, whilst Bhattacharyya [13] has reported results for ship sections. An 'added-mass coefficient' C is frequently defined as:

$$C = \frac{\text{added mass}}{\text{mass of water displaced by a semi circular section with a diameter}}$$
equal to the beam of the object and with the same length

This definition is best illustrated by Fig. 3.4 whilst Havelock's definition of a 'virtual inertia coefficient' k is also illustrated. The coefficient is a function of the geometry of the body and the dimensionless angular frequency $\omega^2 a/g$ where a is an appropriate linear dimension (for example, radius for a cylinder or sphere, beam or half-beam for a ship or rectangular object). Budal and Falnes [17] have demonstrated that the added mass is affected by the interaction between an array of floating bodies. Typical values of added mass coefficient are given in Fig. 3.5, with neither Lewis nor Lamb giving a frequency dependence.

The damping coefficient D, as stated in the first paragraph of section 3.2, depends upon friction, energy extraction and radiation. The friction component D_f caused by fluid viscosity represents a loss of power, but is frequently relatively insignificant. The energy extraction (or applied) damping coefficient D_e is such that the work producing force is $D_e \dot{y}$ and the instantaneous work rate or power is $(D_e \dot{y})\dot{y}$ which is obviously significant. Radiation damping coefficient D_r is related to surface waves which are produced when a body is caused to oscillate at the surface of the fluid. These waves are produced by the alternating displacement volume of the body and also by friction and surface tension. Havelock [69] has shown that the radiation resistance coefficient D_r (kg/s) for an isolated sphere of radius a, floating half-immersed in water is

$$D_r = \frac{2}{3}\pi a^3 \rho \omega \epsilon \qquad (3.25)$$

where $\epsilon = \epsilon(\omega^2 a/g)$.

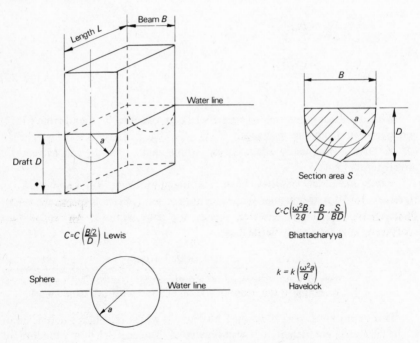

Added mass $= C \times$ Mass of water displaced by half-cylinder
$= C \times \frac{1}{2}\rho\pi a^2 L$
or $= k \times$ Mass of water displaced by hemisphere
$= k \times (\frac{2}{3}\rho\pi a^3)$

Fig. 3.4 — Definition of added mass coefficient.

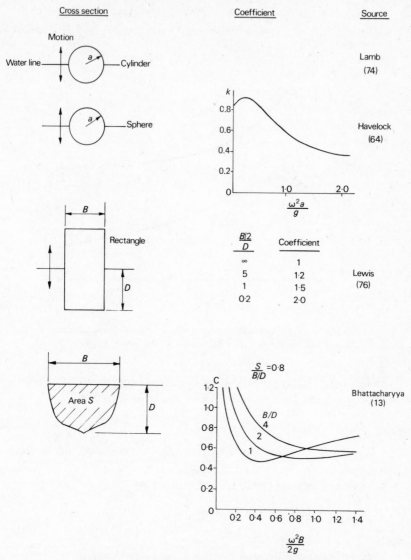

Fig. 3.5 — Added-mass coefficients for heave motion.

ϵ is shown to rise to a maximum value of 0.35 at $\omega^2 a/g = 0.4$ and then fall to 0.11 at $\omega^2 a/g = 2.0$ as shown in Fig. 3.6.

Budal *et al.* [18] propose that the above expression is modified by the factor $\exp(-2kl)$ in the case of a vertical cylinder with a hemispherical bottom and submerged to a cylinder depth l.

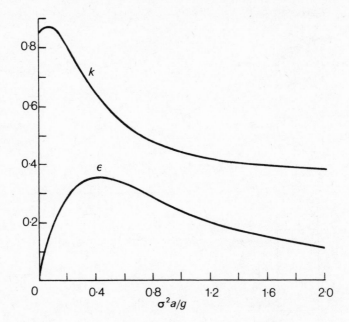

Fig. 3.6 – Variation of virtual inertia coefficient k and damping parameter $2h$ with frequency. From [69] by courtesy of The Royal Society.

Ambli *et al.* [3] have shown that for an array of buoys the radiation resistance coefficient is reduced because of the interaction factor q so that

$$D_{r_{n,\gamma}} = D_{r_1}/q \tag{3.26}$$

where $D_{r_{n,\gamma}}$ = the radiation resistance coefficient for n bodies, with interspaces d, and aligned at angle γ to the incoming wave crests.

For $n \to \infty$, $\gamma = 0$ and $kd < 2\pi$, $q = kd/2$ so that

$$D_{r_{\infty,0}} = D_{r_1}/(kd/2) = D_{r_1}/(\pi d/L) \tag{3.27}$$

for $d < L$.

Thus the radiation resistance coefficient can be estimated from the geometry of the body, the dimensionless angular frequency and in case of an array of devices, from the spacing and alignment of the array to the wave crests.

The energy extraction damping coefficient depends on the instantaneous power loading and can be controlled by the designer of the device. For example a turbine can provide a severe throttling action or can be designed to give a lighter load. Thus the energy extraction damping coefficient D_e can be varied in relation to the sum D_L of the 'loss' coefficients $D_f + D_r$ and a suitable optimum performance condition evaluated.

The instantaneous damping force due to energy extraction $= D_e \dot{y}$ so that the instantaneous energy extraction rate $= D_e \dot{y}^2$. But from (3.16)

$$y = C \cos(\omega t + \epsilon) \tag{3.28}$$

where

$$C = |F| / \sqrt{(S - m\omega^2)^2 + D^2 \omega^2} \tag{3.29}$$

and

$$D = D_e + D_f + D_r = D_e + D_L \tag{3.30}$$

Differentiating (3.28) gives

$$\dot{y} = -C\omega \sin(\omega t + \epsilon) \tag{3.31}$$

Therefore the instantaneous energy extraction rate or power

$$= D_e \dot{y}^2 = D_e C^2 \omega^2 \sin^2(\omega t + \epsilon) \tag{3.32}$$

Hence the mean power $= \overline{D_e \dot{y}^2} = D_e C^2 \omega^2 \overline{\sin^2(\omega t + \epsilon)} \tag{3.33}$

where the overbar represents the average over a period. Now the mean square of a sine wave over a period is $1/2$, and hence the mean power is

$$\bar{P} = D_e C^2 \omega^2 / 2 = \frac{D_e |F|^2 \omega^2 / 2}{(S - m\omega^2)^2 + (D_e + D_L)^2 \omega^2} \tag{3.34}$$

Since $\bar{P} = \bar{P}(D_e, \omega)$ the maximum power is obtained when (i) $\partial \bar{P} / \partial D_e = 0$ and (ii) $\partial \bar{P} / \partial \omega = 0$.

(i) gives

$$[(S - m\omega^2)^2 + (D_e + D_L)^2 \omega^2] |F|^2 \omega^2 / 2$$

$$= D_e |F|^2 \omega^2 [2(D_e + D_L)\omega^2] / 2$$

or

$$(S - m\omega^2)^2 + (D_e + D_L)^2 \omega^2 = 2 D_e (D_e + D_L) \omega^2 \tag{3.35}$$

(ii) gives

$$[(S - m\omega^2)^2 + (D_e + D_L)^2 \omega^2] D_e |F|^2 \omega$$

$$= D_e |F|^2 \omega^2 [2(S - m\omega^2)(-2m\omega) + 2(D_e + D_L)^2 \omega] / 2$$

or

$$(S - m\omega^2)^2 = -2m\omega^2 (S - m\omega^2) \tag{3.36}$$

Thus

$$\omega^2 = \pm S/m \tag{3.37}$$

If $\omega^2 = -S/m$, then $\omega = i\sqrt{S/m}$ and hence $\exp(i\omega t) = \exp(-\sqrt{S/m}\,t)$. Thus the solution (3.16) for y results in an overdamped behaviour, which is of little interest. Hence $\omega^2 = +S/m$ is one condition for maximum power.

Putting this value into (3.35) gives either

$$D_e + D_L = 0 \quad \text{or} \quad D_e + D_L = 2D_e$$

The first solution which implies either D_e or D_L negative is unrealistic whilst the second solution gives $D_e = D_L$.

Thus the conditions for maximum power demand that the undamped natural frequency be matched to the forcing frequency of the waves ($\omega = \sqrt{S/m} = \omega_0$) and that the energy extraction damping coefficient D_e be equal to the sum D_L of the friction D_f and radiation D_r damping coefficients.

Substituting these conditions into (3.34) gives

$$\bar{P}_{max} = |F|^2/8D_L \tag{3.38}$$

Showing that the maximum mean power depends directly on the square of the amplitude of the forcing effect and inversely on the loss coefficient D_L. This implies that the designer should pay particular attention to the radiation and friction losses. It also suggests that the forcing effect amplitude should be considered.

3.2.2 Evaluation of the Forcing-Effect Amplitude

Figure 3.7 illustrates three wave energy devices for which the present analysis is relevant. These are buoys with controlled motion developed in Norway by Budal and Falnes, the oscillating water column of Masuda (Japan) and the National Engineering Laboratory (UK) and the submerged oscillating water column

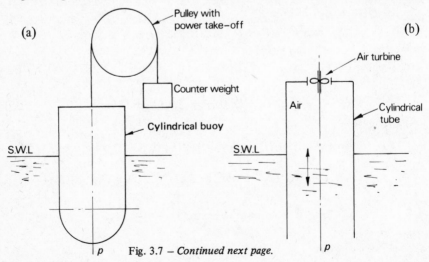

Fig. 3.7 – *Continued next page.*

S.W.L

(c)

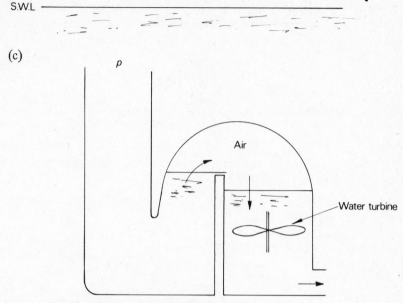

Fig. 3.7 — Three types of wave energy converter.
(a) Buoy-type energy converter.
(b) Oscillating water column.
(c) Submerged oscillating water column.

developed by Vickers in the UK. The force acting on the device is determined from the pressure p of the water surrounding the device (Fig. 3.7(a)) or at the open 'mouth' of the device (Figs. 3.7(b) and 3.7(c)). If the interaction of the incident waves and the device is neglected, the so-called 'Froude-Krylov' hypothesis, then the pressure may easily be evaluated from the linearised progressive wave theory presented in Chapter 2. Even with this simplifying assumption, the pressure may vary significantly across the device in the direction of wave propagation at any instant and the integrated (or mean) effect across the device will be less than the maximum. If the device is circular, as in Fig. 3.7, then the integration over the circle of the force due to the pressure, which varies sinusoidally along a diameter (Fig. 3.8) is

$$F = \int_0^R \int_{-\pi}^{+\pi} \rho g a \exp{(ky)} \sin{\{k(x-ct)\}} r \, dr \, d\theta \tag{3.39}$$

with $x = r \cos \theta$.

$$F = \int_0^R \int_{-\pi}^{+\pi} \rho g a \exp{(ky)} \sin{\{kr \cos \theta - \omega t\}} r \, dr \, d\theta \tag{3.40}$$

where $\omega = kc$.

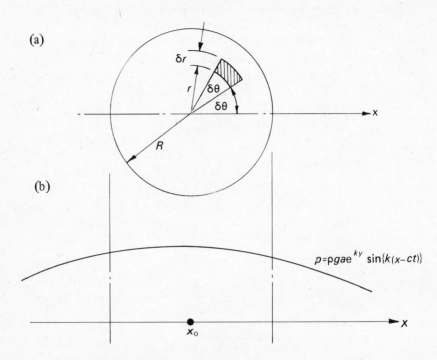

Fig. 3.8 – Variation of pressure across a device of circular plan.
(a) Circular device.
(b) Pressure variation due to waves in deep water at time t such
that $\sin\{k(x - ct)\} = 1$ at x_0.

To integrate $\sin\{kr\cos\theta - \omega t\}$ with respect to θ, it is necessary to expand
the sine as a series in powers of $kr\cos\theta$ and integrate term by term. The result,
with the limits $\pm\pi$, involves a series in powers of kr, which must then be multiplied
by r and integrated with respect to r. The final result, as shown by McCormick
[97], involves a series, which is conventionally defined as a Bessel function of the
first kind of order one.

Conveniently the resultant force can be written

$$F = [\rho g a \exp(ky)](\pi R^2)\left[1 - \frac{1}{2}\left(\frac{\pi R}{L}\right)^2 + \frac{1}{12}\left(\frac{\pi R}{L}\right)^4 - \ldots + \ldots\right]\sin\omega t$$

$$(3.41)$$

which obviously reduces, when $R \ll L$, to

$$F = [\rho g a \exp(ky)](\pi R^2)\sin\omega t \qquad\qquad (3.42)$$

magnitude of	area	periodic
dynamic	of	variation
pressure at	device	
device centreline		

When $R = L/10$ the second term in (3.41) is -0.049 whilst the third term is $+0.0008$, so that an error of less than 5% results from the use of (3.42), which would be adequate for most purposes.

Several authors have now reported analyses which account for the interaction between the device and the incident waves. Newman [111] was concerned with the determination of exciting forces on a ship in waves and his results are applicable to the buoy-type converter of Fig. 3.7(a). When a wave is incident on a rigid body it may be diffracted and a new wave system developed. Furthermore if the body is caused to oscillate, then it will 'radiate' waves and this radiation can be caused by the three linear body motions of surge, sway and heave and by the three angular motions of roll, pitch and yaw as defined in Fig. 3.9.

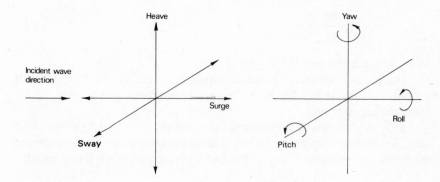

Fig. 3.9 – The linear motions of surge, sway and heave and angular motions of roll, pitch and yaw. Where other authors use different terminology this will be indicated in the text.

Newman defined velocity potentials $\phi_j(x, y, z)$ for each wave component

$j = 0$ for incident wave
$j = 1 \rightarrow 6$ for radiated waves due to surge, sway, heave, roll,
          pitch and yaw respectively
$j = 7$ for the diffracted wave.

He then considered the two independent problems of diffraction and radiation. In the diffraction case, since the appropriate boundary condition is that of zero normal velocity on the body, then on the submerged surface

$$\frac{\partial}{\partial n} (\phi_0 + \phi_7) = 0 \tag{3.43}$$

where n is the unit normal vector into the fluid.

In the radiation case, the potential ϕ_j on the body must have the same normal velocity as the corresponding mode of the body, so that

$$\frac{\partial \phi_j}{\partial n} = f_j(x,y,z) \text{ on the submerged surface } (j = 1,2,\ldots,6) \qquad (3.44)$$

The velocity potentials must satisfy the Laplace Equation (2.6) the surface boundary condition (2.13) and the radiation potentials ϕ_1 to ϕ_6 and the diffraction potential ϕ_7 must each satisfy the radiation condition of outgoing waves at infinity, and must vanish at infinitely large depth in the fluid.

The forces and moments (X_j) can be determined from the hydrodynamic pressure obtained from the Bernoulli Equation (2.8) by removal of the hydrostatic term gy and linearised by neglecting $q^2/2$, so that

$$p = -\rho \frac{\partial \Phi}{\partial t} \qquad (3.45)$$

where $\Phi(x,y,z,t) = \phi(x,y,z) \exp(i\omega t)$ here.

This pressure is integrated over the surface and multiplied by the appropriate geometric factor to resolve in the respective directions and account for the respective moment arms.

Although the complete mathematical treatment is outside the scope of this text, the resultant expression for the exciting-force amplitude is independent of the diffraction potential ϕ_7 and is evaluated from the surface integral at infinity

$$X_j = -i\omega\rho \int\limits_{S_\infty} \int \left(\phi_0 \frac{\partial \phi_j}{\partial n} - \phi_j \frac{\partial \phi_0}{\partial n} \right) \mathrm{d}S \qquad (3.46)$$

The dimensions of ϕ_j and hence f_j, in (3.44), are adjusted so that $f_{1,2,3}$ are dimensionless and $f_{4,5,6}$ have dimensions of length. Thus $X_{1,2,3}$ are forces (N), whilst $X_{4,5,6}$ are moments (Nm).

Since the right-hand side of (3.46) can also be evaluated over the submerged surface S of the body and $\partial\phi_3/\partial n = \cos(n,z)$, for example, then the first term of (3.46) for vertical oscillations gives an amplitude $= -i\omega\rho \int \int \phi_0 \cos(n,z)\mathrm{d}S$ which would be derived from (3.45) if only the effect of the incident wave was considered. The second term in (3.46) represents the effect of the interaction between the device and the incident wave system.

Since the exciting forces X_j are determined from the radiation potentials ϕ_j at infinity (3.46) and the damping forces are also obtained from energy radiation at infinity, a relationship between exciting forces and the damping coefficients can therefore be obtained. Newman [111] thus showed, for example, that the exciting-force amplitude for vertical oscillations (heave) of a body with a vertical axis of symmetry is given by

$$F = a \sqrt{\frac{2\rho g^3}{\omega^3}} D \qquad\qquad (3.47)$$

where a is the wave amplitude (m); ω is the angular frequency (rads/sec); D is the damping coefficient (Ns/m).

The case of the submerged oscillating water column (Fig. 3.7(c)) has been analysed two-dimensionally by Lighthill [84] and the results confirmed experimentally by Knott and Flower [75]. Because the problem has been reduced to two-dimensions by considering infinitely-long parallel plates, the classical methods of conformal mapping can be applied and a relatively straightforward solution obtained. The submerged duct shown in Fig. 3.7(c) has sharp lips in order to facilitate the conformal transformation. Because conformal mapping relates to irrotational flow, there is no separation and hence no energy dissipation at the lip. Although this desirable behaviour can only be achieved in practice by a rounded entrance to the duct, experience with sharp-edged aerofoil theory encourages the use of the method for rounded edges.

Assuming that the duct mouth responds only to local pressure fluctuations, so that the influence of the free surface and the remaining geometry of the device can be neglected, the problem reduces to that of a semi-infinite duct in an otherwise unbounded fluid. Fig. 3.10(a) therefore shows the 'local' model in the complex z plane. The Schwarz-Christoffel transformation, which maps the inside of any polygon in the z plane to the upper half of a new Z plane (Fig. 3.10(b)) is used.

Free surface effectively at $z = x + i\infty$

$z_A = -\frac{nL}{2}$ A y x B $z_B = +\frac{nL}{2}$

O

D

$z_D = -i\infty$

Fig. 3.10(a) – Physical z plane for 'local' model.

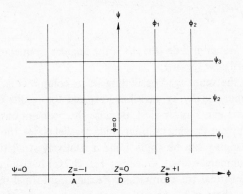

Fig. 3.10(b) — Transformed Z plane (upper half). From [84]
by courtesy of The Syndics of the Cambridge University Press.

The transformation is

$$\frac{\partial z}{\partial Z} = C\Pi(Z-c)^{(\theta-\pi)/\pi} \tag{3.48}$$

where C is a complex constant for adjusting the scale and orientation in the Z plane.

$\Pi[(Z-c)^{(\theta-\pi)/\pi}]$ is a product of terms for each point $Z = c$ on the real axis corresponding to a vertex of the polygon where the interior angle is θ.

For the flow into and out of the duct at A and B the interior angles of the 'polygon' are effectively 2π whilst the interior angle at $D(z = -i\infty)$ is zero. Choosing $Z = \pm1$ at A and B respectively gives

$$\frac{\mathrm{d}z}{\mathrm{d}Z} = \frac{C(Z-1)(Z+1)}{Z} \tag{3.49}$$

It is clear from (3.49), that $\mathrm{d}z/\mathrm{d}Z$ becomes infinite at $Z = 0$ and this mathematical 'singularity' is physically unrealistic. The point $Z = 0$ may be avoided by an infinitessimal diversion around it at radius ϵ as shown in Fig. 3.11.

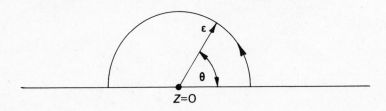

Fig. 3.11 — Avoiding a singularity.

Writing $Z = \epsilon \exp(i\theta)$ so that $dZ = \epsilon i \exp(i\theta)d\theta$ then

$$dz = \frac{C(Z-1)(Z+1)}{Z}dZ = \frac{C[\epsilon^2 \exp(2i\theta) - 1] \, \epsilon i \exp(i\theta)d\theta}{\epsilon \exp(i\theta)}.$$

or

$$dz = C[\epsilon^2 \exp(2i\theta) - 1]i\,d\theta$$

as $\epsilon \to 0$, $dz \to -Ci\,d\theta$ and so the change in z around the diversion is

$$\Delta z = -\int_0^\pi Ci\,d\theta = -Ci\pi \tag{3.50}$$

Now as the point D $(Z = 0)$ in the transformed plane is passed from right to left, the corresponding variation in the physical (z) plane is finite and equal to $-nL$, where n = the ratio of the duct width to wavelength L.

Thus

$$C = nL/\pi i \tag{3.51}$$

and

$$dz = \frac{nL}{\pi i}\left[Z - \frac{1}{Z}\right]dZ \tag{3.52}$$

Integrating gives

$$z = \frac{nL}{\pi i}\left[\frac{Z^2}{2} - \log_e Z\right] + \text{constant}$$

At $Z = +1$, $z = nL/2$ and hence the constant is

$$\frac{nL}{2} - \frac{nL}{2\pi i} = -\frac{nL}{\pi i}\left[\frac{1}{2} - \frac{\pi}{2}i\right]$$

But

$$-\frac{\pi}{2}i = \log_e[\exp(-\pi i/2)] = \log_e[\cos(-\pi/2) + i\sin(-\pi/2)]$$
$$= \log_e(-i)$$

Therefore

$$z = \frac{nL}{2\pi i}\,[(Z^2 - 1) - 2\log_e(-iZ)]$$

$$z = \frac{n}{ki}\,[(Z^2 - 1) - 2\log_e(-iZ)] \tag{3.53}$$

where $k = 2\pi/L$ as usual.

By definition, streamlines and velocity potential lines are orthogonal and since a 'conformal' transformation ensures preservation of angles, the real and imaginary parts of the complex variable in the transformed plane may be taken

to represent the velocity potential ϕ and stream function ψ respectively, as shown in Fig. 3.10(b).

Thus

$$Z = \phi + i\psi = f(x + iy) = f(z) \tag{3.54}$$

For the simple case of zero duct flow (that is, the duct not working) the appropriate boundary condition is

$$\psi = 0 \quad \text{on both walls} \quad (x = \pm nL, \ y < 0) \tag{3.55}$$

Thus the walls of the duct are represented by the real axis in the Z plane and the first term in (3.53) contributes only to the imaginary part iy of z because

$$\frac{n}{ki}[Z^2 - 1] = -\frac{in}{k}[Z^2 - 1]$$

The second term $-(2n/ki)\log_e(-iZ)$ must provide the real part x of z. For real Z this may be written as

$$-\frac{2n}{ki}\log_e[|Z|\exp(i\theta)] = -\frac{2n}{ki}[\log_e|Z| + i\theta]$$

and hence the real part is $-(2n\theta/k) = -(n\theta L/\pi)$. Since this must be equal to $\pm(nL/2)$ then $\theta = \mp(\pi/2)$ or

$$\arg(-iZ) = \mp\frac{\pi}{2} \quad \text{for real } Z \gtrless 0 \tag{3.56}$$

Thus (3.53) for the duct walls becomes

$$z_{\text{walls}} = \frac{n}{ki}\left[(Z^2 - 1) - 2\log_e|Z| + \frac{i\pi Z}{|Z|}\right] \tag{3.57}$$

where $Z \neq 0$ and real.

Following Lighthill's method, $f(z)$ conveniently has two components, the first $f_\infty(z)$ represents the behaviour of the fluid in the physical plane far away from the duct mouth, whilst a second component f_c is introduced to represent a 'local' correction, which will vanish at infinity and also satisfy the boundary condition (3.55) at the duct walls.

In the absence of the duct

$$f_\infty(z) = f_0 \exp(-2\pi i x/L) \exp(2\pi y/L) = f_0 \exp(-2\pi i z/L)$$
$$= f_0 \exp(-ikz) \tag{3.58}$$

where f_0 is the value of $f(z)$ at the point where the mouth of the duct is eventually located ($z = x + iy = 0$).

For a sinusoidal wave travelling in the x direction f_0 is proportional to $\exp{(i\omega t)}$.

From (3.54) and (3.58) it follows that

$$\phi = \text{Re} \{f_0 \exp{(-ikx)} \exp{(ky)}\}$$
$$= \text{Re} \{f_0 [\cos(-kx) + i \sin(-kx)] \exp{(ky)}\}$$
$$= f_0 \exp{(ky)} \cos(kx) \tag{3.59}$$

which for deep water is essentially the same as given by (2.16).

Substituting for z from (3.53) into (3.58) gives

$$f_\infty(Z) = f_0 \exp\langle -ik \{(n/ki)[(Z^2 - 1) - 2\log_e(-iZ)]\}\rangle \tag{3.60}$$

$$f_\infty(Z) = f_0 \exp{[n(1 - Z^2)]} \exp{[2n\log_e(-iZ)]}$$

$$f_\infty(Z) = f_0 \exp{[n(1 - Z^2)]}(-iZ)^{2n} \tag{3.61}$$

The second component of $f_c(Z)$ must correct $f_\infty(Z)$ to ensure $\psi = 0$ on the duct walls, which are represented in the transformed plane by the real axis for Z, and at the same time vanish far from the duct (Z large and complex).

Based on a knowledge of the evaluation of 'residues' at 'singularities', Lighthill selects

$$f_c(Z) = \frac{1}{\pi} \int_{-\infty}^{+\infty} Im \left\{ f_\infty(Z_1) \frac{dZ_1}{(Z - Z_1)} \right\} \tag{3.62}$$

where Im means the imaginary part of the integrand. When $Z \neq Z_1$ the integrand and hence $f_c(Z)$ become zero as Z approaches infinity as required. When $Z = Z_1$ the resultant singularity produces a residue $-Im\{f_\infty(Z)\}$ and the integral is π times that residue, so that $f_c(Z) = -Im\{f_\infty(Z)\}$ which exactly cancels the imaginary component of the first term of $f(Z)$ where

$$f(Z) = f_\infty(Z) + \frac{1}{\pi} \int_{-\infty}^{+\infty} Im \left\{ f_\infty(Z_1) \frac{dZ_1}{(Z - Z_1)} \right\} \tag{3.63}$$

so that $f(Z)$ is real and $\psi = 0$ on the walls as required.

Now at the point D where $z = -i\infty$ and $Z = 0$

$$f_\infty(Z) = 0$$

and hence

$$f_D(Z) = \frac{1}{\pi} \int_{-\infty}^{+\infty} Im \left\{ f_\infty(Z_1) \frac{dZ_1}{-Z_1} \right\} \tag{3.64}$$

$$f_D(Z) = \text{Re}\left\{\frac{i}{\pi}\int_{-\infty}^{+\infty} f_\infty(Z)\frac{dZ}{Z}\right\} \tag{3.65}$$

Now this real part of the complex potential at the bottom of the duct can also be related to the real part of a multiple of the complex potential at the location of the duct mouth when the duct is absent. This multiplying factor is the result required from the analysis and can be expected to involve both amplitude and phase changes.

Thus

$$f_D(Z) = \text{Re}\{K\exp(-i\alpha)f_0\} \tag{3.66}$$

Equating (3.65) and (3.66) and substituting for $f_\infty(Z)$ from (3.61) gives

$$K\exp(-i\alpha) = \frac{i}{\pi}\int_{-\infty}^{+\infty}\exp[n(1-Z^2)](-iZ)^{2n}\frac{dZ}{Z} \tag{3.67}$$

Using (3.56) for real Z gives

$$(-iZ)^{2n} = (Z^2)^n\exp(-in\pi) \quad \text{for } Z > 0$$
$$= (Z^2)^n\exp(+in\pi) \quad \text{for } Z < 0$$

The integral of (3.67) therefore becomes

$$\exp(+in\pi)\int_{-\infty}^{0}\exp[n(1-Z^2)](Z^2)^n\frac{dZ}{Z}$$

$$+ \exp(-in\pi)\int_{0}^{\infty}\exp[n(1-Z^2)](Z^2)^n\frac{dZ}{Z} \tag{3.68}$$

Now since the Z^2 factors in the integrands of (3.68) are the same for $Z \lessgtr 0$, the Z in the denominator affects the sign, but not the magnitude of the integrands.

Thus (3.67) may be written

$$K\exp(-i\alpha) = \frac{i}{\pi}[\exp(-in\pi)-\exp(+in\pi)]\int_{0}^{\infty}\exp[n(1-Z^2)]Z^{2n-1}dZ$$

$$K\exp(-i\alpha) = \frac{2\sin n\pi}{\pi}\int_{0}^{\infty}\exp[n(1-Z^2)]Z^{2n-1}dZ \tag{3.69}$$

Putting $X = nZ^2$ so that $dX = 2nZdZ$ changes the right-hand side of (3.69) to

$$\left(\frac{2 \sin n\pi}{\pi}\right) \frac{\exp(n)}{2n^n} \int_0^\infty \exp(-X) X^{n-1} dX = \left(\frac{2 \sin n\pi}{\pi}\right) \frac{\exp(n)}{2n^n} (n-1)!$$

(3.70)

where the integral is the standard factorial-function integral or gamma function. Thus

$$K \exp(-i\alpha) = \frac{\sin n\pi}{n\pi} \left[\frac{n!}{(n/e)^n}\right]$$

(3.71)

and since the right-hand side is real, then $\alpha = 0$.

If however the average pressure is calculated at the duct mouth assuming no interaction between the duct and the waves the multiplying factor is obtained by averaging the pressure created by the waves in the absence of the duct across the duct mouth as follows

$$\frac{1}{nL} \int_{-nL/2}^{+nL/2} \text{Re} \{\exp(-ikx)\} dx = \frac{1}{nL} \int_{-nL/2}^{+nL/2} \text{Re} \{\exp(-i2\pi x/L)\} dx$$

$$= \frac{\sin n\pi}{n\pi}$$

(3.72)

This factor is always less than 1 as expected. However the multiplying factor defined by (3.71) is greater than that of (3.72) by $[n!/(n/e)^n]$ which is always greater than 1 for positive n. This additional factor can readily be evaluated for positive integer values of n. To allow evaluation at fractional values of n, Lighthill uses the approximation

$$\frac{n!}{(n/e)^n} \approx (2\pi n + 1)^{1/2}$$

(3.73)

which is correct at $n = 0$ and gives less than 5% underestimate elsewhere.

The resultant values for the multiplying factor K as a function of n are tabulated below:

n	0	0.1	0.2	0.3	0.4	0.5	0.6	0.7	0.9	1.0
K	1	1.302	1.448	1.492	1.445	1.315	1.116	0.864	0.284	0

From Lighthill [84].

The helpful amplifying effect over a range of values of n is caused by the duct walls restricting fluid accelerations which would normally be produced by the pressure distribution caused by the waves in the absence of the duct.

It must be recalled that these results relate to a simplified 'local' model for which the duct is far enough from the free surface to avoid distortion of the normal free surface conditions. When this assumption is not valid and when the other assumption of no flow in the duct is not appropriate, K can still be greater than 1, as illustrated by Fig. 3.12 where the predictions of Lighthill [84] for the fully interactive theory are confirmed by the experiments of Knott and Flower [75].

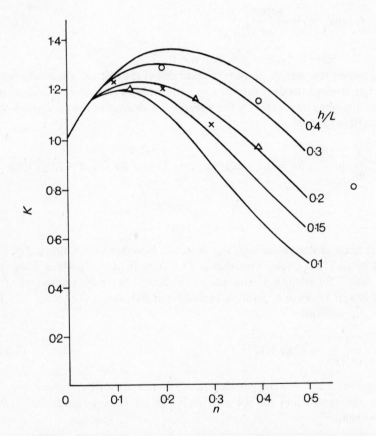

Fig. 3.12 – The pressure modification factor K in the mouth-upwards case, plotted as a function of the ratio n of duct width to wavelength for different values of the ratio h/L of the mouth depth to wavelength. Curves: fully interactive theory. Experimental points $\bigcirc$, $h/L = 0.3$; $\triangle$, $h/L = 0.2$; $\times$, $h/L = 0.15$. From [84] by courtesy of The Syndics of the Cambridge University Press.

A similar analysis by Lighthill for the case represented by Fig. 3.7(b) where the opening is facing downwards gives values of the multiplying factor $K < 1$ for all values of n and all depths of submergence h, as shown in Fig. 3.13, which also shows the phase lead $-\alpha$.

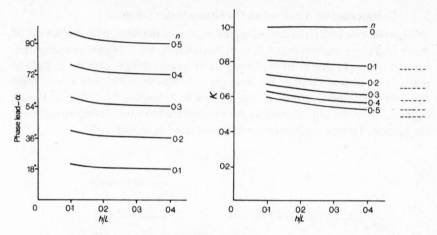

Fig. 3.13 – The pressure modification factor K, and the associated phase lead $-\alpha$, plotted in the mouth-downwards case against the ratio h/L of the mouth depth to wavelength for different values of the width-wavelength ratio. Broken lines: asymptotic values given by the 'local' model. From [84] by courtesy of The Syndics of the Cambridge University Press.

Another important experimental observation, again supported by the 'local' model prediction, is that suitably rounded lips to the duct can enhance the value of the factor K.

It is therefore clear from the foregoing analyses and experiment that the Froude-Krylov hypothesis is not appropriate and that the designer of a wave energy converter must consider the interaction between the incident waves and the device in order to correctly assess the forcing-effect amplitude.

3.3 FURTHER PRIMARY ENERGY CONVERSION PROCESSES

Primary conversion processes have been defined as those which produce the mechanical energy of relative motion of solid-body mechanisms from the energy of the waves. In this respect buoys, which oscillate relative to the sea-bed, have experienced the complete process, and the motion can be analysed and controlled as indicated in sections 3.1 and 3.2.

For oscillating water columns, however, there are further primary conversion processes involving air compression and conversion by means of an air turbine or 'overtopping' of a water column and conversion by means of an hydraulic turbine. Furthermore, since the wave frequency and hence that of any directly-driven solid-body mechanism is so low that efficient conversion to electrical energy is difficult, it is desirable in such cases to interpose hydraulic pumps and motors to effect a suitable speed increase. These further processes to obtain a satisfactory form of mechanical energy are presented in the following sections.

3.3.1 Compression of Air above an Oscillating Water Column

The simpler case of a fixed device, representative of the latest NEL designs and of many laboratory experiments will be presented first. Fig.3.14a shows a simplified form of the upper part of an oscillating water column device, with the air turbine replaced by a simple orifice. By evaluating the kinetic energy rate at exit from the orifice, the performance of the turbine is decoupled from that of the air column, whilst the orifice provides the appropriate 'throttling' effect to represent the turbine. Turbine performance will be discussed in section 3.3.2.

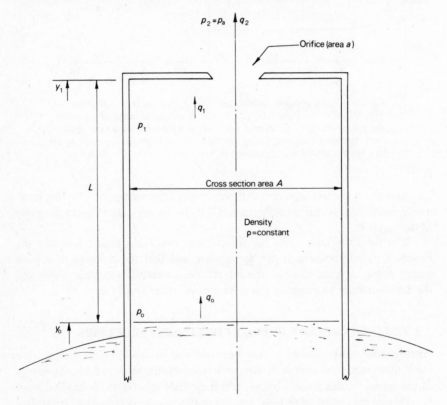

Fig. 3.14a – Upper part of oscillating water column device with a simple orifice to represent the air turbine (at any y, any property across the column is assumed uniform, at any time).

Since the motion of the air within the column is not steady the energy equation will contain the non-steady term representing the acceleration of the fluid, although this term may be relatively insignificant in many cases. Since the pressure variations are small it is permissible to assume that the density is constant in most cases. Thus for the air column up to the orifice

$$\frac{p_o}{\rho} + \frac{q_o^2}{2} + gy_o = \frac{p_1}{\rho} + \frac{q_1^2}{2} + gy_1 + \int_{y_o}^{y_1} \frac{\partial q}{\partial t} dy + (gy_{loss})_{o1} \tag{3.74}$$

where $\int_{y_o}^{y_1} (\partial q/\partial t) dy$ is the energy per unit mass expended in accelerating the air, and gy_{loss} is the energy loss per unit mass due to viscous dissipation. Because the flow is not steady, this loss term would be difficult to estimate from conventional steady flow data, unless the quasi-steady assumption is made. This point will be discussed in more detail in the section 3.3.2 relating to the turbine performance.

The continuity equation, for the assumption of incompressible flow and constant cross-sectional area of the column, gives

$$q_1 = q_o \tag{3.75}$$

whilst q_o can be evaluated as $-dL/dt$.

The acceleration term therefore becomes

$$\int_{y_o}^{y_1} \frac{\partial q}{\partial t} dy = -L \frac{d^2 L}{dt^2} \tag{3.76}$$

and can therefore be evaluated from a record of the length of the air column against time.

Also as a result of (3.75) the kinetic energy terms per unit mass cancel in (3.74) and the potential energy terms per unit mass can be combined since $gy_1 - gy_o = gL$.

If the orifice is assumed to be of negligible thickness so that $y_2 \sim y_1$ and hence also no acceleration term, then the energy equation gives

$$\frac{p_1}{\rho} + \frac{q_1^2}{2} = \frac{p_2}{\rho} + \frac{q_2^2}{2} + (gy_{loss})_{12} = \frac{p_a}{\rho} + \frac{q_2^2}{2} + (gy_{loss})_{12} \tag{3.77}$$

where $p_2 = p_a =$ atmospheric pressure.

Combining (3.74) and (3.77) and taking $y_1 = y_2$ gives

$$\frac{p_o}{\rho} + \frac{q_o^2}{2} + gy_o = \frac{p_a}{\rho} + \frac{q_2^2}{2} + gy_2 - L \frac{d^2 L}{dt^2} + (gy_{loss})_{o2} \tag{3.78}$$

For an orifice area a, the continuity equation for incompressible flow gives

$$Aq_o = C_c a q_2 \tag{3.79}$$

where C_c is the contraction coefficient.

Hence the required kinetic energy per unit mass leaving the orifice is obtained from the rearranged (3.78) with appropriate substitutions.

$$q_2^2/2 = \frac{\left(\dfrac{p_0 - p_a}{\rho}\right) - gL + L\dfrac{d^2L}{dt^2} - gy_{loss}}{\left[1 - \dfrac{C_c^2 a^2}{A^2}\right]} \qquad (3.80)$$

Thus the instantaneous rate of energy leaving the orifice or instantaneous power is

$$P = \dot{m}(q_2^2/2) \qquad (3.81)$$

where $\dot{m}$ = instantaneous mass flow rate, which for incompressible flow and constant column area A, is given by

$$\dot{m} = -\rho A(dL/dt) \qquad (3.82)$$

Thus the instantaneous power becomes

$$P = -\rho A \frac{dL}{dt}\left[\left(\frac{p_0 - p_a}{\rho}\right) - gL + L\frac{d^2L}{dt^2} - gy_{loss}{}^\dagger\right]\bigg/\left[1 - \frac{C_c^2 a^2}{A^2}\right] \qquad (3.83)$$

Since the pressure term $(p_0 - p_a)/\rho$ in the numerator is usually much larger than the remaining terms and since $a \ll A$ for optimum energy extraction, (3.83) can be simplified to

$$P \sim -A\frac{dL}{dt}(p_0 - p_a) \qquad (3.84)$$

Either (3.83) or its approximation (3.84) can be used as the input energy rate to the air turbine, whose performance can be evaluated as shown in section 3.3.2.

McCormick [96] has analysed the more complicated case of an air column within a pneumatic-type wave-energy conversion buoy which is allowed to oscillate in the vertical direction ('heave'). In McCormick's approach, the air is assumed to be incompressible and the viscous dissipation is accounted for by one term which is taken to be proportional to the square of the velocity. Changes of potential energy of the air are neglected and the turbine is included in the air flow analysis. Fig. 3.14b, shows the buoy arrangement and the notation. In particular $\bar{\eta}_1$ is the area-averaged displacement of the internal free surface. z_b is the heaving displacement of the buoy, and $\zeta = \bar{\eta}_1 - z_b$ = the relative motion of the internal free surface. p_1 = internal air pressure relative to atmospheric pressure (that is, gauge).

The instantaneous power or work rate is evaluated as

---

† The expression is similar, except for $+gy_{loss}$, when the air is expanding as the water level in the column falls $(dL/dt > 0)$.

$$P = \frac{dW}{dt} = \rho_a (\pi r_1^2) \dot{\zeta} \left[\frac{p_1}{\rho_a} - \frac{1}{2} \dot{\zeta}^2 \left\{ \left(\frac{A_1}{A_3} \right)^2 - 1 \right\} - g \sum_i \delta_i \dot{\zeta} |\dot{\zeta}| \right.$$
$$\left. - \{ h + L_t (A_1/A_3) - \zeta \} \ddot{\zeta} \right] \qquad (3.85)$$

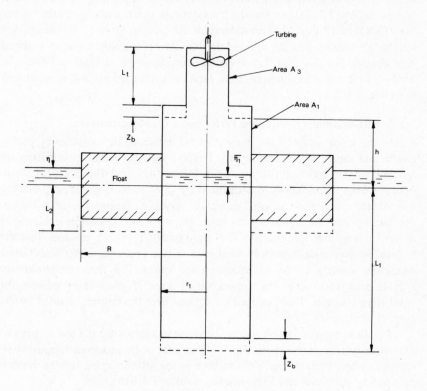

Fig. 3.14b – Pneumatic-type wave energy convertion buoy.

The first term $\rho_a (\pi r_1^2) \dot{\zeta} [p_1/\rho_a]$ is the same as (3.84). The second term within the square brackets accounts for the kinetic energy loss at exit from the turbine and the kinetic energy contribution of the air in the column. The third term is the summation of all the viscous dissipation losses, with δ_i the loss coefficient for a sudden contraction or expansion, wall shear stress, etc. The last term accounts for the acceleration of the air column $(h - \zeta)$ in length, plus the acceleration in the turbine section of length L_t.

McCormick [96] also evaluates the force on the buoy due to the vertical momentum of internal air flow as

$$F_a = \rho_a A_1 \dot{\zeta}^2 + p_1 A_1 \qquad (3.86)$$

This force must be added to the force on the buoy due to the water waves as discussed in section 3.2.2.

Thus with the hydrodynamic pressure p_o determined from the linearised non-steady Bernoulli Equation for the waves, with due allowance for the inter-action effects as described in section 3.2.2, the turbine inlet pressure p_1 can be determined by (3.74) above and the instantaneous power available to the turbine from (3.83) or (3.84). Thus consideration can now be given to the design of a suitable air turbine, bearing in mind that the flow is not only unsteady as with a turbocharger, but also that flow reversals occur. Since gas turbines and hydraulic turbines have much in common, both types of turbomachine will be dealt with in section 3.3.2.

3.3.2 Turbomachinery – General Performance Considerations

Within the scope of this book, only essential details of turbomachinery perfor-mance and design will be presented. Readers seeking further information are referred to the texts of Csanady [33], Dixon [45], and Horlock [70]. Since evidence from turbocharger investigations by Craig *et al.* [31] indicates that the quasi-steady assumption is valid except at very high frequencies of pulsation, this assumption can reasonably be made for wave energy devices operating at relatively very low frequencies. The quasi-steady approach assumes that the turbine behaves instantaneously as though it was operating under steady-state conditions identical to the instantaneous conditions. Thus the mean power over a cycle is obtained from the summation of a set of quasi-steady powers, for small time intervals with averaged conditions over the interval, divided by the number of intervals.

The flow reversal problems can be overcome either by the use of pairs of non-return valves as shown in Fig. 1.6 and 1.14 or by ingenious 'symmetrical' turbine designs such as the Wells turbine or the self-rectifying turbine systems patented by Babinsten and Filipenco (see section 3.3.6).

Continuity, momentum and energy equations are employed in the design of the turbine and ultimately lead, via a set of velocity triangles, to the deter-mination of the appropriate blade or vane shapes for both rotors and stators. The selection of optimum speeds and machine diameters is based on empirical values for 'specific speed' and 'specific diameter', which are derived by dimen-sional analysis. Fortunately both gas and hydraulic turbines can be accommodated by this one approach.

3.3.3 Dimensional Analysis Applied to Turbomachinery

The method of dimensional analysis is described in many engineering textbooks, especially those relating to Fluid Mechanics. The essential advantage of the method is that the physical behaviour of a device, such as a turbine, can be measured and described by dimensionless parameters (or 'groups') fewer in number than the number of variables involved. Additionally, since by definition

the 'groups' are dimensionless, no one particular set of units (SI, Imperial, or c.g.s.) is implied, and any consistent set of units can be used.

Briefly, the method first requires a listing of *all* the variables involved, together with an assessment of their dimensions usually in the fundamental dimensions of mass M, length L and time T. Then one variable V_1 is described as a function of the others in the form of a product of powers of the other variables.

$$V_1 = K(V_2^a . V_3^b . V_4^c \ldots) \tag{3.87}$$

where K, a, b, c etc. are pure numbers, determined by experiment.

In the case of an hydraulic turbine, the variables (with notation, SI units, and fundamental dimensions) are as follows:

Variable	Notation	SI unit	Fundamental dimension
Volume flow rate	Q	m³/s	L^3/T
Head	H	m	L
Diameter	D	m	L
Rotational speed	N	rev/min	$1/T$
Fluid density	ρ	kg/m³	M/L^3
Fluid viscosity	μ	Pa s	M/LT
Efficiency	η	—	—
Gravitational acceleration	g	m/s²	L/T^2

All variables, including efficiency (even though it is already dimensionless) should be included in order to ensure that no important parameter is missed. Equation (3.87) may then be written (excluding the dimensionless parameter η) as

$$Q = K(H^a D^b N^c \rho^d \mu^e g^f) \tag{3.88}$$

or dimensionally as

$$\frac{L^3}{T} \cong L^a L^b \frac{1}{T^c} \frac{M^d}{L^{3d}} \frac{M^e}{L^e T^e} \frac{L^f}{T^{2f}} \tag{3.89}$$

where $\cong$ means dimensionally equal.

For (3.89) to be dimensionally consistent the powers of M must balance and those for L and T also.

Thus

$$\left. \begin{array}{lll} \text{for } M & 0 = d + e \\ \text{for } L & 3 = a + b - 3d - e + f \\ \text{for } T & -1 = -c - e - 2f \end{array} \right\} \tag{3.90}$$

These three simultaneous equations for six unknowns allow three (say b, c and e) to be expressed in terms of the other three, so that (3.88) can be written

$$Q = K(H^a D^{3-a+2d-f} N^{1+d-2f} \rho^d \mu^{-d} g^f)$$

Collecting like powers gives

$$\frac{Q}{ND^3} = K\left[\left(\frac{H}{D}\right)^a \left(\frac{g}{N^2 D}\right)^f \left(\frac{\rho N D^2}{\mu}\right)^d\right] \tag{3.91}$$

Each bracketed group is dimensionless and hence multiplication of two or more groups would produce an *alternative* dimensionless group, which could replace one of the original groups. No new independent group is produced, as the number of independent groups is equal to the number of variables less the number of fundamental dimensions ($8 - 3 = 5$ in this case).

Thus multiplying the first and second groups on the right-hand side of (3.91) gives the more conventional group $gH/N^2 D^2$. Hence, remembering the efficiency η, the dimensionless groups with their conventional names and notation are:

Dimensionless volume flow rate or flow coefficient	$\phi = Q/ND^3$
Dimensionless head or energy coefficient	$\psi = gH/N^2 D^2$
Reynolds number	$\text{Re} = \rho N D^2/\mu$
Head-diameter ratio	$= H/D$
Efficiency	$= \eta$

Although, the analysis is somewhat different for a gas turbine with compressibility significant, the dimensionless groups, above, can easily be modified for an 'incompressible' air turbine. In this case, $Q = Ac_x$ for an axial flow machine, where A is the flow area, dimensionally equivalent to D^2 and c_x is the axial velocity. Also, the pressure drop $\Delta p \triangleq \rho g H$ and the mean blade speed $U \triangleq ND$.

Thus for an incompressible air turbine:

The flow coefficient	$\phi = c_x/U$
The pressure coefficient	$\psi = \Delta p/(\rho U^2/2)$
Reynolds number	$\text{Re} = \rho DU/\mu$

The introduction of the 1/2 in the denominator for ψ is arbitrary and usually introduced because the dynamic pressure (from Bernoulli's Equation) involves 1/2.

The performance of either an hydraulic turbine or an 'incompressible' air turbine is usually presented in the form of graphs of ψ and η against ϕ for various Reynolds numbers, although frequently the effect of Reynolds number

is negligible. Typical curves are shown in Fig. 3.15, which shows an optimum performance (with maximum efficiency). In order to utilise such prior empirical knowledge for the design of a new turbine another dimensionless group — the specific speed — is used.

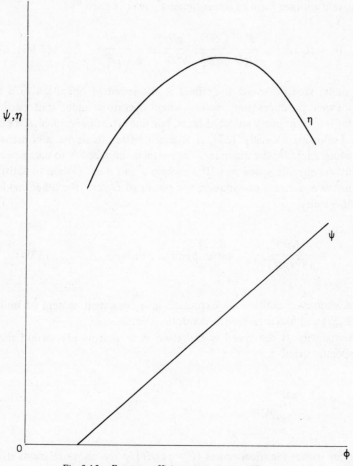

Fig. 3.15 — Energy coefficient or pressure coefficient ψ
and efficiency η against flow coefficient ϕ.

First a dimensionless power is derived by considering the available power from a 'head' of water.

Thus the available power P = rate of change of potential energy of
the water through a head H

= mass flow rate $\times gH$

= ρQgH

therefore a dimensionless power

$$\Pi_1 = \frac{P}{\rho Q g H} \tag{3.92}$$

Alternatively another form of dimensionless power is given by

$$\Pi = \Pi_1 \phi \psi = \frac{P}{\rho Q g H} \cdot \frac{Q}{ND^3} \cdot \frac{gH}{N^2 D^2} = \frac{P}{\rho N^3 D^5} \tag{3.93}$$

Traditionally, specific speed is defined as the speed of operation of a model turbine which produces unit power when operating under unit head. This parameter is used in many standard texts, but since it is dimensional, it is difficult to use. Following Csanady [33], it is much better to devise a dimensionless group, which excludes the diameter D and retains the speed N to unit power.

Thus the specific speed $\nu = \Pi^a \psi^b$ where a and b are chosen to satisfy two simultaneous equations, one making the power of D zero, the other making the power of N unity.

Hence

$$\nu = \frac{NP^{1/2}}{\rho^{1/2}(gH)^{5/4}} \quad \text{for an hydraulic turbine} \tag{3.94}$$

and the various quantities are expressed in a consistent system of units (for example, SI) and N is measured in revolutions per second.

Alternatively, if the speed is expressed as ω radians per second then the radian specific speed

$$\Omega = \frac{\omega P^{1/2}}{\rho^{1/2}(gH)^{5/4}} \tag{3.95}$$

It is better to use the ideal power ($P = \rho g Q H$) in the above relation, although many texts refer to the brake or shaft power. For good performance, there is an empirical relationship between Ω and H as shown in Fig. 3.16. The type of machine suitable for different heads is also shown in the figure with axial-flow Kaplan turbines (Fig. 3.17) most suitable for the low heads associated with wave power.

Thus a radian specific speed Ω of about 5 is typical. For axial-flow gas turbines Csanady [33] suggests radian specific speeds between 0.5 and 2, although Horlock [70] suggests that gas turbine designers find the specific speed (or shape parameter as he prefers to call it) less useful.

There is also a non-dimensional specific diameter

$$\Delta = \frac{\psi^{1/4}}{\phi^{1/2}} = \frac{D(gH)^{1/4}}{Q^{1/4}} \tag{3.96}$$

which is related to Ω as shown in Fig. 3.18. This parameter assists the designer to select the most suitable diameter D for the turbine.

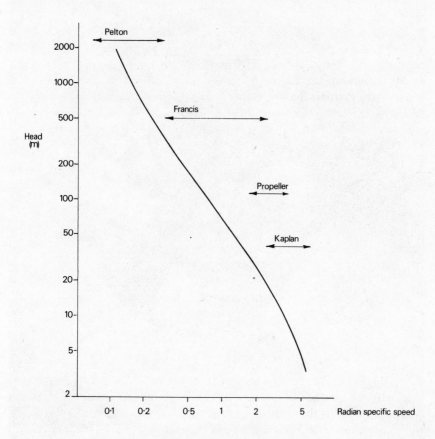

Fig. 3.16 – Hydraulic turbine types and
radian specific speed for various heads.

Fig. 3.17 — Axial-flow Kaplan turbine.
Photograph by courtesy of Escher Wyss.

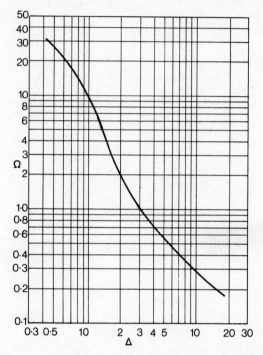

Fig. 3.18 – Cordier diagram showing the empirical relationship between specific speed Ω and specific diameter Δ. From [33] by courtesy of McGraw Hill Book Co. (UK) Ltd.

3.3.4 Design of the Turbine Blades or Vanes

Only axial-flow machines which are appropriate to both air and hydraulic wave-energy systems will be discussed. Essentially an axial-flow turbine has a row of fixed, stator blades which transform either the hydraulic head or the air pressure into kinetic energy of the fluid, which is directed by the stator blades towards the moving row of rotor blades. In the rotor blades a change of direction of the fluid causes a change of angular momentum and hence a torque to be applied to the rotor.

In order to convert the 'head' or 'pressure' into kinetic energy a convergent flow passage is required to accelerate the fluid. If the flow passage between the rotor blades is designed for no further acceleration of the fluid in the rotor, the turbine is described as a zero-reaction machine, whilst machines with flow accelerations in the rotor have varying degrees of reaction, defined effectively by the fraction of the acceleration which takes place in the rotor. Fig. 3.19 shows typical rotor and stator blades in the opened or 'developed' peripheral $x\theta$ plane together with the appropriate velocity triangles.

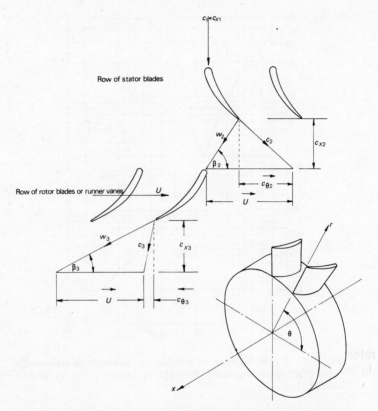

Fig. 3.19 – Velocity triangles and blade shapes for an axial-flow turbine. Viewed in the 'developed' θx plane at mean radius r_m. c = absolute velocity; w = velocity relative to blades; c_x = axial component of velocity; c_θ = tangential component of velocity; U = rotor blade speed.

The torque on the rotor T = rate of change of angular momentum, according to Newton's law.

Now the angular momentum per unit mass is the product of the tangential or peripheral velocity and the radius, $c_\theta r$. Thus the change in angular momentum across the rotor, per unit mass is

$$\overrightarrow{c_{\theta 2}}\, r_2 - \overrightarrow{c_{\theta 3}}\, r_3 \tag{3.97}$$

where the arrows $\rightarrow$ indicate a consistent vectorial direction (thus in Fig. 3.19 the tangential velocity $\overleftarrow{c_{\theta 3}}$ is negative).

If the mass flow rate is $\dot{m}$, then the torque or rate of change of angular momentum is

$$T = \dot{m}(\overrightarrow{c_{\theta 2}} r_2 - \overrightarrow{c_{\theta 3}} r_3) \tag{3.98}$$

and hence the power or work rate is

$$P = T\omega = \dot{m}(\vec{c}_{\theta 2}\,\omega r_2 - \vec{c}_{\theta 3}\,\omega r_3) \tag{3.99}$$

Now $\omega r = U$ the blade (peripheral) speed and in an axial-flow machine $r_2 = r_3 = r$. Hence

$$P = \dot{m}U(\vec{c}_{\theta 2} - \vec{c}_{\theta 3}) \tag{3.100}$$

Equation (3.100) must be multiplied by the mechanical efficiency η_m to obtain the shaft power.

The continuity equation $\dot{m} = \rho A c_x$ allows $\dot{m}$ to be evaluated provided the flow area A is known and the axial velocity is determined from the velocity triangles. For steady, incompressible flow and constant area A, it follows that c_x is constant through the machine. The turbomachine designer can also choose a number of design conditions such as:

(1) Minimum exit kinetic energy loss per unit mass $(c_3^2/2)$, which means that c_3 is axial and equal to c_{x3} and hence $c_{\theta 3} = 0$.

(2) Shock-free entry or zero incidence to the blades which means that β_2, the relative flow angle at entry to the rotor, is also the inlet blade angle.

(3) Some suitable variation of the tangential velocity c_θ with radius, such as the so-called 'free-vortex' condition for which $c_\theta r$ is constant, for each particular axial location. Since ω is obviously constant, it follows that $c_\theta U$ is constant and (3.100) can be used without the necessity to integrate with respect to r for elemental mass flows through elemental annuli of thickness δr.

This 'free-vortex' condition is derived from consideration of radial equilibrium of the flow and constant axial velocity c_x with respect to radius.

3.3.5 Relevant Background for Turbine Design

Tidal-power systems, such as the one at the estuary to the River Rance near Dinard on the northern coast of France, employ low-head Kaplan turbines, which must operate in the head range 2–8 m. Experience with these machines can usefully be employed for wave-energy systems. Milne [104] has reported the performance characteristics of the turbines used for the Rance system and has presented the results in appropriate non-dimensional form as shown in Fig. 3.20. Thus the off-design performance of a Kaplan turbine, with a design point selected by the specific speed parameter, can be anticipated.

The turbines of a diesel-engine turbocharger provide the best experience for the air turbines, associated with the oscillating water column and other devices. Design pressure ratios are of the order of 1.6 and turbochargers also operate under pulsating conditions. An alternative to the energy coefficient is frequently used by gas turbine designers, who substitute an ideal kinetic energy $(c_i^2/2)$ for the potential energy (gH) per unit mass.

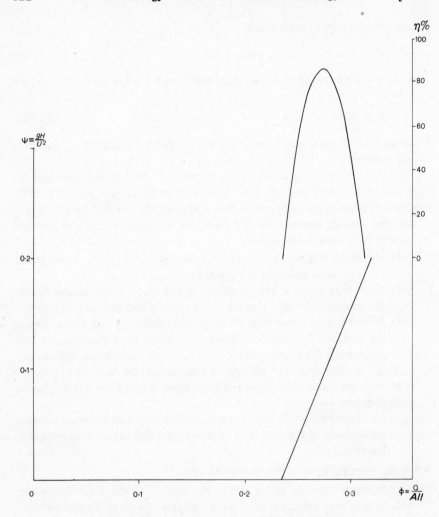

Fig. 3.20 — Energy coefficient ψ and efficiency η against flow
coefficient ϕ for River Rance tidal power turbines.

Thus

$$\psi = \frac{gH}{N^2 D^2} \quad \text{becomes} \quad \frac{c_i^2}{2U^2}$$

and the velocity ratio U/c_i is used in place of ψ.

3.3.6 Turbines for Reversing Flows

As suggested in section 3.3.2 a number of 'symmetrical' turbines have been
devised to accommodate the reversing flow associated with wave energy devices.
Fig. 3.21 shows a single-stage Wells turbine with velocity triangles similar to

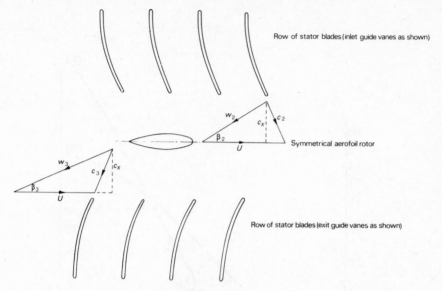

Fig. 3.21 – Single-stage Wells turbine.

those of a conventional turbine stage (Fig. 3.19), but having symmetrical aerofoil rotor blades with chords aligned in the direction of rotation. A second row of stator blades act as exit guide vanes as shown, but on flow reversal they become the inlet guide vanes. Provided that the relative velocity w_2 has a suitable angle of incidence to the aerofoil, the flow around the aerofoil produces a pressure distribution giving a resultant force with a small component in the direction of rotation. This driving force is still in the forward direction when the flow reverses and the angle of incidence is not too small. During the cylclic flow reversal, however, the angle of incidence falls to zero and the aerodynamic forces then oppose the motion. This can be seen from Fig. 3.22 which shows the tangential force F_θ as a function of the angle of incidence i_2 as reported by Grant *et al.* [64]. The steady-state performance of the single-stage Wells turbine is shown in Fig. 3.23 as a non-dimensional plot of pressure coefficient ψ and efficiency η against flow coefficient ϕ. The implied negative efficiencies for low flow-coefficient correspond to the negative tangential forces at low angles of incidence, which would reduce the mean cycle power. The reversing-flow characteristics of the Wells turbine, when available, should clarify the extent of this reduction.

To avoid the period of opposing tangential force, the symmetrical aerofoil can be replaced by a cambered blade alike the rotor blade of an impulse turbine as shown in Fig. 3.24. For the impulse stage there is no further expansion in the rotor blade row and in the absence of friction the 'equiangular' blade ensures that $w_3 = w_2$. With the vectorial addition of the blade velocity $\overline{U}$ it is clear that

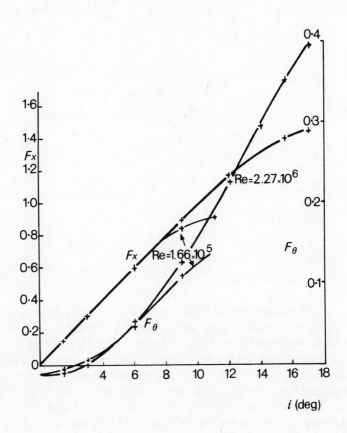

Fig. 3.22 – Measured force coefficients. From [64] by
courtesy of The Institution of Electrical Engineers.

the angle of the absolute velocity at exit α_3 is larger than the angle α_2 at inlet. Hence the second stator row, designed as inlet guide vanes for the reverse flow, is ill-designed to function as exit guide vanes for the original flow direction. As exit guide vanes, they function with negative incidence, which would be increased by friction losses in the rotor and by inlet guide vane deviation (that is, the difference between blade angle and fluid angle at exit). A design, such as this, has been patented by I. A. Babinsten (1975) in the US, whilst G. D. Filipenco patented a 'velocity-compounded' version, also in 1975 in the US, and McCormick [98] has described a counter-rotating turbine design.

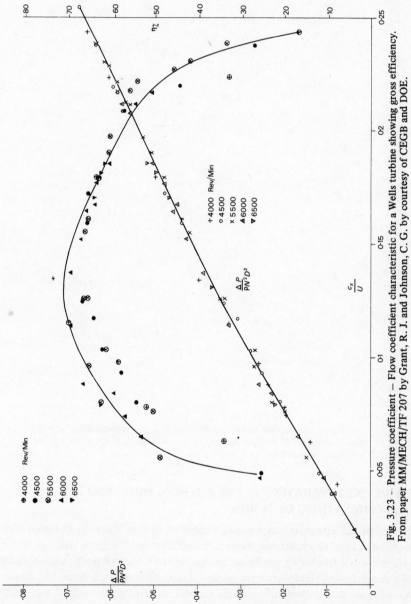

Fig. 3.23 – Pressure coefficient – Flow coefficient characteristic for a Wells turbine showing gross efficiency. From paper MM/MECH/TF 207 by Grant, R. J. and Johnson, C. G. by courtesy of CEGB and DOE.

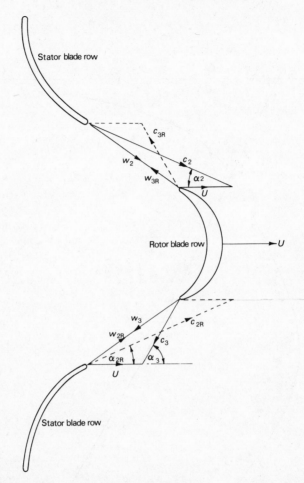

Fig. 3.24 – Symmetrical turbine for reversing flow. c = absolute velocity; w = relative velocity; U = blade velocity; $_2$ = rotor inlet; $_3$ = rotor exit; $_{2R}$ = reversed flow rotor inlet; $_{3R}$ = reversed flow rotor exit.

3.4 DEVICES OPERATING IN THE PITCHING MODE AND IN COMBINATIONS OF MODES

In section 3.2 attention was focussed mainly on devices operating in the heaving (vertical) mode of oscillation. Several potentially good devices operate in the pitching mode, including the Salter Ducks and the Cockerell Rafts, whilst others like the Bristol Cylinder operate in the combined modes of surge and heave. As affirmed at the beginning of this chapter, detailed mathematical treatment is inappropriate to this text, but nevertheless an understanding of the physical behaviour of the devices is essential for all designers of wave energy converters.

3.4.1 Salter Ducks

Mynett *et al.* [110] have analysed the behaviour of the Salter Duck with a fixed shaft, so that it is free to operate in the pitching mode only (referred to as 'roll' in [110]) and also when it is free to move in surge ('sway' in [110]), heave and pitch. Their conclusions for a fixed shaft confirmed Salter's experiments, which indicated high efficiency over a broad frequency range. For a Salter Duck, which is only partially constrained, Mynett *et al.* suggest that the added degrees of freedom can reduce both the efficiency and the reacting force.

Other efficiency predictions by Count [27], Glendenning [62] and Mei and Newman [101] have indicated that movement of the duck mountings reduces the performance. Salter [122, 124] however conducted a series of experiments which clearly demonstrated that there is *not* a continuous degradation of performance from absolute rigidity to total freedom. These exeriments were initiated by Salter after discussions with Dr. David Evans, whose Bristol Cylinder device operates in surge and heave. The 'duck' was supported by a mounting, which allowed separate control of rigidity in surge and heave, and measurements of efficiency made at different frequencies and different combinations of rigidity. Fig. 3.25 shows a typical performance plot rescaled to represent a 10 m diameter duck in a monochromatic sea with a wave period of 12s. Rigidity of the mounting is expressed as force per unit width of duck per unit deflection (N/m^2), but the reciprocal, compliance (m^2/N), is more convenient and is used by Salter. The performance plot shows two regions of high efficiency, both at moderate surge compliance $(3-5 mm^2/N)$, with one at negligible heave compliance, and the other at relatively large heave compliance $(\sim 100 mm^2/N)$. Between the two regions there is a region of very low efficiency, when the heave compliance is $10-20 mm^2/N$. At higher frequencies (shorter periods and wavelengths), the efficiency contours move closer to the origin, or point of total rigidity, whilst for longer waves the contours move towards greater compliance. Greenhow [65] has applied the method of Mynett *et al.* [110] to specific designs of Salter's Duck and has shown that theoretical and experimental results agree as regards the shape of the efficiency contours at high frequencies (period $T = 8.7$ seconds) although the experimental efficiency is less than the theoretical value, because of friction, turbulence and viscous losses. At slightly lower frequencies ($T = 10.2$ seconds) the theoretical and experimental results do not agree at high heave compliance, due to significant non-linearity in the springs under these conditions.

A number of observations must now be made regarding the behaviour of the Salter Duck. First, since a rigid backbone for the device is impractical at sea and by Fig. 3.25 undesirable, there is an increase in the number of degrees of freedom which includes a seventh due to the motion of the duck relative to the backbone. This latter (relative) rotational motion has the same axis as that for the pitching of the device as a whole, and is referred to as 'nod'.

Second, since short wavelengths are usually associated with short crest lengths and hence short intercepts on the duck, such waves will find the duck

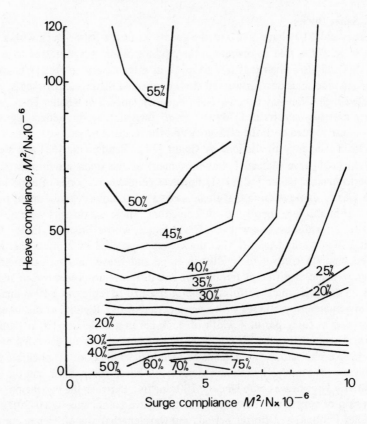

Monochromatic sea: $T = 12$ s. $L/d = 22$
Data rescaled to represent 10m diameter duck

Fig. 3.25 – Efficiency of Salter Duck with variation of surge and heave compliance.
From [124] by courtesy of the Institution of Electrical Engineers.

string relatively rigid, which is fortunately in agreement with Salter results. Furthermore, the longer wavelengths with longer intercepts, will find the backbone more compliant as required for good performance.

Third, the low efficiency region of Fig. 3.25, might well provide a safe operating condition for particularly large waves.

Salter has given a good physical explanation of this performance of the ducks, by considering the behaviour of cylindrical devices with horizontal axis, which are driven so as to move in surge and heave. Ogilvie [112] had shown that when a cylinder is driven in a circular orbit, waves are generated in only one direction (the direction of motion of the cylinder at the top of its orbit) and

Evans and others have since used this device as an experimental wave-maker. Salter therefore concludes that when the duck is partially constrained, so that it moves in surge and heave to produce waves which are the inverse of those which propagate below the duck, then the water to the rear of the device will be calm, and the energy conversion at its best.

The different performance characteristic at different frequencies (or wavelengths) is accounted for by the different energy distributions with depth. For short waves (L small) the water movement is concentrated near the surface, because of the exponential decrement $[\exp(2\pi y/L, \, y < 0)]$, so that very little energy passes beneath the duck and hence a more rigid mounting is appropriate.

Further details regarding the design of the duck and the associated hydraulic pump-motor system will be given in section 3.5.1, since there are common features with the systems for other devices.

3.4.2 Cockerell Rafts

Haren and Mei [67] have developed a theory for a two-dimensional device consisting of a number of rafts, whose wave-induced rotation about the hinges is employed for the primary energy-conversion process. They employed the relatively-simple linearised shallow-water theory (see Stoker [129] for example), and evaluated the velocity potential and total pressure under the raft. The velocity and the velocity potential under the free surface, adjacent to the raft, were then related to the velocity and velocity potential under the raft, so as to satisfy the boundary conditions for continuity and dynamic pressure at the raft edges. A single raft, hinged at a fixed wall was considered first, as shown in Fig. 3.26, and use made of conservation of angular momentum of the raft in the form

$$I\ddot{\Theta} + \bar{\alpha}\dot{\Theta} + M = 0 \qquad (3.101)$$

where I = moment of inertia of the raft about the hinge; Θ = angular deflection; $\bar{\alpha}$ = energy extraction coefficient or damping rate; M = the dynamic moment, caused by the dynamic pressure under the raft.

The three resultant equations were then solved for the three unknowns:

(i) Reflection coefficient R (originating in the free-surface conditions, because of reflection from the raft).

(ii) A constant of integration C (originating from the integration of $\partial\Phi/\partial X$ to obtain Φ).

(iii) The amplitude of the angle of deflection $|\Theta|$.

Then since the instantaneous power extracted is determined from the product of the moment due to energy extraction $\bar{\alpha}\dot{\Theta}$ and the angular velocity $\dot{\Theta}$, and Θ varies periodically with angular velocity Ω, the time-averaged power extracted is evaluated as

$$P = \frac{1}{2}\bar{\alpha}\Omega^2|\Theta|^2 \tag{3.102}$$

which can then be compared with the incident wave power to give an ideal efficiency of conversion, as shown in Fig. 3.26.

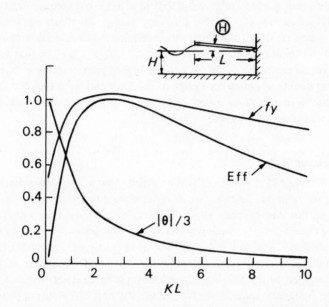

Fig. 3.26 – Optimum raft hinged to a sea wall or to another infinitely long raft, $d = D/L = 0.01$, $h = H/L = 0.1$. The normalised extraction rate at the hinge is $\alpha = 0.278$, f_y = normalised vertical force at the hinge, $|\theta| = |\Theta L/A|$ normalised angular displacement. From [67] by courtesy of CML Publications Ltd.

The analysis also demonstrates that for maximum efficiency the raft must operate under resonant conditions and that the energy extraction rate must equal the radiation damping rate (as demonstrated previously). For these optimum conditions the reflection coefficient is zero. For the assumption of negligible draft and hence inertia, it was also shown that the raft length should be about 40% of the wavelength for best efficiency.

Haren and Mei also analysed the behaviour of a train of N rafts and employed a numerical theory for arbitrary wavelength in order to check the shallow water theory. The main conclusions of this investigation were:

(1) Two or three rafts are sufficient. The addition of further rafts does not help significantly.
(2) The ideal efficiency is comparable or better than that of the Salter Duck, while mooring forces are much less.
(3) For the same wavelength, the effect of water depth is slight.

(4) For a sample double-peaked spectrum, it is most cost effective to extract energy from the short wave peak.

Cockerell *et al.* [25] have reported practical developments of the raft system as already described in Chapter 1. Tests with a 1/50th scale model gave high efficiencies (~80%) at a period of 1 s, which would represent just over 7 s at full scale in a real sea. The efficiency however fell to about 35% at a period of 1.5 s (equivalent to about 10.5 s at full scale). They also made a number of other experimental observations which suggested that:

(1) The raft weight made little difference to performance, once a minimum value was exceeded, because of the significant 'added mass' of water.
(2) The rafts were insensitive to the form and value of the damping produced by the power take-off over quite a wide range.
(3) The rafts were insensitive to marine fouling.
(4) The form and position of the mooring did not affect the power performance significantly.
(5) There was little to gain in power by having more than two hinge lines.

Following from this last observation, a raft system with a single hinge line was designed, as shown in Fig. 3.27. Two leading rafts (~25 m wide) were

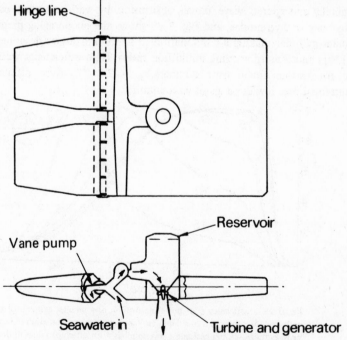

Fig. 3.27 – Latest design of wave-contouring raft.
From [25] by courtesy of HMSO and DOE.

connected to a common back section, with a double-acting oscillating-vane pump extending right across the raft and forming an integral part of the structure. Sea water flows from the pump into a transverse main and then to a central reservoir on the rear raft. The water then flows through an axial-flow Kaplan turbine (see section 3.3.3) mounted with its axis vertical and located below the reservoir.

3.4.3 The Bristol Cylinder Device

Ogilvie [112] had shown that when a submerged cylinder is driven so that its axis moves in a circle, of small radius, about an axis parallel to the cylinder axis, the waves produced on the free surface travel away from the cylinder in one direction only. In fact this effect can be achieved for any shape of body, for any given frequency, by a suitable combination of the horizontal (surge) and vertical (heave) motions so as to produce a cancellation of the waves produced by the two separate motions at infinity in one direction. This point has already been discussed in section 3.4.1 in connection with the effect of surge and heave compliance on the performance of Salter's Duck.

It is logical to expect that this process of wave-making can be reversed and that by constraining a circular cylinder in such a way as to allow motion in a circular orbit, it will act as an efficient absorber of incident waves. Evans [50] originally considered wave power absorption by various bodies oscillating in either one or two modes, and Fig. 3.28 shows the encouraging prediction for a circular cylinder making a combination of heave and surge (described as 'sway' in [50]) motions of varying amplitude ratios. High efficiencies were predicted and for certain tuned wave numbers $\nu_0 = (2\pi a/L)_0$ these efficiencies were maintained over a wide range of wave number.

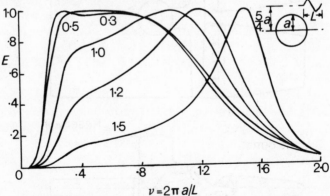

Fig. 3.28 — Efficiency E of power absorption of a circular cylinder of radius a with $m = M$, submerged to a depth $5a/4$ and making a combination of heave and sway motions, vs. dimensionless wavenumber ν for different values of the tuned wavenumber ν_0. From [50] by courtesy of The Syndics of the Cambridge University Press.

Thus for deep water waves of 10s period and hence 156m wavelength, a cylinder of 8m radius, giving $\nu_0 = 0.32$, would be suitable, provided the correct ratios of heave to surge amplitude were maintained, as shown in Fig. 3.29.

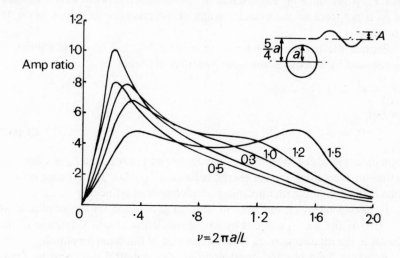

Fig. 3.29 — Ratio of the heave or sway amplitude to the incident wave amplitude $|\xi_i/A|$, $i = 1, 2$, for a cylinder of radius a, with $m = M$, submerged to a depth $5a/4$ and making a combination of heave and sway motions, vs. wavenumber ν for different values of the tuned wavenumber ν_0. From [50] by courtesy of The Syndics of the Cambridge University Press.

In a subsequent paper, Evans *et al.* [53] have described the performance of the submerged cylinder wave energy device. In the theoretical approach, a circular cylinder of radius a is submerged so that its centre is at depth $h > a$ and it is constrained to make small horizontal and vertical oscillations under springs of stiffness S_i and dampers of damping constants D_i, where $i = 1$ for the horizontal x direction and $i = 2$ for the vertical y direction. The incident waves have amplitude A at infinity ($x = +\infty$). With ζ_i the time-dependent displacement of the centre of the cylinder from its equilibrium position in the two directions ($i = 1, 2$), the equations of motion of the cylinder (in the form of (3.2)) are

$$m\ddot{\zeta}_i + D_i\dot{\zeta}_i + S_i\zeta_i = F_i \qquad (i = 1, 2) \tag{3.103}$$

where m is the mass per unit length of the cylinder, which is assumed to be neutrally buoyant and F_i is the total periodic hydrodynamic force on the cylinder per unit length.

As discussed in section 3.2.2, the force F_i is affected by the interaction between the incident waves and the device and account must be taken of the waves 'radiated' by the surge and heave motions of the cylinder. Thus

$$F_i = F_{is} + \sum_{j=1}^{2} F_{ij} \tag{3.104}$$

where F_{is} is the force on the cylinder in the ith direction when held stationary and F_{ij} is the force on the cylinder in the ith direction due to motion in the jth direction.

Because the circular cylinder is symmetric, there are no forces induced in one direction by motions in the other direction and hence

$$F_{ij} = 0 \quad \text{for } i \neq j$$

However

$$F_{ii} = -a_{ii}\ddot{\xi}_i - b_{ii}\dot{\xi}_i \tag{3.105}$$

where a_{ii} is the added mass of the cylinder per unit length, and b_{ii} is a damping coefficient, accounting for the energy radiated away from the cylinder because of the oscillation in the ith direction per unit length of cylinder.

F_{is} is dependent on the incident wave amplitude and on the amplitude, at $x = +\infty$, of the wave produced by forced oscillation of unit amplitude of the cylinder in the ith direction. b_{ii} is also a function of this latter amplitude.

Based on these physical considerations, the analytical treatment by Evans yields the following expression for the efficiency of the device.

$$\eta = 2 \sum_{i=1}^{2} D_i b_{ii} / |Z_i|^2 \tag{3.106}$$

where $Z_i = (D_i + b_{ii}) + i[(m + a_{ii})\omega - S_i/\omega]$.

The optimum performance occurs when

$$S_i = (m + a_{ii})\omega^2 \quad \text{and} \quad D_i = b_{ii} \quad (i = 1, 2) \tag{3.107}$$

and then $\eta_{\max} = 100\%$.

Although Evans' notation has been partly retained above in order to avoid excessive subscribing, D_i would be $(D_e)_i$ and b_{ii} would be $(D_r)_{ii}$ in the notation of section 3.2 where a_{ii} was included within m. The similarity of the optimum conditions is then apparent. Again the energy extraction damping coefficient should be equal to the loss coefficient; in this case, the radiation damping coefficient.

For equal spring coefficients $S_1 = S_2$ and equal damping coefficients $D_1 = D_2$, Evans *et al.* [53] additionally show that the cylinder orbit is circular, with no reflection of the incident wave at any frequency. At the tuned frequency ω_0 there is also no transmission.

The experiments conducted by Evans *et al.* [53] to support the theoretical treatment just described, confirmed the predictions for infinitessimal waves as regards the 100% maximum efficiency and the broad bandwidth, but for finite-

amplitude waves several other important effects were observed to adversely affect the performance. These experiments were undertaken in a wave tank 10m long, 30cm wide and 60cm deep at the Department of Mechanical Engineering, University of Edinburgh, and made use of the experimental apparatus developed for the Edinburgh wave power project. To separate incident wave measurement from reflected wave measurement, two wave-height gauges were used at a fixed 1/4 wavelength separation. Movement of the fixed pair of gauges in the direction of wave propagation, until the maximum difference in wave amplitudes measured by the two gauges was achieved, allowed evaluation of the incident wave amplitude as the mean of the two readings, whilst half the difference of the two readings gave the reflected wave amplitude. Allowance was also made for the attenuation of the wave amplitude along the tank between the gauges and the model, and the theory required some modification to allow for the additional mass of the support structure of the surge-heave-pitch rig employed.

For the model used, a neutrally-buoyant circular cylinder 10cm in diameter and slightly narrower than the tank, Fig. 3.30 shows the variation of efficiency with the ratio of wavelength to cylinder diameter for different incident wave amplitudes. The broken line represents the theoretical prediction, excluding the

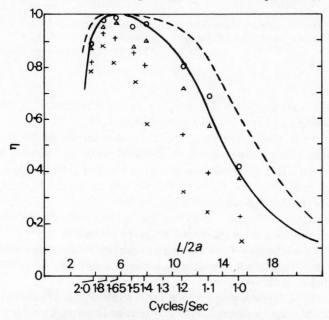

Fig. 3.30 – Variation of efficiency of power absorption η vs. wavelength to cylinder diameter ration, $L/2a$, for different incident wave apmplitues A. Cylinder axis submerges to depth h = 6.35cm so that a/h = 4/5.Cylinder tuned to 1.65 Hz or $L/2a$ = 5.7; $A/a \doteq$ ○, 0.033; △, 0.054; +, 0.096; ×. 0.18; ——, m_1 = 1.36; m_2 = 2.26; -----, m_1 = m_2 = 1.0. From [53] by courtesy of CML Publications Ltd.

effect of the added structural mass, whilst the full line indicates the prediction when structural mass is considered. Fig. 3.31 shows the variation of efficiency with the ratio of wave amplitude to cylinder radius for two different depths of submergence at a fixed frequency. The following effects on performance can be observed from these curves and from other observations recorded:

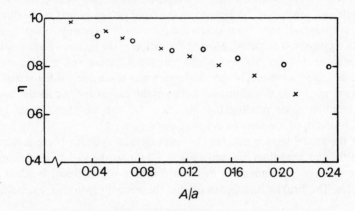

Fig. 3.31 – Variation of maximum efficiency of power absorption η vs. wave amplitude ratio A/a, for two different depth of submergence ratios a/h. Cylinder tuned to 1.5 Hz or $L/2a = 7.1$. a/h: ×, 0.8; ○, 0.67. From [53] by courtesy of CML Publications Ltd.

(1) As the wave amplitude increases, the theory is inadequate and actual efficiencies are lower and the bandwidth narrower.

(2) Also for increasing amplitude, the waves downstream of the cylinder contain higher harmonics, generally with twice the incident wave frequency. This occurred because the submerged cylinder acted as a beach and caused the waves to steepen (see section 2.1.5) and hence degenerate into higher harmonic components.

(3) Comparison of the full and broken lines of Fig. 3.30 indicates that the added structural mass reduces the efficiency bandwidth.

(4) For frequencies away from the tuned frequency, the damping coefficient decreases rapidly with depth of submergence and thus the efficiency bandwidth is narrowed.

(5) For a fixed frequency near to the tuned value, Fig. 3.31 indicates that the more deeply submerged cylinder can cope better with steeper waves, because it acts less like a beach (point (2) above).

(6) The cylinder caused very little reflection and most of the power loss occurred by transmission. This implies that mean horizontal second-order forces on the cylinder are lower than would be the case for a surface device which reflects more of the incident wave momentum.

3.5 FURTHER ENERGY-CONVERSION PROCESSES FOR SLOW-SPEED DEVICES

The oscillating buoy (section 3.2.2), Salter's Duck (section 3.4.1) and the Bristol Cylinder (section 3.4.3) all convert the wave energy into the energy of mechanical motion at the wave frequency ($\sim 0.1\,$Hz), which is far too low for conventional electricity generation at 50Hz. Electrical generation and other methods of utilising wave energy are discussed in Chapter 4, whilst immediate attention is directed to methods for increasing the speed within the primary energy-conversion process. Since gear boxes with high ratios of speed increment and good efficiency are difficult to make, attention has been directed towards the use of hydrostatic transmission systems, which are described by Korn [77] and Turnbull [132]. Some of the essential construction and performance characteristics of such systems are given in the following section, whilst the inclusion of a gyroscopic system is discussed in section 3.5.2.

3.5.1 Hydrostatic Transmission Systems

When power is transmitted by a fluid and positive displacement pumps and motors are employed, the process is defined as **hydrostatic transmission**. The process can be controlled by means of valves in the delivery or inlet lines or by variation of the stroke when a piston-type unit is used. The alternative hydrokinetic (or rotodynamic or turbomachine) type of unit is not appropriate for wave energy systems, as it is less efficient and generally more suited to very large flow rates.

The characteristics of most positive displacement pumps and of most positive displacement motors are similar, with the overall efficiency η_o given by the product of the volumetric efficiency η_v and the mechanical efficiency η_m. The volumetric efficiency accounts for leakage losses whilst the mechanical efficiency accounts for both viscous fluid friction and solid friction losses. Turnbull [132] gives the following simplified expressions for overall efficiency:

For the pump

$$\eta_o = \frac{1 - C_s/S}{1 + C_D S + C_f} \qquad (3.108a)$$

and for the motor

$$\eta_o = \frac{1 - C_D S - C_f}{1 + C_s/S} \qquad (3.108b)$$

where C_s = the leakage or 'slip' coefficient; C_D = the viscous drag coefficient; C_f = the solid friction coefficient, and $S = \mu N/p$ = a form of Sommerfeld number; μ = the fluid viscosity (Pas); N = the speed (rev/sec); p = the fluid pressure (Pa).

Pressure p is usually relatively high (up to 20MPa) with moderate or low flow rates Q (less than 0.4m³/min) giving powers pQ up to 130kW. Typical pump and motor characteristics are shown in Fig. 3.32. Although there are several different types of positive displacement pump and motor, the radial-piston type is more suitable for low-speed, high-torque applications and was therefore recommended by Salter *et al.* [125] for the power take-off pump. The axial-piston motor is better suited to high-speed, high-power conditions and the variable-angle swashplate type was selected by Salter *et al.* [125] to provide the constant speed drive suitable for electrical generation. These particular pumps and motors are shown in diagrammatic form in Figs. 3.33 and 3.34.

In a later design, Salter [124] recommends the use of a modified version of a ring cam pump, in which a ring cam with inward facing lobes drives roller followers, which in turn activate linkages which drive low-speed piston-type pumps as shown in Fig. 3.35.

3.5.2 Gyroscopic Energy-conversion Systems

In the words of Salter [124] "The axis of spin of a gyro defines one direction. We can consider the two other axes perpendicular to the spin axis as the 'ports' of a transforming device which converts torque into angular velocity". To appreciate this statement it is pertinent to recall the derivation of the gyroscopic relation from Newton's second law for rotational motion, which may be stated as "the rate of change of angular momentum is proportional to, and in the direction of, the applied torque".

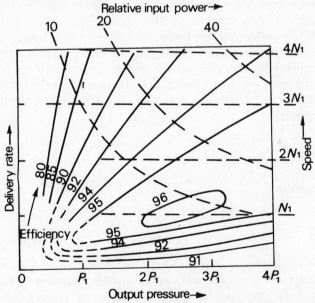

General pump performance charachteristics

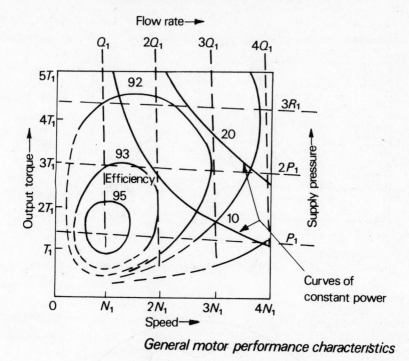

General motor performance characteristics

Fig. 3.32 – Typical pump and motor characteristics. From
[132] by courtesy of Butterworth and Co. (Publishers) Ltd.

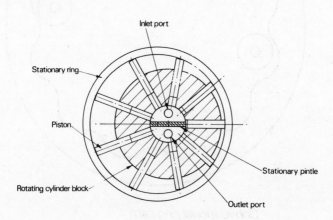

Fig. 3.33 – Radial-piston pump or motor.

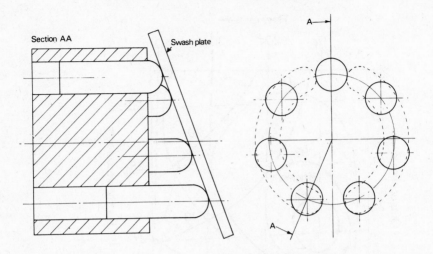

Fig. 3.34 — Axial-piston pump or motor.

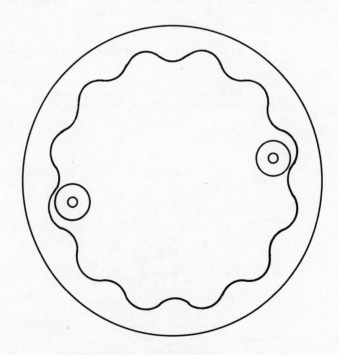

Conventional ring cam

Fig. 3.35 — continued next page.

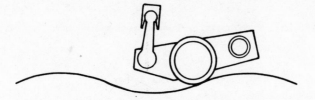

Roller follower and link which drives low speed pump

There are 384 units in each duck

Fig. 3.35 – Ring cam and roller follower. From [124]
by courtesy of The Institution of Electrical Engineers.

Now angular velocity, angular momentum and torque have directional significance, as well as scalar magnitude, and must therefore be represented as vector quantities. The isometric view of a gyroscope shown in Fig. 3.36(a) illustrates this point, with each vector drawn along the appropriate axis using the conventional right-hand screw rule to define the direction.

In view of Newton's law, the small change in angular momentum in the small time interval δt will be $T\delta t$ and as shown in Fig. 3.36(b) this will be

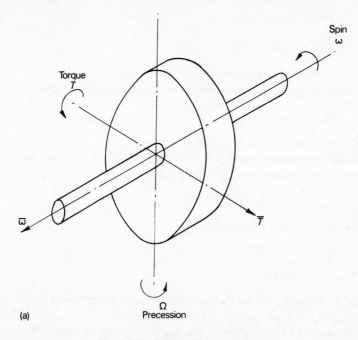

(a)

Fig. 3.36 – continued next page.

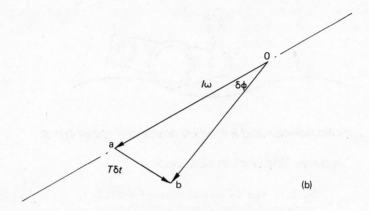

Fig. 3.36 – The behaviour of a simple gyroscope.

represented by a vector with the direction of the torque vector, whilst the initial angular momentum vector $I\omega$ will be directed along the spin axis. Vectorially adding the two vectors $I\omega$ and $T\delta t$ gives a resultant vector Ob and as $\delta t \to 0$, the magnitude is $I\omega$ but the direction is changed by the small angle $\delta\phi$.

Thus from the geometry

$$T\delta t = I\omega . \delta\phi \text{ as } \delta t \to 0 \tag{3.109}$$

or

$$T = I\omega . \Omega \tag{3.110}$$

where $\Omega = \mathrm{d}\phi/\mathrm{d}t$ = angular velocity of precession.

When the gyroscope has precessed by angle ϕ (3.110) becomes

$$T_{\text{in}} = I\omega . \Omega_{\text{out}} \cos\phi \tag{3.111}$$

for an input torque giving an output precession.

Since gyroscopes can equally function in the reverse manner, an input precession can produce an output torque so that

$$T_{\text{out}} = I\omega . \Omega_{\text{in}} \cos\phi \tag{3.112}$$

Salter [124] thus showed that

$$I\omega = \frac{\kappa}{r \cos\phi} \tag{3.113}$$

where $\kappa = T_{\text{in}}/\Omega_{\text{in}}$ = the hydrodynamic damping coefficient of the duck and $r = \Omega_{\text{out}}/\Omega_{\text{in}} = T_{\text{in}}/T_{\text{out}}$ = an equivalent gear ratio.

Equation (3.113) indicates that the ratio r can be varied by changing the speed of rotation ω of the gyroscope. Salter suggests that this ratio r could be

varied between a value of six for calm conditions and three for conditions near to the power limit. Furthermore, with pairs of gyroscopes spinning in opposite directions, the opposed output torques can be accommodated within the duck, without transmission to the backbone of the device.

3.6 OTHER DEVICES AND TECHNIQUES FOR WAVE-ENERGY CONVERSION

In the preceding sections of this chapter, devices which operate in heave, surge, pitch and nod have been discussed. There are however many devices which cannot be classified in this way, and some of these, especially the French flexible bag device, which is most competitive in terms of cost per unit power, require further treatment.

3.6.1 The French Flexible Bag Device

As described in section 1.6, this device is along, shallow structure (about one wavelength long by 0.05 wavelength deep) aligned in the direction of wave propagation. The port and starboard sides of the device are flexible and hence will deflect inwards under the hydrodynamic pressure of the wave crest and outwards in the region of the trough. Although the small finite depth of the device makes hydrodynamic analysis difficult, French [57] and Chaplin and French [23] have reported an analysis for waves *entering* a channel whose flexible walls extend downwards indefinitely and move horizontally and normally to the direction of wave propagation in simple harmonic motion, so extracting energy from the waves (see Fig. 3.37).

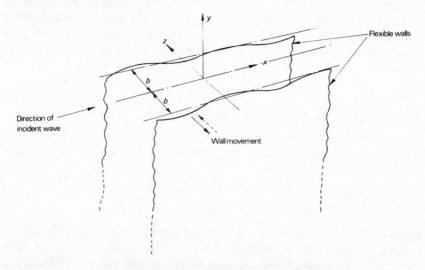

Fig. 3.37 – Flexible-sided channel of infinite depth.

The velocity potential ϕ which satisfies Laplace's Equation (2.6) and the surface boundary condition (2.13) and which must now also satisfy the conditions for attenuation in the direction of wave propagation (x) and sinusoidal variation, in the x direction, of the velocity normal to the walls (z direction in the notation of this text) is

$$\phi = \text{Re}\{\cosh[(1 + i)\alpha z]\exp[-sx + ny + ik(x - ct)]\} \qquad (3.114)$$

where c = phase velocity; k = wave number = $2\pi/L$; s = attenuation factor; $\alpha = \sqrt{ks}$, and $k^2 = s^2 + n^2$.

The power per unit area of absorbing surface is evaluated as the product of the velocity of the surface $(-\partial\phi/\partial z)$ and the hydrodynamic pressure $(\rho\partial\phi/\partial t)$. For a narrow channel, with breadth $2b$ less than one quarter wavelength, and with $s \sim 0.06k$, the resultant expression for the power developed in a channel of length l becomes

$$P = \frac{1}{2}\rho g a^2 bc[1 - \exp(-2sl)] \qquad (3.115)$$

where a = wave amplitude.

Chaplin and French [23] have reported the results of tests made on a 1/40th scale model floating free in heave only, with the tube height 75% immersed when in still water. At the most favourable frequency the model power was 1/3rd the tank power, with improved performance at the expense of pitch stability as the immersion was increased to 100%.

Since the device produces a low-pressure air flow from the various air-bag compartments, the primary conversion process to mechanical energy will be completed by means of two single-stage air turbines, the design of which has been already described in section 3.3. Chaplin and French [23] however recommended adjustable nozzle blades, closing the blade passage to give low reaction for high waves and opening them to give about 50% reaction for low waves.

3.6.2 Techniques for Focusing Wave Energy

The prospect of long, continuous lines of wave energy converters of the 'terminator' type encourages research into methods of focusing the wave energy, which may be classified as

(1) radiation methods
(2) refraction methods

Budal [16] dealt comprehensively with the former method. He considered a number of rigid, spaced, oscillating bodies, which could be partly or fully submerged. The incident wave, the total diffracted wave and the total radiated wave were each represented by separate velocity potentials in a similar manner

to Newman, as demonstrated in section 3.2.2. The power absorbed by the system was evaluated by summing the products of pressure × area × velocity normal to the area for the totality of the wetted surfaces of the N bodies.

Thus with

$$\Phi_i = \phi_i \exp(i\omega t) \quad \text{for the incident wave}$$
$$\Phi_d = \phi_d \exp(i\omega t) \quad \text{for the diffracted wave}$$
$$\Phi_r = \phi_r \exp(i\omega t) \quad \text{for the radiated wave} \qquad \cdot$$

the hydrodynamic pressure $p = \Sigma - \rho(\partial\Phi/\partial t) = -i\rho\omega(\Phi_i + \Phi_d + \Phi_r)$

the velocity vector $\overline{q} = \nabla(\Phi_i + \Phi_d + \Phi_r)$

and the power absorbed by the system

$$P = \int_s \overline{\text{Re}\{p\}\,\text{Re}\{\overline{q}\} \cdot \overline{dS}} \tag{3.116}$$

where the overbar indicates the time averaged value.

Although the complete mathematical treatment is outside the scope of the present text, the result of the analysis has already been shown in Fig. 2.15 and is repeated as Fig. 3.38. The fact that the oscillating bodies can absorb all the incident energy, even though they are spaced apart by distances substantially greater than their own diameter, is accounted for physically by the radiated waves and incident waves interfering in such a way that the flux of energy in the ocean is directed towards the bodies. When correctly operated the oscillating bodies become 'sinks' for the incident power, in a manner analogous to the absorption of electromagnetic power by the elements of an antenna array.

The physical phenomena on which refraction methods are based can be explained by reference to Fig. 2.6(a), which shows that as the waves enter shallower water, so the phase velocity c and the wavelength L decrease. Thus, if waves approach a beach with the line of their crests at an angle to the sea-bed contours, that part of the crest line which first encounters the shallower water will begin to move more slowly and the crests will come closer together (shorter wavelength). As a result the crest line will turn and tend to become parallel with the sea-bed contours, as shown in Fig. 3.39.

Refraction of waves by islands and shoals with circular bottom contours was reported by Arthur [7] and the phenomenon employed by Wirt of the Lockheed Corporation [143] as described in section 1.6. Fig. 3.40 from a Lockheed proposal [85] shows the refraction patterns for the Dam-Atoll wave energy device, whilst Fig. 3.41 gives a cross-section view of the device.

Mehlum and Stamnes [100] also suggest a method for employing the diffraction technique in order to focus ocean swells. Their approach is analogous to an optical lens and consists of a number of plates placed horizontally at

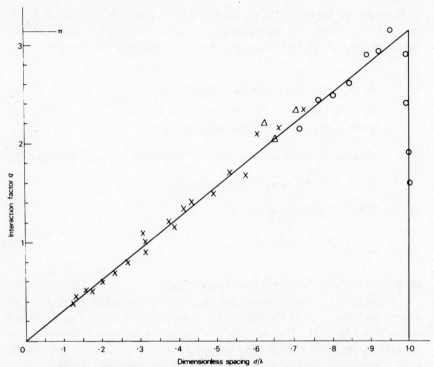

Fig. 3.38 – Interaction factor as function of buoy spacing. From [18] by courtesy of The Group of Wave Energy Research, Chalmers University of Technology, Gothenburg.

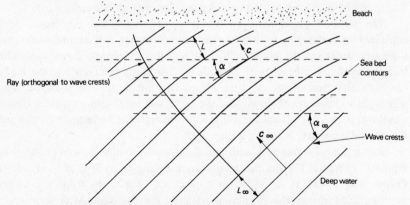

Fig. 3.39 – Refraction of waves with crests initially inclined to the sea-bed contours. L_∞ = wavelength in deep water; c_∞ = phase velocity in deep water; α_∞ = initial angle between wave crests and parallel sea-bed contours; L = wavelength in shallower water; c = phase velocity in shallower water; α = angle between wave crests and sea-bed contours in shallower water.

different depths below the surface, so as to focus the waves and thereby concentrate the wave energy for extraction by a device which is much smaller than the length of the crest line of the incident waves.

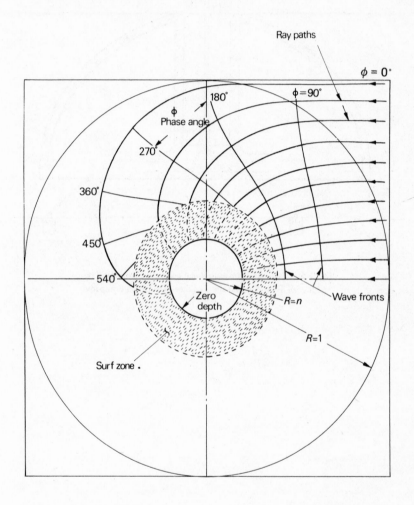

Fig. 3.40 – Refraction patterns with superimposed surf zone. From [85] by courtesy of L. S. Wirt and the Lockheed California Company.

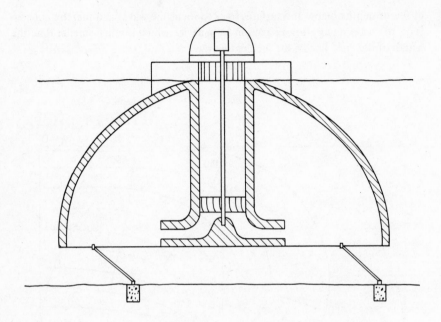

Fig. 3.41 — Dam-Atoll cross-sectional schematic. From [85] by
courtesy of L. S. Wirt and the Lockheed California Company.

CHAPTER 4

Mechanical energy conversion to other usable forms of energy

4.1 INTRODUCTION

The randomness of wave heights and frequencies was illustrated in Chapter 2 (section 2.3) and since the power in the waves is proportional to the square of the height times the period, and the efficiency of the device is frequency-dependent, then the variation with time of the power extracted by the device will be large (see Fig. 4.1). The design of the power take-off system to accommodate

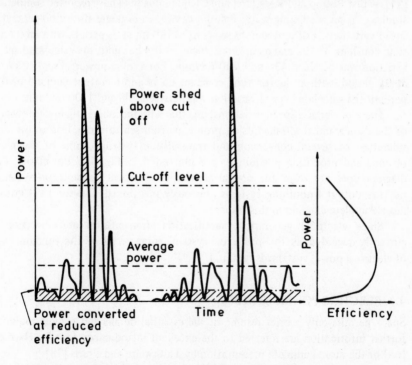

Fig. 4.1 – Interaction of the conversion characteristic and the power extracted by the device. From [42] by courtesy of the HMSO and the DOE.

these variations involves a compromise, requiring some shedding of power and an efficiency-power charactersistic suited to the average power level, as shown in Fig. 4.1. Smoothing of the output is obviously desirable and should preferably be arranged as soon as possible in the conversion-transmission chain. Smoothing can be achieved in the primary conversion process by:

(1) interconnection of several devices
(2) storage of hydraulic fluid
(3) inertial energy storage.

The effect of the inertia of a system is described by the **Inertia Time Constant**

$$H = \frac{\text{Energy stored at the rated speed}}{\text{Rated power}} \quad \text{(seconds)}$$

where the power for an electrical machine would be the apparent power in volt-amperes.

Power variation and smoothing are discussed more completely by Dawson [37], whilst Bishop and Rees [15] and Glendenning [61] have reported simulation studies, for an oscillating water column device, to evaluate the turbo-generator speed variations. For a moderate sea state, 35 kW/m at 7s period, with an inertia time constant of 10s and a current demand of 0.4 per unit, the calculated speed variation was between 430 and 700 rev/min. For a more powerful sea, 90kW/m at 9s period, with an inertia time constant of 5s and a current demand of 0.5 per unit the calculated speed variation was between 500 and 1100 rev/min.

These power and speed variations, together with the inherently low frequency of the device and the transmission problems from sea to shore, lead to the consideration of several conversion and transmission systems. Some of the more obvious and promising possibilities are illustrated in Fig. 4.2. For clarity, this diagram does not show the several alternative electrical transmission systems, nor the output smoothing systems previously mentioned. Dawson [37] gives a more complete diagram in this respect.

Since electrical generation, rectification, transmission and inversion is currently regarded as the preferred system, some recall of the fundamentals of electrical power systems is required.

4.2 ELECTRIC POWER SYSTEMS

Space permits only a brief resumé of the essential details and readers requiring further information are referred to the excellent introductory text by Harrison [68] or the more complete presentation by Laithwaite and Freris [78].

The e.m.f. generated by a simple single-phase generator is evaluated by considering a coil of N turns and area A square metres, rotating in a magnetic

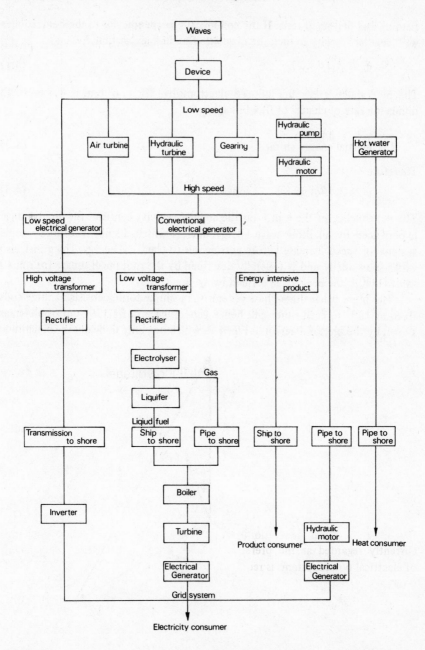

Fig. 4.2 – Conversion and Transmission systems.

field of flux density B tesla. If the coil initially perpendicular to the field, rotates with angular velocity ω then the magnetic flux linkage, at time t, is

$$\Phi = NAB \cos \omega t \tag{4.1}$$

The by Faraday's law the induced electromotive force, or e.m.f., e is equal to minus the rate of change of flux linkage, or

$$e = -\frac{\mathrm{d}\Phi}{\mathrm{d}t} \tag{4.2}$$

Therefore

$$e = NAB\omega \sin \omega t \quad \text{(volts)} \tag{4.3}$$

The dependence of the e.m.f. on the angular velocity confirms the disadvantage experienced by all those wave energy devices which do not incorporate some system for speed increase before conversion to electrical energy. The e.m.f. also varies sinusoidally and is generally described by the root mean square (or r.m.s.) value (that is, the peak value divided by $\sqrt{2}$).

The more usual three-phase generator, in simple form, consists of three coils fixed at 120° to each other and hence generating e.m.f.'s 120° out-of-phase, as shown by the phasor diagram in Fig. 4.3, which not only indicates the magnitude

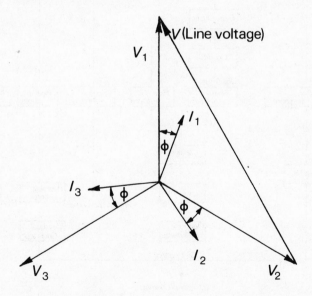

Fig. 4.3 – Phasor diagram for a star-connected three-phase generator. V_1, V_2, and V_3 are phasors representing the voltages induced in coils 1, 2 and 3 respectively, each having a magnitude V_p (the phase voltage).

of the voltage induced in each coil, but also the phase relationship. The currents in each of the three phases are also included and shown as lagging the voltage by an angle ϕ. If similar ends of the coils are connected together and the other ends are brought out to form the three terminals of the three-phase generator, the so-called 'star' connection, then the line voltage is determined as shown and is $\sqrt{3}$ times the phase voltage, whilst the line current is equal to the phase current. For the alternative 'delta' connection, the line voltage is equal to the phase voltage, but the line current is $\sqrt{3}$ times the phase current.

Since the current in a pure inductance lags the voltage by 90° ($v = L[di/dt]$) and the current in a pure capacitance leads the voltage by 90° ($i = C[dv/dt]$), whilst the current through a pure resistance is in phase with the voltage, it is convenient to represent the impedance phasor Z of an electric power circuit by the complex number

$$Z = R + jX \tag{4.4}$$

where $j = \sqrt{-1}$ is used by electrical engineers to avoid confusion with i representing current; $R =$ the resistive component; $X =$ the reactive component (>0 for an inductance, <0 for a capacitance).

Unless $X = 0$, there will be a phase angle ϕ between the voltage and current phasors as shown in Fig. 4.3. The real power P in any one phase is then $V_p I_p \cos\phi$ and hence for the three phases, the real power, in terms of the phase voltage V_p and phase current I_p is

$$P = 3V_p I_p \cos\phi \tag{4.5}$$

Since either $V = \sqrt{3}V_p$ and $I = I_p$ for a star connection or $V = V_p$ and $I = \sqrt{3}I_p$ for a delta connection, the real power can be expressed in terms of the line quantities as

$$P = \sqrt{3}\,VI\cos\phi \quad \text{(watts)} \tag{4.6}$$

For convenience in power system calculations, two other quantities are defined.

the apparent power $S = \sqrt{3}\,VI$ (volt-amperes) $\tag{4.7}$

and

the reactive power $Q = \sqrt{3}\,VI\sin\phi$ (volt amperes reactive) $\tag{4.8}$

Although the sign of Q is arbitrary, convention defines an electrical load with inductance as consuming both real and reactive power, whilst a capacitor supplies reactive power to the system. For transmission lines, the equivalent circuit for one phase of a short length of line is shown in Fig. 4.4. For cables, the capacitance is dominant and leads to large reactive power generation and to charging currents which limit the length of the cable. Alternatively for long

cables, reactive power compensation must be provided by means of shunt inductance. Not only does this compensation add up to 25% to the cost of an a.c. cable installation, but it is difficult to apply to undersea cables.

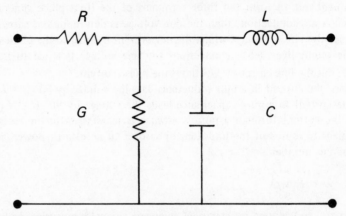

Fig. 4.4 – Equivalent circuit for one phase of a short length of cable. R = resistance of conductor; L = inductance due to magnetic field surrounding the conductors; G = shunt conductance due to leakage currents in the insulation; C = capacitance due to electric field between conductors.

Obviously an a.c. power system has the outstanding advantage that it allows the voltage to be stepped up or down, using a transformer to suit each particular part of the system:

- generation at 11kV–22kV to suit the machine designer
- transmission at 132kV, 275kV or 400kV to keep the I^2R losses small in the transmission lines
- distribution to the consumer at 240V or 415V.

To avoid the reactive power problem of the transmission cables d.c. cables may be used, even though rectifiers are needed to convert a.c. to d.c. and then inverters required to reconvert to a.c. Such a system has the added advantage that it can be used to interconnect two a.c. systems which are not synchronised.

4.3 CONVERSION AND TRANSMISSION SYSTEMS

The various possible systems have been identified in Fig. 4.2 and each can now be examined and assessed, by considering the separate parts of the complete process.

4.3.1 Low-speed Electrical Generation

Conventional machines for electrical generation cannot operate economically at frequencies below about 10Hz, because the ohmic losses are then significant. With wave frequencies of about 1/10Hz, it is clear that conventional machines

directly driven from device motions are impractical. Unconventional machines making use of the phenomenon of superconductivity may however permit low-speed generation. Several elements and many more compounds have resistivities which fall rapidly to zero within a few degrees of absolute zero. Thus, machines with superconducting windings will have no ohmic loss and no lower frequency limit. This technique has been discussed by Wilson [139] who concluded that preliminary studies revealed no insuperable problems and that costs would be reasonable. Wilson considered two schemes: one using dipole windings for both the field coil and the armature, and rotating in a similar manner to a conventional generator. The other scheme employed two solenoid coils, with the inner one having linear reciprocating motion. Because of the problem of transmitting the driving force from ambient temperature surroundings to the low temperature environment, the armature would be difficult to operate in the superconducting state and Wilson illustrates a specific design with only the field coil superconducting.

Binns [14] suggested the use of permanent magnet generators and concluded that although there were many problems, this type of machine would be relatively efficient. Bishop and Rees [15] however considered these machines would only be economical if high grade magnet material was used and that at high ratings there would be demagnetisation problems. Low-speed electrical generation is therefore not considered competitive at the present time.

4.3.2 Conventional Electrical Generation

The use of conventional generators implies a speed increase of the order of 100, and direct gearing is ruled out because of the high inertial loads and overspeed conditions. Air and hydraulic turbines and hydraulic pumps and motors are all acceptable devices for effecting the necessary speed increase (see Chapter 3). The choice of generator must then be made between d.c. machines, induction generators and synchronous a.c. generators. However, d.c. machines are ruled out because of the relatively low terminal voltages at which they can generate. There is also a danger of flashover of the commutator under overspeed conditions. They would however be suitable for local loads.

Induction generators although cheap and robust, have limited efficiency and problems of control, compensation and stability.

The choice of a.c. synchronous machines is dictated by their flexibility of operation, efficiency and cost. They are however most unlikely to be synchronised with the grid, and will operate at arbitrary frequencies, varying from one machine to another.

4.3.3 Electrical Transmission Systems

In section 4.2, the reactive power limitation on a.c. transmission cable length was noted. Thus oil-impregnated paper-insulated cables, which are uncompensated, are limited to a length of about 40km. Cure and Sullivan [34] indicate

that this figure can be increased to 100km by the use of XPLE insulated cables. For a string of Salter Ducks, they therefore recommend synchronous a.c. generation at 3.3kV with grouping of machine outputs at a 3.3/132kV transformer. Transformers would then be connected together using flexible cables to a connecting chamber located on the sea bed, and the power transmitted ashore at 132kV by a small number of high capacity cables, for connection to the grid in a conventional switching station. Cure and Sullivan conclude that this would be a less costly scheme than one employing d.c. transmission, although they confirm that flexible cables for operation at 132kV have not yet been developed.

The more widely advocated transmission system is shown schematically in Fig. 4.5, with generation by synchronous a.c. machine at 3.3kV and transfor-

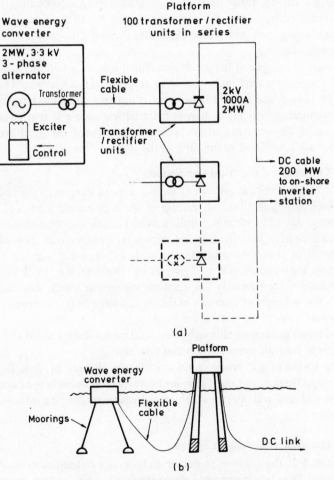

Fig. 4.5 – d.c. electrical transmission system.
From [42] by courtesy of HMSO and the DOE.

mation on the wave energy converter to a higher voltage ($\sim$22kV). Power is then transmitted by flexible cables, which according to Bishop and Rees [15] have a maximum rating at present of 20MVA, 22kV, to either sea-bed or platform mounted transformer/rectifier units. Dawson [37] then suggests that the d.c. outputs are connected in series as shown in Fig. 4.5 to give 200MW at 200kV for transmission to shore. Bishop and Rees [15] suggest 250MW at $\pm$250kV d.c. at peak rating and recommend the use of two separate $\pm$250kV, 2000A bipole thyristor inverters at the onshore station.

Glendenning [61], McIlhagger [99] and Wallace and Whittington [136] all accept that the variable frequency of generation and the reactive power problem of a.c. cables demand that the d.c. transmission system is used. Wallace and Whittington also discuss cables, cable laying and choice of route.

4.3.4 Fuel Production and Transmission

Glendenning [60] stated that the concept of a 'floating factory' was first introduced by Denton et al. [40] in 1975, although it would appear that Winer [141] also considered the manufacture of synthetic fuels in connection with ocean thermal energy conversion (OTEC) schemes at about the same time.

Figure 4.2 indicates the complete process, starting with the generation of electricity at medium voltage for use by the electrolyser. Since the electolysis of sea water is not a practical proposition, it would be essential to include a desalination process, followed by electrolysis to produce hydrogen at a pressure of 3MPa. Alternative fuels, such as methanol, methane and gasoline, could then be produced by catalytic combinations of hydrogen and carbon oxides. Gaseous fuels could then be transmitted to shore by pipeline and liquid fuels conveyed ashore by ship, to be used in a boiler-turbine-generator system to produce electricity. The limitation imposed by the Second Law of Thermodynamics on the reconversion from thermal energy at the boiler to mechanical energy at the turbine is an obvious disadvantage of this process and in any case Glendenning [61] estimates that the fuel costs would be more than four times normal fossil fuel costs.

4.3.5 Energy Intensive Products

The hydrogen, produced as indicated above, could be combined by catalytic reaction with nitrogen to produce ammonia, which forms the basis for fertilisers vital to the economy of the UK. Dawson [37] estimates that future demand for such fertilisers will require a power output approaching 3GW, but Glendenning [61] suggests that the production cost would be about twice that of production from coal and hence this process is not viable.

Other energy intensive products such as aluminium could be produced on a 'floating factory', or uranium fuel could be extracted from the sea water. Glendenning [60] suggested these possibilities, as did Winer [141] in connection with ocean thermal energy conversion (OTEC) schemes. Winer also suggested

that lithium batteries could be employed to transport the energy by electro-chemical methods, and detailed consideration appears to have been given to this idea in the US, especially when the energy converter is much more than 100km from the shore.

4.3.6 Hydraulic Transmission

As shown in Fig. 4.2 the hydraulic pump and motor pair can be separated, so that the hydraulic motor and all the electrical generation equipment are located on shore. Both filtered sea water and conventional hydraulic oils have been considered for the power transmission, with the sea water system found to be more efficient, since no return pipe is required and since water has the lower viscosity. Dawson [37] reported that for a 1.2m diameter pipe. 24km long and operating at a pressure of 15MPa, with an 80MW power input, the losses amount to about 14MW ($\eta \sim 83\%$). Based on North Sea oil technology such a fluid transmission system is considered feasible, but the pipe would have to be laid in a trench and provided with a protective overlayer of concrete. As a result, the cost is considered to be two or three times that of electrical transmission, although the rectifier and inverter of the d.c. electrical transmission system would be eliminated.

4.3.7 Thermal Transmission

In this method, the original device motion would be converted to thermal energy using a friction brake. Heated water or oil could then be applied to an insulated storage vessel for transportation ashore, where it could be used for district heating, power station preheating or conversion to electricity. Since the friction brake converts high-grade mechanical energy to low-grade thermal energy, the reconversion to electrical energy would result in very low overall efficiencies. Furthermore, district heating demands are generally not adjacent to wave energy supply locations and thus thermal transmission is regarded as the least promising method.

4.3.8 Other Possible Conversion Systems

This chapter would not be complete without some mention of other possible conversion systems. Leishman and Scobie [81] gave a very comprehensive survey of the situation up to 1976 and this included the linear generator device patented by The University College of North Wales, which has also been described by Omholt [113]. Piezoelectric methods have also been suggested, whilst Salomon and Harding [120] considered the use of gas concentration cells.

CHAPTER 5

Construction and mooring of devices

5.1 INTRODUCTION

The designer of any device must first analyse the forces and moments which have to be sustained by that device. He must next assess the effects of the local environment on the materials he might use and then within the overall constraint of economic viability, he must produce a suitable design solution. Since the basic requirement is to use powerful waves, forces will generally be large. Furthermore, since the waves are so random, these forces will be difficult to predict, especially when the waves break or the device lifts from the surface to 'slam' back into the water. The environment is not only corrosive and erosive, but can cause severe problems due to marine fouling. It is therefore apparent that the designers of wave energy converters must ultimately rely on a wide range of experimental investigations, both at sea and in the laboratory. Experiments conducted on models in the laboratory or at sea must be carefully planned in order to preserve dynamical similarity (see Appendix B) and in some cases complete similarity may not be possible. For example, stresses increase in proportion to linear dimensions, because wave forces increase as the cube of the linear dimension, whilst areas only increase as the square of the linear dimension. This occurs even for a correctly scaled model in correctly scaled waves.

Both mooring and maintenance can contribute significantly to the overall costs of many wave energy devices and hence must be taken into account early in the overall design considerations.

Attention will therefore be directed in this chapter to the various points identified above and to the existing background of experience which may prove relevant.

5.2 DETERMINATION OF WAVE-INDUCED FORCES

Forces on floating and submerged objects were discussed in section 2.1.5 and the appropriate equation (2.34) is repeated below:

$$F = \frac{1}{4}\rho g(a_i^2 + a_r^2 - a_t^2) \qquad (5.1)$$

where F = the horizontal force per unit width of device; a_i = the amplitude of the incident wave; a_r = the amplitude of the reflected wave; a_t = the amplitude of the transmitted wave.

This analytical expression, based on linear theory, holds for waves of small amplitude, but as observed in section 2.1.5 for waves of higher amplitude, the forces may be less than predicted in the case of the circular cylinder device because of second harmonics in the transmitted waves and because of wave 'set-up'. Similar behaviour has been observed for ducks. Salter [124] has indicated that, for a 10 m duck in waves of small to moderate amplitude, the mean horizontal force is about 13 kN per metre width, but that the force tends to fall with larger amplitudes and even become negative for extreme irregular waves. The reduction is attributed to energy transmitted to the leeward by waves created by the movement of the duck mounting and by the large angular movements of the duck. The ultimate negative values are accounted for by the waves breaking over the duck to give waves with higher frequency (lower period) and hence, for energy conservation, higher amplitudes.

On the other hand, impulsive forces induced by 'slamming' could be large. It is therefore apparent that the designer may well be able to calculate the cyclic forces due to waves of small amplitude and hence determine possible fatigue damage, but that the effect of forces due to extreme conditions may only be determined by experiment as suggested by Smith [127]. Nevertheless, Dawson [37] has indicated that theoretical studies on breaking waves and slamming have been carried out at Cambridge University, the National Maritime Institute and the Hydraulics Research Station.

Although there is a considerable background of experience concerning wave-induced forces on ships and off-shore structures, there are two essential differences in the case of wave-energy converters, namely:

(1) Some wave-energy converters lie 'broadside' to the waves by choice.
(2) Some wave-energy converters consist of more than one part, with relative motion between the parts and hence more than six degrees of freedom.

The need for continuing experimental work on specific devices is clear and Dawson [37] confirmed that both wave tank and intermediate scale experiments were planned by the Technical Advisory Group responsible for structures and fluid loading in support of the UK Wave Energy Research and Development Programme.

5.3 DETERMINATION OF STRUCTURAL STRESSES AND STRAINS

For most practical purposes, the relatively-simple methods of conventional 'mechanics of solids' may be employed to determine the stresses and strains within the structure of the device. Such methods would seem to be particularly

justified in view of the difficulty of prediction of the wave-induced forces, to which must be added the normal still-water forces due to the different distributions of weight and buoyancy.

For advanced analysis, the more complex finite-element method might be employed. This method has already been incorporated in a number of computer programs, originally developed for other purposes but adaptable to suit wave energy devices. An example is the NASA Structural Analysis program (NASTRAN) described by MacNeal [92]. The cost of computing time might however restrict usage of such programs to the checking of the simpler methods in a few specific cases.

5.4 STRUCTURAL MATERIALS AND MANUFACTURING METHODS

The two main structural materials are concrete and steel, which have already been extensively used in many applications at sea. Glass-reinforced plastics, currently used in the construction of small boats, might also be employed. The relative merits of these materials must be assessed in relation to the following problems posed by the device environment and operational conditions:

(1) Salt water is very corrosive, especially in the 'splash zone', where the structure is exposed alternately to water and then air.

(2) Wave energy converters are subject to fluctuating forces so that fatigue endurance is important.

Furthermore corrosion can affect the fatigue life of a component, especially in the presence of stray electrical currents created by the generation and transmission equipment. Hudson [71] has reported the results of the UK Offshore Steels Research Project which showed crack growth rates six times the 'dry' rates for structural steel in sea water at frequencies of 0.1Hz. However in other tests, cathodic protection was shown to restore the 'dry' fatigue characteristics.

(3) Marine fouling by the settlement and growth of marine plants and animals can increase the mass of a device by as much as $50kg/m^2$ every year, and could influence corrosion and corrosion fatigue.

5.4.1 Concrete

Reinforced concrete ships of the 1914–18 war, with lives of 50 years and more, and concrete forts of the 1939–45 war have demonstrated the durability and corrosion resistance of this material. Concrete can also be easily formed into complicated shapes and the negligible tensile strength can be improved by reinforcing or prestressing. It is however expensive, unless production line techniques are used and it is heavy. There may also be problems due to fatigue and due to stray currents in the reinforced concrete.

5.4.2 Steel

Steel is obviously a well-proven material for use at sea, although there may be fatigue problems and appropriate corrosion protection must be provided. This involves the use of epoxy-resin based paints and cathodic protection.

Cockerell *et al.* [25] have suggested that in principle such protection should give a 25-year life, although the corrosion protection would add substantially to the costs of the hull. Their raft design in steel consisted of a gridwork of transverse and longitudinal bulkheads at approximately 13m centres, typical of shipbuilding practice. This arrangement of the bulkheads conveniently provides the required ballast tanks.

5.5 MOORING

The designer's first consideration must be to assess the magnitude of the forces to be sustained by the mooring system, as in section 5.2, where horizontal forces of up to 13kN per metre width of Salter Duck were predicted. Dawson [37] suggests that these forces might be as high as 100kN/m for oscillating water columns and rafts. As well as these wave-induced forces there may be forces due to currents and, to a lesser extent, due to winds. The next consideration relates to the compliance of the mooring system, especially as regards limitations imposed by the flexibility of any electrical cables and by the proximity of adjacent converters.

Three types of conventional mooring system, which could be used for wave energy devices are:

(1) catenary
(2) taut elastic
(3) tethered buoyant-structure

as shown in Fig. 5.1. Dynamic positioning by propulsion or active mooring are other possibilities.

5.5.1 Catenary Moorings

A considerable background of experience exisits with this type of system, including the mooring of semi-submersible platforms used in some North Sea oil fields. As can be seen from Fig. 5.1 and the following analysis, there is a near-horizontal tension at the sea bed and this ensures good location by 'drag' anchors. Catenary moorings also provide 'spring' in the system and this compliance would generally be a desirable characteristic. It is essential that this type of mooring line has significant weight per unit length and this is assumed in the analysis.

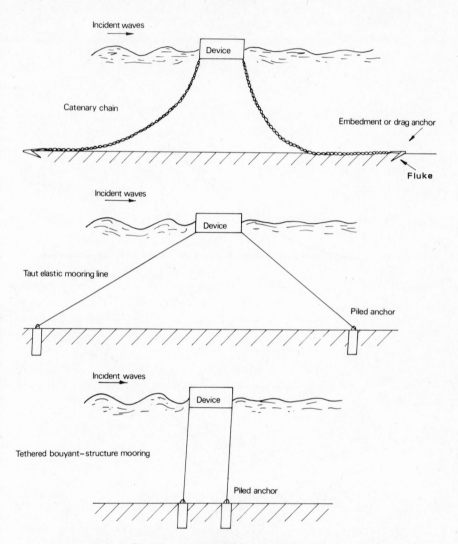

Fig. 5.1 – Mooring and anchoring methods.

Consider the catenary mooring line shown in Fig. 5.2 which has an 'effective' weight w per unit length (that is, weight of the line less the weight of water displaced per unit length). In the absence of other forces such as those due to fluid drag, the elemental section is in equilibrium when

$$T + w\delta s \sin\phi = (T + \delta T) \cos\delta\phi \tag{5.2}$$

by resolving tangentially, and

$$(T + \delta T) \sin\delta\phi = w\delta s \cos\phi \tag{5.3}$$

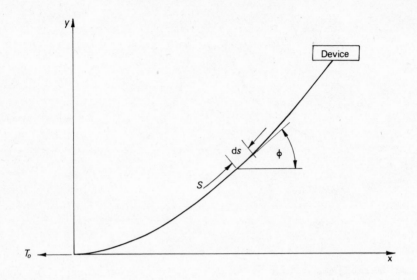

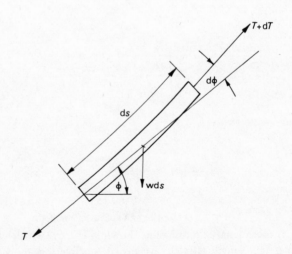

Fig. 5.2 – Catenary mooring line.

by resolving along the normal.

As $\delta s \to 0$, then $\delta\phi \to 0$, $\cos\delta\phi \to 1$, $\sin\delta\phi \to \delta\phi$ and hence

$$\frac{dT}{ds} = w\sin\phi \qquad\qquad (5.4)$$

and
$$\frac{d\phi}{ds} = \frac{w}{T}\cos\phi \tag{5.5}$$

Also
$$\int_{T_0}^{T}\frac{dT}{T} = \int_{0}^{\phi}\tan\phi\,d\phi$$

and hence
$$\log_e\frac{T}{T_0} = \log_e(\sec\phi)$$

or
$$T = T_0\sec\phi \tag{5.6}$$

Substituting (5.6) into (5.5) gives
$$\int_{0}^{\phi}\frac{d\phi}{\cos^2\phi} = \int_{0}^{s}\frac{w}{T_0}\,ds$$

Thus
$$\tan\phi = \frac{ws}{T_0} \tag{5.7}$$

And since $\tan^2\phi + 1 = \sec^2\phi$, (5.6) and (5.7) give
$$\left(\frac{ws}{T_0}\right)^2 + 1 = \left(\frac{T}{T_0}\right)^2$$

or
$$\frac{T}{T_0} = \sqrt{\left(\frac{ws}{T_0}\right)^2 + 1}$$

Now
$$x = \int_{0}^{s} ds\cos\phi = \int_{0}^{s}\frac{T_0}{T}\,ds = \int_{0}^{s}\frac{ds}{\sqrt{(ws/T_0)^2 + 1}}$$

Therefore
$$x = \frac{T_0}{w}\sinh^{-1}\left(\frac{ws}{T_0}\right) \tag{5.8}$$

Since
$$\frac{dy}{dx} = \tan\phi = \frac{ws}{T_0}$$

Then
$$y = \int_{0}^{x}\frac{ws}{T_0}\,dx$$

and from (5.8)

$$\frac{ws}{T_o} = \sinh \frac{wx}{T_o}$$

Therefore

$$y = \int_0^x \sinh\left(\frac{wx}{T_o}\right) dx = \frac{T_o}{w}\left[\cosh\left(\frac{wx}{T_o}\right) - 1\right] \tag{5.9}$$

A curve whose equation has the form of (5.9) is called a catenary and gives the name to this type of mooring. If the line is too short to ensure that $\phi = 0$ at the sea bed, the above equations may be used from the origin to find x_1, y_1, s_1, ϕ_1, at the sea bed position.

Further detail concerning the statics and dynamics of mooring line can be found in the text by Berteaux [12] and the analysis of multicomponent mooring systems has been given by Ansari [6].

5.5.2 Taut Elastic Moorings

Man-made fibre ropes, which are neutrally buoyant (or nearly so), could be used for mooring purposes. In this case the ropes are essentially straight and rely on the elasticity of the material for the necessary compliance. The main background of experience relates to berthing situations however.

5.5.3 Tethered Buoyant-Structure Moorings

As shown in Fig. 5.1, the buoyancy of the floating structure maintains the mooring lines under tension and thus the heave motion is reduced. The reduced compliance would however probably make this type of mooring unsuitable for wave energy devices.

5.5.4 Dynamic Positioning

Dynamic positioning can either be achieved by means of a set of computer-controlled propellers activated to maintain position over a group of sonic transducers on the sea-bed, or by means of several mooring lines connected to computer-controlled winches aboard the device. The power requirements and the expense of the control equipment discourage the use of this system for wave energy converters.

5.5.5 Anchors

There are essentially three types of anchor — deadweight, drag or embedment and piled. The choice depends primarily on the soil composition of the sea bed and hence requires extensive sampling at each particular site. Drag anchors with 'flukes' which 'dig' into the sea bed can be used except where rock is encountered. Then either deadweight (or clump) anchors or rock piles must be used.

5.5.6 Mooring Line Materials

Chain, wire rope and fibre ropes are all suitable materials. Chain has been used traditionally for mooring to anchors, but the use of wire rope is increasing, because of the ease of handling and the saving in weight. Man-made fibres, such as nylon, polyester, polypropylene and parafil, all have excellent corrosion resistance, but inferior abrasion resistance compared with chain wire. As yet little experience has been gained in using fibre ropes for mooring to anchors.

More extensive discussion of mooring and anchoring can be found in Dawson [37] and Hancock [66].

CHAPTER 6

Environmental, social and industrial considerations

6.1 INTRODUCTION

Any significant human activity interacts with other natural and human activities and it is prudent to anticipate this interaction and avoid any possible serious consequence. In the UK, a Technical Advisory Group of the Wave Energy Steering Committee has considered these aspects of wave energy conversion and although it will naturally take several years to complete some investigations, Dawson [36, 37] reports that no serious problem has yet been identified. In the US, environmental problems have been related more to ocean thermal energy conversion, as reported by Dugger [46] or to more general ocean energy projects as reported by Lewis and Waite [83], whilst the effect of waves on the coastline is extensively covered by the US Army Coastal Engineering Research Center [134].

The major environmental and social problems associated with wave energy will be identified and then assessed in relation to the problems experienced by other energy conversion processes. In particular consideration will be given to the effects of wave energy converters on:

- the physical state of the adjacent coastline;
- the visual amenity;
- the ecological balance;
- navigation;
- the fishing industry;
- the off-shore oil industry;
- the social wellbeing of local communities.

6.2 EFFECTS ON THE ADJACENT COASTLINE

Coastlines consiting of beaches of sand or shingle are most affected by wave action, and there are two major results. First, the waves create a flow along the shoreline, called the along-shore littoral current, and second, they transport the beach material to or from the shoreline depending upon the type of wave. Short steep waves, normally created by a storm near the coast, tend to remove

beach material, whilst long waves (swells) tend to move material from deep water onto the beach. The offshore (erosion) process may occur more frequently in winter storms, whilst the onshore (accretion) process occurs in summer.

The along-shore littoral current results from the angle of approach of the waves to the beach, and the associated littoral drift of material usually has a dominant direction. Caldwell [19] gives the average net rate of drift along the south shore of Long Island as over $3 \times 10^5 m^3$/year to the west, whilst the US Army indicate that some shorelines experience rates five times that value.

To determine the effect of wave-energy converters on the waves reaching the shoreline requires a knowledge of:

(1) the height, direction, and frequency of the waves transmitted by the devices;
(2) the diffraction of waves passing around the devices;
(3) wave regeneration by the wind between device and shoreline;
(4) the sea-bed contour lines.

Consequently mathematical analysis is not easy, but Dawson [36] reported a calculation by The Hydraulics Research Station for a force 7 storm situation. In this specific case, the waves became less steep because the significant wave height is reduced from 5.9m to 4.6m whilst the down-crossing period increased from 8.4s to 9.0s. Such a reduction in wave steepness would reduce erosion. For the shorelines of North and South Uist and Benbecula in the Outer Hebrides (North-West Scotland) the net tendency to cause accretion is considered to be beneficial rather than deterimental, but this conclusion might not apply to other coastlines.

6.3 EFFECTS ON THE VISUAL AMENITY

It is unlikely that wave-energy converters themselves will be visible from the shore, unless they are sea-bed located and hence close inshore. The associated shore terminal for the reception and transmission of the energy or energy-intensive products and for maintenance purposes could be suitably designed to be aesthetically acceptable. Thus the visual amenity might only suffer because of the overhead electricity transmission lines which would have to be routed through some of the most scenically beautiful parts of Scotland.

6.4 EFFECTS ON THE ECOLOGY

The greatest concern must be for the fish population of any particular location, although bird-life and sea-bed plant-life might also be affected directly or indirectly by wave-energy converters. Whereas the bottom-feeding (demersal) fish such as cod and haddock and shellfish such as lobster and crab are unlikely to be affected, fish that spend the greater part of their lives nearer the surface require more careful consideration. Herring spawn on clean gravel and after hatching the lavae

rise from the sea-bed to be transported by currents to a new location. Eventually the mature fish return to the spawning grounds. If wave energy converters affected the currents between the spawning and feeding grounds this natural cycle could be upset. Certainly disturbance of the gravel spawning grounds would be inadvisable.

Salmon, commercially important to Scotland, travel from feeding grounds in the oceans to rivers where they spawn. En route, they probably swim near the surface and might be diverted by wave energy devices, or devoured by predatory birds or seals, which might themselves be attracted to the devices.

Provided that the number of wave-energy converters in any particular location increased in a controlled and systematic manner, any harmful effects could be detected and appropriate action taken.

On the other hand for the shell-sand beaches along the west coast of the Uists, Probert and Mitchell [117] suggest that the reduced wave impact would increase the diversity and density of the fauna, and might allow the establishment of some species of mollusc.

Wildlife could be endangered by the electricity transmission system and Probert and Mitchell [116, 117] have reported that certain animals may be deterred from crossing power line corridors because of the audible hum due to corona (air ionisation). There are also significant mortalities of some bird species caused by the birds striking the high-level earth wire during poor visibility and at night. For this reason, they recommend that consideration be given to burying appropriate stretches of powerline.

6.5 EFFECTS ON NAVIGATION, THE FISHING AND OFF-SHORE OIL INDUSTRIES

The primary hazard to shipping must be the risk of collision due to the low free board of the wave-energy devices making them undetectable either by direct sighting or by radar. Elevated warning lights and radar reflectors will be required and navigation channels between lines of converters will need to be particularly well marked. A second hazard for small boats relates to wave reflection from the converters causing standing waves of increased amplitude (see (2.39) of Chapter 2). Transmitted waves of increased amplitude may also occur in certain circumstances, as mentioned in section 5.2. Thus, except for maintenance purposes, shipping would have to be excluded from the proximity of the devices.

Interference to shipping would obviously depend on location. Whereas fishing boats would be disadvantaged off the Outer Hebrides and in the Moray Firth in Scottish waters and off the southern Cornish coast, major international shipping routes would be affected by wave-energy converters off the Scilly Isles in the English Channel. Although wave energy devices will offer little hindrance to off-shore oil exploration, they could interfere with the transport of that oil by ship, as for example from Sullom Voe in the Shetland Isles.

6.6 EFFECTS ON LOCAL COMMUNITIES

The development of a major new industrial activity in an area, such as the Outer Hebrides, which has little industry, a declining population and relatively high unemployment, must generally be to the advantage of the local community. Apart from the obvious need for workers to construct, operate and maintain any new industrial development, there is a second advantage in the case of a power producing system, in as much as the power can be used locally for other new industries.

Although remote sites with small local populations and few port facilities may initially appear unattractive, Dawson [36] gives examples of previous successful developments of a similar nature, such as the Dounreay nuclear power station on the northern coast of Scotland and the Sullom Voe oil terminal in the Shetland Isles. Skilled manpower with experience in all branches of engineering, and divers would need to be brought to the area, but the necessary seafaring experience would be provided by the local community.

6.7 CONCLUSIONS

The foregoing sections of this chapter have identified some of the more important environmental and social problems created by wave-energy devices and even though Probert & Mitchell [117] suggest that wave-energy conversion is not necessarily environmentally benign, it is clear that the problems are much less severe than occur with many other energy conversion processes.

One of the anticipated problems is the prospect of an oil tanker striking a wave-energy device. Such an accident is however unlikely to occur, as wave-energy devices will not exist in significant numbers until oil supplies decline, partly by plan, but mainly because of the relatively long development time for new energy technologies ($\sim$ 20 years).

Concern for the unsightly appearance of overhead electricity transmission lines in areas of great scenic beauty and the danger of these overhead lines to wildlife is justifiable and the recommendation by Probert & Mitchell [117] that these powerlines be buried must be accepted in certain locations. This will of course add to the cost of the transmission system, since underground cables are more expensive than overhead cables by a factor of between 10 and 15, because of the poor insulation provided by wet earth compared with air. However for a typical electrical network, the transmission system accounts for 25% of the total capital cost and the distribution system, which accounts for a further 25% of the cost, is by underground cable in built-up areas. Thus the additional cost of underground transmission over limited distances should not be prohibitive.

Although the adverse effects of wave-energy devices on the fish population must be minimised by careful location and installation of the devices, such adverse effects should be assessed by comparison with conventional thermal power stations (both fossil and fissile). Because of their low efficiencies (section

1.2), thermal power stations must reject large amounts of energy as heat transfer to the environment. For direct water cooling, Eden *et al.* [48] have indicated that the effects are diverse and not fully understood, but report that Wilson & Jones [140] have indicated changes of fish species with higher river and estuary temperatures, fish deaths due to sudden temperature gradients and the chlorine used for condenser cleaning, and disturbances to breeding patterns and food chains. To avoid these problems, cooling towers are frequently used, with heat transfer mainly to the atmosphere and consequent cloud formation, loss of visual amenity and loss of land for the cooling ponds. When the problems of air pollution due to carbon dioxide, sulphur dioxide and fly-ash with fossil-fueled stations are also considered, the environmental effects of wave-energy devices are relatively much less harmful.

With the effects of wave-energy extraction on local coastlines more likely to be beneficial than detrimental and the development of new industrial activity to the advantage of the local community, wave-energy conversion becomes a most acceptable energy conversion process on environmental and social grounds.

Linearised theory for progessive water waves

Wind blowing over the sea generates waves by means of both normal (pressure) forces and tangential (shear) forces, in a complex manner which is still not entirely understood. However molecular viscosity is small and the water can reasonably be regarded as inviscid. Thus if the original motion is assumed to have been generated only by normal forces, then the motion of the water particles will be initially irrotational and will remain so, except near the sea-bed in shallow water, when viscosity becomes significant.

Water has a bulk modulus $K \sim 2\,\text{GPa}$ and since the hydrodynamic pressure variation near the surface is $\pm \rho g a$, then

$$\frac{\mathrm{d}\rho}{\rho} = \frac{\mathrm{d}p}{K} \quad \text{can be written} \quad \frac{\Delta\rho}{\rho} \sim \pm \frac{10^4 a}{2 \times 10^9}$$

where a = wave amplitude in metres.

This density variation is clearly negligible and the water can be taken to be incompressible.

Over reasonable distances along the wave crests, the waves may be considered to be uniform, so that in the notation of this text, no variation occurs in the z direction.

Thus for the two-dimensional motion of an incompressible fluid the equation of continuity gives

$$\frac{\partial u}{\partial x} + \frac{\partial v}{\partial y} = 0 \tag{A.1}$$

Whilst the condition of irrotationality is satisfied by

$$\frac{\partial v}{\partial x} - \frac{\partial u}{\partial y} = 0 \tag{A.2}$$

It is then possible to define a scalar quantity ϕ, called the velocity potential, which satisfies (A.2), as follows:

$$u = \frac{\partial \phi}{\partial x} \quad \text{and} \quad v = \frac{\partial \phi}{\partial y} \tag{A.3}$$

Substituting the appropriate differentials of (A.3) in (A.2) gives

$$\frac{\partial^2 \phi}{\partial x \, \partial y} - \frac{\partial^2 \phi}{\partial y \, \partial x} = 0 \tag{A.4}$$

Since the order of the partial differentiation does not affect the result, the condition of irrotationality is satisfied.

Substituting the appropriate differentials of (A.3) in (A.1) then gives

$$\frac{\partial^2 \phi}{\partial x^2} + \frac{\partial^2 \phi}{\partial y^2} = 0 \tag{A.5}$$

This is Laplace's Equation in two-dimensions and can be solved by the method of separable solutions. Fig. A.1 and physical reasoning suggests that ϕ is a function of x and t taken together, multiplied by a function of y.

Therefore let

$$\phi = X(x - ct)Y(y) \tag{A.6}$$

where c = a constant = the phase velocity.

Substituting the appropriate partial derivatives of (A.6) in (A.5) gives

$$X_{xx} Y + X Y_{yy} = 0 \tag{A.7}$$

where

$$X_{xx} = \frac{\partial^2 X}{\partial x^2} \quad \text{and} \quad Y_{yy} = \frac{\partial^2 Y}{\partial y^2}$$

(A.7) can be rewritten

$$\frac{X_{xx}}{X} + \frac{Y_{yy}}{Y} = 0 \tag{A.8}$$

Now

$$\frac{X_{xx}}{X} = f_1(x - ct) \quad \text{and} \quad \frac{Y_{yy}}{Y} = f_2(y)$$

Therefore

$$f_1(x - ct) = -f_2(y) \tag{A.9}$$

This functional relationship can only hold for all x, y and t, if $f_1 = -f_2 =$ constant. This constant is then chosen as $-k^2$ in order to suit the physical phenomenon that the wave is periodic in x and t.

Thus

$$\frac{X_{xx}}{X} = -k^2 \quad \text{and} \quad \frac{Y_{yy}}{Y} = +k^2 \qquad\qquad \text{(A.10)}$$

The solutions to these two differential equations are

$$X = a \cos \{k(x - ct) + \epsilon\} \qquad\qquad \text{(A.11)}$$

and

$$Y = b \cosh k(y + h) \qquad\qquad \text{(A.12)}$$

where a, b, h and ϵ are constants to be determined.

Thus

$$\phi = A \cosh k(y + h) \cos \{k(x - ct) + \epsilon\} \qquad\qquad \text{(A.13)}$$

where $A = ab$.

The equations of motion must also be satisfied. Since the water is incompressible and inviscid and the motion two-dimensional ($\partial/\partial z = 0$) and the only body force per unit mass is due to gravity ($F_y = -g$) the two equations are:

$$-\frac{1}{\rho}\frac{\partial p}{\partial x} = \frac{\partial u}{\partial t} + u\frac{\partial u}{\partial x} + v\frac{\partial u}{\partial y} \qquad\qquad \text{(A.14)}$$

$$-g - \frac{1}{\rho}\frac{\partial p}{\partial y} = \frac{\partial v}{\partial t} + u\frac{\partial v}{\partial x} + v\frac{\partial v}{\partial y} \qquad\qquad \text{(A.15)}$$

Equation (A.14) may be converted to an equation containing only partial derivatives with respect to x as follows:

$$\frac{\partial u}{\partial t} = \frac{\partial}{\partial t}\left(\frac{\partial\phi}{\partial x}\right) = \frac{\partial}{\partial x}\left(\frac{\partial\phi}{\partial t}\right)$$

$$\frac{\partial u}{\partial y} = \frac{\partial v}{\partial x} \quad \text{from (A.2)}$$

Thus since ρ is constant and

$$u\frac{\partial u}{\partial x} = \frac{\partial}{\partial x}\left(\frac{u^2}{2}\right) \quad \text{etc.}$$

$$\frac{\partial}{\partial x}\left(\frac{p}{\rho} + \frac{\partial\phi}{\partial t} + \frac{u^2}{2} + \frac{v^2}{2}\right) = 0 \qquad\qquad \text{(A.16)}$$

Equation (A.15) may be converted to an equation containing only partial derivatives with respect to y as follows:

$$-g = \frac{\partial}{\partial y}(-gy)$$

$$\frac{\partial v}{\partial t} = \frac{\partial}{\partial t}\left(\frac{\partial \phi}{\partial y}\right) = \frac{\partial}{\partial y}\left(\frac{\partial \phi}{\partial t}\right)$$

$$\frac{\partial v}{\partial x} = \frac{\partial u}{\partial y} \quad \text{from (A.2)}$$

Thus

$$\frac{\partial}{\partial y}\left(gy + \frac{p}{\rho} + \frac{\partial \phi}{\partial t} + \frac{u^2}{2} + \frac{v^2}{2}\right) = 0 \tag{A.17}$$

Integrating (A.16) with respect to x and (A.17) with respect to y gives respectively:

$$\frac{p}{\rho} + \frac{\partial \phi}{\partial t} + \frac{q^2}{2} = f_1(y, t) \tag{A.18}$$

$$gy + \frac{p}{\rho} + \frac{\partial \phi}{\partial t} + \frac{q^2}{2} = f_2(x, t) \tag{A.19}$$

where $q =$ the resultant velocity $= \sqrt{u^2 + v^2}$.

In order that (A.18) and (A.19) can be satisfied simultaneously it is necessary that

$$f_1(y, t) = -gy + f(t)$$

and

$$f_2(x, t) = f(t)$$

Hence

$$gy + \frac{p}{\rho} + \frac{\partial \phi}{\partial t} + \frac{q^2}{2} = f(t) \tag{A.20}$$

satisfies both (A.18) and (A.19).

The $f(t)$ on the right-hand side of (A.20) would not create pressure gradients, which would affect the water motion and hence may be taken as zero without loss of physical correctness.

Thus

$$\frac{p}{\rho} + \frac{q^2}{2} + gy + \frac{\partial \phi}{\partial t} = 0 \tag{A.21}$$

This is the Bernoulli equation with the inclusion of the non-steady term $\partial \phi / \partial t$.

It is now necessary to consider the boundary conditions in order to determine A, h, c and ϵ of (A.13). It will be assumed that the sea bed is horizontal and that surface tension can be neglected.

The first condition is that there is no velocity perpendicular to the sea bed at the sea bed.

Thus

$$\frac{\partial \phi}{\partial y} = v = 0 \tag{A.22}$$

at the sea bed.

The second condition is that fluid particles at the free surface cannot move relative that surface.

To simplify this condition and avoid a non-linear term it is necessary to assume that the waves are not steep. Fig. A.1 shows a water particle at time t and at time $(t + \Delta t)$. The vertical velocity of that particle

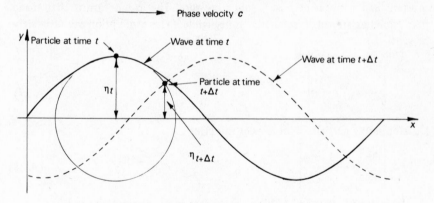

Fig. A.1 – Progressive water wave showing movement of a water particle located in the free suface.

$$v = \underset{\delta t \to 0}{\text{Limit}} \left(\frac{\eta_{t+\delta t} - \eta_t}{\delta t} \right) = \frac{D\eta}{Dt} \tag{A.23}$$

Since

$$\eta = \eta(x, t)$$

then

$$\frac{D\eta}{Dt} = \frac{\partial \eta}{\partial t} + \frac{\partial \eta}{\partial x} \frac{\partial x}{\partial t}$$

Now $\partial \eta / \partial x =$ slope of the free surface and this is small for waves that are not steep.

Thus

$$v \sim \frac{\partial \eta}{\partial t} \tag{A.24}$$

at the free surface.

But v is also determined by the velocity potential as

$$v = \frac{\partial \phi}{\partial y} \tag{A.25}$$

at the free surface.

Equating (A.24) and (A.25) gives

$$\left. \frac{\partial \phi}{\partial y} \sim \frac{\partial \eta}{\partial t} \right|_{y=\eta} \tag{A.26}$$

The third boundary condition is that the pressure at the free surface is constant and conveniently zero gauge pressure. The assumption is then made that velocities are small, so that q^2 is negligible. (This assumption can ultimately be verified.)

Thus (A.21) becomes

$$\left. gn + \frac{\partial \phi}{\partial t} \sim 0 \right|_{y=\eta} \tag{A.27}$$

Differentiating partially with respect to t gives

$$\left. \frac{\partial \eta}{\partial t} \sim -\frac{1}{g} \frac{\partial^2 \phi}{\partial t^2} \right|_{y=\eta} \tag{A.28}$$

Equating (A.26) and (A.28) gives the free-surface boundary condition

$$\left. \frac{\partial^2 \phi}{\partial t^2} + g \frac{\partial \phi}{\partial y} = 0 \right|_{y=\eta} \tag{A.29}$$

For waves of small steepness (A.26) can be written approximately as

$$\left. \frac{\partial \eta}{\partial t} \sim \frac{\partial \phi}{\partial y} \right|_{y=0} \tag{A.30}$$

and the right-hand side can be determined by differentiating (A.13) partially with respect to y and putting $y = 0$.

Thus

$$\frac{\partial \eta}{\partial t} \sim Ak \sinh kh \cos \{k(x - ct) + \epsilon\} \tag{A.31}$$

Integrating and putting $-(A/c) \sinh kh = a$ and $\epsilon = 0$ gives

$$\eta = a \sin \{k(x - ct)\} \tag{A.32}$$

(the equality sign will be used subsequently even though the result is strictly an approximation).

The free-surface thus takes the form of a sine wave of amplitude a, and the velocity potential is

$$\phi = -\frac{ac \cosh k(y + h)}{\sinh kh} \cos \{k(x - ct)\} \tag{A.33}$$

Substituting the appropriate partial derivatives of ϕ into the free-surface boundary conditions (A.29) gives

$$k^2 c^2 \left[\frac{ac \cosh k(\eta + h)}{\sinh kh} \right] \cos \{k(x - ct)\}$$
$$= gk \left[\frac{ac \sinh k(\eta + h)}{\sinh kh} \right] \cos \{k(x - ct)\}$$

Since $\eta \ll h$ (except for shallow water) then

$$c^2 = \frac{g}{k} \tanh kh \tag{A.34}$$

To satisfy the definition of wavelength L and period T, (A.32) requires that

$$k = \frac{2\pi}{L} \quad \text{and} \quad kc = \frac{2\pi}{T}$$

Thus (A.34) can be written as

$$c^2 = \frac{gL}{2\pi} \tanh kh \tag{A.35}$$

This is known as the dispersion relation, as it indicates that longer wavelengths give higher phase velocities and waves of different wavelength travel at different speeds.

Now the sea-bed condition $v = \partial\phi/\partial y = 0$ can be determined by partial differentiation of (A.33) with respect to y.

Thus it follows that $\sinh k(y + h) = 0$ or $y = -h$ at the sea bed, and all the arbitrary constants of (A.13) have now been determined.

Deep water conditions

For deep water $h \to \infty$ some simplifications can be made because

$$\sinh kh \to \exp(kh)/2, \cosh k(y+h) \to \exp[k(y+h)]/2$$

and $\tanh kh \to 1$.

Thus

$$\phi = -ac \exp(ky) \cos\{k(x-ct)\} \tag{A.36}$$

and

$$c^2 = \frac{g}{k} \tag{A.37}$$

Dimensional analysis applied to model tests

In section 3.3.3 the method of dimensional analysis was applied to turbo-machinery in order to group a number of variables together and so permit a more concise presentation of the performance characteristics, whilst in section 5.1 attention was drawn to a problem of using a model of reduced scale. Since wave-energy converters and many other machines and devices are frequently tested as scaled models, it is pertinent to discuss briefly the correct method of modelling and some of the inherent difficulties of interpretation of model results.

Essentially the model must be geometrically similar to the full-scale device (that is, all linear dimensions scaled by the same factor). There should also be dynamical similarity so that forces are correctly scaled, kinematic similarity so that motions are correctly modelled. There may also be the need for thermal and electrical similarlity.

After ensuring geometrical similarity between the model and the full-scale prototype, it is necessary to arrange for dynamical similarity. For a body which is partly submerged in an incompressible viscous fluid the appropriate independent variables are:

Variable	Notation	SI unit	Fundamental dimensions
The imposed force	F	N	ML/T^2
Length	L	m	L
Density of fluid	ρ	kg/m^3	M/L^3
Viscosity of fluid	μ	Pas	M/LT
Velocity	V	m/s	L/T
Gravitational acceleration	g	m/s^2	L/T^2

Thus by dimensional analysis (as in section 3.3.3) the functional relationship between these variables is

$$\frac{F}{\rho V^2 L^2} = f\left\{\frac{\rho VL}{\mu}, \quad \frac{V}{\sqrt{gL}}\right\} \tag{B.1}$$

Newton   Reynolds Froude
number   number   number

The physical significance of these dimensionless groups can be appreciated as follows:

$$\text{Inertia force} = \text{mass} \times \text{acceleration} = (\rho L^3)(dV/dt)$$

$$= (\rho L^3)\left(V\frac{dV}{dL}\right) \propto \rho V^2 L^2$$

$$\text{Viscous force} = \text{shear stress} \times \text{area} = \left(\mu\frac{dV}{dL}\right)L^2 \propto \mu VL$$

$$\text{Gravitational force} = \text{mass} \times \text{gravitational acceleration}$$

$$= (\rho L^3)g = \rho g L^3$$

Thus

$$\text{the Newton number } N = \frac{\text{imposed force}}{\text{inertia force}}$$

$$\text{the Reynolds number } Re = \frac{\text{inertia force}}{\text{viscous force}}$$

and

$$\text{the Froude number } Fr = \left(\frac{\text{inertia force}}{\text{gravitational force}}\right)^{1/2}$$

For complete dynamical similarity, the functional relation (B.1) must apply to both model and prototype. This implies that the Reynolds number must be the same for model and prototype and that the Froude number of model and prototype is also the same.

$$\text{If the geometric scale factor } s = \frac{L_m}{L_p} \qquad (s < 1 \text{ here})$$

where L_m = a typical model dimension; L_p = the corresponding prototype dimension.

Then since g is constant, equality of Froude number requires

$$\frac{V_m}{V_p} = \sqrt{\frac{L_m}{L_p}} = s^{1/2}$$

whilst equality of Reynolds number additionally requires

$$\frac{\nu_m}{\nu_p} = \left(\frac{\mu_m}{\rho_m}\right) \bigg/ \left(\frac{\mu_p}{\rho_p}\right) = \frac{V_m L_m}{V_p L_p} = s^{3/2}$$

Thus for a laboratory experiment with a 1/100th scale model, the fluid used would require a kinematic viscosity of 1/1000th that of water. This impractical, if not impossible, situation is avoided by using water in the model tests, and measuring the wave-induced forces with the correct Froude number. Theoretical readjustment can then be made to the viscous component of the forces, based on a knowledge of the variation of skin friction with Reynolds number which would of course be in error in the model tests. Such reassessment of viscous forces may however be unnecessary, if these are small compared with the wave-induced forces.

Now for geometrical modelling by a scale factor s and dynamical similarity based on the Froude number, then

$$\frac{V_m^2 L^2}{V_p^2 L_p^2} = s^3$$

and if the fluid density remains the same, then

$$\frac{F_m}{F_p} = \frac{\rho_m V_m^2 L_m^2}{\rho_p V_p^2 L_p^2} = s^3$$

Thus the imposed force varies as the cube of the geometric scale factor, whereas the areas obviously only increase as s^2. Hence stresses vary as s and are thus smaller for the model than for the prototype (see section 5.1). There is strictly also a small correction to be made because of the difference in density (by 2% to 3%) between sea water and fresh water.

To ensure kinematic similarity the frequency f (or period T) should be added to the variables already considered and this leads to the formation of another dimensionless group:

the Strouhal number $S = \dfrac{fL}{V}$ or $\dfrac{L}{VT}$

Thus for a wave-energy device of diameter (or dimension) d operating in waves with

amplitude a
wavelength L
period T
phase velocity c

and moving with velocity V in water of depth h and negligible viscosity, complete similarity is ensured if the following ratios are preserved:

Geometric similarity $\dfrac{a}{L}, \dfrac{h}{L}, \dfrac{d}{L}$

Kinematic similarity $\dfrac{TV}{L}$ or $\dfrac{V}{c}$

Dynamical similarity $\dfrac{V}{\sqrt{gL}}$ or $\dfrac{c}{\sqrt{gL}}$

Some of the similarity ratios have already been established in previous analysis. For example, (2.14) shows that

$$c^2 \triangleq \frac{g}{k} = \frac{gL}{2\pi} \quad \text{or} \quad \frac{c}{\sqrt{gL}} \quad \text{is dimensionless.}$$

SI and Imperial units

SI UNITS
The Seven Primary Units

Quantity	Unit	Symbol
length	metre	m
mass	kilogram	kg
time	second	s
electric current	ampere	A
thermodynamic temperature	kelvin	K
luminous intensity	candela	cd
amount of substance	mole	mol

Some Special Derived Units

Quantity	Unit	Symbol	Definition
plane angle	radian	rad	$180/\pi$ degrees
frequency	hertz	Hz	s^{-1}
force	newton	N	$kg\,m/s^2$
pressure, stress	pascal	Pa	N/m^2
dynamic viscosity	pascal second	Pa s	Ns/m^2
work, energy, quantity of heat	joule	J	Nm
power, heat flow rate	watt	W	J/s
electric charge	coulomb	C	As
electric potential difference	volt	V	W/A
electric resistance	ohm	Ω	V/A
electric conductance	siemens	S	A/V
electric capacitance	farad	F	As/V
magnetic flux	weber	Wb	Vs
inductance	henry	H	Vs/A
magnetic flux density	tesla	T	Wb/m^2

Fractions and Multiples

Fraction	Prefix	Symbol	Multiple	Prefix	Symbol
10^{-1}	deci	d	10	deca	da
10^{-2}	centi	c	10^2	hecto	h
10^{-3}	milli	m	10^3	kilo	k
10^{-6}	micro	μ	10^6	mega	M
10^{-9}	nano	n	10^9	giga	G
10^{-12}	pico	p	10^{12}	tera	T
10^{-15}	femto	f			
10^{-18}	atto	a			

IMPERIAL UNITS
The Six Primary Units

Quantity	Unit	Symbol
length	foot	ft
mass	pound	lbm
time	second	s
electric current	ampere	A
temperature	degree Rankine	°R
luminous intensity	candela	cd

Some Special Derived Units

Quantity	Unit	Symbol	Definition
force	pound	lbf	$(1/g_0)$ lbm ft/s^2
work, energy	foot pound	ft lbf	ft lbf
quantity of heat	British thermal unit	Btu	J ft lbf
power	horsepower	hp	550 ft lbf/s

Notes

(1) $(1/g_0)$ is the constant of proportionality in Newton's second law of motion so that:

$$1\,\text{lbf} = \frac{1\,\text{lbm} \times 32.174\,\text{ft/s}^2}{g_0}$$

Therefore

$$g_0 = \frac{32.174}{\text{lbf s}^2} \text{ lbm ft}$$

(2) J is Joule's equivalent and relates heat units to work units in the imperial system so that:

$$1 \text{ Btu} = 778 \text{ ft lbf}$$

or

$$J = 778 \text{ ft lbf/Btu}$$

Conversion Factors (4 figure accuracy)

	Imperial unit		SI unit
length	1 in	=	2.540 cm
	1 ft	=	0.3048 m
	1 mile	=	1.609 km
area	1 in^2	=	6.452 cm^2
	1 ft^2	=	0.0929 m^2
volume	1 in^3	=	16.39 cm^3
	1 ft^3	=	0.02832 m^3
velocity	1 ft/s	=	0.3048 m/s
	1 mile/h	=	1.609 km/h
mass	1 lbm	=	0.4536 kg
	1 slug	=	14.59 kg
density	1 lbm/ft^3	=	16.02 kg/m^3
	1 slug/ft^3	=	515.4 kg/m^3
force	1 lbf	=	4.448 N
pressure	1 lbf/in^2	=	6.895 kPa
	1 in H_2O	=	249.1 Pa
	1 in Hg	=	3.386 kPa
energy	1 ft lbf	=	1.356 J
	1 Btu	=	1.055 kJ
power	1 hp	=	745.7 W

REFERENCES

[1] Airy, G. B. (1845), Tides and waves, *Encyc. Metrop., Art*, **192**, 241-396.

[2] Altmann, H. and Farley, F. J. M. (1979), *Progress report on the Triplate wave energy converter*, Royal Military College of Science Report.

[3] Ambli, N., Budal, K., Falnes, J., Sørenssen, A. (1977), Wave power conversion by a row of optimally operated buoys, *Proceedings 10th World Energy Conference, Istanbul*, Paper 4.5-2.

[4] Anon. (1970), New concept for harnessing ocean waves, *Ocean Industry*, **March**, 62-63.

[5] Anon. (1979), Is this the ultimate wave machine?, *Solar Energy Digest (2)*, **June**.

[6] Ansari, K. A. (1979), How to design a multi-component mooring system, *Ocean Industry*, **March**, 60-68.

[7] Arthur, R. S. (1946), Refraction of water waves by islands and shoals with circular bottom contours, *Trans. American Geophysical Union*, **27**, 2, 168-177.

[8] Bellamy, N. W. (1978), The Loch Ness trials of the duck, *Proceedings Wave Energy Conference, London*, 29-34.

[9] Bellamy, N. W. (1981), A second generation wave energy device – the Clam concept, *Proceedings Third International Conference on Future Energy Concepts*, IEE.

[10] Bendat, J. S. and Piersol, A. G. (1966), *Measurement and analysis of random data*, John Wiley & Sons, Inc.

[11] Benjamin, T. B. and Feir, J. E. (1967), The disintegration of wave trains on deep water, *J. Fluid Mech.*, **27**, 417-430.

[12] Berteaux, H. O. (1976), *Buoy Engineering*, J. Wiley & Sons, New York.

[13] Bhattacharyya, R. (1978), *Dynamics of Marine Vehicles*, Wiley-Interscience.

[14] Binns, K. J. (1979), The use of permanent magnet machines for low speed generation, *Proceedings First Symposium on Wave Energy Utilization, Gothenburg, Sweden*, 161-166.

[15] Bishop, H. W. and Rees, G. R. (1979), An electrical generation and transmission scheme for wave power, *Proceedings First Symposium on Wave Energy Utilization, Gothenburg, Sweden*, 167-189.

[16] Budal, K. (1977), Theory for absorption of wave power by a system of interacting bodies, *J. Ship Research*, **21**, 4, 248-253.

[17] Budal, K. and Falnes, J. (1979), Interacting point absorbers with controlled motion, *Power from Sea Waves, Proceedings I.M.A. Conference 1979 Edinburgh*, Academic Press.

[18] Budal, K., Falnes, J., Kyllingstad, A. and Oltedal, G. (1979), Experiments with point absorbers, *Proceedings First Symposium on Wave Energy Utilization, Gothenburg, Sweden*, 253-382.

[19] Caldwell, J. M. (1963), Shore processes and coastal engineering, *Proceedings Conference on Ocean Wave Spectra, Maryland, 1961*, National Academy of

Sciences, 305–307.

[20] Cartwright, D. E. and Longuet-Higgins, M. S. (1956), The statistical distribution of the maxima of a random function, *Proceedings Roy. Soc. Lond. A.*, **237**, 212–232.

[21] Central Electricity Generating Board (1980), *Annual Report and Accounts 1979–80*, CEGB.

[22] Central Policy Review Staff (1974), *Energy Conservation*, HMSO.

[23] Chaplin, R. V. and French, M. J. (1979), Aspects of the French flexible bag device, *Power from Sea Waves – Proceedings I.M.A. Conference, Edinburgh, 1979*, Academic Press.

[24] Chester-Browne, C. V. (1978), The Vickers device, *Proceedings Wave Energy Conference, London*, 55–58.

[25] Cockerell, Sir Christopher, Platts, M. J. and Comyns-Carr, R. (1978), The development of the wave-contouring raft, *Proceedings Wave Energy Conference, London*, 7–16.

[26] Cottrill, A. (1981), Wave energy: Main UK contenders line up for 1982 decision, *Offshore Engineer*, **Jan.**, 25–36.

[27] Count, B. M. (1979), The absorption of energy from ocean waves, *Proceedings First International Conference on Future Energy Concepts*, IEE Conference Publication No. 171, 96–99.

[28] Count, B. M. (1979), Wave power, *Power from Sea Waves – Proceedings I.M.A. Conference, Edinburgh, 1979*, Academic Press.

[29] Crabb, J. A. (1978), A review of wave measurement and analysis methods relevant to the wave energy programme, *Proceedings Wave Energy Conference, London*, 107–111.

[30] Crabb, J. A. and Fortnum, B. C. H. (1979), South Uist wave climate – a summary of recent results, *Wave Energy Steering Committee Report*, WESC(79) DA 89.

[31] Craig, H. R. M., Edwards, K. J., Horlock, J. H., Janota, M., Shaw, R. and Woods, W. A. (1969), An investigation of steady and unsteady flow through a Napier turboblower turbine under conditions of full and partial admission, *Proceedings I.Mech.E.*, **183**, 1.

[32] Crapper, G. D. (1979), Energy and momentum integrals for progressive capillary-gravity waves, *J. Fluid Mech.*, **94**, (1), 13–24.

[33] Csanady, G. T. (1964), *Theory of turbomachines*, McGraw-Hill Book Co.

[34] Cure, J. R. and Sullivan, J. A. (1981), Generation and transmission of electricity from wave energy schemes, *Proceedings Third International Conference on Future Energy Concepts*, IEE Conference Publication No. 192, 135–146.

[35] Danel, P. (1952), On the limiting clapotis, gravity waves, *National Bureau of Standards Circular No. 521*, 35–38.

[36] Dawson, J. K. (1978), The environmental and some social aspects of wave-power generating stations, *Proceedings Wave Energy Conference, London*,

135-142.

[37] Dawson, J. K. (1979), Wave energy, *Energy Paper No. 42*, DOE, HMSO.

[38] Dean, R. G. (1974), Evaluation and development of water wave theories for engineering application, *Report SR-1, US Army Corps of Engineers*, Coastal Engineering Research Center, Fort Belvoir, Virginia.

[39] Dean, W. R. (1948), On the reflection of surface waves by a submerged cylinder, *Proceedings Camb. Phil. Soc.*, **44**, 483-491.

[40] Denton, J. D. *et al.* (1975), The potential of natural energy resources, *CEGB Research, Number 2*, 28-40.

[41] Department of Energy (1979), Energy technologies for the UK, *Energy Paper Number 39*, HMSO.

[42] Department of Energy (1979), Wave energy, *Energy Paper Number 42*, HMSO.

[43] Department of Energy (Sept. 26, 1980), *Press Notice*, Reference 191.

[44] Department of Energy (1981), *Energy Trends*, **Nov.**

[45] Dixon, S. L. (1978), *Fluid Mechanics, thermodynamics of turbomachinery* (3rd Edn.), Pergamon Press.

[46] Dugger, G. L. (1979), Ocean thermal energy for the 80's, *Proceedings 6th OTEC Conference*, US Department of Energy, Washington DC.

[47] Eden, R. J. (1981), World energy outlook – alternative strategies and changing perceptions, *Proceedings Institute of Petroleum Conference, University of Cambridge, England.*

[48] Eden, R., Posner, M., Bending, R., Crouch, E., and Stanislaw, J. (1981), *Energy economics*, Cambridge University Press.

[49] Esso Petroleum Co. Ltd. (1981), UK energy outlook, *Esso Magazine Supplement*, **Winter**, 1981/82.

[50] Evans, D. V. (1976), A theory for wave-power absorption by oscillating bodies, *J. Fluid Mech.*, **77**, 1-25.

[51] Evans, D. V. (1978), The submerged cylinder wave device, *Proceedings Wave Energy Conference, London*, 121-122.

[52] Evans, D. V. (1979), Some analytic results for two and three dimensional wave-energy absorbers, *Power from Sea Waves – Proceedings I.M.A. Conference, Edinburgh, 1979*, Academic Press, 213-249.

[53] Evans, D. V., Jeffrey, D. C., Salter, S. H. and Taylor, J. R. M. (1979), Submerged cylinder wave energy device: theory and experiment, *Appl. Ocean Res.*, **1**, 1, 3-12.

[54] Farley, F. J. M. (1978), The Triplate wave energy converter, *Proceedings Wave Energy Conference, London*, 129-131.

[55] Farley, F. J. M. (1980), *Wave energy conversion by flexible resonant rafts*, Royal Military College of Science report.

[56] Flower, J. O. and Knott, G. F. (1978), Development of the Sussex wave energy converter, *Proceedings Wave Energy Conference, London*, 123-125.

[57] French, M. J. (1977), Hydrodynamic basis of wave-energy converters of

channel form, *J. Mech. Eng. Sci.*, **19**, 2, 90-92.

[58] French, M. J. (1978), The flexible bag wave power device, *Proceedings Wave Energy Conference, London*, 59-60.

[59] French, M. J. (1979), The search for low-cost wave energy and the flexible bag device, *Proceedings First Symposium on Wave Energy Utilization, Gothenburg, Sweden*, 364-377.

[60] Glendenning, I. (1977), Ocean wave power, *Applied Energy*, **3**, 197-222.

[61] Glendenning, I. (1978), Generation and transmission, *Proceedings Wave Energy Conference, London*, 79-90.

[62] Glendenning, I. (1979), Wave power – some practical considerations, *Proceedings First International Conference on Future Energy Concepts*, IEE Conference Publication No. 171, 109-114.

[63] Government Statistical Service, DOE (1980), *Digest of United Kingdom Energy Statistics 1980*, HMSO.

[64] Grant, R. J., Johnson, C. G. and Sturge, D. P. (1981), Performance of a Wells turbine for use in a wave energy system, *Proceedings Third International Conference on Future Energy Concepts*, IEE Conference Publication No 192, 135-146.

[65] Greenhow, M. J. L. (1981), Efficiency calculations for a Salter's Duck on a compliant axis, *Appl. Ocean. Res.*, **3**, 3, 145-7.

[66] Hancock, R. (1979), The mooring of large scale wave power stations, *Proceedings First Symposium on Wave Energy Utilization, Gothenburg, Sweden*, 298-324.

[67] Haren, P. and Mei, C. C. (1979), Wave power extraction by a train of rafts: hydrodynamic theory and optimum design, *Appl. Ocean Res.*, **1**, 3, 147-157.

[68] Harrison, J. A. (1980), *An introduction to electric power systems*, Longman.

[69] Havelock, Sir T. (1955), Waves due to a floating sphere making periodic heaving oscillations, *Proceedings Roy. Soc.*, **A231**, 1-7.

[70] Horlock, J. H. (1966), *Axial flow turbines*, Butterworths.

[71] Hudson, J. A. (1978), Materials aspects of wave energy converters, *Proceedings Wave Energy Conference, London*, 99-104.

[72] International Energy Agency (1975), Statistical data and projections. World energy consumption and supply, *IEA submission to the 2nd session of the CIEC Energy Commission.*

[73] Isaacs, J. D., Castel, D. and Wick, G. L. (1976), Utilization of the energy in ocean waves, *Ocean Engineering*, **3**, 175-187.

[74] Jefferys, E. R. (1979), Device characterisation, *Power from Sea Waves – Proceedings I.M.A. Conference, Edinburgh, 1979*, Academic Press.

[75] Knott, G. F. and Flower, J. O. (1979), Wave tank experiments on an immersed, vertical parallel-plate duct, *J. Fluid Mech.*, **90**, 327-336.

[76] Komar, P. D. (1976), *Beach processes and sedimentation*, Prentice-Hall.

[77] Korn, J. (Ed.) (1969), *Hydrostatic Transmission Systems*, Intertext Books, London.

[78] Laithwaite, E. R. and Freris, L. L. (1980), *Electric energy: its generation, transmission and use*, McGraw-Hill Book Co. (UK).

[79] Laitone, E. V. (1960), The second approximation to cnoidal and solitary waves, *J. Fluid Mech.*, **9**, (3), 430–444.

[80] Lamb, H. (1945), *Hydrodynamics*, Dover Publications, New York.

[81] Leishman, J. M. and Scobie, G. (1976), *The development of wave power – a techno-economic study*, Department of Industry, National Engineering Laboratory Report, EAU M25.

[82] Lewis, F. (1929), The inertia of water surrounding a vibrating ship, *Trans. Soc. Naval Architects and Marine Engrs.*, **37**.

[83] Lewis, L. F. and Waite, K. G. (1980), Ocean energy technology: An environmental overview, *Proceedings 26th Meeting of the Institute of Environmental Science, Philadelphia*.

[84] Lighthill, Sir James (1979), Two-dimensional analyses related to wave-energy extraction by submerged resonant ducts, *J. Fluid Mech.*, **91**(2), 253-317.

[85] Lockhead-California Company (1979), Proposal for Dam-Atoll Ocean Wave Energy Extraction, *Lockheed Report LR 28932*.

[86] Long, A. E. and Whittaker, T. J. T. (1978), The Belfast device, *Proceedings Wave Energy Conference, London*, 61-64.

[87] Longuet-Higgins, M. S. (1952), On the statistical distribution of heights of sea waves, *J. Mar. Res.*, **11**(3), 245-266.

[88] Longuet-Higgins, M. S. (1956), The refraction of sea waves in shallow water, *J. Fluid Mech.*, **1**, 163-76.

[89] Longuet-Higgins, M. S. (1977), The mean forces exerted by waves on floating or submerged bodies with applications to sand bars and wave power machines, *Proceedings Roy. Soc. Lond. A*, **352**, 463-480.

[90] Longuet-Higgins, M. S., Cartwright, D. E. and Smith, N. D. (1961), Observations of the directional spectrum of sea waves using the motions of a floating buoy, *Ocean Wave Spectra – Proceedings of a Conference National Academy of Sciences*, 111-136, Prentice-Hall.

[91] Longuet-Higgins, M. S. and Stewart, R. W. (1964), Radiation stresses in water waves; a physical discussion, with applications, *Deep-Sea Research*, **11**, 529-562.

[92] MacNeal, R. H. (1970), *The NASTRAN theoretical manual*, NASA SP-221.

[93] Madsen, O. S. (1971), *The Breaking criteria of Miche*, Unpublished Memorandum for Record Coastal Engineering Research Centre, Washington DC, 28 September 1971.

[94] Masuda, Y. (1972), Study of wave activated generator and future view as an island power source, *2nd International Ocean Development Conference*, Preprints, **2**, 2074-2090.

[95] Masuda, Y. (1979), Experimental full scale result of wave power machine

KAIMEI in 1978, *Proceedings First Symposium on Wave Energy Utilization, Gothenburg, Sweden*, 349-363.

[96] McCormick, M. E. (1974), Analysis of a wave energy conversion bucy, *J. Hydronaut. (AIAA)*, **8**, 3, 77-82.

[97] McCormick, M. E. (1976), A modified linear analysis of a wave-energy conversion buoy, *Ocean Eng.*, **3**, 133-144.

[98] McCormick, M. E. (1978), Ocean wave energy conversion concepts, *Proceedings Oceans '79 Conference, San Diego, California*, (MTS-IEEE), 553-557.

[99] McIlhagger, D. S. (1981), Output optimization from a group of wave energy converters, *Third International Conference on Future Energy Concepts*, IEE Conference Publication No. 192, 309-312.

[100] Mehlum, E. and Stamnes, J. (1979), Power production based on focusing of ocean swells, *Proceedings First Symposium on Wave Energy Utilization, Gothenburg, Sweden*, 29-35.

[101] Mei, C. C. and Newman, J. N. (1979), Wave power extraction by floating bodies, *Proceedings of the First Symposium on Wave Energy Utilization, Gothenburg.*

[102] Meir, R. (1978), The development of the oscillating water column, *Proceedings Wave Energy Conference, London*, 35-44.

[103] Miche, R. (1944), Mouvements ondulatoires des mers en profondeur constante ou décroissante, *Annales des Ponts et Chausseés.*

[104] Milne, A. J. (1978), Tidal power in Scottish lochs, *BHRA International Symposium on Wave and Tidal Energy, Canterbury, England*, Paper C2.

[105] Mitsuyasu, H., Tasai, F., Suhara, T., Mizuno, S., Ohkusu, M., Honda, T. and Rikiishi, K. (1975), Observations of the directional spectrum of ocean waves using a cloverleaf buoy, *J. Phys. Ocean.*, **5**, 750-760.

[106] Miyazaki, T. and Masuda, Y. (1980), Tests on the wave power generator "Kaimei" ,*12th Annual Offshore Technology Conference, Houston, Texas*, Paper OTC 3689.

[107] Moody, G. W. (1979), The N.E.L. oscillating water column − Recent developments, *Proceedings First Symposium on Wave Energy Utilization, Gothenburg, Sweden*, 283-297.

[108] Morley, J. G. (1978), SRC-supported work on wave energy at Nottingham University, *Proceedings Wave Energy Conference, London*, 127-128.

[109] Munk, W. H. (1949), The solitary wave theory and its application to surf problems, *Annals of the New York Academy of Sciences*, **51**, article 3, 376-424.

[110] Mynett, A. E., Serman, D. D., and Mei, C. C. (1979), Characteristics of Salter's cam for extracting energy from ocean waves, *Appl. Ocean Res.*, **1**, 1, 13-20.

[111] Newman, J. N. (1962), The exciting forces on fixed bodies in waves, *J. Ship Research*, **6**, 3, 10-17.

[112] Ogilvie, T. F. (1963), First- and second-order forces on a cylinder submerged under a free surface, *J. Fluid Mech.*, **16**, 451–472.

[113] Omholt, T. (1978), A wave activated electric generator, *Proc. "Ocean 78", Marine Tech. Conference Washington DC*, 585–589.

[114] Palme, A. (1920), Wave motion turbine, *Power*, **52** (18), 700–701.

[115] Pierson, W. J. Jr., and Moskowitz, L. (1964), A proposed spectral form for fully developed wind seas based on the similarity theory of S. A. Kitaigorodskii, *J. Geophys. Research*, **69** (24), 5181–5190.

[116] Probert, P. K. and Mitchell, R. (1979), Nature conservation implications of siting wave energy converters off the Outer Hebrides, *Nature Conservancy Council, Chief Scientist's Team Notes*, Number 15.

[117] Probert, P. K. and Mitchell, R. (1981), Environmental implications of wave energy proposals for the Outer Hebrides and Moray Firth, *Second International Symposium on Wave and Tidal Energy, University of Cambridge, England*.

[118] Putz, R. R. (1952), Statistical distributions for ocean waves, *Trans. Am. Geophys. Union*, **33** (5), 685–692.

[119] Rance, P. J. (1978), The development of the H.R.S. rectifier, *Proceedings Wave Energy Conference, London*, 49–54.

[120] Salomon, R. E. and Harding, S. M. (1979), Gas concentration cells for the conversion of ocean wave energy, *Ocean Engineering*, **6**, 3, 317–327.

[121] Salter, S. H. (1974), Wave power, *Nature*, **249** (5459), 720–724.

[122] Salter, S. H. (1978), The development of the duck concept, *Proceedings Wave Energy Conference, London*, 17–28.

[123] Salter, S. H. (1979), Recent progress on ducks, *Proceedings First Symposium on Wave Energy Utilization, Gothenburg, Sweden*, 36–76.

[124] Salter, S. H. (1980), Recent progress on ducks, *IEE Proc.*, **127**, **A**, 5, 308–319.

[125] Salter, S. H., Jeffrey, D. C. and Taylor, J. R. M. (1976), The architecture of nodding duck wave power generators, *The Naval Architect*, **Jan.**, 21–24.

[126] Scott, M. K. (1965), Electricity from waves, *Sea Frontiers*, **11**, (4), 202–207.

[127] Smith, C. S. (1978), Structural design of wave energy devices, *Proceedings Wave Energy Conference, London*, 91–94.

[128] Stahl, A. W. (1892), The utilization of the power of ocean waves, *Trans. ASME*, **13**, 438–506.

[129] Stoker, J. J. (1957), *Water waves*, Wiley-Interscience, New York.

[130] Stokes, Sir G. G. (1880), On the theory of oscillatory waves, *Mathematical and Physical Papers I*, Cambridge University Press.

[131] Taylor, R. J. (1981), Wave energy: the influence of maintenance/repair requirements, *Second International Symposium on Wave and Tidal Energy, University of Cambridge, England*.

[132] Turnbull, D. E. (1976), *Fluid Power Engineering*, Newnes-Butterworths.

[133] Ursell, F. (1950), Surface waves on deep water in the presence of submerged circular cylinder, *Proc. Camb. Phil. Soc.*, **49**, 141-152.

[134] US Army Coastal Engineering Research Center (1977), *Shore Protection Manual* (3rd Edition), Fort Belvoir, Virginia.

[135] US Department of Commerce (1980), *Statistical abstract of the United States 1980*.

[136] Wallace, A. R. S. and Whittington, H. R. (1981), Routing of submarine cables for wave power transmission, *Third International Conference on Future Energy Concepts*, IEE Conference Publication No. 192, 123-126.

[137] Walton Bott, A. N., Hailey, J. F. M., Hunter, P. D. (1978), The Mauritius wave energy project — Research results and proposed outline design, *Proceedings International Symposium on Wave and Tidal Energy, Canterbury*, F2-15-38.

[138] Wiegel, R. L. (1964), *Oceanographical Engineering*, Prentice-Hall.

[139] Wilson, M. N. (1979), Slow speed generators with superconducting windings, *Proceedings First Symposium on Wave Energy Utilization, Gothenburg, Sweden*, 127-139.

[140] Wilson, R. and Jones, W. J. (1974), *Energy, ecology and the environment*, Academic Press.

[141] Winer, B. M. (1975), Electrical energy transmission from ocean thermal power plants, *Proceedings Third Workshop on Ocean Thermal Energy Conversion, Houston, Texas*, 103-105.

[142] Winter, A. J. B. (1979), The wave energy resource. Some calculations from the Met. Office model, *Wave Energy Steering Committee Report*, WESC (79) DA84.

[143] Wirt, L. S. (1979), Wave-powered motor, *US Pat. 4,152,895*, 8th May 1979.

[144] Woolley, M. V. and Tricklebank, A. H. (1981), Mass production of concrete wave energy devices, *The Structural Engineer*, **59A**, 2, 57-68.

[145] Workshop on Alternative Energy Strategies (1976), *Energy demand studies. Major comsuming countries*, MIT Press.

[146] Workshop on Alternative Energy Strategies (1977), *Energy. Global prospects 1985-2000*, McGraw-Hill.

[147] Energy Research Group, Cambridge (1977), World Energy Demand to 2020 in *World energy resourses 1985-2020* (papers presented at the World Energy Conference 1978), IPC Science and Technology Press.

Subject Index

Author Index